The Regulation of Arms and Dual-Use Exports
Germany, Sweden and the UK

sipri

Stockholm International Peace Research Institute

SIPRI is an independent international institute for research into problems of peace and conflict, especially those of arms control and disarmament. It was established in 1966 to commemorate Sweden's 150 years of unbroken peace.

The Institute is financed mainly by the Swedish Parliament. The staff and the Governing Board are international. The Institute also has an Advisory Committee as an international consultative body.

The Governing Board is not responsible for the views expressed in the publications of the Institute.

sipri

Stockholm International Peace Research Institute
Signalistgatan 9, SE-169 70 Solna, Sweden
Cable: SIPRI
Telephone: 46 8/655 97 00
Telefax: 46 8/655 97 33
Email: sipri@sipri.se
Internet URL: http://www.sipri.se

The Regulation of Arms and Dual-Use Exports
Germany, Sweden and the UK

Ian Davis

sipri

OXFORD UNIVERSITY PRESS

2002

OXFORD
UNIVERSITY PRESS

Great Clarendon Street, Oxford OX2 6DP
Oxford University Press is a department of the University of Oxford.
It furthers the University's objective of excellence in research, scholarship,
and education by publishing worldwide in

Oxford New York
Athens Auckland Bangkok Bogotá Buenos Aires Cape Town
Chennai Dar es Salaam Delhi Florence Hong Kong Istanbul Karachi
Kolkata Kuala Lumpur Madrid Melbourne Mexico City Mumbai Nairobi
Paris São Paulo Shanghai Singapore Taipei Tokyo Toronto Warsaw
and associated companies in Berlin Ibadan

Oxford is a registered trade mark of Oxford University Press
in the UK and certain other countries

Published in the United States
by Oxford University Press Inc., New York

British Library Cataloguing in Publication Data
Data available

Library of Congress Cataloguing-in-Publication Data
Data available

ISBN 0-19-925219-X

Typeset and originated by Stockholm International Peace Research Institute
Printed in Great Britain on acid-free paper by
Biddles Ltd., Guildford and King's Lynn

Contents

Part I. Setting the context

Part II. The development of common regulatory policies within the European Union

Part III. Regulations in practice: national export controls in the UK, Germany and Sweden

**8. A comparative analysis of the regulatory regimes in the UK,   219
Germany and Sweden: the convergence–divergence mix explained**

9. Conclusions   265

Part IV. Appendices

**Appendix A. National and multilateral statements on controlling   281
arms exports**

Preface

This book, written by Ian Davis, the Director of the British American Security Information Council (BASIC), assesses the development of common policies for the European Union (EU) governing arms and dual-use export controls. The changes that have taken place the world over, in particular the end of the cold war and the collapse of the bipolar system, have not left arms export control policies unaffected. This study analyses the reasons for and the broad implications of the post-cold war reforms of arms and dual-use export controls within the EU. It conceptualizes the arms export policy process as a policy system involving the interaction of three basic elements: the policy environment, policy stakeholders and public policies.

Three national case studies on the UK, Germany and Sweden explore the major problems and paradoxes of practical regulatory activity. The differences in their regulatory approaches—including variations in the export control criteria, controlled goods, decision-making bodies, licensing decisions and enforcement procedures—are rooted in each state's unique historical normative framework. Evidence is also presented of policy convergence within the EU as a whole. While COCOM (the Coordinating Committee on Multilateral Export Controls) was the main instrument of convergence during the cold war, the most significant instrument of convergence in the 1990s was EU integration.

The degree of convergence towards a common framework varies between the three countries. The book assesses the changing nature of the convergence–divergence 'mix' in the three states, and draws the principal conclusions that: (*a*) the process of European integration in the 1990s led to a significant but incomplete convergence of the three states' arms and dual-use export controls; (*b*) convergence is more advanced in the case of dual-use technologies than in that of military goods; (*c*) convergence accelerated during the late 1990s as a result of the introduction of the EU Code of Conduct on Arms Exports and common measures to combat illicit trafficking in small arms; (*d*) convergence is more advanced for policy-making structures than for policy-execution structures; and (*e*) further convergence can be expected in the next decade.

The author bases his analyses—in addition to the primary sources and publications—on a large number of interviews with policy stakeholders in three countries under consideration and within the European Commission. Most of the primary research for this study was carried out in 1997 and 1998, supplemented by additional interviews and research in 1999 and 2000. Some of the material has also been revised and expanded to take account of changes that occurred in European arms and dual-use export controls during the first half of 2001. The main conclusion of the volume is that reaching the consensus among the EU member states was a difficult process but the Union is now in a position to shape a cooperative model for arms and dual-use export controls.

Adam Daniel Rotfeld
Director of SIPRI
December 2001

Acknowledgements

This research was first conceived and written as a doctoral study. Many teachers, friends and colleagues influenced my thinking over the lifetime of the project. The University of Bradford Department of Peace Studies, my intellectual home for most of the past decade, and a grant from the Economic and Social Research Council made it possible for me to undertake this research. In particular, I must record my deep gratitude to my supervisor, Malcolm Chalmers, for his guidance throughout the preparation of the thesis and for his astute comments on successive drafts. I also owe a debt of thanks to former colleagues including Paul Dunne, Owen Greene, Steve Schofield and Peter Southwood.

I benefited from visits to the Bonn International Center for Conversion (BICC), the Peace Research Institute Frankfurt and the Stockholm International Peace Research Institute (SIPRI) during 1997. Ian Anthony at SIPRI and Michael Brzoska at BICC also gave me timely comments and helpful suggestions at various crucial stages in the research.

The transformation from doctoral thesis to book took place while working for Saferworld. I would like to thank all my colleagues there, and especially Paul Eavis and Elisabeth Clegg, for their continuing support and encouragement of a project that never seemed finished. My involvement in arms export control research and advocacy at Saferworld kept me close enough to the events and key stakeholders to make it possible to include the most up-to-date knowledge and evaluation. This made the task of finalizing the book all the more rewarding.

Finally, I am particularly grateful to Eve Johansson at SIPRI for her helpfulness and encouragement to an author in travail.

Ian Davis
Washington
December 2001

Acronyms and abbreviations

ACDA	Arms Control and Disarmament Agency (USA: from April 1999 Bureau of Arms Control)
AL	Ausfuhrliste (Export List , Germany)
APM	Anti-personnel mine
ASEAN	Association of South-East Asian Nations
AWG	Aussenwirtschaftsgesetz (Foreign Trade Act, Germany)
AWP	Arms Working Party (UK)
AWV	Aussenwirtschaftsverordnung (Foreign Trade Statutory Order, Germany)
BAe	British Aerospace
BAFA	Bundesausfuhramt (Federal Export Office, Germany)
BAW	Bundesamt für Wirtschaft (Federal Office of Economics, Germany)
BDI	Bundesverband der Deutschen Industrie (Federation of German Industries)
BMWi	Bundesministerium für Wirtschaft und Technologie (Federal Ministry of Economics, Germany)
C^3	Command, control and communications
CBW	Chemical and biological weapons
CDU	Christlich Demokratische Union (Christian Democratic Union (Germany)
CFE	Treaty on Conventional Armed Forces in Europe (1990)
CFSP	Common Foreign and Security Policy (EU)
CGEA	Community General Export Authorisation
COARM	Council of Ministers' Group for Co-operation in the Field of Armaments and the Harmonisation of European Export Policies (EU)
COCOM	Coordinating Committee on Multilateral Export Controls
COREPER	Committee of Permanent Representatives (EU)
CSCE	Conference on Security and Co-operation in Europe
CSU	Christlich Soziale Union (Christian Social Union, Germany)
DAC	Development Assistance Committee (OECD)
DESO	Defence Export Services Organisation (UK)
DESS	Defence Export Services Secretariat (DESO)
DEU	Declaration by End-User (Sweden)
DFID	Department for International Development (UK)
DM	Deutsche mark
DMA	Defence Manufacturers Association (UK)
DTI	Department of Trade and Industry (UK)
DUEC	Dual-Use and Related Goods (Export Control) Regulations (UK)

EC	European Community
ECGD	Export Credits Guarantee Department (UK)
ECO	Export Control Organisation (DTI)
ECOWAS	Economic Community of West African States
ECSC	European Coal and Steel Community
EDC	European Defence Community
EDIG	European Defence Industry Group
EEC	European Economic Community
EGCO	Export Goods Control Order (UK)
EKN	Exportkreditnämnden (Export Credits Guarantee Board, Sweden)
EP	European Parliament
EPC	European Political Co-operation
ERT	European Round Table of Industrialists
EU	European Union
EUU	End-User Undertaking
FCO	Foreign and Commonwealth Office (UK)
FDP	Freien Demokratischen Partei (Free Democratic Party, Germany)
FMV	Försvarets Materielverk (Defence Matériel Administration, Sweden)
FRG	Federal Republic of Germany
GATT	General Agreement on Tariffs and Trade
GDP	Gross domestic product
HADDEX	*Handbuch der Deutschen Exportkontrolle* [Handbook of German export controls]
ICBL	International Campaign to Ban Landmines
IGC	Intergovernmental Conference (EU)
IOL	Individual Open Licence (Sweden)
ISP	Inspektionen för Strategiska Produkter (National Inspectorate of Strategic Products, Sweden)
KMI	Krigsmaterielinspektionen (Military Equipment Inspectorate, Sweden)
KOBRA	Kontrolle Bei Der Ausfuhr (computerised export data collection system, Germany)
KWKG	Gesetz über die Kontrolle von Kriegswaffen (Weapons of War Control Act, Germany)
LFZ	Licence-free zone
MEC	Military equipment for combat purposes (Sweden)
MEP	Member of the European Parliament
MOU	Memorandum of Understanding
MTCR	Missile Technology Control Regime
MOD	Ministry of Defence (UK)
MOU	Memorandum of understanding
MP	Member of Parliament

MTCR	Missile Technology Control Regime
NATO	North Atlantic Treaty Organization
NBC	Nuclear, biological and chemical
NGO	Non-governmental organization
NPT	Non-Proliferation Treaty (1968)
NSG	Nuclear Suppliers Group
OAS	Organization of American States
OECD	Organisation for Economic Co-operation and Development
OGEL	Open General Export Licence
OGL	Open General Licence
OIEL	Open Individual Export Licence
OME	Other military equipment (Sweden)
OSCE	Organization for Security and Co-operation in Europe
P5	The five permanent members of the UN Security Council
PoCo	Political Committee (EU)
QMV	Qualified majority voting
R&D	Research and development
SEK	Swedish crowns
SEM	Single European Market
SFS	Svensk författningssamling
SIEL	Standard Individual Export Licence
SITC	Standard Industrial Trade Classification
SPD	Sozialdemokratische Partei (Social Democratic Party, Germany)
TARIC	Integrated Community Tariff
TDS	Tulldatasystemet
UAE	United Arab Emirates
UN	United Nations
UNDC	UN Disarmament Commission
UNICE	Union of Industrial and Employers' Confederations of Europe
WEU	Western European Union
WMD	Weapons of mass destruction
WTO	World Trade Organization
ZKA	Zollkriminalamt (Customs Criminal Investigation Service, Germany)
ZKI	Zollkriminalinstitut (Customs Investigation Service, Germany)

Glossary

Arms exports The dispatch of conventional weapons, weapon platforms and related equipment (that would normally be found on a military list of controlled goods) from one country to another.

Buyer's market A situation where the market supply exceeds general demand so that sellers are at a disadvantage relative to a buyer's options to shop around.

Communication Method used by the European Commission to submit policy proposals to other EU institutions (such as the Council and European Parliament) with the purpose of initiating an intergovernmental policy debate at ministerial level.

Conditionality Provisions that require certain policies, such as reduced defence spending, in exchange for agreement to provide financial or military assistance.

Council of Ministers The key decision-making body for EU policy. It comprises ministers from each member government, the exact minister depending on the subject under discussion.

Dual-use exports The dispatch of conventional dual-use goods and technologies that are licensable from one country to another. Although 'dual-use' can refer to any technology that has current *or* potential military *and* civilian applications, here it is used only to refer to those technologies that are licensable.

End-use certificates Statements associated with arms and dual-use export licence applications which set out expected behaviour regarding the final destination and uses allowed for the goods.

European Commission The functional equivalent of an executive civil service, consisting of commissioners (appointed by member governments) and supporting staff. Commissioners act independently of governments and of the European Council, but may be collectively removed by the European Parliament with a two-thirds majority vote. The Commission makes proposals for Community laws, monitors compliance with the treaties and administers the Community finances.

European Community/European Union The institutional changes and somewhat complicated terminology created by the 1991 Treaty of European Union (the Maastricht Treaty) have led to some confusion over the difference between the European Union (EU) and the European Community (EC). After ratification of the Maastricht Treaty in 1993, the EC (formerly the European Economic Community) became one of the three European Communities (along with the European Coal and Steel Community (ECSC) and the European Atomic Energy Community (Euratom). The Council of Ministers became the Council of the European Union at this point. The Commission remains the Commission of the European Communities. Issues involving the single market, competition and external trade still fall under the EC, and the EU is the collective union of member states. The correct usage of 'EU' and 'EC' therefore depends on the context under discussion.

European Council Heads of state and government, assisted by their foreign ministers, meet at the European Council two or three times a year to discuss major issues and to set parameters for the future direction of the Union. It has no formal powers as such and must implement its proposals via the Council of Ministers.

European Court of Justice Including judges from all the EU countries, the ECJ passes judgement on disputes arising from the application and interpretation of Community laws.

European Parliament The EU's directly elected assembly with consultative and oversight powers.

European Political Co-operation A strictly intergovernmental process of coordination within the European Communities between 1970 to 1991, when it was replaced by the CFSP.

Extraterritoriality A US concept which involves the US authorities demanding the right to impose penalties on companies in allied countries which re-export or transfer US technologies to another user without the permission of the US Government.

Framework Agreement The Framework Agreement Concerning Measures To Facilitate the Restructuring and Operation of the European Defence Industry, signed in July 2000 by the defence ministers of France, Germany, Italy, Spain, Sweden and the United Kingdom.

Harmonization A specific conception of EU economic integration by which national administrators, the European Commission and private organizations seek to achieve common technical standards for products. It was a specific policy goal of the European Commission from 1968 to the early 1990s, but meagre results saw the adoption of 'mutual recognition' as a new approach after 1992.

Horizontal proliferation The spread of weapons to more and more countries.

Indigenous Produced or originating inside a given country.

Multilateral Involving cooperation between more than two countries.

Mutual recognition An alternative conception of EU economic integration (arising from the limitations of 'harmonization') in which national regulations and standards for products and services are framed in a way that respects minimum European requirements.

Political Committee Representatives from the foreign ministries of member states who meet once a month to define and implement the Common Foreign and Security Policy (and formerly European Political Co-operation).

Re-export The export of arms or dual-use goods that were originally obtained by import.

Regimes Although the orthodox usage refers to agreements or the joint development of organizations among countries to regulate international behaviour or outcomes, here it is also used to conceptualize the national regulation of arms and dual-use exports.

Vertical proliferation The transfer and spread of higher levels of weapon technology in the international system.

1. Introduction

I. Background

This book explores one aspect of the European integration process—the development of common policies for the European Union (EU) governing arms and dual-use export controls.

While common policies have been developed in some areas of EU policy, such as trade, member states' strategic export control policies and regulatory mechanisms have traditionally fallen within the remit of national sovereignty. The lack of common policies in security-related export controls became more problematic as a result of the creation of a Single European Market in 1992 and the progressive removal of internal barriers to trade. This raised the potential of opportunist manufacturers producing strategic equipment in, and applying for export licences from, the EU member states with the most relaxed arms-related export controls.

In addition, the importance of multilateral arms and dual-use export control regimes was highlighted by the 1991 Persian Gulf War, when on occasions troops from EU member states faced weapons of EU origin. This turn of events suggested to governments a need to avoid export loopholes and the stockpiling of weapons by unstable regimes. Thus, it was seen to be in the interest of EU member states to pursue convergence in a policy area of universal concern. This book sets out to evaluate the extent to which such convergence has occurred so far and the prospects for further harmonization in the future.

The purpose of this introductory chapter is to provide the orientation for the rest of the book by discussing some of the issues that shaped its content and direction. It begins by outlining some of the key arguments and reasons for conducting the study, including a brief review of the relevant literature (section II). This is followed by a discussion of the scope, method and conduct of the study (section III).

II. The rationale for this study

The core aim of this book is to assess the reforms of export controls for arms and dual-use goods and technologies currently taking place within the EU, and to analyse the reasons for and the broad implications of those reforms. In support of this, the three national case studies (of national arms and dual-use export control policies in the United Kingdom, Germany and Sweden) raise the major problems and paradoxes of practical regulatory activity and highlight the often-differing attitudes and policy positions among principal government agencies.

In short, is the process of European integration (and in particular, the harmonization of regulatory policies within the EU) leading to a convergence of national arms and dual-use export control regimes in member states and, if so, what are the likely consequences for international efforts to control the proliferation of conventional weapons and dual-use technologies? In considering this question, the book also addresses a number of supplementary questions:

1. Why do countries differ in the ways in which they engage in regulation of arms and dual-use goods transfers?

2. Do these differences have consequences for the diffusion of arms and military-related technology?

3. What are the main obstacles to agreement on EU arms and dual-use export control regimes?

4. Is the current framework for harmonizing European arms and dual-use export controls based on intergovernmentalism, supranationalism or a 'middle way'?

5. What are the norms and control standards around which convergence is taking place?

6. What policy measures (depending on the answers to the previous two questions) are needed in order to achieve credible and effective EU control regimes? In particular, what changes would be necessary in the oversight and regulatory functions of the various national government departments and agencies of member states whose responsibilities touch on arms and dual-use export controls?

7. Will the EU need to cooperate with other major suppliers outside the EU (particularly the USA) and, if so, what form should that cooperation take?

The answers to these questions are developed in the chapters which follow and drawn out in the conclusions of each chapter. For the sake of clarity, the final chapter also returns to and directly addresses them again.

There are a number of reasons why the development of common European arms and dual-use export controls is worthy of such a detailed examination at this time. First, the recent introduction of separate and partial EU control regimes for arms and dual-use items provides a unique and timely opportunity to examine this issue in detail.[1] Second, the widening of the EU in 1995 to include another important arms supplier—Sweden, which is discussed in chapter 7—provides an opportunity to examine the issue from a new perspective. Third, the further enlargement of the EU is certain to result in other important supplier states (such as the Czech Republic and Poland) becoming members of the Union, and this study can suggest ways in which EU norms and regimes could affect their policies. Finally, the development of common European policies could do much to influence the effectiveness of evolving international controls on military and dual-use goods.

---

[1] The Regulation and Joint Action on Dual-Use Goods and Technologies came into force on 1 July 1995 and are discussed in chapter 3. The 1997 EU Programme for Preventing and Combating Illicit Trafficking in Conventional Arms, the 1998 EU Code of Conduct on Arms Exports and the 1998 EU Joint Action on Small Arms are discussed in chapter 4.

Existing studies on arms export control policies

Existing studies of security-related export control policies are extremely diverse. Three broad types of empirical investigation can be distinguished: analysis at the level of international systems;[2] those based around some aspect of the political economy of international security (including economic studies and trade theory);[3] and those that focus on regulatory issues, such as the general arms control and disarmament literature, elements of strategic studies, international relations and regime theory, and work on bureaucratic and 'high' politics.[4] However, most of this literature is only concerned indirectly with the everyday politics and administration of export controls, and even then the focus is generally on East–West technology transfer or the proliferation of nuclear, biological and chemical (NBC) weapons.[5]

There are also a number of case studies of individual countries' arms export policies.[6] Within the EU, in addition to Kolodziej's study of France,[7] some of the most important studies are concerned with the three countries discussed in this book. Two of the most significant in relation to British arms export controls are Pearson's study in the early 1980s[8] and more recently Miller's case study of British arms export policy, which is both a general analysis of that policy (in the aftermath of the Scott Report on the 'Arms to Iraq' affair) and a detailed

[2] The first comprehensive analysis of the development of the international arms transfer and production *system* was provided by Harkavy, R., *The Arms Trade and International Systems* (Ballinger: Cambridge, Mass., 1975), but for a more recent treatment see Krause, K., *Arms and the State: Patterns of Military Production and Trade* (Cambridge University Press: Cambridge, 1992); and Laurance, E., *The International Arms Trade* (Lexington Books: New York, 1992).

[3] See, e.g., Keller, W., *Arm in Arm: The Political Economy of the Global Arms Trade* (Basic Books: New York, 1995); and Pearson, F., *The Global Spread of Arms* (Westview Press: Boulder, Colo., 1994).

[4] See, e.g., Carlton, D. *et al.* (eds), *Controlling the International Transfer of Weaponry and Related Technology* (Dartmouth: Aldershot, 1995); Brauch, H. G. *et al.* (eds), *Controlling the Development and Spread of Military Technology: Lessons from the Past and Challenges for the 1990s* (VU University Press: Amsterdam, 1992); and Nolan, J. (ed.), *Global Engagement: Cooperation and Security in the 21st Century* (Brookings Institution: Washington, DC, 1994).

[5] Compendiums of national export control policies concerned with the proliferation of weapons of mass destruction (WMD), and particularly nuclear materials, have been published by a number of scholars. In particular, see the work of Harald Müller and the Peace Research Institute Frankfurt, including Müller, H., (ed.), *Nuclear Export Controls in Europe* (European InterUniversity Press: Brussels, 1995); and Müller, H. (ed.), *European Non-Proliferation Policy 1993–1995* (European InterUniversity Press: Brussels, 1996). See also Bailey, K. and Rudney, R. (eds), *Proliferation and Export Controls* (University Press of America: Lanham, Md., 1993). On East–West technology controls see the work of Gary Bertsch and his colleagues at the Center for East–West Trade Policy at the University of Georgia in the USA. Particularly noteworthy are: Bertsch, G., Vogel, H. and Zielonka, J. (eds), *After the Revolutions: East–West Trade and Technology Transfer in the 1990s* (Westview Press: Boulder, Colo., 1991); Bertsch, G. and Elliott-Gower, S. (eds), *Export Controls in Transition: Perspectives, Problems, and Prospects* (Duke University Press: Durham, Ga., 1992); and Bertsch, G., Cupitt, R. and Elliott-Gower, S. (eds), *International Cooperation on Nonproliferation Export Controls: Prospects for the 1990s and Beyond* (University of Michigan Press: Ann Arbor, Mich., 1994).

[6] Outside the EU most of the case studies focus on the USA—see, e.g., Heinz, J., *US Strategic Trade: An Export Control System for the 1990s* (Westview Press: Boulder, Colo., 1991)—or the countries of the former Soviet Union and Central and Eastern Europe (see note 5).

[7] Kolodziej, E., *Making and Marketing Arms: The French Experience and its Implications for the International System* (Princeton University Press: Princeton, N.J., 1987).

[8] Pearson, F., 'The question of control in British defence sales policy', *International Affairs*, vol. 59, no. 2 (spring 1983), pp. 211–38.

account of British controls in relation to Iran and Iraq.[9] Arguably the most significant of all the British studies, however, is the officially-sanctioned Scott Report, which foreshadowed a major political change in the UK's arms export controls (as discussed in chapter 5).[10]

Several scholars have published detailed studies on German export controls, including Pearson, Brzoska, Müller and Hofhansel.[11] Sweden has attracted less scholarly interest, although a number of comparative studies touch on Swedish export controls.[12]

There is a surprising paucity of careful empirical studies of cross-national regulatory policies where the proliferation of conventional arms and dual-use goods and technologies is a central feature of the analysis. There are at least eight recent notable exceptions, however. The volume edited by Anthony was the first book ever to document and explain the practice of arms export regulation, and includes descriptions of 24 different national arms export control regimes and a number of multilateral arms transfer control regimes.[13] A similar publication by Vastera Ltd (a UK-based company, formerly known as Deltac Ltd, and trading as Export Control Publications) drew together practical information on export control policy and procedures in countries that participate in multilateral export control regimes. There have been several editions since the first edition of 1991 and the guide now includes profiles of over 40 countries.[14] Both these volumes concentrate primarily on describing the legal frameworks that exist to regulate the export of arms and pay only secondary attention to government policy, the pattern of exports and the influences of structure and agency.

This is not the case with the other six contributions, which take a more analytical and 'theoretically informed' approach. The volume edited by Bertsch, Cupitt and Elliott-Gower explores 10 different national export control perspectives from around the world with the aim of assessing whether multilateral export controls can be designed that will promote democracy, economic prosperity and military security.[15] Similarly, the volume edited by Bertsch and Grillot explores the developing export control systems in the 15 states of the

---

[9] Miller, D., *Export or Die: Britain's Defence Trade with Iran and Iraq* (Cassell: London, 1996).

[10] British House of Commons, *The Right Honourable Sir Richard Scott, Report of the Inquiry into the Export of Defence Equipment and Dual-Use Goods to Iraq and Related Prosecutions: Return to an Address of the Honourable the House of Commons dated 15th February*, HC 1995/96 115 (Her Majesty's Stationery Office: London, 1996), 5 vols and index (hereafter the Scott Report).

[11] Pearson, F., 'Of leopards and cheetahs: West Germany's role as a mid-sized arms supplier', *Orbis* (spring 1985); Brzoska, M., 'The erosion of restraint in West German arms transfer policy', *Journal of Peace Research*, vol. 26, no. 2 (1989), pp. 165–77; Müller, H. *et al.*, *From Black Sheep to White Angel? The New German Export Control Policy*, PRIF Reports no. 32 (Peace Research Institute Frankfurt: Frankfurt, Jan. 1994); and Hofhansel, C., *Commercial Competition and National Security: Comparing US and German Export Control Policies* (Praeger: Westport, Conn., 1996).

[12] See, e.g., Hagelin, B., 'Sweden's search for military technology', eds M. Brzoska and P. Lock, SIPRI, *Restructuring of Arms Production in Western Europe* (Oxford University Press: Oxford, 1992); and van Dassen, L., 'Sweden', ed. Müller, *Nuclear Export Controls in Europe* (note 5).

[13] Anthony, I. (ed.), SIPRI, *Arms Export Regulations* (Oxford University Press: Oxford, 1991).

[14] The most recent edition is *Worldwide Guide to Export Controls 1998/1999* (Export Control Publications: Chertsey, May 1999).

[15] Bertsch, Cupitt and Elliott-Gower (note 5).

former Soviet Union.[16] Although this book focuses on efforts to reduce the risk of proliferation of weapons of mass destruction (WMD), it also explores a number of theoretical approaches and methods for measuring and comparing export control development. In a similar vein, Hofhansel provides an in-depth comparative study of German and US export control policies.[17]

Of more direct relevance to this book is the 1991 comparative study for the European Parliament in by Bauer, Brzoska and Karl, which contains an overview of the arms export policies of each of the European Community (EC) member states and goes on to outline some of the options for a common arms export policy within the EC.[18] Similarly, the study by Cornish examines West European attempts to regulate the trade in arms and dual-use goods and evaluates the obstacles to effective multilateral coordination.[19] Finally, a small number of European-based research institutes and non-governmental organizations (NGOs) have been at the forefront of policy research and advocacy in the field of European arms and dual-use export controls, and have published a wide variety of relevant briefings, reports and journal articles.[20]

III. The scope, method and conduct of the study

The existing literature suggests that policy making in the field of arms export controls is best understood as a diffuse and multi-level process. As Parsons notes: 'To think analytically about public policy we have to be sensitive to the existence of "reality" as a construction within a multiplicity of frameworks'.[21]

Thus, the orientation of this research is pragmatic, critical and inter-disciplinary. It attempts to integrate the previous ways in which scholars have conceived of export controls. It does not set out to advance new theories or interpretations on export controls, nor does it presume to incorporate all the important themes and writings of scholars in the various academic disciplines

---

[16] Bertsch, G. and Grillot, S. (eds), *Arms on the Market: Reducing the Risk of Proliferation in the Former Soviet Union* (Routledge: New York, 1998).

[17] Hofhansel (note 11).

[18] Bauer, H., Brzoska, M. and Karl, W., *Co-ordination and Control of Arms Exports from EC Member States and the Development of a Common Arms Export Policy*, Study Prepared for the European Parliament, Directorate General for Research, European Parliament Research Project no. 4/90/9, Arbeitspapiere/Working Papers no. 48 (Berghof Foundation: Berlin, 1992).

[19] Cornish, P., *The Arms Trade and Europe*, Chatham House Papers (Royal Institute of International Affairs and Pinter: London, 1995).

[20] See, e.g., the reports and briefings published by Saferworld, including: Anthony, I., Eavis, P. and Greene, O., *Regulating Arms Exports: A Programme for the European Community* (Saferworld: London, Sep. 1991); Eavis, P. (ed.), *Arms and Dual-Use Exports from the EC: A Common Policy for Regulation and Control* (Saferworld: London, Dec. 1992); and Eavis, P. and Shannon, A., 'Arms and dual-use export controls: priorities for the European Union', Saferworld Briefing, London, June 1994. See also Adam, B. (ed.), *European Union and Arms Exports* (Groupe de Recherche et d'Information sur la Paix et la Sécurité (GRIP): Brussels, Dec. 1995). In addition, the yearbooks published by the Stockholm International Peace Research Institute (the SIPRI Yearbook) and the International Institute for Strategic Studies (*The Military Balance*) often contain useful material on national and multilateral export controls.

[21] Parsons, W., *Public Policy: An Introduction to the Theory and Practice of Policy Analysis* (Edward Elgar: Aldershot, 1995), p. 58.

which touch upon the issue.[22] It does, however, elaborate on and synthesize certain established themes and interpretations that are considered to be of central importance in providing a contextual focus for understanding regulatory activity in the contemporary European arms market. This synthesis involves a shift from 'specific' to 'holistic' (or interdisciplinary) research, where a range of factors impinging on the research subject, as well as past and present networks of relationships, are taken into consideration.

This study is concerned specifically with the policy process, that is to say, the stages through which the arms export policy passes, and the influence of different factors on policy formulation. The literature on foreign policy and export controls suggests that a very large array of variables may influence the formulation of export control policy, thereby making a cross-national model of export control policies problematic. From their review of the theoretical perspectives that shape multilateral export controls, for example, Bertsch, Cupitt and Elliott-Gower conclude that a combination of 'political, military, economic, and technological forces at the international and domestic levels and the institutional setting interact to form the policy-making environment'.[23] Given that export control policies are clearly complex political phenomena, an approach is required that 'stresses the dynamics of individual national policy processes, the interaction of multiple political and economic objectives, and the current policy-making environment'.[24]

A 'policy system' approach

This study is therefore structured around a conceptual model of the arms export policy process as a policy system (as shown in figure 1.1). According to Dunn a policy system is 'the overall institutional pattern within which policies are made' and involves the interrelationship between three elements: (*a*) public policies—the long series of more or less related choices, including decisions not to act, made by government bodies and officials; (*b*) policy stakeholders— individuals or groups which have a stake in policies because they affect and are affected by governmental decisions); and (*c*) policy environments—the specific context in which events surrounding a policy occur influences and is in turn influenced by policy stakeholders and public policies.[25]

The interactions that take place between these three elements are crucial to understanding the formulation of arms export control policy.[26]

---

[22] E.g., this study does not examine the role of the media and public opinion in the policy agenda-setting process.

[23] Bertsch, Cupitt and Elliott-Gower (note 5), pp. 11–12.

[24] Bertsch, Cupitt and Elliott-Gower (note 5), p. 21.

[25] Dunn, W., *Public Policy Analysis: An Introduction*, 2nd edn (Prentice-Hall: Englewood Cliffs, N.J., 1994), p. 70.

[26] For a discussion of the notion that causality lies in interactions rather than in individual parts see Scholte, J. A., *International Relations of Social Change* (Oxford University Press: Oxford, 1993), especially chapter 6, 'Facets of world-systemic social transformation', pp. 100–18.

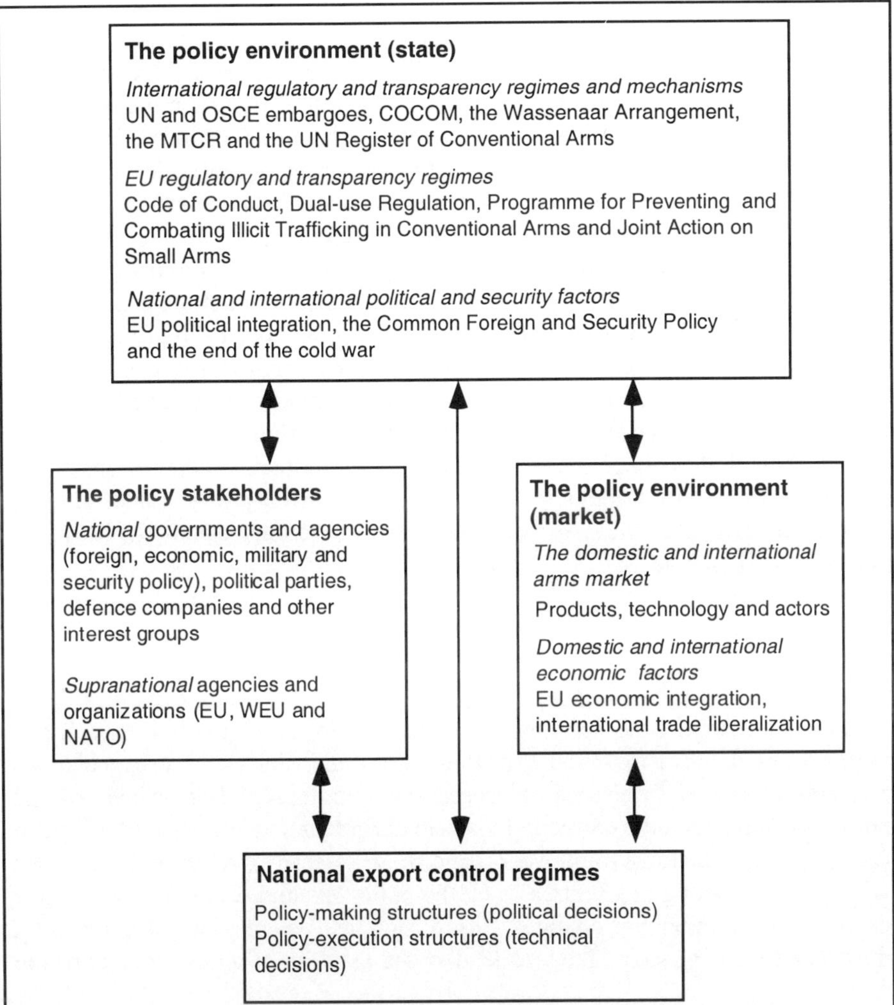

Figure 1.1. A model of the arms and dual-use export control policy system

Source: Adapted by the author from Bertsch, G., Cupitt, R. and Elliott-Gower, S. (eds), *International Cooperation on Nonproliferation Export Controls: Prospects for the 1990s and Beyond* (University of Michigan Press: Ann Arbor, Mich., 1994), pp. 11–12.

The 'public policy' under examination here has two basic elements: policy making and policy execution.[27] Policy making in the field of arms export controls is about deciding what goods should be subject to control in respect of which destinations and under which conditions. These are essentially political decisions of a normative nature. It is important to note, however, the difference

[27] This distinction is suggested by Wenzel, J., 'The European Community's approach to export controls', eds Bailey and Rudney (note 5), pp. 95–96.

between the study of policy as opposed to the study of decision making. Policy may occasionally be identifiable in terms of a decision, but very often it involves either groups of decisions or what may be seen as little more than a general predisposition to respond in a particular way.[28] For example, when the British Government says that it has adopted an ethical dimension to its foreign policy (see chapter 5), it is stating an intention to make specific decisions with this attitude in mind. It is not announcing a decision as such. In fact, the practical 'decisions' may turn out to be quite different.[29]

In contrast, policy execution in the field of arms export controls is about establishing and operating procedures capable of ensuring that the export of the designated goods is effectively controlled to the proscribed destinations. While these are essentially technical decisions, they remain highly politicized. This is because arms export control policies often involve a level of technical complexity in their normal operation that requires government officials to make critical choices at the implementation stage. (The question whether or not this is the intention of policy makers is addressed later in chapter 8, for as Hague, Harrop and Breslin conclude, 'window dressing' is one reason for having a policy in the first place.[30])

Thus, it is often difficult to draw a clear distinction between policy making and policy execution. Nevertheless these two basic elements provide a useful analytical tool which is further enhanced by the conceptualization of this public policy area as a regime. Although there are many theories about regimes,[31] one common treatment is to see them as 'sets of implicit or explicit principles, norms, rules and decision-making procedures around which actors' expectations converge in a given issue area of international relations'.[32] The 'principles and norms' are understood to provide the basic defining characteristics of a regime (i.e., the policy-making framework), and these effectively underpin the 'rules and decision-making procedures' (i.e., the policy-execution framework). Thus, changes in the latter are changes within regimes, whereas major changes in norms and principles are likely to lead to the creation of a new regime or the

---

[28] Ham, C. and Hill, M., *The Policy Process in the Modern Capitalist State*, 2nd edn (Harvester Wheatsheaf: Brighton, 1984), p. 10.

[29] Similar ambiguity was captured by Brzoska in his categorization of German export policy on 3 different levels: the level of declarations, expressed in the official rules and regulations; the bureaucratic level, embodied in the customs and practices of agencies granting licences; and the 'real' level, where the most important motivations of officials are reflected in overall patterns of sales. Brzoska (note 11), pp. 165–77.

[30] Hague, R., Harrop, M. and Breslin, S., *Comparative Government and Politics: An Introduction*, 3rd edn (Macmillan: London, 1994), p. 397.

[31] Much of the disagreement and abstraction about international regimes stems from deeper epistemological and ontological differences among commentators. See, e.g., Krasner, S. (ed.), *International Regimes* (Cornell University Press: Ithaca, N.Y., 1983), pp. 1–21; and Buzan, B., 'From international system to international society: structural realism and regime theory meet the English school', *International Organization*, vol. 47, no. 3 (summer 1993), pp. 227–52.

[32] 'Principles are beliefs of fact, causation and rectitude. Norms are standards of behaviour defined in terms of rights and obligations. Rules are specific prescriptions or proscriptions for action. Decision-making procedures are prevailing practices for making and implementing collective choice.' Krasner (note 31), p. 2.

disappearance of a regime from a given issue area.[33] The arms export control regimes in the UK (chapter 5), Germany (chapter 6) and Sweden (chapter 7), and the extent to which a new regime is being created at the EU level (chapters 3 and 4), are the focus of this study, including the 'bargains'[34] between policy stakeholders (domestic and international, political and economic, corporate and interstate) that underlie the regimes.

The main 'policy stakeholders' are political parties, national governments, government agencies (both national and supranational), policy analysts, defence companies and NGOs. It will become clear in later chapters (especially 5, 6 and 7) that there are common and divergent interests and views not only between national governments in different countries but also within each EU member state. It is rare to find a unified national perspective on this issue, so it is important to attempt to differentiate between widely held views and minority views on export controls. This study is also concerned with charting arms export 'policy networks'[35] both at the national and at the European level.

Finally, the 'policy environment' involves a number of different levels of analysis: the domestic policy environment within the context of the nation state (chapters 5, 6 and 7); the macro–regional policy environment within the EU and the North Atlantic Treaty Organization (NATO) (chapter 3); and the global or international policy environment. In the latter, the evolving multipolar security structure and the international political economy form much of the context for national regulatory policies, and particularly the international arms market and multilateral regulatory regimes (briefly discussed in chapter 2). The EU is, however, the most important multilateral context for national policy making (chapters 3 and 4).

The importance of definitions: understanding the terms 'arms' and 'dual-use'

In considering arms export control policy in the EU, a central problem is the absence of any standard definition of both the 'arms' and the 'dual-use' trade. The starting point in most of the arms control literature is to separate WMD from so-called conventional armaments. This study is only concerned with the regulation of conventional weapons and associated 'dual-use' equipment and technology. It does not examine the regulation of NBC materials that can be used in the construction of WMD.

Having disregarded WMD, there are still considerable problems in defining what is meant by the conventional arms trade and dual-use transfers.

---

[33] A further distinction is the *weakening* of a regime, either because of incoherence in both its norms and its rules or because actual practice is inconsistent with those norms and rules. Krasner (note 31), pp. 3–4.

[34] Strange, S., 'Political economy and international relations', eds K. Booth and S. Smith, *International Relations Theory Today* (Polity Press: Cambridge, 1995), p. 160; and Strange, S., 'Cave! hic dragones: a critique of regime analysis', ed. Krasner (note 31), pp. 353–54.

[35] For a discussion of policy network analysis see Parsons (note 21), pp. 184–92.

There are a number of possible definitions and meanings attributable to 'arms' and 'dual-use', and, as Anthony concludes, 'until standard definitions gain more widespread acceptance, the arms trade will continue to mean different things to different people'.[36] Moreover, the identification and categorization of the various 'commodities' that make up the arms trade is a problem which has practical as well as theoretical implications. Without a common understanding of how and where to draw the line between goods and services which should be controlled and those that can be traded freely, it is difficult to forge EU-wide agreements in this area. For most states, arms and dual-use goods are defined in national legislation in accordance with national lists of goods and technologies. As later chapters make clear, one of the most potent issues but also one of the most difficult is the harmonization of such national lists of controlled goods.

The narrowest definition of the arms trade would be linked purely to lethal equipment or weapons of war. However, since it is generally accepted that a wide array of combat support equipment and a considerable number of dual-use components and technologies are integral to the effectiveness of a country's armed forces, this narrow definition is now rarely used. Indeed, many countries have modified their export regulations in recent years to reflect this reality of modern warfare.[37] Of course, including dual-use equipment and technologies does mean that at some levels the 'arms trade' is virtually inseparable from trade generally. As will become clear later this complexity is a central feature of the current regulatory environment. 'Dual-use' is a term which has variously been applied to products, to the results of research, to technology (itself a term with multiple meanings) and even to raw materials. A recent study applied a broad definition of technology (which included both capital and labour assets) to the term 'dual-use', and in turn defined dual-use technology as 'any technology that has current *or* potential military *and* civilian applications'.[38]

Given these complexities, this study follows the lead taken within the EU (as discussed in chapter 3), in that it draws a distinction between the trade in 'arms' and the trade in 'dual-use' goods. Thus, unless a particular context specifies otherwise, the term 'arms' is used to refer only to conventional weapons and weapons platforms and related equipment (which would normally be found on a national military list of controlled goods). Similarly, the term 'dual-use' is

---

[36] Anthony (note 13), p. 4. See also the discussion by Lowe, V., 'The definition of restricted exports' in Eavis (note 20), pp. 25–43.

[37] In Sweden, e.g., a distinction is made between 'military equipment', i.e., equipment designed primarily for a military purpose, and 'defence equipment', which may also have non-military applications but is procured by the defence forces. Only the former is specified in law and subject to export controls. A new and expanded concept of 'military equipment' was introduced in 1993, so those items are now classified either as 'military equipment for combat purposes' or as 'other military equipment'. See the discussion in chapter 7.

[38] Mollas-Gallart, J. and Perry Robinson, J., 'Assessment of dual technologies in the context of European security and defence', PE 166 819/Final, European Parliament, Directorate General of Research, Luxembourg, Oct. 1997, p. 15. The forms of technology covered by their definition include: products (final systems, major subsystems, components and materials, tools and machinery); blueprints, designs, scientific and technological (codified) knowledge; 'know-how', skills; management techniques and systems; and management and organizational 'principles'.

generally applied in a narrow sense, to refer only to those conventional dual-use goods and technologies that are licensable.

While the latter is a useful working definition for this study, in the context of the practical application of export controls, it raises once again the question how to identify and categorize the various 'technologies' that make up the dual-use trade. In the case of consumer electronics, for example, personal computers, software and know-how all fall within the definition of dual-use technology. However, since they are everyday tools which are mass-produced throughout the world there is often little to be gained by imposing export restrictions. Increasingly, therefore, conventional dual-use technologies are only controlled if they are indispensable within a weapon system or programme, cannot be substituted easily and are not easily available. More detailed discussions of the problems raised by dual-use technology transfers are undertaken in subsequent chapters, that is, in relation to the EU Regulation on Dual-use Goods and Technologies (chapter 4) and the national case studies (chapters 5, 6 and 7).

In addition to the problems in identifying the commodities to be included in any description of the arms trade, two other distinctions need to be highlighted: that between legal and illegal trade; and that between *inter*national and *intra*-national trade.

First, this study is only indirectly concerned with the illegal or covert arms market (also known as 'grey' and 'black' arms transfers). Although the illicit trade in arms is an important and growing area of concern, the multiple and complex processes driving or permitting illicit arms trafficking are beyond the scope of this study.[39] Second, while the primary focus in much of the arms control literature is normally the weapons traded between states, domestic procurement (the purchase of weapons by governments for their own national armed forces) is also important. That the two issues are inextricably linked was highlighted in the political debate over the setting up of the UN Register of Conventional Arms. In short, developing countries wanted to know why those states that import significant amounts of weapons should be subjected to more scrutiny than those that manufacture most of their own armaments. Moreover, as Hartung has pointed out, 'if limits on arms sales to the Third World are not matched by reductions in arms production and interventionary capacity in the industrial nations, arms-transfer restraint could come to be viewed as a mere adjunct to a renewed policy of big-power interventionism, another point of leverage to be used by the nations of the North in policing and manipulating conflicts in the South for their own benefit'.[40]

---

[39] Illicit arms trafficking exists on a large scale and is closely associated with recent war, insecurity, crime, terrorism and social violence in Europe as well as in other regions of the world. See, e.g., Klare, M., 'Secret operatives, clandestine trades: the thriving black market for weapons', *Bulletin of the Atomic Scientists*, vol. 44, no. 3 (Apr. 1988), pp. 16–25; Naylor, R. T., 'Loose cannons: covert commerce and underground finance in the modern arms black market', *Crime, Law and Social Change*, vol. 22 (1995), pp. 1–57; and Greene, O., *Tackling Illicit Trafficking in Conventional Arms: Strengthening Collective Efforts by EU and Associate Countries* (Saferworld: London, Apr. 1999).

[40] Hartung, W., 'Curbing the arms trade: from rhetoric to restraint', *World Policy Journal*, vol. 9, no. 3 (spring 1992), p. 236.

Problems with the data on arms and dual-use exports

The difficulties in defining the arms and dual-use trade inevitably lead to problems of measurement. These are exacerbated by the absence of reliable data on arms and dual-use exports in national foreign trade statistics.[41] There are, however, several publicly available, multi-country statistical sources on international arms transfers, including the UN Register, the US Congressional Research Service (CRS), the US Bureau of Arms Control—formerly the Arms Control and Disarmament Agency (ACDA)—and the Stockholm International Peace Research Institute (SIPRI) arms transfers database.[42] Since most of these sources tend to concentrate on major conventional weapons, a significant part of the arms trade is excluded from the data, including most transfers of dual-use technologies and small arms.[43] However, even though the major conventional weapons market receives the most attention, problems still remain with the data and there are often large discrepancies in the comparable numbers reported by different sources.[44]

The treatment of transfers involving dual-use technology or collaborative production can exacerbate problems of consistency in the data. Are aircraft parts and electronic components, for example, treated as a transfer of civil, military or dual-use goods? How should market shares be calculated in collaborative projects such as the Tornado aircraft? In the case of the former, some sources,

[41] The trade classifications used by most countries—the Standard Industrial Trade Classification (SITC) and the Harmonised System (HS)—do not clearly identify military-related trade. Happe and Wakeman-Linn conclude that 'for most countries, customs data in their present form cannot be used as a source for information on military trade'. Happe, N. and Wakeman-Linn, J., 'Military expenditure and arms trade: alternative data sources, Part I', *Peace Economics, Peace Science and Public Policy*, vol. 1, no. 4 (1994), p. 7.

[42] For further information on the UN Register of Conventional Arms see, e.g., the annual reports of the UN Secretary-General on the register—most recently UN document A/55/299, 15 Aug. 2000, available on the UN Internet site at URL <http://www.un.org/Depts/dda/CAB/register.htm>—and the Bradford Arms Register Studies series of publications—most recently Chalmers, M. and Greene, O., *In Need of Attention: The UN Register in its Seventh Year*, BARS Working Paper no. 7 (Bradford University: Bradford, Feb. 2000). The CRS publishes annual reports on arms transfers to the Third World, *Trends in Conventional Arms Transfers to the Third World*. The US Bureau of Arms Control publishes an annual report on global arms transfers, most recently in *World Military Expenditures and Arms Transfers 1998* (US Department of State: Washington, DC, Feb. 2000). ACDA became the Bureau of Arms Control, a part of the US State Department, in Apr. 1999. SIPRI publishes its findings on the international trade in major conventional weapons in its *Yearbook*, most recently *SIPRI Yearbook 2001: Armaments, Disarmament and International Security* (Oxford University Press: Oxford, 2001). Significant differences exist in the methods used by these organizations to gather and estimate information on arms transfers and in the scope and coverage of the resulting data. For a comparative analysis of the data sources and their limitations see Happe and Wakeman-Linn (note 41), pp. 3–38; Laurance (note 2), pp. 16–45; Brzoska, M., 'Arms transfer data sources', *Journal of Conflict Resolution*, vol. 26, no. 1 (Mar. 1982), pp. 77–108; and Anthony, I., 'Measuring conventional arms transfers: definitions, data and evaluation', *Strategic Analysis* (Mar. 1995), pp. 1453–79.

[43] The exception is the Bureau of Arms Control data, which include deliveries of weapons, components of weapons, support equipment, other commodities designed for military use, dual-use equipment if the primary use is deemed to be military, production technology and licensing fees in certain cases, and construction, training and technical support.

[44] Some organizations, such as the UK's Defence Export Services Organisation (DESO), measure the flow of *new orders* (sometimes referred to as *agreements*). SIPRI measures only *deliveries* of defence equipment while the 2 US governmental agencies (the Bureau of Arms Control and the CRS) attempt to measure both *agreements* and deliveries.

such as SIPRI, use the identity of the buyer as the criterion, and a dual-use transfer is treated as 'military' if the recipient is from the armed forces or paramilitary forces of the country concerned. In the latter example, the transfer of Tornadoes to Saudi Arabia in the late 1980s was listed in most data sets as a supply from the UK even though the aircraft were built by a multinational consortium (Panavia) involving companies based in Germany, Italy and the UK.

Problems with the poor quality of data on the quantity and type of weapons and defence-related goods transferred are exacerbated by difficulties in establishing transaction prices, which are rarely publicized. Hence, national arms export figures are very difficult to analyse, with cross-source comparisons being particularly difficult because of the extent of the differences between sources.[45] This said, however, the available data do allow for some analysis of trends in arms transfers. The US Bureau of Arms Control and SIPRI are the two main data sources used throughout this study.

Structure of the study

This study is structured in four parts. Part I (chapter 2) provides an overview of the nature and effectiveness of international arms and dual-use export controls, both past and present. It also addresses the question why states, and EU member states in particular, impose export controls and the imperatives that are driving cooperation between states in this area. The aim of this first chapter is to provide a better understanding of the key trends affecting the international regulatory climate prior to an analysis of specific supranational and national control regimes in subsequent chapters.

Part II (chapters 3 and 4) seeks to understand the problems in the development of common export policies within the EU governing the transfer of conventional weapons and dual-use goods and technologies. It analyses what has happened so far, what is happening now and the potential for future cooperation in this area. It is divided into three historical periods. In the first, 1957–89, arms export controls were singularly a matter for national governments, although in the 1980s limited coordination of arms embargoes against specific countries did take place in the framework of European Political Co-operation. The second period, 1990–95, was when real progress began to be made on this issue for the first time, particularly within the framework of the Intergovernmental Conference (IGC) leading up to the 1991 Treaty on European Union (the Maastricht Treaty). It was also the period in which consideration of dual-use exports was formally separated from that of conventional weapon exports. These first two periods are discussed in chapter 3.

Chapter 3 also examines the development of common EU export controls on dual-use goods and technologies. It begins by describing the protracted and difficult negotiations which led to the introduction of an EU Regulation and

---

[45] Happe and Wakeman-Linn (note 41), p. 18. For a recent analysis of the difficulties of comparison see Wezeman, P. D. and Brandt-Hansen, A., 'Government and industry statistics on national arms exports', *SIPRI Yearbook 2001* (note 42), p. 404.

Joint Action on Dual-Use Goods and Technologies (which came into force on 1 July 1995), and this is followed by an analysis of the main regulatory clauses and annexes which make up the new control regime. The chapter also examines how the new regime worked in practice over the first five years and assesses the findings from a recent review by the European Commission. Drawing on these lessons from the initial implementation phase, it also considers the effectiveness of the Regulation and Joint Action and in particular the extent to which economic, security and harmonization objectives have been met.

Chapter 4 takes up the history of the development of common arms export control policies in the EU. The production of and trade in armaments are closely linked to defence and foreign policy considerations of member states and by implication, therefore, to progress in the development of a European security and defence policy. The chapter begins by exploring some of these linkages, but the main focus of the discussion is the intergovernmental debates that took place in the period 1995–2000, including the efforts under the Dutch and British presidencies which led to the agreement on an EU Code of Conduct on Arms Exports in 1998.

The evolving policies in Britain, Germany and Sweden are examined and then compared in Part III. Chapters 5, 6 and 7 discuss the different regulatory approaches in the UK, Germany and Sweden, respectively. Each case study begins with a review of the domestic and external policy environment, including the role of policy stakeholders, the evolution and current status of national arms exports, and the government arms export promotion function. This is followed by an analysis of the national regulatory regime, including a description of the policy-making and policy-execution structures. Finally, because officially stated policy is not always reflected in the policy actually implemented—witness the failings in all three countries' regulatory regimes—the 'unofficial' arms export policy in each country is also scrutinized for evidence of the broader (and often unwritten) political and economic principles that shape (and sometimes undermine) the written regulations. In short, each case study concludes with an appraisal of policy outcomes.

These three chapters provide a unique in-depth study of the arms export control regimes of the countries concerned and serve to highlight areas of agreement as well as the existence of anomalies and differences. Chapter 8 explains the reasons for this mix of divergence and convergence. It begins by exploring two broad explanations for continuing divergence—national differences in the cultural and political norms associated with policy making and administration; and persistent differences in foreign and defence policies as between the three countries. It then summarizes the reasons for convergence—principally the increasing importance of multilateral export controls and changes of practice arising from European integration. Finally, the chapter draws on some examples to assess which of these themes have tended to dominate the shaping of each national policy system.

Chapter 9 provides a summary of the evidence and arguments presented in the study. It also discusses the implications and indicates some of the possible options for future EU arms export control policy. Finally, Part IV provides background documentation and a bibliography.

Method

If an eclectic mix of the different normative and philosophical traditions associated with policy analysis, international relations and political economy provides the epistemological foundation for the research, comparative public policy provides the method. The study adopts a policy-centred approach using focused comparisons of the regulatory policies of three EU member states—the UK, Germany and Sweden. The focused comparative approach has several benefits. Not only will it help to improve existing classifications and explanations of regulatory processes in the countries concerned, but it should also reveal any patterns of common preferences conducive to the development of cooperative European export control arrangements. As Hague, Harrop and Breslin conclude, 'focused comparisons remain sensitive to the details of particular countries and policies while retaining some ability to form, and test, explanations'.[46]

The three countries selected for the case studies are among the five largest and most long-established suppliers of armaments in the EU.[47] Moreover, they have enough in common to make comparison possible but sufficient diversity (for instance, in terms of military and economic stature) to make comparison interesting. They also have contrasting positions in regard to EU integration generally, as discussed in more detail in Part III of the study.

A number of different sources have been used, including official government documents and statements, newspaper and journal articles, and other secondary sources specifically relating to arms export control policy, the arms trade and European integration. Independent and government data sources on arms production and transfers were also accessed, including SIPRI Yearbooks, national arms production and export statistics, as well as transnational compilations such as the UN Register. Given that the most interesting and important information in this field is not always published, and if it is published often dates very quickly, the information strategy chosen in the study also included a large number of interviews with policy stakeholders within the three focus states and within the European Commission.

Focused—i.e., non-schedule-structured[48]—interviews were conducted with five different groups of current and historical policy stakeholders in each of the

---

[46] Hague, Harrop and Breslin (note 30), p. 40.

[47] The other 2 are France and Italy.

[48] There are 4 main characteristics of focused interviews. First, they take place with respondents who are known to have been involved in a particular experience. Second, they refer to situations that have been analysed prior to the interview. Third, they proceed on the basis of an interview guide specifying topics related to the research hypotheses. Fourth, they focus on the subjects' experiences regarding the situations under study. Frankfort-Nachmias, C. and Nachmias, D., *Research Methods in the Social Sciences*, 4th edn (Edward Arnold: Sevenoaks, 1992), pp. 224–25. Interview methods used in this research also drew on May, T., *Social Research: Issues, Methods and Process* (Open University Press: Buckingham, 1993),

selected countries: (*a*) academics; (*b*) representatives of NGOs; (*c*) regulators (civil servants) in government departments and agencies; (*d*) political representatives (members of parliament, members of the European Parliament (MEPs), activists, trade unionists and researchers); and (*e*) representatives from defence-related trade associations. Key officials in EU institutions and representatives from Brussels-based NGOs supplemented this sample.

Interviewees were identified from public records or were recommended by other policy stakeholders. The interview objectives were: (*a*) to discover what was currently happening in terms of both operational procedures and policy making within the British, German and Swedish arms export control regimes; (*b*) to piece together recent history concerning the development of common controls within the EU, particularly the Regulation on Dual-Use Goods and Technologies, and the Code of Conduct on Arms Exports; and (*c*) to test attitudes of policy stakeholders towards the arms trade and export controls and, in particular, to discover the level of awareness about the dynamics that drive the arms trade; the level of support for common export control policies; and the extent to which systemic factors affect such attitudes in order to identify crucial divergent and convergent interests.

Overall, therefore, a total of 44 interviews were conducted with a representative sample of key officials and other policy stakeholders during 1997 and 1998.[49] Many of the interviews, particularly with government officials, were carried out on a non-attributive basis.

This study is by no means exhaustive. Cross-national comparison as a method does have some shortcomings. The 'same' behaviour can mean different things in different countries, and there are problems of political bias and political values when comparing politics in different countries. Moreover, the comparison contains none of the southern member states (for instance, Greece, Italy, Portugal or Spain) where export controls are often thought to be weakest. Since it is quite possible that a different selection of countries might well have produced a different set of findings, great care must be exercised in extrapolating the research results across the EU as a whole.

especially chapter 6; and Sapsford, R. and Jupp, V. (eds), *Data Collection and Analysis* (Sage: London, 1996), especially chapter 4.

[49] Some follow-up discussions and additional interviews were carried out in 1999 and 2000 through the author's work for the UK-based independent foreign policy think tank, Saferworld.

Part I
Setting the context

2. Regulation of the global arms market: national and multilateral defence-related export controls past and present

I. Introduction

Regulation of trade, both civil and military, is nothing new. During the period of mercantilism in the 17th century, for example, the English Navigation Act of 1651 reserved for the home country the right to trade with the colonies and prohibited the import of goods of non-European origin unless transported in ships flying the English flag. Even in the modern neo-liberal era, those governments that do not appear to be regulating their trade exchanges in any positive way are usually doing so negatively by the imposition of tariffs and non-tariff barriers against outside producers and by subsidies and grants in aid of their own producers. In the case of civil trade, most of the world's countries have agreed to negotiate down the barriers to trade—through global and regional trade agreements, such as the General Agreement on Tariffs and Trade (GATT), its successor, the World Trade Organization (WTO), the Multilateral Agreement on Investment (MAI), the EU Single European Market, the North American Free Trade Agreement (NAFTA) and so on—but there remains the tendency to retain those forms of protection that are regarded as the most important for their own economies. However, the most complex and restrictive kind of regulatory regimes are usually applied to military-related trade.

The Persian Gulf War in March 1991 refocused international attention on how best to prevent the spread or 'proliferation' of conventional and NBC weapons as well as dual-use technologies. This chapter is concerned with the 'why' and the 'how' questions concerning the development and application of export controls on arms and dual-use transfers. The aim is to provide a better understanding of why countries attempt to control the transfer of conventional arms and dual-use goods and how they have set about doing so. This will provide the context for a more detailed analysis of the emerging EU control regimes in Part II of the study.

Section II of this chapter begins by outlining how two opposing forms of social organization—the state and the market—are of crucial importance in understanding why states impose export controls. Section III then attempts to clarify why states seek to control the trade in arms and dual-use goods and reviews some of the main reasons for so doing. Section IV looks at the elements that go into making a typical national arms export control regime, and section V assesses the effectiveness of current efforts to apply common controls at the international level. Finally, some conclusions are drawn in section VI.

II. Why do states develop export controls?

Explanations as to why states develop export controls can be found in a number of theoretical approaches.[1] The following brief discussion of the political economy of export controls aims to provide a useful context for the subsequent discussion of why and under what circumstances states specifically seek to control arms and dual-use transfers.

For the past 500 years the nation state has been the primary organizing principle of the international political order and the market has been the primary means for organizing economic relations.[2] These two opposing forms of social organization—state interests and market forces—are of crucial importance in shaping the international regulation of the arms trade. For some states—those with large national production capabilities or secure access to imports—regulations on the transfer of arms are a useful part of ensuring national security. For others—those that rely on arms imports—regulations on the transfer of arms are often perceived as preventing national autonomy. In both cases the market is exerting pressure for the elimination of as many of the political and regulatory obstacles to the operation of the price mechanism as possible.[3] It is the tension between these two fundamentally different ways of ordering human relationships that underpins many of the problems associated with the contemporary arms trade.

Most of the literature on the highly controversial issue of the interaction between state and market divides the subject into three broad theoretical perspectives or 'ideologies' of political economy: the nationalist (or neo-mercantilist) perspective; the liberal (or orthodox) perspective; and the Marxist (or radical) perspective.[4] What then, are the dominant ideologies that have

---

[1] See, e.g., the review of realism/neo-realism, rational institutionalism, domestic politics and liberal identity by Grillott, S., 'Explaining the development of nonproliferation export controls: framework, theory and method', eds G. Bertsch and S. Grillot, *Arms on the Market: Reducing the Risk of Proliferation in the Former Soviet Union* (Routledge: New York, 1998), pp. 3–10.

[2] The termss 'nation state' and market' are not single concepts and are used here as 'ideal types'. The link between nation and state can take many forms, and markets differ according to the degree of freedom of participants to enter the market and also the extent to which particular buyers or sellers can determine the terms of the exchange. Buzan, B., *People, States and Fear* (Wheatsheaf Books: London, 1991), pp. 57–96; and Gilpin, R., *The Political Economy of International Relations* (Princeton University Press: Princeton, N.J., 1987), pp. 16–18.

[3] Put simply, the price of a commodity is the result of the opposing forces of supply and demand. The reality, of course, is somewhat more complicated. Demand in civil markets is often created or stimulated through the general pressure of materialism and the specific thrusts of mass advertising. In economic terms these pressures are known as 'supply push' and 'demand pull'. The global arms market is even further removed from any theoretical notion of the free market. Moravcsik, e.g., describes it as a highly regulated oligopoly with a number of inherent market imperfections. Moravcsik, A., 'The European armaments industry at the crossroads', *Survival*, vol. 32, no. 1 (Jan./Feb. 1990), p. 72.

[4] See, e.g., Gilpin (note 2); and Kapstein, E. B., *The Political Economy of National Security: A Global Perspective* (McGraw-Hill: New York, 1992). There is also a more recent body of literature that encompasses a range of 'new' economic thinking, from theories of 'disorganized capitalism' to feminist and Green critiques of the existing paradigms of political economy. While the 'new economic thinking' is not sufficiently advanced and coherent to form a new general perspective of political economy, it seems unlikely that we have reached the 'end of history'. Michael Barratt Brown, e.g., describes 10 different models of capitalist economies, 5 different models of attempted socialist economies and 4 potential future

shaped the international economy in recent years? Since the early 1980s the framework in which economic development has occurred in most countries in all parts of the world has been 'globalization'.[5] Although globalization is often treated as an economic phenomenon rather than a political act, the key economic processes—the internationalization of production, trade, distribution and finance—were triggered by political decisions resulting from a neo-liberal model of political economy. Thus, trade-driven free-market economic reforms, and particularly the emphasis on privatization, fierce competition and deregulation (and re-regulation[6]), have severely weakened the autonomy of national policy makers to control or influence key economic processes.

While this dominant paradigm in the international political economy suggests that an expanding international economy is good for all states,[7] the key exception to this understanding has traditionally been the military sector. In this sector the belief that national security could potentially be undermined by international commerce in advanced weapons and military technology had widespread support and meant that military industrial aspects of international security could not be left to market forces (particularly during the cold war). Privatization of defence industries in the UK and elsewhere during the 1980s represented a partial break with that tradition, but most international defence transactions continue to fall outside the remit of GATT and other mechanisms that affect international commerce. Why is this the case?

One answer can be found in international relations theory. While neo-liberalism dominated thinking on the international economy throughout the 1980s and 1990s, the 'neo-realist' rationale, its ideological room-mate,[8] has dominated thinking in the international political system for much longer. According to realist theory, states are the most important actors in international politics and they act in a 'rational' way in attempting to preserve and improve

models for building a new social order. Barratt Brown, M., *Models in Political Economy*, 2nd edn (Penguin: London, 1995).

[5] The literature on economic globalization is vast and there are various interpretations. Hirst and Thompson challenge extreme versions of the globalization thesis and argue that major nation states remain central to governance of the international economy. The present author shares their view that 'a world economy with a high and growing degree of international trade and investment is not necessarily a globalised economy'. Instead, what we seem to have is a 'highly internationalised economy in which most companies trade from their bases in distinct national economies' which thereby still allows a fundamental role for 'nation states, and forms of international regulation created and sustained by nation states'. Hirst, P. and Thompson, G., 'Globalization and the future of the nation state', *Economy and Society*, vol. 24, no. 3 (Aug. 1995), pp. 408–42.

[6] The past 20 years have seen fierce regulatory reform rather than deregulation per se, that is, independent regulatory bodies and supranational regulation have tended to replace regulation by public ownership or through government departments. Majone, G. *et al.*, *Regulating Europe* (Routledge: London, 1996).

[7] Free trade and economic exchange are regarded by liberals as a source of peaceful relations among nations because, first, all nations are said to gain in absolute terms (although it is recognized that the relative gains will differ), and, second, such mutual benefits are thought to foster cooperative relations and economic interdependence.

[8] On the relationship between neo-liberalism and neo-realism see Baldwin, D. (ed.), *Neorealism and Neoliberalism: The Contemporary Debate* (Columbia University Press: New York, 1993), especially chapter 1.

their power relative to that of other states.[9] Neo-realism, while moderating the assumption that power is the only (or primary) objective of state behaviour, asserts that states continue to act in a self-interested manner, but within a structured system of states.[10] The system is said to be defined by specific principles, such as decentralization and anarchy, and the relative positions of states within it are increasingly a function of their technological and economic development. This approach not only continues to dominate the study of international relations but also informs most of the policy making in relation to the arms trade.

Thus, while EU member states are increasingly adopting the logic of economic liberalism and the global division of labour in their pursuit of prosperity,[11] most remain largely committed to retaining national autonomy in foreign and military affairs. There is, therefore, an underlying tension between nationalistic (state-centred) conceptions of security and the Europeanization (and globalization) of economic activity, which the member states in the EU have yet to resolve. The UK, Sweden and Germany, for example, have all combined some measure of liberalization and economic nationalism in their defence policies. Nowhere is this tension more pronounced than in respect of ongoing attempts to deepen EU integration, particularly with regard to military union. This issue is discussed in greater detail in the next two chapters.

In short, in keeping with this neo-realist paradigm most, if not all, governments with major domestic defence industries are required to undertake two contradictory roles: the regulation and control of military exports, on the one hand, and the promotion of foreign sales, on the other. A further dichotomy is that supplier states normally want to export as many arms as possible in order to keep their defence industries vibrant and unit costs to a minimum, while at the same time seeking to retain the technological superiority they enjoy.

Once we move beyond these theoretical explanations of why states develop export controls, we still have to deal with the complex search for principles or criteria around which an arms and dual-use export control regime can be based.

III. Why do states control arms and dual-use exports?

It is possible to identify at least three potential causes or 'dynamics' that drive the proliferation of arms and dual-use technologies—the supply-side dynamic, the demand-side dynamic and technological imperatives.[12] While there is little agreement as to which of these three causes is the most important, and in most

---

[9] The classic text on realism (first published in 1948) is Morgenthau, H., *Politics Among Nations* (Alfred Knopf: New York, 1973).

[10] Waltz, K., *Theory of International Politics* (Addison-Wesley: Reading, Mass., 1979).

[11] Economic liberalism would seem to be the guiding principle for the EU treaties—hence the Single Market project—although protectionism is still a factor in respect of external trade.

[12] The relationship between technological change and proliferation is complex. See, e.g., Gleditsch, N. P. and Njølstad, O. (eds), *Arms Races: Technological and Political Dynamics* (Sage: London, 1990); Wander, W. T., Arnett, E. and Bracken, P. (eds), *The Diffusion of Advanced Weaponry: Technologies, Regional Implications, and Responses* (American Association for the Advancement of Science: Washington, DC, 1994); and Sperling, J., Louscher, D. and Salomone, M., 'A reconceptualization of the arms transfer problem', *Defense Analysis,* vol. 11, no. 3 (1995), pp. 293–311.

examples of proliferation elements of all three dynamics can be found, this study is only concerned with supply-side controls. It is clear, however, that export controls alone are unlikely to prevent the continuing proliferation of weapons, and measures to address the other two dynamics will also normally be necessary. Controlling the global proliferation of small arms and light weapons, for example, not only requires measures to restrict legal transfers and combat illicit arms trafficking, but also necessitates initiatives to address the demand for such weapons.

Given these proliferation dynamics, under what circumstances and against whom should export controls be applied? A useful starting point in answering this question is the right of states to self-defence under international law. Both Article 51 of the UN Charter and Article 3 of the resolution establishing the UN Register of Conventional Arms recognize the right of states to self-defence, 'which implies that States also have the right to acquire arms with which to defend themselves'.[13] In this respect there is a clear difference between conventional armaments and weapons of mass destruction. Given the strong normative prohibition against both possession and use of the latter, efforts to control such weapons can take elimination as their ultimate goal. Conventional weapons are different, however.[14] The 'right' of states to possess conventional weapons for the purpose of self-defence is seldom disputed, and most governments therefore see no need to avoid arms transfers, as highlighted by Sir Alan Thomas, former head of the UK's Defence Exports Services Organisation (DESO): 'All countries have a right under the UN Charter, Article 51, to defend themselves and therefore to obtain the means necessary for defence. The UK claims that right itself and it would be hypocritical to deny it to others'.[15]

As a result, the conventional defence trade is treated as almost a standard form of commerce for all but the most sensitive destinations and the most sensitive weapons and technologies.

In what relation, if any, does this trade stand to ethical and moral issues? How far should moral laws govern the organization of industry or control the mechanisms of trade? The simplest moral attitude to the arms trade—and therefore to all military preparations, killing and warfare (which is organized killing)—is that in any circumstances it is wrong, irrespective of its profitability or political expediency. This pacifist view is entirely rational (i.e., a blanket ban on arms sales should be matched by a parallel ban on the possession of arms, thereby ensuring a level playing field) but is far from commonly sanctioned, particularly by states. Only Costa Rica and Iceland come close to the purely pacifist position, although even here there are some doubts concerning the 'arming' of the national guard in Costa Rica, and fisheries protection and NATO member-

---

[13] United Nations, General Assembly Resolution 46/36 L, 9 Dec. 1991, Article 3. On the UN Register of Conventional Arms see section V of this chapter.

[14] Despite some blurring at the edges as a result of the destructiveness of some modern conventional weapons (e.g., area-impact munitions), the distinction between conventional weapons and WMD is still a useful one.

[15] Thomas, A., 'Attacked from all sides: the UK 20 per cent in the arms market?', *RUSI Journal*, Feb. 1994, p. 45.

ship in Iceland. Instead, the majority of states (and individuals) appear to take a more pragmatic position by arguing that the arms trade and military preparations are prima facie right but not always so. This diluted moral attitude clearly implies a qualified acceptance of the arms trade, which in turn transfers debate to the question in what circumstances arms transfers are not justified. Moral absolutes and moral certainties then become dissolved in political and economic discussions that produce compromises around individual transactions and particular weapon systems. In one form or another, therefore, the idea that some arms transfers are good and others bad has been the orthodoxy that has underlined government efforts to regulate the arms trade in the 20th century.

In the 21st century, under what circumstances is this 'right' to 'legitimate' arms sometimes overridden by a duty not to supply? Just as states have motives for trading in arms, they also have interests in restricting access to them. These interests are mainly related to national security concerns and include international treaty obligations, regional stability, terrorism, international law and the risk of diversion. Among many states, however, there are also a growing number of normative and moral concerns that are leading to constraints on the use of force generally[16] and more restrictive export controls. For example, a major and increasing concern for many exporting states is the internal situation of the recipient country as a function of the existence of human rights violations, internal armed conflict or economic underdevelopment. As these national security interests and humanitarian concerns are the main criteria around which EU member states have sought to base their cooperation, a brief discussion of them is useful here.[17] It should be remembered, however, that the following general reservations about exports may be (and often are) outweighed by the perceived political and commercial benefits of a particular sale.

National security

Consideration of the potential effect of a proposed export on the defence and security interests of the exporting state (and those of its friends and allies) has been a long-standing criterion applied by most EU member states. Decisions to deny exports on national security grounds are normally taken because of the risk that the goods might later be used against the exporting state's own military forces. 'Rogue' or 'enemy' states (actual or potential) are normally denied weapons for this reason.[18]

---

[16] In the post-cold war euphoria some political scientists were moved to predict the end of 'major war'. See, e.g., Mueller, J., *Retreat from Doomsday: The Obsolescence of Major War* (Basic Books: New York, 1989). However, while most 'minor wars' now involve 'internal' issues, it is premature to conclude that international war has become obsolete. The conflict in Kosovo, e.g., started out as a classic 'minor' internal war but then escalated to a conflict with international dimensions. See also Wallensteen, P. and Sollenberg, M., 'The end of international war? Armed conflict 1989–95', *Journal of Peace Research*, vol. 33, no. 3 (1996), pp. 353–70.

[17] See the 8 EU criteria and the EU Code of Conduct in appendix A, and the discussion in chapter 4.

[18] Application of the term 'rogue state' is highly politicized. Chomsky, N., 'West embraced the rogue it now reviles', *The Observer*, 22 Feb. 1998.

Regional stability

National security depends on stability on both the regional and the global level. To the extent that easy access to weapons can give rise to a breakdown in that stability, states have a strong interest in promoting constraints on conventional weapon transfers, particularly to regions of tension. Although the role of weapons in the outbreak of conflict is a contentious issue (most serious analyses of the causes of war recognize a multiplicity of possible causes[19]) there is a great deal of evidence that the *unevenness* of trade in arms encourages arms races and transforms political conflicts into war, either by encouraging the ambitions of aggressor states or by increasing apprehension among insecure states.[20] In that sense, many of the wars that have occurred since 1945 have been started, escalated or prolonged as a result of arms transfers.[21]

In the post-cold war era the regional threat posed by large-scale offensive operations with major conventional weapons has become a major concern of EU (and other) states, particularly in relation to the Middle East and Asia. The EU arms embargo on China, for example, is in part linked to the perceived need to handicap Chinese military modernization in regard to its neighbours. In practice, however, this criterion has been very difficult to determine and there is very little international agreement as to how it should be interpreted (although a Working Group within the Wassenaar Arrangement has recently looked at this question).[22] While it has often been difficult to reach common ground on distinguishing between 'destabilizing accumulations' and more benign forms of weapons acquisition in regions of tension (such as the gradual replacement of obsolete weapons, or the gradual modernization of armed forces), some weapon sales are clearly more sensitive than others. The intense US pressure on Russia not to sell aircraft carriers to China in the early 1990s is illustrative of the concern with offensive weapons.[23]

[19] For a partial 'road map' on the causes of war see Stoessinger, J., *Why Nations Go To War,* 4th edn (St Martins Press: London, 1985); and Howard, M., *The Causes of Wars,* 2nd edn (Temple Smith: London, 1983).

[20] E.g., the Indo-Pakistani War over Kashmir in 1965 was fuelled by large quantities of modern weapons available to both sides. The UK was a major supplier to both sides prior to the outbreak of war: India received 220 jet fighters and 68 bombers (71% of its air attack force) while Pakistan received 60 bombers (25% of its air force). In addition, both their navies were almost totally equipped by British companies. Thayer, G., *The War Business: The International Trade in Armaments* (Simon & Schuster: New York, 1969), p. 274. Other regional conflicts that appear to have been dominated by the 'security dilemma' include the Arab–Israeli conflict, the Iraq–Iran War of 1980–88 and several smaller conflicts in Africa and Asia.

[21] There have been a number of studies on the effects of arms transfers on the course of wars. See, e.g., Brzoska, M. and Pearson, F., *Arms and Warfare: Escalation, De-escalation and Negotiation* (University of South Carolina: Columbia, S.C., 1994); and Sample, S., 'Military buildups, war, and realpolitik', *Journal of Conflict Resolution,* vol. 42, no. 2 (Apr. 1998), pp. 156–75.

[22] E.g., EU member states were unable to agree a common interpretation of the arms ban against China and the scope of that ban is left to national interpretation. On the 1996 Wassenaar Arrangement on Export Controls for Conventional Arms and Dual-Use Goods and Technologies see section V of this chapter.

[23] Kan, S. A., Bolkcom, C. and O'Rourke, R., *China's Foreign Conventional Arms Acquisitions: Background and Analysis,* Report for Congress (Library of Congress, Congressional Research Service: Washington, DC, 10 Oct. 2001); and Sakhuja, V., 'Dragon's dragonfly: the Chinese aircraft carrier', *Strategic Analysis,* vol. 24, no. 7 (2000), pp. 1367–86.

Terrorism and international law

EU member states have generally denied exports of arms to governments that support or engage in international terrorism. The recipient country's behaviour as regards respect for international law and its commitment to non-proliferation may also contribute to the exporting state's decision to deny an export.

The risk of diversion

This criterion addresses the risk that equipment may be diverted within the buyer country or re-exported under undesirable conditions. It is thus predominantly linked to the national security and terrorist concerns discussed above. However, the less-than-rigorous application of end-use provisions in EU member states (and elsewhere) suggests that this issue has not been given sufficient priority in the past, as is made clear in later chapters.

Internal armed conflicts

Just as there has been a growing recognition of the destabilizing impact of arms in the regional context, there has also been a growing consensus among EU member states that exports will not be granted which would provoke or prolong armed conflicts in the country of final destination. There are many explanations for this normative change. Some have to do with the projection of European values and culture, particularly notions of 'good governance' and 'democratization'. Arms exports to states involved in internal armed conflict may undermine such aims, by, for example, strengthening the political power of oppressive regimes.[24] The refusal to sell arms to a country can therefore send political signals of disapproval of and dissociation from a particular regime and its practices. Of course, it may also be designed to weaken a government vis-à-vis a rebel group, as in the case of the EU arms embargo against Sudan.

Human rights

Similarly, respect for human rights in the country of final destination has become an increasingly important normative restraint on Western arms transfers. While some European suppliers, particularly the Scandinavian countries, have a long tradition of denying arms to countries which fail to adhere to established international human rights instruments, many EU member states (especially France and the UK) are more recent converts to this criterion. In the three countries which provide the case studies in this volume, domestic politics

---

[24] There are few systematic and comparative studies on the impact of arms transfers on developing states, but one such study suggests that they facilitate the occurrence of *coups d'état* and help prolong periods of military rule. In the period covered by the study (1963–80), 39 of the 49 coup-affected states had received significant amounts of arms before a *coup d'état*. Maniruzzaman, T., 'Arms transfers, military coups, and military rule in developing states', *Journal of Conflict Resolution*, vol. 36, no. 4 (Dec. 1992), pp. 733–55.

and the increasing influence of NGOs are largely responsible for this normative shift. Even where restrictions on supply may have very little military impact—as in the case of the partial arms embargo against Indonesia applied by the USA and some EU suppliers during the 1990s—there may still be a political effect if a country or group of countries say that they will not supply unless human rights improve.

Economic development in the recipient country

The opportunity costs, both economic and political, of military expenditure by developing states during the cold war have probably been substantial. Between 1960 and 1987, for example, military spending in developing countries rose three times faster than in industrial countries—from $24 billion to $145 billion, an increase of 7.5 per cent a year, compared with 2.8 per cent for the industrialized countries. As a result, the developing countries' share of world military expenditure rose from 7 per cent to 15 per cent during this period.[25] It is also doubtful whether these high levels of military spending by developing countries actually increased the security of the average citizen. The 1994 UN *Human Development Report* revealed, for example, that in developing countries the chances of dying from social neglect (malnutrition and preventable diseases) were 33 times greater than the chances of dying in a war from external aggression.[26] Moreover, countries which spend very little on defence and much more on human development, such as Costa Rica and Mauritius, have in modern times been more successful at defending their national sovereignty than those which spend heavily on arms, such as Iraq and Somalia.

Despite the publication of several influential reports during the cold war drawing attention to the negative effects of arms exports on the global economy, and particularly the importing economies in the South, the impact on the behaviour of most supplier states was negligible.[27] Again, however, there has been a noticeable normative shift in the last decade. Many aid donors, including the World Bank, the International Monetary Fund (IMF), the Organisation for Economic Co-operation and Development (OECD) countries and the EU have begun to adopt the concept of *military conditionality*—providing aid only if the recipient does not spend 'excessively' on defence.

In particular, the work done over recent years by the OECD Development Assistance Committee (DAC) has moved the debate forward significantly. Concerned about the negative impact of 'excessive' military expenditure on development, in 1995 the DAC approved a set of guidelines on donor activities to reduce military expenditure and address imbalances in the economic and

---

[25] United Nations Development Programme (UNDP), *Human Development Report 1994* (Oxford University Press: Oxford, 1994), p. 49.

[26] *Human Development Report 1994* (note 25), p. 50.

[27] See, e.g., Palme, O., *Common Security: Report of the Independent Commission on Disarmament and Security Issues* (Pan Books: London, 1982); and Thorsson, I., Chairwoman, UN Group of Government Experts, *The Relationship Between Disarmament and Development* (United Nations: New York, 1982).

political roles of civilians and the military.[28] The DAC Task Force on Conflict, Peace and Development Co-operation is continuing to examine security sector-related issues, including the identification of manageable levels of military expenditure.[29] In addition, some national development agencies, including the UK's Department for International Development (DFID), are increasingly using military and other specialists to determine genuine security needs on a case-by-case basis.[30] One of the DFID's core aims in this respect is to assist countries and regions to make reasonable judgements about the extent of the security threats they face and the appropriate level of defence spending required to meet them. Such thinking is also beginning to be reflected in arms export control policy. All EU member states now look at whether the proposed export would seriously hamper the development of the recipient country.

International treaty obligations

Finally, respect for the international non-proliferation commitments of other like-minded states has been a strong normative tradition in EU member states' arms export controls, especially with regard to UN sanctions and international agreements covering WMD. For conventional arms and dual-use technologies there is currently no multilateral regime or international organization with authority to decide on specific transfers. Some guidelines, principles and norms have been established in the framework of the UN, the Organization for Security and Co-operation in Europe (OSCE), the EU and the Wassenaar Arrangement, and these are reviewed below. The common positions developed within the EU framework are, of course, a central concern of this study, and are discussed in detail in Part II. However, for most international transfers of conventional arms and dual-use technologies, national export control regimes are crucial in deciding what kind of control will be exerted over such transfers.

IV. Elements of a typical national arms export control regime

First developed by major suppliers in the 1930s (including European states such as Belgium, France, Sweden and the UK),[31] national export controls are the basis of all controls on the international arms trade. Indeed, it is a requirement of membership of the UN and the Wassenaar Arrangement that states have such

---

[28] Organisation for Economic Co-operation and Development, Development Assistance Committee, *Participatory Development and Good Governance*, Development Co-operation Guidelines Series (OECD: Paris, 1995).

[29] See, e.g., Organisation for Economic Co-operation and Development, Development Assistance Committee, *Military Expenditure in Developing Countries: Security and Development* (OECD: Paris, 1998).

[30] See the Speech by the Rt Hon. Clare Short, MP, on 9 Mar. 1999 in *Security Sector Reform and the Elimination of Poverty* (Centre for Defence Studies, King's College: London, 1999).

[31] Anthony, I., SIPRI, *Arms Export Regulations* (Oxford University Press: Oxford, 1991), p. 9.

controls in order to be able to comply with UN arms embargoes and controls against 'pariah' states, respectively.[32]

A national export control regime allows a decision to be made whether or not to permit the export of a designated item. Although there is no detailed blueprint for a national export control regime, there are certain features which most have in common: (*a*) a policy-making structure, including: a legal basis; a policy-making mechanism; a list of items subject to control; a list of sensitive or restricted destinations; and export criteria; and (*b*) an administrative (policy-execution) structure, including: a decision-making mechanism (for licence applications); and compliance and enforcement mechanisms.

The policy-making structure

Legislation is used to transform national interests and international obligations into norms that regulate the behaviour of corporate bodies and individual citizens. Primary legislation gives the state the legal authority to interfere in the affairs of exporting companies and usually sets out the scope and limitations of that interference. Legislation may also be used to codify government thinking on how to balance competing interests in arms export control policy, for example, by setting detailed parameters for each government department or agency. Alternatively, legislation can be minimal in order to allow officials greater discretion in establishing the core principles that underpin arms export policy. Secondary legislation is normally used to provide more specific guidance—on the export criteria for deciding individual licence applications, for example, or the list of items subject to control—and allows frequent and limited revisions to be made without the necessity of a more extensive legislative review.

Having instituted the legal authority, governments are also required to establish policy-making mechanisms for managing the general oversight and direction of arms export policy. In many states, the national arms export policy-making process is (in theory, at least) wholly under ministerial (and therefore strict political) control. In practice, however, policy is often 'shaped' on an ad hoc basis by networks of committees and advisory groups, some within ministries, some within industry and some crossing national boundaries. In some countries policy is developed in consultation with a wide number of participants; in others the whole process is usually well insulated from parliamentary and public scrutiny.

The administrative (policy-execution) structure

The main administrative instrument for implementing agreed policy is usually an export licence. While 'individual' export licences are normally required for

---

[32] While it is an explicit requirement of membership of the Wassenaar Arrangement, it is only an indirect obligation of UN membership (Article 2.5 of the UN Charter). Anthony (note 31), p. 1.

the most sensitive exports, many licensing authorities are making greater use of 'open' or 'general' export licences as part of a more flexible approach in respect of non-sensitive destinations. The decision whether or not to grant an export licence tends to be based on two overall factors—the nature of the recipient and the sensitivity of the equipment to be exported. For example, weapon systems may be ranked in terms of technological sensitivity and prospective customers ranked in terms of security risk and political acceptability. Applicants are normally obliged to supply information on the type of goods, the end-user and the end-use to which they will be put.

Although a single specialized agency or ministerial department is usually designated to manage the application procedure, inter-agency cooperation and consultation are also the norm. This cooperation can take several forms, but usually involves the lead agency seeking advice on specific defence, foreign policy or economic criteria from the relevant ministry or intelligence services, or a similar consultation on the technical specifications of the proposed export.

Compliance and enforcement mechanisms are a crucial component of the administrative framework. Most arms export control regimes operate to a large degree on the basis of voluntary compliance, that is, procedures are designed so that exporters understand what is expected of them, and officials are able to monitor the movement of controlled items and inspect the necessary documentation at the point of export. Because voluntary compliance cannot be assumed in all cases, however, most regimes have mechanisms to enforce export controls. Enforcement aspects can include border controls, monitoring of telecommunications, criminal investigations and computer surveillance.

Technical weaknesses in national export control regimes include limited or non-existent transparency of actual shipments, inaccessible or secretive official decision making, lax enforcement, and lack of effective end-use verification. For example, end-use restrictions are applied by many states, although enforcement is rare because of the possible threat to market position that would follow if a country became known as an unreliable supplier. However, seemingly tight control regimes may still produce questionable arms export decisions when other pressures are brought to bear. The situation is particularly complex for states with major domestic defence industries. The study returns to these issues in the discussion of the national export control regimes in the three focus countries—the UK, Germany and Sweden—in Part III.

V. Current efforts to apply common controls: how effective are they?

Most states have developed export controls based around a conception of the national interest. The fact that national interests, including the underlying foreign, security and industrial policy frameworks, usually differ has generally meant that, with the exception of the denial of arms to countries which are the subject of a mandatory UN arms embargo and a number of limited multilateral agreements (discussed below), there has been an almost complete absence of any universally agreed norms or principles governing the regulation of conventional arms transfers. Discussions between states regarding radical changes to national approaches to arms export policy have been rare, as have negotiations aimed at harmonizing export control procedures. Even among like-minded states, such as the EU member states or participant states within the Wassenaar Arrangement, most of the discussions around the criteria reviewed in section III above are relatively recent (post-cold war) and a clear conceptual framework for common interpretation of them is only now beginning to emerge.

An attempt by the five permanent members of the UN Security Council (known as the P5—China, France, Russia, the UK and the USA) to create a more comprehensive supplier regime in the early 1990s ultimately ended in failure, but eight restraining conditions for arms transfers were agreed during discussions in 1991.[33] Although never fully implemented, the guidelines clearly influenced the development of the EU's own arms export guidelines.

In the post-cold war era the main rationale for international cooperation in export controls has been the non-proliferation of specific weapons such as ballistic missiles and dual-use items to certain 'pariah' states, mainly located in the South. Of course, regulatory structures differ, not only as between end-users but also as between different types of equipment. The transfer of components for WMD, for example, is heavily restricted: nuclear weapons are covered by the 1968 Non-Proliferation Treaty (NPT) and the London Suppliers Group, chemical weapons by the 1993 Chemical Weapons Convention (CWC) and the Australia Group, biological weapons by the 1972 Biological and Toxin Weapons Convention (BTWC) and long-range missiles by the 1987 Missile Technology Control Regime (MTCR); but major conventional weapon systems, dual-use equipment and small arms continue to carry fewer restrictions.

EU member states participate in the only multilateral supplier regime that covers conventional arms—the Wassenaar Arrangement—and mandatory UN arms embargoes. In addition, several regional regimes (including the non-proliferation discussions within the OSCE) also receive the support of EU member states. There are also a number of initiatives that involve the development of global norms and principles for controlling international arms transfers or increasing transparency. All these initiatives and regimes impinge on arms export control policy in the EU either directly or indirectly.

Arms embargoes

An arms embargo is one form of sanction which can be adopted either in conjunction with broader economic sanctions or independently. The application of sanctions has several merits but can also pose several difficult challenges. Article 41 of the UN Charter gives broad authority to the UN Security Council to impose them, and they can be an important consensus-building tool.

---

[33] The guidelines for international arms transfers developed by the P5 are reproduced in appendix A.

However, the effective implementation, monitoring and enforcement of sanctions has often proved difficult in practice, and the humanitarian side effects of economic sanctions in particular are a regular bone of contention among the international community. Sanctions can also backfire, and instead of improving a target country's behaviour can make matters worse by uniting the populace behind the governing elite.

During the cold war the UN Security Council imposed mandatory and comprehensive economic sanctions only once, against Rhodesia in 1965, and an arms embargo on South Africa in 1978.[34] Since 1990, however, use of these tools has increased considerably, with the imposition of comprehensive sanctions against Iraq and Serbia, and mandatory arms embargoes against Angola, Haiti, Liberia, Libya, Rwanda, Sierra Leone, Somalia, Sudan and all six republics of the former Yugoslavia. While the effectiveness of UN arms embargoes is often regarded as uneven (largely because of problems with implementation[35]), all have either slowed or prevented arms transfers to proscribed destinations.

Embargoes can also be imposed through regional groupings, such as the OSCE or the EU, or nationally. The EU member states have sometimes applied arms embargoes collectively as a Joint Action under their Common Foreign and Security Policy (the CFSP, which is discussed in greater detail in chapter 3) and individually as a result of national concerns (for instance, the UK's national embargo against Argentina in 1982 as a result of the Falklands conflict). Of course, the broader the coalition of states adhering to the embargo, the more effective it is likely to be.

The Wassenaar Arrangement

Multilateral supply-side regulation of the conventional arms trade is undertaken in an attempt to coordinate the scope and application of national export controls. According to arms control theory, multilateral efforts to control conventional proliferation are hampered by two major difficulties: the 'free rider' and 'lowest common denominator' problems.[36] These serious problems for supply-side restraint and are discussed in more detail in chapters 3 and 4. There is currently only one multilateral supplier regime that is intended to control proliferation of conventional arms and sensitive military equipment and

---

[34] There are 2 types of UN embargo—mandatory, binding on all nations, and voluntary. For a discussion of the mandatory arms embargo against South Africa see Wulf, H., 'United Nations arms embargoes against the Republic of South Africa', ed. Anthony (note 31), pp. 238–44.

[35] Such problems range from different national interpretations of the scope of the embargo to non-compliance on the part of some states. On the limited effectiveness of the sanctions against the União Nacional para a Independência Total deAngola (National Union for the Total Independence of Angola, UNITA), e.g., see United Nations, Report of the Panel of Experts on Violations of Security Council Sanctions against UNITA, UN document S/2000/203, 10 Mar. 2000; and Human Rights Watch, *Angola Unravels* (Human Rights Watch: New York, 1999).

[36] 'Free riders' are said to take advantage of more restrictive policies in order to increase their own export opportunities. The level of the lowest common denominator is the potential outcome of policy coordination and harmonization because of downward pressures exerted by vested interests.

technology—the Wassenaar Arrangement, which has its roots in the earlier Coordinating Committee on Multilateral Export Controls (COCOM) regime.

From its establishment in 1949 until its dissolution in 1994, COCOM provided the institutional context within which all NATO countries (except Iceland) and a number of other countries managed their export control policies—including the three states that are the focus here.[37] Throughout its history, COCOM was largely shaped and driven by US leadership.[38] For example, a number of other like-minded countries (including Sweden) had working arrangements with the USA to control exports in line with COCOM norms.[39] The aim of COCOM was to impose restrictions on the export of 'sensitive' technologies to communist countries in Eastern Europe, Asia and the former Soviet Union[40] in order to 'maintain a technological gap in the conception, design and development of military materials'.[41] It operated on an informal basis and its meetings and decision making were shrouded in secrecy.[42]

Central to the regime were three lists that banned or limited the export of goods associated with nuclear energy (the International Atomic Energy List), goods and technologies associated with direct military use (the International Munitions List), and dual-purpose goods and technologies (the International Industrial List). These lists were included in member states' national export control regimes, effectively creating a partial trade embargo to proscribed countries. Requests by member states for an exemption from the embargo were forwarded to the COCOM secretariat (of approximately 30 people) located at the US Embassy in Paris.[43] A standing committee composed of national delegations from member states met on a weekly basis to review requests for exemptions. The standing committee was not a decision-making body, however. National delegates simply channelled requests for exemptions from other countries back to their own national licensing authorities for a decision. The

---

[37] Although Sweden was never a member of COCOM, it nonetheless shaped the behaviour of Swedish companies and the design of Swedish export controls for dual-use goods. See chapter 7; and Stankovsky, J. and Roodbeen, H., 'Export controls outside CoCom', eds G. Bertsch, H. Vogel and J. Zielonka, *After the Revolutions: East–West Trade and Technology Transfer in the 1990s* (Westview Press: Boulder, Colo., 1991), pp. 85–86.

[38] Zielonka, J., 'Introduction: Eastern Europe in transition', eds Bertsch, Vogel and Zielonka (note 37), pp. 7–8.

[39] Austria, Finland, Hong Kong, Ireland, New Zealand and Switzerland had such arrangements.

[40] Although COCOM did not publish a list of proscribed destinations, the following countries are known to have been targeted, for all or part of the duration of the regime: Afghanistan, Albania, Bulgaria, Cambodia, China, Czechoslovakia, Estonia, the German Democratic Republic (GDR), Hungary, North Korea, Laos, Latvia, Lithuania, Mongolia, Poland, Romania, the Soviet Union and Viet Nam. Not all destinations were proscribed equally over time, however. Some received preferential treatment (e.g., China after 1985) and some were subject to a firm 'no exceptions' policy (e.g., the Soviet Union 1980–89). Bertsch, G., Cupitt, R. and Elliott-Gower, S. (eds), *International Cooperation on Nonproliferation Export Controls: Prospects for the 1990s and Beyond* (University of Michigan Press: Ann Arbor, Mich., 1994), p. 36.

[41] Altes, P., *Access to Outer Space Technologies: Implications for International Security*, UNIDIR Research Paper no. 15 (United Nations Institute for Disarmament Research: Geneva, Dec. 1992), p. 110.

[42] COCOM was not a treaty and there was no documentary foundation for the committee. Anthony, I., 'The Coordinating Committee on Multilateral Export Controls', ed. Anthony (note 31), pp. 207–11.

[43] Some exemptions (i.e., those below certain technological or monetary thresholds) did not require the formal consent of other member states.

national licensing authority then had 12 weeks (reduced to eight weeks in 1991) in which to register an objection.

With the end of the cold war, COCOM lost its justification and was wound up in 1994, although members agreed to maintain the control lists and apply them on a global basis through their national regulations pending the formation of a successor regime. The successor negotiations, known as the New Forum, sought to establish a mechanism for regular exchanges of information and consultation regarding conventional arms and certain sensitive technologies. Finally, in December 1995, representatives of 28 countries agreed to establish the Wassenaar Arrangement on Export Controls for Conventional Arms and Dual-Use Goods and Technologies as a successor to the COCOM regime.[44] The first plenary meeting, held on 2–3 April 1996, ended without agreement,[45] although, most significantly, Russia was included in the negotiations for the first time. At the second meeting on 11–12 July 1996 representatives of 33 states[46] eventually reached agreement on the 'initial elements' of the regime.[47] These set out the purpose of the Arrangement, which is to contribute to regional and international security by: (*a*) promoting transparency and greater responsibility with regard to transfers of conventional arms and dual-use goods and technologies, thus preventing destabilizing accumulations; (*b*) seeking through national policies to ensure that transfers of these systems do not contribute to the development or enhancement of military capabilities which undermine these goals and are not diverted to support such capabilities; (*c*) complementing and reinforcing, without duplication, the existing control regimes for weapons of mass destruction and their delivery systems, as well as other internationally recognized measures designed to promote transparency and greater responsibility, by focusing on the threats to international and regional peace and security which may arise from transfers of armaments and sensitive dual-use goods and technologies where risks are judged greatest; and (*d*) enhancing cooperation to prevent the acquisition of armaments and dual-use items for military end-uses if the situation in a region or the behaviour of a state is or becomes a cause for serious concern to the participating states.

[44] The regime is named the Wassenaar Arrangement after the town outside The Hague in the Netherlands where preliminary agreement was reached in Dec. 1995. It has a small secretariat based in Vienna. On the membership see the glossary in successive editions of the SIPRI Yearbook.

[45] The main obstacle to agreement was thought to be Russia's reluctance to agree a 'no undercutting without consultation' rule for sensitive dual-use goods. 'Undercutting' is the practice of one country granting an export that another has turned down. See, e.g., 'Failure to agree new rules for arms control', *Saferworld Update*, summer 1996, p. 6; and 'Export accord blocked by Russians', *Jane's Defence Weekly*, 17 Apr. 1996. Other reports highlight a range of issues under dispute, including a lack of consensus on barring transfers to 'pariah states' (Iran, Iraq, North Korea and Libya). Goldring, N., 'Wassenaar Arrangement in limbo', *BASIC Reports* (British American Security Information Council), no. 52 (13 May 1996).

[46] The 33 participating states as at 1 Apr. 1999 were the 15 member states of the EU, Argentina, Australia, Bulgaria, Canada, the Czech Republic, Hungary, Japan, South Korea, New Zealand, Norway, Poland, Romania, the Russian Federation, Slovakia, Switzerland, Turkey, Ukraine and the USA.

[47] The Wassenaar Arrangement on Export Controls for Conventional Arms and Dual-Use Goods and Technologies, Initial Elements, as adopted by the Plenary of 11–12 July 1996, available on the SIPRI Internet site at URL <http://projects.sipri.se/expcon/wass_elements.htm>.

Further details of the arrangement were slow to emerge, although more substantive official documentation can now be found on the official Internet site.[48] One of the most controversial issues is that all members must ban exports of arms and sensitive technologies to the four so-called pariah states, Iran, Iraq, Libya and North Korea. Similar cooperation is expected in denying arms and technology transfers to any other state or region that becomes a serious cause for concern. It seems clear, therefore, that while COCOM was designed to prevent transfers to the former Soviet bloc, the new arrangement is targeted principally at 'rogue' or pariah states in the developing world. Another important difference, however, is that while membership of COCOM was severely limited, the Wassenaar Arrangement is 'open, on a global, non-discriminatory basis, to all countries meeting the agreed membership criteria'.[49] Indeed, the arrangement has already expanded from the 23 states that participated in the initial New Forum discussions to the current level of 33 member states.

Wassenaar has two 'pillars', one relating to dual-use goods (the List of Dual-Use Goods and Technologies) and the other to conventional arms (the Munitions List). The dual-use pillar is divided according to the sensitivity of the items. The Basic list (tier 1) has two annexes: a Sensitive list (tier 2) and a Very Sensitive list (a subset of tier 2). All member countries are obliged to incorporate these lists into their national export control systems. Wassenaar does not allow for vetoes of proposed exports (as was the case with COCOM) but relies on national export regulations and transparency of transactions to control activity, that is, the decision to transfer or deny a transfer of any item is the sole responsibility of each participating state. Member governments are expected to focus their efforts on sharing intelligence on 'clandestine projects and dubious acquisition trends' as well as on regular exchanges of more detailed information about transfers of sensitive dual-use goods to non-member countries.[50] Members are notified of any denials: for tier 2 items within 60 days (but preferably within 30 days) of denial on a case-by-case basis; and for tier 1 items twice yearly on an aggregate basis. Aggregate information on approved tier 2 transfers is also to be exchanged twice yearly. A major weakness is the failure to agree a 'no undercutting rule' for sensitive goods.[51] Instead, members have agreed to inform all other members, within 60 days, of an approval of a licence that has been denied by another member during the previous three years.[52]

For arms transfers, the arrangements are even more modest. They simply require twice-yearly information exchanges of transfers of major weapons as defined by the 1990 Treaty on Conventional Armed Forces in Europe (the CFE

[48] URL <http://www.wassenaar.org>.

[49] Davis, L., 'The Wassenaar Arrangement: Address by Undersecretary of State for Arms Control and International Security Affairs, Lynn Davis', Carnegie Endowment for International Peace, Washington, DC, 23 Jan. 1996.

[50] In most participating states the greater part of this information is collected by government officials from export licence applications.

[51] On undercutting see note 45.

[52] Greene, O., 'Launching the Wassenaar Arrangement: challenges for the new arms export control regime', Saferworld Briefing, London, Mar. 1996, p. 4.

Treaty) and the UN Register of Conventional Arms, with the inclusion of slightly more detail, such as descriptions of the model involved. In addition, there is expected to be 'more intrusive information sharing' on arms transfers among some major suppliers—the USA, the UK, Russia, France, Germany and Italy.[53] So far, however, these informal meetings by this 'small group on conventional arms' have failed to make much progress. They rejected, for example, a proposal by the USA for pre-notification of transfers. However, other general working groups within the Wassenaar Arrangement have been useful for discussing issues of common concern. One such working group, for example, has studied the criteria for assessing destabilizing accumulations of major conventional weapons within the context of regional security.[54] Participating states have also exchanged information during working group meetings on national practices in relation to the 1998 ECOWAS (Economic Community of West African States) moratorium on the import, export and manufacture of small arms;[55] the control of small arms and light weapons; end-use controls; the disposal of surplus military equipment; and sensitive emerging technologies.

At the 1999 Wassenaar Plenary meeting a number of priorities for enhancing the Arrangement were discussed.[56] Deepening links between existing members is the main priority, including increased transparency in the arms pillar, and especially enhanced information exchange on small arms, diversion and illicit trafficking routes. Other priorities include strengthening consultation on regions and countries of concern, and clarifying the circumstances for circulating denial notifications for transfers to such countries. In 2000 progress was made on establishing a safe computer system for internal communication within the framework of the Arrangement. It was expected to be operational in 2001.

As the first post-cold war security framework, the Wassenaar Arrangement is presently rather ill-defined. Many key issues remain vague and unresolved. Very little progress was made during the 1999 review process. However, stronger guidelines and structures are likely to be developed over time and, given that Wassenaar includes most of the important supplier states, it remains the most promising forum for multilateral discussions currently available.

Regional control regimes

Several regional regimes have, either directly or indirectly, the goal of arms transfer restraint. In the Americas, for example, the 12-member Rio Group and the 1997 Organization of American States (OAS) Convention are important

---

[53] Davis (note 49).

[54] The 1998 Wassenaar Arrangement Plenary approved 'Elements for Objective Analysis and Advice Concerning Potentially Destabilising Accumulations of Conventional Weapons', WA PLM (98) RU2 rev., 3 Dec. 1998.

[55] Lodgaard, S. and Rønnefeldt, C., *A Moratorium on Lights Weapons in West Africa* (Norwegian Institute of International Affairs and Norwegian Initiative on Small Arms Transfers: Oslo, 1998).

[56] In addition to the regular annual review, the 1999 Wassenaar Plenary concluded the first overall assessment of the functioning of the Arrangement. 'Public statement for 1999 Plenary', available at URL <http://www.wassenaar.org/docs/press_5.html>.

initiatives.[57] In Asia, the Association of South-East Asian Nations (ASEAN) Regional Forum (the ARF) is also making progress in this area, and other modest discussions are taking place in the Middle East and in parts of Africa. In contrast to multilateral supplier regimes, some of these emerging regional regimes also include recipients in the negotiations. It is in Europe, however, that the most significant attempts to build agreement on regional standards for arms exports are being made. Many of the European security treaties and institutions that emerged from the cold war have a non-proliferation component, especially the CFE Treaty and the 1992 CFE-1A Agreement.[58] In terms of specific regional arms transfer controls, however, the multilateral supplier regimes that are being developed within the OSCE and the EU are the most important.

The OSCE Principles Governing Conventional Arms Transfers

The OSCE (formerly the Conference on Security and Co-operation in Europe, CSCE) is the most comprehensive of the European security institutions, both in scope and in membership.[59] Including in its membership all the major supplier countries except China, it is well placed to develop a comprehensive supply-side conventional arms transfer control regime. In addition to an ongoing programme of confidence- and security-building mechanisms (CSBMs) which already provide for exchange and discussion of data on armed forces, arms production and defence budgets, the OSCE has issued several declarations and documents on conventional proliferation. At the 1992 Prague Council meeting of CSCE ministers, for example, a Declaration of the CSCE Council on Non-Proliferation and Arms Transfers committed member states to a number of non-proliferation measures.[60] This was followed in November 1993 by the adoption of a set of Principles Governing Conventional Arms Transfers which instructed member states to avoid transfers that would be used to suppress human rights, prolong or aggravate a conflict, introduce destabilizing military capabilities into a region, contribute to regional instability or encourage terrorism.[61] These principles represent an attempt to harmonize national policies around common

[57] The Rio Group includes Argentina, Bolivia, Brazil, Chile, Colombia, Ecuador, Mexico, Panama, Paraguay, Peru, Uruguay and Venezuela. Negotiators are seeking a regional agreement to prohibit the purchase, transfer and manufacture of new generations of advanced conventional weapons and to implement regional CSBMs, including the establishment of a centre to monitor arms sales and production.

Agreed in Nov. 1997, the Inter-American Convention Against the Illicit Manufacturing of and Trafficking in Firearms, Ammunition and Explosives, and Other Related Material seeks to promote and facilitate cooperation and information exchange between OAS member states.

[58] On the CFE Treaty and the 1992 Concluding Act of the Negotiation on Personnel Strength of Conventional Armed Forces in Europe (the CFE-1A Agreement) see *SIPRI Yearbook 2001: Armaments, Disarmament and International Security* (Oxford University Press: Oxford, 2001), glossary.

[59] The membership expanded from the original 35 countries to 52 after the collapse of the Soviet Union and Yugoslavia. On the membership see the glossary in successive editions of the SIPRI Yearbook.

[60] Conference on Security and Co-operation in Europe, 'Compendium of documents and measures adopted by the Special Committee of the Forum for Security Co-operation since September 1992', Budapest, Dec. 1994.

[61] Conference on Security and Co-operation in Europe, 'Principles governing conventional arms transfers', 25 Nov. 1993, from 'Compendium of documents and measures adopted by the Special Committee of the Forum for Security Co-operation since September 1992' (note 60). The Principles are reproduced in appendix A.

norms and principles. However, follow-up seminars within the OSCE Forum for Security Co-operation (FSC) in June 1995 and December 1996 failed to take the principles forward in any meaningful way.[62]

Following a decision taken at its Istanbul Summit Meeting in November 1999, the OSCE turned its attention to the problem of small arms and light weapons. At an FSC seminar in April 2000, experts considered among other things common norms and principles for restraining legal small arms transfers, and improved transparency. These norms were later reflected in the OSCE Document on Small Arms and Light Weapons of November 2000.[63] If properly implemented this document should prove a significant advance in supplier coordination of small arms transfers among OSCE member states.

Supplier coordination within the EU

A great deal of progress has been made in developing supplier coordination in the EU. Eight common criteria governing arms exports were established in 1991 and 1992[64] and later included in a new EU Regulation governing the export of dual-use goods that entered into force in July 1995 and formed the basis of the EU Code of Conduct on Arms Exports agreed in June 1998.[65] The development of these and other common measures within the EU are the focus of Part II of this study, especially chapters 3 and 4.

Global norms and principles: the role of the UN and other actors

The UN has been a focal point for many recent studies and initiatives that have attempted to shape the normative framework governing arms transfers. The most significant initiative has been the setting up of the UN Register of Conventional Arms, although the arms transfer guidelines produced by the UN Disarmament Commission (UNDC) are also noteworthy. Two other global initiatives worthy of comment in the context of this study are the international ban on landmines and the international Code of Conduct on arms transfers developed by a group of Nobel Peace Prize laureates.

The UN Register of Conventional Arms

Support for conventional arms transparency via a UN register of transfers was galvanized among major industrial states following the ceasefire in the Persian

---

[62] Organization for Security and Co-operation in Europe, 'Seminar on Principles Governing Conventional Arms Transfers', FSC.DEC/10/95, *Forum for Security Cooperation Journal*, no. 10, Point no. 5 (26 Apr. 1995); and Organization for Security and Co-operation in Europe, 'Decision by the FSC on the follow up to the Seminar on Principles Governing Conventional Arms Transfers', FSC.DEC/14/95, *117th Plenary Meeting Forum for Security Cooperation Journal*, no. 21, Point no. 5 (1995), para. I.

[63] Adopted at the 308th Plenary Meeting of the FSC on 24 Nov. 2000. FSC.JOUR/314. The document is available on the OSCE Internet site at URL <http://www.osce.org> and is reproduced in *SIPRI Yearbook 2001* (note 58), pp. 590–98.

[64] The European Union Common Criteria for Arms Exports are reproduced in appendix A.

[65] The Code of Conduct on Arms Exports is reproduced in appendix A and discussed further in chapter 4.

Gulf War. General Assembly Resolution 46/36 H of December 1991 contained a concrete proposal for a register and was approved by 150 member states with no dissenting voices. Seven categories of conventional weapons have to be reported: battle tanks; armoured combat vehicles; large-calibre artillery systems; combat aircraft; attack helicopters; warships; and missiles and missile launchers. The first register was published in 1993, based on data from 82 countries on the weapons they had transferred (exported and imported) in the previous year. Since then annual registers have been published.[66] Although the number of replies rose steadily each year, reaching a peak of 95 states replying in 1998 (including all the main exporters except China[67]), in 1999 participation declined to 77 states. This decline is largely explained by the failure of key OECD states to remind and encourage other states to participate rather than by disaffection with the register.[68] Moreover, 147 states have reported to the register in at least one year.

The register has a number of weaknesses, including: problems with defining what constitutes a transfer; incomplete information or insufficient detail (supplier and recipient reports of the same transfer often do not match); the exclusion of financial data (weapons are reported by number rather than by value); the exclusion of several categories of weapons (small arms and ground-to-air missiles, for example, do not have to be reported); the exclusion of transfers of components and subsystems; and the failure of many countries (particularly in the Middle East and Sub-Saharan Africa) to report their imports.

Despite these weaknesses, the UN Register is an important breakthrough. It is the first mechanism by which governments have made such data public since the 1930s and it has clearly influenced the debate in the EU on the role of transparency in arms export controls (as will become clear in later chapters). The register also has the potential to form the basis of a more complete reporting system. For example, the establishment of regional registers in Asia, Africa, Europe and Latin America and the inclusion of small arms and light weapons[69] would be significant steps forward. Pressure also needs to be applied on a number of non-participants, especially those which are significant recipients of transfers. However, any attempt to move beyond the current requirements is likely to increase the rate of non-participation. So far, therefore, only small incremental improvements in the register have been possible, the most important being the inclusion of production and holdings in the last three registers (which has gone some way to alleviating developing countries' concerns over its discriminatory nature). There has also been incremental progress

---

[66] See the UN Internet site at URL <http://www.un.org/Depts/dda/CAB/register.htm>.

[67] China suspended participation in response to the USA's inclusion of its exports to Taiwan in 1997 in a footnote to its own submission. Chalmers, M. and Greene, O., *A Maturing Regime? The UN Register in its Sixth Year*, BARS Working Paper no. 6 (University of Bradford: Bradford, Jan. 1999), p. v.

[68] Chalmers, M. and Greene, O., *In Need of Attention: The UN Register in its Seventh Year*, BARS Working Paper no. 7 (Bradford: University of Bradford, Feb. 2000), p. v.

[69] On the advantages and disadvantages of having small arms and light weapons in the UN Register see Goldring, N., 'Developing transparency and associated control measures for light weapons', eds M. Chalmers, M. Donowaki and O. Greene, *Developing Arms Transparency: The Future of the UN Register* (University of Bradford: Bradford, 1997), pp. 213–31.

in the quality of the information provided, with all but two reporting states including data on weapon types and models in the 1999 register. A review by a Group of Governmental Experts in 2000 provided an opportunity to develop the register in a number of these areas. The group reported its findings to the UN General Assembly in August 2000. Unfortunately, the group was unable to reach consensus on broadening the range of equipment covered by the UN Register and deferred this question for further consideration at the next review.

The UN Disarmament Commission

The UNDC undertook intensive efforts in the first half of the 1990s to identify common norms and principles governing both dual-use and arms transfers.[70] Starting in 1991, it worked for four years on guidelines and recommendations concerning 'the role of science and technology in the context of international security, disarmament and other related field'. A document containing some fairly general principles governing dual-use transfers was produced in 1994 but narrowly failed to command a consensus within the UNDC.[71]

Also starting in 1991, the UNDC was asked by the UN General Assembly to develop a set of arms transfer guidelines. It was not until 1996, however, that a document containing the guidelines was agreed and adopted by the UNDC. Moreover, it mainly consists of an agenda for controlling illicit arms trafficking, although it does contain a number of 'principles' that states are asked to 'bear in mind' when making international arms transfers.[72] These principles are rather vague and open to subjective interpretation by governments, and are unlikely therefore to overly influence the arms export behaviour of many states.

The global ban on landmines

The use of specific weapons considered excessively inhumane or indiscriminate in their effects is forbidden under international humanitarian law. Issues of international law and common humanity have already influenced some countries not to develop certain weapons. The suspension of the development of the neutron bomb and the prohibition of the dumdum bullet in the late 1970s, for example, may have been motivated in part by such considerations. In the mid-1990s, however, the humanitarian crisis caused by anti-personnel mines (APMs) generated widespread public outrage and focused diplomatic attention on an international ban on the production and transfer of this specific weapon system.

---

[70] Conventional arms control is one of 3 issues currently before the UNDC. The Commission does not have the authority to negotiate conventions but aims to produce (by consensus) guidelines on disarmament strategies.

[71] Iburg, H., 'Controlling high-technology with military application', eds M. Chalmers *et al.*, *Developing the UN Register of Conventional Arms* (University of Bradford: Bradford, 1994), p. 117; and UN Disarmament Commission document A/CN.10/1994/WG.II/CRP10, 9 May 1994.

[72] United Nations Disarmament Commission, Guidelines for International Arms Transfers in the Context of General Assembly Resolution 46/36 H of 6 December 1991, UN document A/CN.10/1996/CRP.3, 3 May 1996. Excerpts from the guidelines are reproduced in appendix A.

The 1981 Inhumane Weapons Convention governs the use of landmines.[73] Two review conferences in 1995 and 1996 attempted to address the widely accepted shortcomings of the convention but failed to reach consensus. This prompted a broadly-based coalition of NGOs, the International Campaign to Ban Landmines (ICBL), to press for a global ban on the production, stock-piling, transfer and use of APMs. This objective of a complete ban was also shared by the International Red Cross, the UN Secretary-General and several states, most notably Canada. Following an initiative know as the Ottawa Process that was launched by the Canadian Government in October 1996 and strongly supported by the ICBL, agreement was finally reached on a convention which bans APMs in September 1997.[74] Although the APM Convention is a disarmament agreement which aims to eliminate (rather than limit) this whole category of weapons, signatories to the convention are obliged to modify their export controls in order to enforce a complete ban on the transfer of all APMs and their component parts.

The Nobel Peace Laureates' International Code of Conduct

In 1995, Dr Oscar Arias Sànchez, former President of Costa Rica, convened a Commission of Nobel Laureates[75] to actively build support for an International Code of Conduct on arms transfers. The International Code (which is repro-duced in appendix A) draws on the highest standards of international law and is the most detailed and comprehensive attempt yet at creating a universal set of norms and principles for governing arms transfers. It was formally launched in New York in May 1997 and continues to be promoted by the laureates and a number of NGO partners as a standard against which regional codes can be measured.[76] So far, only one regional code (the EU Code of Conduct) has been agreed, but others may well be forthcoming. Efforts continue, for example, to establish a restrictive US Code of Conduct, which may have the potential for regional or even wider application.[77]

---

[73] The proper title of the Inhumane Weapons Convention (also known as the Convention on Certain Conventional Weapons) is the Convention on Prohibitions or Restrictions on the Use of Certain Conventional Weapons which May Be Deemed to Be Excessively Injurious and to Have Indiscriminate Effects. The Convention's Protocol on Prohibitions or Restrictions on the Use of Mines, Booby Traps and Other Devices (the Landmines Protocol) restricts the indiscriminate use of anti-personnel mines and prohibits their use against civilian targets. On the signatories to the convention see *SIPRI Yearbook 2001* (note 58), annexe A.

[74] The Convention on the Prohibition of the Use, Stockpiling, Production and Transfer of Anti-Personnel Mines and on their Destruction (the APM or Ottawa Convention). For the text of the convention and a discussion of the successful Ottawa Process see Lachowski, Z., 'The ban on anti-personnel land-mines', *SIPRI Yearbook 1998: Armaments, Disarmament and International Security* (Oxford University Press: Oxford, 1998), pp. 545–74.

[75] The 16-member Commission included the Dalai Llama, former Polish President Lech Walesa and John Hume, former leader of the Social Democratic and Labour Party in Northern Ireland. *Arms Control Today*, Oct. 1996; and *The Guardian*, 21 Oct. 1996.

[76] *Saferworld Update*, no. 19 (autumn 1997), p. 6.

[77] NGOs built up support for a Code of Conduct in the US Congress throughout the 1990s. While several versions of a US Code have been tabled in the past, the House International Relations Committee finally approved in Mar. 1999 an Arms Trade Code of Conduct, sponsored by Congressman Sam Gejdenson. This weakened version (of an earlier code tabled by Congresswoman Cynthia McKinney) ties

Although the Nobel Code is arguably the clearest statement yet of a potentially global normative framework for arms transfers, universal acceptance of the principles and norms it contains remains some way off.

VI. Conclusions

Unlike the case of nuclear and chemical weaponry, there is no taboo against conventional weapons. The arms trade is an economic activity which, although permitted in general, must be regulated to avoid potentially negative consequences. This chapter shows that such regulation is primarily carried out at the national level but is more effective when suppliers coordinate their controls. Indeed, the rise in the number of supplier–recipient relationships and the obvious cross-cutting of a range of interests suggest that most of the meaningful regulatory measures will have to be created within, or conform to, a specific regional context. Furthermore, many of the multilateral arms transfer controls discussed in this chapter are key pointers to what might be possible within the EU. The P5, UNDC and OSCE principles, the international ban on landmines and recent revisions to some national export control regimes reflect concerns with interstate and regional conflicts or with the humanitarian dimension of intra-state conflict and human rights, or both.

However, the development of effective, harmonized and politically legitimate conventional non-proliferation regimes continues to be a highly controversial political goal, hampered by major obstacles. Some multilateral regimes appear to be marking time for want of proper implementation. The slow progress being made within the Wassenaar Arrangement and the UN Register, for example, is testimony to the continuing difficulty in building internationally agreed norms against which to measure behaviour and regulate the market.

Part II of this study examines whether the EU has fared any better at building such cooperation among its member states.

any move to strengthen US export controls to a negotiated agreement among US allies, principally within the Wassenaar Arrangement. *Saferworld Update*, no. 19 (note 76), p. 6; *Saferworld Update*, no. 24 (autumn 1999), p. 3; Jones, S., 'EU and US codes of conduct on arms transfers: status and review', *Non-proliferation, Demilitarization, and Arms Control*, fall 1998, pp. 23–31; and *Arms Trade News*, Mar. 1999, p. 3.

Part II

The development of common regulatory policies within the European Union

3. The EU Dual-Use Regulation: breaking the supremacy of national sovereignty in arms and dual-use export controls

I. Introduction

EU member states have traditionally retained almost total sovereignty in defence policy matters, including arms export controls. However, significant developments in the 1990s led to the elaboration of two outline frameworks or EU regulatory regimes for governing arms and dual-use exports. This chapter discusses those developments up to the mid-1990s and focuses on the development of common EU export controls on dual-use goods and technologies, and in particular the Regulation and Joint Action which came into force on 1 July 1995. Chapter 4 takes up the story of how attempts to harmonize arms export controls within the EU in the latter half of the 1990s culminated in the establishment of an EU Code of Conduct on Arms Exports in June 1998.

The study of common EU arms export controls can be divided into three periods. In the first period, 1957–89 (discussed in section II of this chapter), arms export controls were singularly a matter for national governments, although in the 1980s coordination of arms embargoes against specific countries did take place within the framework of European Political Co-operation. Although such coordination was important, the second period, 1990–95 (discussed in section III), was when real progress began to be made on this issue, particularly within the framework of the IGC leading up to the 1991 Maastricht Treaty. It was also the period in which consideration of dual-use exports was formally separated from that of arms exports. Finally, in the third period (1996–2000) the process of reform accelerated, particularly under the Dutch and British presidencies in 1997 and 1998. This third period is the focus of chapter 4.

Section IV of this chapter takes up the story of the development of common EU export controls on dual-use goods and technologies. It describes the protracted and difficult negotiations which led to the introduction of the EU Regulation and Joint Action on dual-use goods and technologies, and this is followed in section V by an analysis of the main regulatory clauses and annexes which made up the new control regime. Section VI examines how the new regime actually worked in practice over the first five years and why new rules were introduced in June 2000 (including the repeal of the Joint Action). It also considers the extent to which economic, security and harmonization objectives were met during this period.

II. The period 1957–89: the supremacy of national sovereignty in arms export control

The EU began as a small group of states that banded together for reasons of economic self-interest and political stability. The desire to overcome the historical hostility between France and Germany was probably the most important driving force in its early development, and the Franco-German relationship continues to be at the centre of the European integration process.[1] The emergence of the European Economic Community (EEC), the European Coal and Steel Community (ECSC) and the European Atomic Energy Community (Euratom) in the 1950s was also closely dependent on the emergence of NATO (and vice versa), as indeed is the current expansion of the EU. Much of the underlying convergence of European political systems in the early years following World War II was encouraged—even forced—by the USA, and made urgent by the growing threat of the Soviet Union. These historical events clearly made EU and NATO integration possible, and have had an enduring legacy in shaping integration, not least in the acceptance of the governments in question that war is no longer an option between them. The preference for transatlantic defence integration through NATO over European defence integration through the EU is also a historically formed reality.

While early blueprints for European integration, such as the ECSC and the European Defence Community (EDC), were largely stimulated by strategic issues, the potential development of a common European defence policy became 'squeezed' by the conditions of the cold war. With NATO assuming responsibility for collective security, the concept of European integration changed from 'defence first' to 'defence last'. Throughout the 1960s and 1970s, therefore, integration in the foreign policy and security fields played second fiddle to integration in the less contested field of economics.

Finally, the distinction between the EC and the EU, which is important in the context of arms control, needs to be explained. The institutional changes and somewhat complicated terminology created by the Maastricht Treaty have led to some confusion. This book adopts the guidelines outlined by Carolyn Rhodes and Sonia Mazey.[2] After ratification of the Maastricht Treaty in 1993, the EEC became the European Community (EC), one of the three European Communities along with the ECSC and Euratom (although the term European Community was already in general use). The Council of Ministers became the Council of the European Union[3] (and the European Commission still remains

---

[1] Wood, P. C., 'The Franco-German relationship in the post-Maastricht era', eds C. Rhodes and S. Mazey, *The State of the European Union, Vol. 3: Building a European Polity?* (Longman: Harlow, 1995), pp. 221–43; and *Jane's Defence Weekly*, 5 Feb. 1997.

[2] Rhodes and Mazey (note 1), p. ix. On the respective responsibilities of the EC and the EU in the context of arms export controls see, in particular, Anthony, I., 'Multilateral weapon and technology export controls', *SIPRI Yearbook 2001: Armaments, Disarmament and International Security* (Oxford University Press: Oxford, 2001), pp. 626–28.

[3] Hereafter, 'Council' is used to refer to the Council of Ministers after entry into force of the Maastricht Treaty.

the Commission of the European Communities). Issues involving the Single Market, competition and external trade still fall under the EC. References to the EC are appropriate, therefore, in the context of the community of member states before ratification of the Maastricht Treaty, and the EU is the collective union of member states after ratification. Issues covered by the Maastricht Treaty, such as the CFSP, refer to the EU. Thus, the correct usage of 'EC' and 'EU' depends on the context.

The obstacle of Article 223 and the exclusion of military goods from EC competence

Historically, therefore, the issue of arms exports has not directly concerned the EC.

The EC has always influenced certain aspects of security policy in the widest sense through measures concerning, for example, freedom of movement, trade, energy and research. However, this involvement has been specifically limited in relation to the production and trade in arms and certain related materials by Article 223 of the 1957 Treaty of Rome, which founded the EEC. Over the years it has been generally recognized that Article 223 allows (but does not oblige) a member state to exclude 'the production of or trade in arms, munitions and war material' from Community competence where 'it considers it necessary for the protection of the essential interests of its security'. Article 36 also refers to exports which can be excluded from the implementation of the Treaty of Rome, and this can involve arms exports, but the most important articles are articles 223–225. These provisions (which are reproduced in full in appendix B) have been subject to a number of different legal interpretations.

The Treaty of Rome required the Council of Ministers of the EEC to 'draw up a list of products' to which the Article 223 derogation would apply. This military products list (which has never been formally published but is basically the 1958 COCOM Munitions List) was adopted by the Council of Ministers on 31 March 1958 and has not been changed since.[4] This means that all other goods (i.e., non-Article 223 goods, including all dual-use goods that are subject to control under the different multilateral control regimes) should fall within the EC's remit.[5] The European Commission considers that, based on a strict legal interpretation of Article 225, the powers given to the member states may not be used improperly and, in particular, that they should not be used to distort 'the conditions of competition in the common market'. Thus, as is the rule for other dispensatory measures, Article 223 should be interpreted by member states in a

---

[4] For the 1958 list of products referred to in Article 223 see Allebeck, A. C., 'The European Community: from the EC to the European Union', ed. H. Wulf, SIPRI, *Arms Industry Limited* (Oxford University Press: Oxford, 1993), pp. 214–16. Proposed changes to the 15 different categories of goods in the list can be submitted by the European Commission but require unanimous approval from the Council of the European Union. To date, however, no consensus has been reached on any changes. This means that the list bears little resemblance to the realities of military equipment available today. In practice, therefore, each state has its own list of controlled goods which it interprets as being covered by Article 223.

[5] This includes 'soft' defence procurement—procurement of goods not of a uniquely military nature purchased by national defence ministries, such as word processors.

restrictive way. Indeed, where the member states have not remained within the limits given by articles 223–225, the same articles allow the Community institutions (especially the Commission and European Court of Justice) to intervene and examine how the measures might be adjusted.

In practice, however, most states appear to have deviated significantly from this strict legal interpretation in at least two respects. First, exemptions have been applied to a wider range of products than those covered in the 1958 list. Second, some member states have interpreted Article 223 as implying that all areas covering national security are beyond the scope of the treaties. The Commission has always contested this approach[6] and appeared to be vindicated by two European Court of Justice judgements in the mid-1990s which confirmed that dual-use goods fall within the scope of the common commercial policy defined by Article 113 of the treaty (see the discussion in section V below).

However, because Article 223 is effectively used to reinforce member states' sovereignty in economic aspects of defence policy, its deletion or amendment has never been widely discussed. Hence, as an official within the Commission concludes, 'any changes of substance or interpretation of Article 223 are more likely to follow agreement on wider aspects of armaments policy'.[7]

European Political Co-operation and the Single European Act

The growing realization that economic convergence could not be achieved without a minimum of foreign policy coordination led member governments to review the situation in 1969. This review led to the setting up in October 1970 of a strictly intergovernmental process of coordination, known as European Political Co-operation (EPC).[8] The EPC consisted (after 1974) of the European Council—the heads of state and government of the member states—as the primary decision-making body to provide guidelines and resolve controversial issues. At a secondary level, decisions were prepared and made by foreign ministers who met separately during European Council meetings and on at least two other occasions during each presidency. At the next level, representatives from the foreign ministries of member states met once a month in the Political Committee (PoCo) to define and implement the EPC. Finally, below PoCo a number of working groups were established, such as the working group on non-proliferation (focusing on the spread of nuclear weapons) which was initiated in 1981 following an Anglo-Dutch proposal. Today, under the CFSP, there are approximately 20 groups of experts which work in a similar way. These include

---

[6] See, e.g., European Commission, 'The challenges facing the European defence-related industry', COM(96)10 final, Jan. 1996, p. 14.

[7] van Orden, G., 'European arms export controls?', eds P. Cornish, P. van Ham and J. Krause, *Europe and the Challenge of Proliferation*, Chaillot Paper no. 24 (Western European Union, Institute for Security Studies: Paris, May 1996), p. 69.

[8] A set of procedural ground-rules and common positions established in 3 reports agreed by ministers (at Luxembourg in 1970, Copenhagen in 1973 and London in 1981) together with the accumulated experience of over 2 decades (during the 1970s and 1980s) of negotiations towards common political positions on a variety of international issues provided the core dynamics of EPC-style integration.

the CONUC group, which is responsible for nuclear issues, CONOP (non-proliferation), CODUN (global disarmament and arms control) and COARM, the Council of Ministers' Group for Co-operation in the Field of Armaments and the Harmonisation of European Export Policies, which was established in 1991 to examine arms exports (and is discussed in greater detail in chapter 4).

The EPC began life as a purely voluntary intergovernmental process without any legal foundation (the European Court of Justice had no role, for example).[9] It was also many years before the European Parliament became involved in the EPC, reflecting the unwillingness of member states to yield sovereignty in this area. However, the introduction of the Single European Act,[10] which came into force on 1 July 1987, changed the informal character of the EPC. The act formalized the linkage between the Community and the EPC by, among other things, authorizing representatives of the European Commission to participate at EPC meetings and upgrading the European Council to the supreme decision-making body for the Community institutions (although it remained subordinate to the Council of Ministers).[11] The Commission also became responsible for enforcing economic sanctions imposed by the EPC, and the European Parliament became entitled to receive reports from the presidency and to ask specific questions on EPC matters. This slight shift towards Community-led integration was consolidated by the establishment of small secretariats in the Commission's headquarters in Brussels for both the Council of Ministers and the EPC. In turn, the Commission itself established a new Directorate-General (DGIA) with responsibility for foreign and security affairs, including non-proliferation issues.

Moreover, the Single European Act not only authorized the EPC process to prepare common positions on issues of common interest, including economic aspects of security; it also appeared to adopt a position that is close to the restrictive interpretation of Article 223. Article 30, paragraph 6 of the act, for example, announces that: '(*a*) The High Contracting Parties . . . are ready to coordinate their positions more closely on the political and economic aspects of

---

[9] The 2 main problems with the EPC were the decision-making system (which relied on consensus, and thus on the political discretion of each of the member states) and the difficulties of taking external action. External leverage such as economic assistance, sanctions and military support had to be 'borrowed' from national, EC, Western European Union (WEU) or NATO sources. These shortcomings often prevented cohesive and forceful action.

[10] Adopted in 1985, the Single European Act, as well as being the legal driving force behind the Single European Market, strengthened the Treaty of Rome by providing for increased use of qualified majority voting (QMV) in the Council of Ministers. The act introduced a series of some 300 measures to remove barriers by the end of 1992. These measures can be placed in 4 broad groups: measures to enable the free movement of capital Community-wide; measures to open up public procurement to Community-wide competition (which means that member states are now compelled to use competitive tender throughout the Community for many of their purchases); measures directed at the harmonization of regulations, technical norms, and quality and safety standards (either involving agreement of new EC standards or the 'mutual recognition' of existing national standards); and measures towards tax harmonization.

[11] The European Council meets at least once in each (6-month) presidency to discuss major issues and set the parameters for the future direction of the EU. It has no formal powers as such and must implement its proposals through the Council of the European Union, which comprises ministers from each of the member states. The composition of the latter depends on the subject under discussion. See the EU Internet site at URL <http://europa.eu.int>.

security; (*b*) [they] are determined to maintain the technological and industrial conditions necessary for their security. They shall work to that end both at national level and, where appropriate, within the framework of the competent institutions and bodies'.[12]

In addition, the Single European Act envisaged greater collaboration between foreign embassies of member states, and the formation of caucuses during international conferences and in permanent international organizations. However, the Commission did not immediately realize that export controls might be a significant issue within the emerging Single European Market (SEM). Hence, other than some references to nuclear export controls, the SEM documents emerging from the Commission in the mid-1980s contained no reference to export controls.

The main concern at this stage was the bureaucratic nature of European export controls and the wide range of individual licences, import certificates and delivery certificates needed even for intra-Community trade. Encouraged by the Commission, the European Parliament began to take an interest and tabled several reports and resolutions.[13] It was only towards the end of the 1980s, however, that the European Commission fully realized some of the export implications of intra-community trade. In particular, difficulties were envisaged between the effective functioning of COCOM (and especially the requirement for European firms to apply for a re-export licence from the US Commerce Department for intra-Community trade involving US technology or components) and the goal of a market without internal borders.[14]

Thus, at the end of the 1980s, the Commission ordered several studies on the impact of COCOM on internal EC trade (none of which was published[15]), and in the summer of 1989 it convened a PoCo working group to examine the problems that the SEM might pose for member states' arms and dual-use export controls. Article 223 was also examined (prompted mainly by concerns about

---

[12] Article 30.6, Title III of the Single European Act, reproduced in *Treaties Establishing the European Communities, Treaties Amending these Treaties and Documents Concerning the Accession* (Office of Official Publications of the European Communities: Luxembourg, 1987), p. 1049.

[13] Throughout the 1980s the European Parliament gave the most thorough attention to the issue of arms export controls. See, e.g., European Parliament, 'Report drawn up on the behalf of the Political Affairs Committee on arms procurement within a common industrial policy and arms sales, Rapporteur Adam Fergusson', PE 78.344/fin., Strasbourg, 27 June 1983; and European Parliament, 'Report drawn up on behalf of the Political Affairs Committee on European arms exports, Rapporteur Glyn Ford', document A2-0398/88, PE 118.374/fin., Strasbourg, 22 Feb. 1989. See also the resulting European Parliament resolution in *Official Journal of the European Communities*, C96 (17 Apr. 1989), p. 34.

[14] One reason why the Commission was slow to make these links was its almost total exclusion from COCOM activities. Nötzold, J. and Roodbeen, H., 'The European Community and CoCom: the exclusion of an interested party', eds G. Bertsch, H. Vogel and J. Zielonka, *After the Revolutions: East–West Trade and Technology Transfer in the 1990s* (Westview Press: Boulder, Colo., 1991), pp. 119–39. Nonetheless, the Commission would have been aware of some of the long-standing tensions within COCOM—as discussed in chapter 2 of this volume—and the continuing extraterritorial extension of US export regulations (highlighted, for instance, by the Urengoi natural gas pipeline dispute between the USA and European members of COCOM in 1981–82). However, while the EPC process was never used to develop a common EC policy in response to US sanctions, the Commission did fashion a coordinating role for itself in the subsequent discussions with the USA on the problem of US extraterritorial jurisdiction. Nötzold and Roodbeen, pp. 132–33.

[15] Nötzold and Roodbeen (note 14), p. 128.

import duties for weapon transfers) and informal discussions took place between the Commission and the most important member states.

Despite these sensitive and complex discussions and the promising shifts in the Community's institutional framework, the Single European Act failed to change the status quo concerning Article 223 (mainly because of the intransigence of the British and French negotiators). The next question, therefore, was whether the Maastricht negotiations would also leave national competencies concerning arms exports and production unchanged.

III. The period 1990–95: Maastricht and the first steps towards common arms export policies

The Persian Gulf War and other catalysts for change

There are political, military, economic and technological benefits to be had both from restricting the free flow of weapons and weapon-related technologies and from their export. National governments have traditionally had to balance these competing demands within their respective national export control regulations. However, as will be shown in greater detail in Part III of this study, the different underlying attitudes to the desirability of control measures have resulted in different priorities for member states in their export control policies, leading to inconsistencies within the Community as a whole. Indeed, the tendency has been for member states to permit exports except where they directly prejudice their own political or security interests (or where UN embargoes or COCOM rules dictate restraint).

Several developments in the early 1990s pointed to the growing inadequacy of this predominantly national approach to export controls within the EU.

First, the 1991 Persian Gulf War was a timely reminder of the inadequacy of national policies, and particularly those of the larger suppliers—France, Germany, Italy and the UK. While some of this mainly dual-use trade with Iraq occurred clandestinely (particularly from Germany), the majority of arms and technology transfers occurred legally and under the guidance of national governments (particularly from the UK, as discussed in chapter 5, and from France).[16] As a result of these destabilizing transfers to Iraq (and of having had to face weapons of Coalition origin during Operation Desert Storm), there was a great deal of enthusiasm among several member states for tighter controls in the first half of 1991. Germany, for example, tightened its national controls on dual-use transfers and pressed others to do the same (see chapter 6), while both France and the UK were participants in the multilateral P5 negotiations aimed at tighter controls on transfers to the Middle East.

Second, the end of the cold war not only resulted in increasing liberalization of COCOM controls but also provided the political space for the development

---

¹⁶ The former Soviet Union and China were also important suppliers of arms and dual-use materials to Iraq at this time. Timmerman, K., *The Death Lobby: How the West Armed Iraq* (Fourth Estate: London, 1992).

of European options in this area. In other words, instead of being bound by a tight bipolar regulatory and ideological framework, member states were much freer to plot their own regulatory path on arms exports. It also allowed far closer coordination of policies between former enemies (as shown most recently by the willingness of several Central and Eastern European states to adhere to the principles of the EU Code of Conduct: see chapter 4).

Third, the growing integration of Europe's arms industry, including more permanent links among companies and the growing number of collaborative development projects, meant that national controls were becoming increasingly ineffective. In theory, companies with divisions in several countries could choose the country with the weakest legislation from which to export their goods (and the growing tendency of defence firms to be located in multinational corporations raised the issue of how to control the movement of defence-related goods within such corporations). The Swedish company Saab, for example, is producing its Gripen JAS-39 fighter aircraft in a joint project with BAE Systems, thus giving the Swedish company access to BAE's large international sales network (see chapter 7). Another example is the Franco-German manufacturer, Euromissile, which exported 20 000 assorted missiles (anti-tank and surface-to-air) to India and Iraq in the early 1990s. These missiles were jointly produced by Euromissile and the German manufacturer MBB (which held a 50 per cent stake in Euromissile). These exports, which would have been forbidden under German law, were subject to a 1971 Franco-German treaty that stipulates that neither of the two governments will obstruct the other country's export of arms that have been jointly produced to third countries.[17]

Similar problems also arise from government-to-government agreements setting up collaborative projects. In the past, these agreements often contained a provision that allowed each partner government to veto an export from its own production on condition that it then transferred to its partners the manufacturing information to enable the project to be completed. However, given the impracticality of this provision, states were reluctant to use it. Instead, in the mid-1980s a number of secret, bilateral memoranda of understanding were signed between France, Germany and the UK under which the signatories expunged the right to a national veto over exports of collaborative projects, except in cases of extreme national concern.[18]

In practice this sometimes meant that the export policy for collaborative projects was determined by the member state with the weakest controls, as was the case with the export of Tornado aircraft to Saudi Arabia by the British Government, despite German restrictions on such sales (see chapters 5 and 6). The different national controls on the intra-Community transfer of components and subsystems between partner states also affected the competitiveness of

---

[17] Wulf, H., 'The Federal Republic of Germany', ed. I. Anthony, SIPRI, *Arms Export Regulations* (Oxford University Press: Oxford, 1991), p. 77.

[18] Taylor, T., 'European co-operation and conventional arms control', Paper for discussion at the International Institute for Strategic Studies Conference on Conventional Arms Proliferation, Barnet Hill, UK, 5–7 May 1993 (unpublished).

European collaborative projects and led to calls from industry for a licence-free zone (LFZ) for such transfers (discussed in section IV below).

Fourth, the impending free movement of goods within the SEM also threatened to undermine national controls as it raised the possibility of goods being moved to, and exported from, the country with the weakest legislative or administrative system. This situation was and continues to be exacerbated by the changing nature of the international arms trade and, in particular, the growing importance of components and other physically small items such as small arms.

Fifth, the emerging discussions on European political union not only provided another important political catalyst for a heightened EC interest in arms export controls at this time but also offered a process through which common action in this area could progress. These discussions and their impact on the arms export practices of member states are reviewed below.

Emerging perspectives on the problem of Community-level export controls

Thus, in the early 1990s, many European political leaders believed that it was now necessary to reinforce controls on arms exports, and there was 'a view' within the EC that there might be a window of opportunity for the introduction of a common Regulation on this issue. The desire for a common approach was even acknowledged by some defence industrialists, given that the system of different national controls placed some companies in countries with tighter regulation at a competitive disadvantage.[19] At the Council of Ministers meeting in Rome on 14–15 December 1990 (which prepared the ground for the subsequent IGC for the Maastricht Treaty) a list of four fields were specified as integral to the future development of a CFSP. The list, known as the Asolo List, included two fields that are relevant here—economic and technological cooperation in the armaments field, and coordination of armaments export policy and non-proliferation.[20]

The inclusion of the latter field was particularly significant as it was the first explicit mention of coordination of arms export policy within the emerging CFSP. During the first half of 1991, several proposals on the future treaty on European political union included paragraphs that sought to further clarify these two fields. A joint draft proposal by the foreign ministers of France and Germany,[21] and draft proposals by Luxembourg (at the time president of the

---

[19] E.g., the Daimler-Benz technology group wrote an open letter in Mar. 1991 to the President of the European Commission, Jacques Delors, proposing the introduction of harmonized export controls throughout the Community under the guidance of a European Arms Export Control Authority. *Atlantic News*, 27 Mar. 1991, p. 5. See also the European Round Table of Industrialists (ERT) policy paper, 'Towards a single European export control system: harmony or chaos?', ERT, Brussels, June 1991, which is discussed in greater detail in chapter 6 .

[20] 'Presidency conclusions', European Council, Rome, 14–15 December 1990, Part 1, SN 424/1/90, pp. 5–6.

[21] 'Note des délégations allemande et française en date de février 1991 à la Conférence inter-gouvernemental sur l'Union politique, Conférence des représentants des gouvernements des États Membres–union Politique' [Note by the German and French delegations dated February 1991 to the

European Council),[22] the Netherlands and the UK, all cited arms export policy as an area for possible joint action. The European Commission considered going even further by proposing (on 27 February 1991) a formal common arms export policy and the deletion of Article 223.[23] The proposal was also supported by a resolution of the European Parliament on 18 April 1991.[24] At this stage the Commission in particular was beginning to look at the problems which export controls posed for the Community from two perspectives—as an internal technical problem and as an external political problem.[25] Solutions that were applicable in one area were thought likely to have a spillover effect on the other, so the two perspectives were clearly linked.

The internal technical problem

The internal technical problem arose from the fact that export controls were being applied by each member state on a broad range of goods to a number of proscribed destinations and that, to reduce the risk of diversion, the majority of controls in the Community were between member states rather than between individual member states and the proscribed destinations.[26] In particular, the Commission saw the application of such an extensive system of controls on exports in non-Article 223 goods between member states as being incompatible with both the Treaty of Rome and the completion of the SEM. The Commission also recognized, however, that if controls on intra-EC trade were to be abolished all member states would have to apply effective controls based on common standards on the export of controlled goods to non-EC countries.[27]

Intergovernmental Conference on Political Union, conference of representatives of the governments of the member states, Political Union], 4 Feb. 1991, CONF-lup 1718/1/91, pp. 3–4. For a translation of the key parts of the text see Allebeck, A. C., 'The European Community and arms export regulations', ed. Anthony (note 17), p. 215.

[22] 'Draft treaty articles with a view to achieving political union presented by Luxembourg on 15 Apr. 1991 to the Conference of the Representatives of the Governments of the Member States–Political Union', Non-paper CONF-UP 1800/91, Annexe 1, p. 84.

[23] The European Commission had earlier proposed the abolition of Article 223 in a preparatory paper for the IGC on political union in Oct. 1990. Commission of the European Communities, 'Commission opinion of the 21 October 1990 on the proposal for amendment of the Treaty Establishing the European Economic Community with a view to political union', COM(90)600 (final), Brussels, 23 Oct. 1990.

[24] The resolution appeared in European Parliament, 'Report drawn up on behalf of the Political Affairs Committee on the outlook for a European security policy: the significance of a European security policy and its implications for European political union, Rapporteur Hans-Gert Poettering', PE 146.269/fin., Strasbourg, 29 Apr. 1991, and was adopted with all-party support. It called for the abolition of Article 223; Community initiatives to regulate arms exports to the Third World; a ban on exports of arms and dual-use goods to countries which violate human rights; Community support for the UN Register of Conventional Arms; and closer coordination of European procurement policies with a view to reducing excess capacity. *Official Journal of the European Communities*, C129 (20 May 1991), p. 139.

[25] Lennon, P. (Adviser to the European Commission), 'Export controls and the European Community', Paper for the Centre for European Policy Studies (CEPS) Meeting on Controlling the Export of Sensitive Dual-Use Technologies, Brussels, 21 Oct. 1991, p. 3 (unpublished).

[26] The 2 exceptions were intra-Benelux trade and trade from Ireland to the UK (but not vice versa).

[27] Lennon (note 25) p. 4; and Wenzel, J., 'The European Community's approach to export controls', eds K. Bailey and R. Rudney, *Proliferation and Export Controls* (University Press of America: Lanham, Md., 1993), p. 96.

The external political problem

In addition to pressure to complete the Single Market by 1992, the growing pressure (as described above) for more effective non-proliferation controls also located the export control issue in a wider political context. This external political problem was (and continues to be) essentially about what goods should be subject to control in respect of which destinations and under what conditions. The key area of uncertainty at this point was the extent to which this responsibility should be transferred from national competence to the Community. One possibility, for example, would have been to differentiate between policy making and policy implementation, with the former being monitored and coordinated at the EU level and the latter (i.e., licensing, customs, penalties and fines) remaining under the auspices of national governments.[28] However, member states continued to envisage different forms of cooperation, and most feared that Community-level rules would be either more lax or more restrictive than their existing national regulations.

The separation of dual-use goods (and the internal technical problem) from military goods (and the external political problem)

On 8 March 1991, the Vice-President of the Commission, Martin Bangemann (a German commissioner), published an article in the French newspaper *Les Échos* that provoked further speculation that solutions to both these problems might be possible.[29] In particular, he suggested that the expected abolition of internal frontiers at the end of 1992 to create the SEM justified 'to a large extent the urgency of establishing European common rules on arms exports towards non European countries', and that 'the most important objective of a common system of control for the Twelve EC countries is to reach a limitation on arms exports. Common rules being observed by all member countries are a better guarantee for peace in the world than the present dissimilar national norms'.[30]

Bangemann also proposed the setting up of a 'Community system of exports control for armament goods' and Community measures to support defence

---

[28] See, e.g., the discussion in Bauer, H., Brzoska, M. and Karl, W., *Co-ordination and Control of Arms Exports from EC Member States and the Development of a Common Arms Export Policy, Study Prepared for the European Parliament, Directorate General for Research, European Parliament Research Project no. 4/90/9*, Arbeitspapiere/Working Papers no. 48 (Berghof Foundation: Berlin, 1992); and Wenzel (note 27), pp. 95–99.

[29] The most significant extracts from this article are reproduced in Adam, B. (ed.), *European Union and Arms Exports* (Groupe de Recherche et d'Information sur la Paix et la Sécurité (GRIP): Brussels, Dec. 1995), p. 74. As Vice-President of the Commission and responsible for industrial affairs, Bangemann carried a great deal of influence. Given also that it is unusual for commissioners to make public utterances without prior consultation, it was thought that his comments would be the prelude to a formal announcement by the Commission and member states. However, during a personal interview with a Commission official (Brussels, 1997) the present author was informed that it was never the Commission's intention to include conventional weapons in the Regulation. This indicates either that Commissioner Bangemann was badly advised or that (not unlike the situation in national bureaucracies) there were different perspectives within the Commission.

[30] Quoted in Adam (note 29), p. 74.

conversion.[31] However, both proposals were only partially implemented. First, as discussed in section IV below, Bangemann was forced to limit his proposal for a common system of control to dual-use goods (thus addressing mainly the internal, technical problem), and even this watered-down regulation was only adopted two years after the creation of the SEM. Second, there was no agreement within the Commission or the Council of Ministers on the initiation of a conversion programme. It was the European Parliament that took the initiative to start the two defence industry diversification programmes known as PERIFRA and KONVER (although the Commission subsequently agreed to manage them).

In short, it was not possible to implement Commissioner Bangemann's proposals because a number of basic disagreements on the exact nature of the external political problem and the precise steps needed to tackle it continued to divide the member states (and even members of the Commission) during the IGC discussions on political union. The repercussions of the Gulf War and the other catalysts described above remained insufficient to forge consensus in this area and, in particular, to threaten the strict interpretation of Article 223.

Broadly speaking, there were two bodies of opinion within member states. One opinion, championed by France and the UK, was that arms export policies designed within the EC framework should be restricted to military security concerns in general and the prevention of WMD proliferation in particular. This view saw ethical concerns about conventional arms exports and questions of global politics as matters for national governments to decide and not something that should be imposed on member states.[32] A second opinion, promoted by Germany and the Netherlands, was that EC export control policy needed to be extended to conventional weapons and should involve the drafting of specific criteria to establish a common framework for export licence decisions by member states. These differences need to be seen in the context of the broader debate over the future of European integration and the mechanics for decision making on CFSP matters that was taking place at that time.

However, it was clear that the first opinion was in the ascendancy. Bangemann's original proposals were therefore discarded, and the Commission announced on 29 May 1991 that it was working on a more pragmatic solution limited to the standardization of technical and administrative procedures for dual-use goods (thus leaving the external political problem for future intergovernmental cooperation).[33] This effectively split consideration of dual-use goods from conventional weapons. The subsequent intergovernmental debates that led to the development of eight common criteria on arms export controls are discussed in chapter 4.

---

[31] Adam (note 29), p. 74.

[32] See, e.g., 'France/UK block export policy', *Jane's Defence Weekly*, 23 Feb. 1991.

[33] 'Export controls and the completion of the internal market', Communication of Martin Bangemann to the Commission, 29 May 1991.

IV. The development of a common regulation

As discussed above, the European Commission first began to examine the issue of export controls on dual-use goods in the late 1980s as a consequence of the emerging SEM. In May 1991 Commissioner Bangemann submitted some proposals which the Commission then used as the basis for a statement published later the same month.[34] The statement declared that after completion of the SEM at the end of 1992, dual-use goods and technologies (which accounted for about 5 per cent of intra-EC trade[35]) should no longer be subject to controls at internal Community borders. It also announced that the Commission's approach would be to seek 'a pragmatic answer to a complex problem' and that this would be limited to ensuring uniform control procedures for exports of dual-use goods to third countries. This implied the adoption of certain common rules, and throughout the remainder of 1991 the Commission carried out fact-finding missions to member states to determine the comparative strengths and weaknesses of their dual-use export controls. These missions were normally of two days' duration and included meetings with government officials and visits to exporting companies and customs offices to see how controls actually operated in practice. These consultations enabled the Commission to begin thinking about how much of the control system needed to be harmonized (for example, whether lists of controlled products, licences and penalties should be identical in all member states or whether marginal variations could be permitted) and whether any additional measures were necessary to close potential loopholes.

The Commission was not alone in thinking about these matters at this time. Industrial organizations, such as the Union of Industrial and Employers' Confederations of Europe (UNICE)[36] and the European Round Table of Industrialists (ERT),[37] were beginning to play a crucial role in the development of European export control legislation (as they still do), by way of position papers and frequent contacts with officials. For example, in an initial ERT policy paper, to which UNICE subscribed, it was suggested that: 'Industrial efficiency and compatibility with the concept of Europe 1992 as a truly common market without internal borders dictates that all controlled commodity trade within the European Community takes place within a licence free zone. In turn, the licence free zone should operate within a supranational export control system created to regulate proliferation of high-tech dual-use products and technologies'.[38]

In order to create this LFZ, in which all licences for all commodities transferred within the EC (and later, possibly, within what was then the European

---

[34] 'Export controls and the completion of the internal market' (note 33).

[35] *Financial Times*, 17 Feb. 1992.

[36] Created in 1958, UNICE is made up of representatives from the 33 main national federations of business and employers from 25 European countries. Its main purposes are to promote European business interests at the EU and national levels, and to influence European legislation and institutions.

[37] The ERT members are company representatives within Europe.

[38] European Round Table of Industrialists (note 19), p. ii.

Economic Area, and eventually COCOM) would be abandoned,[39] the ERT also called for the establishment of: (*a*) a single control list of commodities for export from the LFZ; (*b*) a single list of proscribed customers; (*c*) common standards for export control systems in the member states; and (*d*) a supranational Export Control Agency to regulate the LFZ.[40] In addition, a three-tier system of controls was suggested for the licensing of exports from the LFZ: (*a*) 'partial controls' on exports to other COCOM member countries; (*b*) 'tighter controls' on exports to other, non-proscribed, countries; and (*c*) 'stringent controls' on exports to proscribed destinations.[41]

The ERT proposals were in keeping with a simultaneous evolution of more liberalized international controls on dual-use goods that was taking place in the post-cold war era. This liberalization took two forms—relaxation in export controls on West-to-East and West-to-West trade. In the former case, the EU Dual-Use Regulation was clearly being developed in the shadow of debates about a successor to COCOM, particularly as those member states which were also part of COCOM had already introduced simplified licensing for exports of sensitive goods to other COCOM partners and COCOM cooperation countries. Industrial lobby groups such as UNICE were also arguing for global harmonization of dual-use export controls at this time at much lower levels of restriction. In the latter case, general rather than individual licences for a large number of controlled commodities were increasingly facilitating export controls on trade between Western countries.

Other broad trends and issues in the global economy were also influencing the trade in dual-use goods during the late 1980s and early 1990s. First, the growth rate in the volume of global exports was twice that of cumulative gross domestic product (GDP), and the growth rate in the volume of foreign direct investment (which tends to facilitate technology transfer) was twice that of exports. The cumulative effect of these two trends was clear—a flourishing global trade in dual-use goods and technologies.[42] Second, the USA was pushing hard in the OECD and GATT to liberalize controls on high-technology goods. The USA had a clear advantage in this area (at least over Europe) and one way in which it sought to maintain it was by stopping EU subsidies for such industries. Thus, Commission officials were involved in informal discussions with US officials on export controls at this time.[43]

It was in this climate and in preparation for the introduction of the SEM in January 1993 that on 31 January 1992 the Commission published its first official Communication on the issue. It was divided into three main sections: a

---

[39] The ERT did, however, envisage the need for exporting companies to have reliable and auditable internal export control systems for trade within the LFZ. European Round Table of Industrialists (note 19), pp. 8–9.

[40] European Round Table of Industrialists (note 19), pp. 4–5.

[41] European Round Table of Industrialists (note 19), pp. 5, 10–12.

[42] Roberts, B., 'Rethinking export controls on dual-use materials and technologies: from trade restraints to trade enablers', *The Arena*, no. 2 (June 1995), p. 3.

[43] Personal interview with an official in the European Commission, Oct. 1997.

description of the current situation in the EC; an outline of the nature of the required solution; and a number of proposed actions.[44]

The first section also presented the conclusions of the above-mentioned fact-finding missions to member states. In short, these were that:

1. A 'solid legal basis for applying export controls' existed in all member states.

2. Some member states had comprehensive control systems and a wealth of experience in operating controls, while others had less sophisticated control systems and little practical experience in operating them.

3. The considerable variations in export control practices in member states—including differences in the product lists, attitudes towards third countries, the type of licences available to exporters, penalties, customs procedures, mechanisms for the exchange of information and administrative cooperation—were threatening the completion of the SEM.[45]

The second section outlined the main objectives to be achieved—resolution (or partial resolution in the latter case) of both the internal technical problem and the external political problem discussed above. To recap, first, because dual-use goods were covered by the Treaty of Rome and were outside the scope of Article 223, they would have to move freely between member states. However, a wide range of dual-use goods and technologies were still subject to export controls at this time when traded between member states. Second, an essential requirement for the elimination of controls on intra-EC trade was the establishment of effective external controls based on common standards. This second objective was particularly important given that the external perimeter was only likely to be as strong as the export control practices adopted at the weakest point in the Community. The growing volume of dual-use trade and the use of sealed containers[46] for the transfer of small items and components increased the problems of detecting illegal shipments, which would inevitably migrate (having been allowed to move freely throughout the EU) to external EU borders where customs scrutiny was weakest. Although the Communication did not identify the member states with the least rigorous controls, countries on Europe's southern flank, such as Greece and Portugal, were widely thought to fall into that category. Thus, while it would not be necessary for controls at the external perimeter to be identical throughout the EU, they would have to present a similar level of deterrence or a minimum standard at every point of exit.

---

[44] European Commission, 'Export controls on dual-use goods and technologies and the completion of the internal market', Communication from the Commission to the Council and the Parliament, SEC(92)85 final, 31 Jan. 1992.

[45] European Commission (note 44), pp. 1–3.

[46] In 1989, e.g., over 9.5 million sealed containers moved through the 10 largest EC ports alone. Institute of Shipping Economics and Logistics, *Shipping Statistics* (Institute of Shipping Economics and Logistics: Bremen, Dec. 1990), p. 49, quoted in Anthony, I., Eavis, P. and Greene, O., *Regulating Arms Exports: A Programme for the European Community* (Saferworld: London, Sep. 1991), p. 27.

In the third section the Commission set out a list of measures to be taken to achieve these two objectives. In particular, it considered that the following were essential: (*a*) a common list of dual-use goods and technologies subject to control; (*b*) a common list of proscribed or authorized destinations; (*c*) common criteria for the issuing of licences; (*d*) a forum or mechanism in which to coordinate member states' licensing and enforcement policies and procedures; and (*e*) explicit procedures for administrative cooperation between customs and licensing offices throughout the Community.[47]

The Commission also recognized the need for a number of other supporting measures, two of which were particularly important. First, in order to strengthen member states' control regimes, the Commission announced the start of a technical assistance programme including seminars, training courses and exchanges between officials. Second, to support the Community's external perimeter, the Commission considered that an EC-wide information system would be needed to provide information on potential fraud and violations, as well as more basic information about the products to be controlled and the different destinations. It was suggested that two existing information systems might be utilized for this purpose—SCENT/CIS and the Integrated Community Tariff (TARIC).[48]

After a generally favourable reaction to the Communication, the Council of Ministers recruited an Ad Hoc High Level Working Party in February 1992 to explore the substantive proposals in greater detail. The Working Party included representatives from the Council of Ministers, the Commission and member states. Following recommendations made by this Working Party, the Commission presented on 31 August 1992 a proposed Council 'framework Regulation'[49] which was to be followed later by implementing regulations. This proposal was confined to what was necessary at the Community level to meet the essential requirements for the completion of the SEM. Further work on the Commission's proposal took place in two forums: the Ad Hoc High Level Working Party undertook a detailed, line-by-line, examination of the proposal; and a series of informal intergovernmental meetings sought to draw up the common list of goods, destinations and authorization criteria.

However, continuing disagreement among member states over a number of issues, including the legal structure of the Regulation (see the discussion in section V below), whether the 'catch-all' clause should be obligatory or optional, and the make-up of both the common list of dual-use goods and the list of proscribed or authorized destinations, prevented the Regulation from

[47] European Commission (note 44), p. 5.

[48] The Secure System for Customs Enforcement/Cutsoms Information System (SCENT/CIS) system was designed to exchange confidential information in order to combat fraud. Although up and running, in the early 1990s at least, it had still to be expanded in Greece, Ireland, Portugal and Spain. European Commission (note 44). The TARIC system was introduced in the late 1980s as part of the harmonization of customs tariffs. In addition to the standard 8-digit commodity codes it can process additional requirements, e.g., new agricultural controls or special taxes.

[49] European Commission, 'Proposal for a Council Regulation (EEC) on the control of exports of certain dual-use goods and technologies of certain nuclear products and technologies', COM(92)317, 31 Aug. 1992, *Official Journal of the European Communities*, C253 (30 Sep. 1992), p. 13.

coming into force in time for the opening of the SEM.[50] Instead, on 21 December 1992, the General Affairs Council released a statement that, with effect from 1 January 1993, dual-use goods and technologies 'will no longer be subject to internal frontier controls within the Community but solely to checks carried out as part of the normal control procedures applied in a non-discriminatory fashion throughout Community territory'.[51] In effect, without waiting to adopt the Regulation that would establish the legal conditions for the elimination of controls on intra-Community transfers of dual-use goods, the 12 member states had agreed to end such controls (on the basis that national controls for such exports to non-member countries would be maintained).

Although the Council of Ministers also announced on 21 December 1992 that member states would intensify their efforts to implement a Regulation by 31 March 1993, this (and other) deadlines came and went because no agreement could be reached. France and the UK, in particular, were of the opinion that the proposal did not allow the states enough competence.[52] Industrial representatives, on the other hand, were concerned that the draft Regulation was beginning to drift away from their ideal of an internal LFZ with a common control system at external borders.[53] In the transitional period at least there was no clear list of controlled commodities and no 'negative' destination list, and the number of national exemptions and exceptions for which different licensing procedures would apply was continuing to grow. Thus, Peter Lennon, a senior official within the European Commission (DGIII-A) and one of the major architects of the Regulation, wrote rather gloomily at this time:

The discussions in the Ad Hoc High Level Working Party would suggest that there are in fact a relatively small number of differences between certain member states in respect of certain goods, destinations and licensing requirements. If these could be resolved most, perhaps all, of the problems with which we are faced would disappear. I am convinced that they can be resolved if the will to do so is there. However, if the will to do so is not there, I fear that any solution which is acceptable to all member states would require complex administrative procedures which would impose a greater burden on exporters, and on the licensing and enforcement authorities than is at present the case. I am not sure that the Commission would wish to be associated with such a solution.[54]

It was during the Danish presidency of the EU in the first half of 1993 that member states decided to split the legal base between a Regulation and an inter-

[50] For a full list of the issues in dispute at this time see Lennon, P., 'Dual-use export controls and the European Community', Paper for the CEPS/Saferworld Conference, Brussels, 18 June 1993, pp. 4–6 (unpublished).

[51] European Communities, Council of Ministers, 'Council statement on the completion of the internal market in dual-use goods and technologies', 21 Dec. 1992, *Bulletin of the European Communities*, Dec. 1992, p. 60.

[52] Adam (note 29), p. 78.

[53] E.g., this was the view of Dr Paul Merkelbach, Head of Corporate Bureau, Export Controls, Philips International, based on the minutes of a seminar co-hosted by Saferworld and the Centre for European Policy Studies in June 1993 on Arms and Dual-Use Export Controls: Common Policies for Europe?

[54] Lennon, P., 'Export controls and the European Community', Paper for a Seminar on Defence Export Controls, Defence Manufacturers Association, London, 3 Nov. 1993, pp. 7–8 (unpublished).

governmental Decision (on the basis of the Joint Action procedure).[55] The aim was to establish a division of competence between those aspects that fell to the Community as a whole and those that should remain solely within the scope of the member states. It was also agreed that the annexes (which would contain the control lists and export criteria) should be linked to the Joint Action and therefore kept under member states' control.

This decision to split responsibility between the member states and the Commission was in keeping with the hybrid nature of much of European integration and meant that the proposal was now a reflection of both the functionalist[56] and the intergovernmental routes to integration. Many of the technical decisions (i.e., policy execution) in respect of the control of dual-use exports were to be centralized and standardized (and coordinated by the Commission), but member states would retain sole responsibility for the political decisions (i.e., policy making), including the drawing up of lists of goods, destinations and the criteria to be applied in licensing exports. Negotiations on the text then began in earnest during the Belgian presidency in the latter half of 1993. An indication of the new level of resolve was the involvement at this time of the Committee of Permanent Representatives (COREPER), which also began to look for solutions to outstanding problems regarding the duration of the transitional period and the means to combat fraud.[57]

In the meantime, during the second half of 1992, the European Parliament had also studied the proposal, and on 17 December 1992 reached agreement on 23 amendments to it.[58] These were contained in a report tabled by Gérard Fuchs (a French Socialist Member of the European Parliament, MEP) on 3 December 1992,[59] but a final vote on the report was delayed while the Parliament tried to put pressure on the Council and the Commission to allow it to be consulted on the lists of dual-use goods, destinations and export criteria contained in the annexes. In response, the Council pointed out that the member states had sole jurisdiction over the contents of the lists, which would be negotiated in an intergovernmental framework. Somewhat reluctantly, therefore, the European Parliament finally passed the report on 14 September 1993 without having the opportunity to officially consider the lists.[60]

---

[55] Under articles J2 and J3 of the Maastricht Treaty. On the Joint Action procedure, see Anthony, I., 'European Union approachs to arms control, non-proliferation and disarmament', *SIPRI Yearbook 2001* (note 2), p. 601.

[56] On the functionalist approach to integration see, e.g., Haas, E., *Beyond the Nation-State: Functionalism and International Organization* (Stanford University Press: Stanford, Calif. 1964).

[57] European Parliament, Directorate-General for Research, 'International transfers of dual-use technologies: CoCom and the European Community', External Economic Relations Series, DOC_EN\DV\239\239598, W-5 10/1993, p. 22.

[58] 'Minutes of the sitting of 17 Dec. 1992', *Official Journal of the European Communities*, C21 (25 Jan. 1993), p. 183.

[59] European Parliament, 'Report of the Committee on Economic and Monetary Affairs and Industrial Policy on the Commission proposal for a Council regulation on the control of exports of certain dual-use goods and technologies and of certain nuclear products and technologies, Rapporteur Gerard Fuchs', document A3-0398/92, Part A and Part B, PE 201.553/fin., Strasbourg, 3 Dec. 1992.

[60] *Official Journal of the European Communities*, C268 (4 Oct. 1993), p. 26. See also European Parliament, Directorate-General for Research (note 57), p. 22.

After two years of intensive discussions the Council finally agreed the texts of both the Regulation and the Joint Action during the Greek presidency in June 1994. Although the package of measures was due to come into effect on 1 January 1995, member states had still to agree the contents of all the annexes. These were agreed in August 1994, but subsequent requests for last-minute amendments, together with problems arising from the translation of the 180-page Annex I list of controlled goods into all the Community languages meant that the start date was put back to 1 March 1995. On 19 December 1994, during the German presidency, the General Affairs Council formally adopted the Regulation and the Joint Action.[61] However, in the second half of February 1995 the Commission notified the member states that the Regulation would not be published in the *Official Journal of the European Communities* by 1 March, and the implementation date was postponed again. Thus, an additional Regulation and two further Council decisions were adopted on 10 April 1995, postponing implementation until 1 July 1995.[62]

V. The legal structure of the Regulation and Joint Action

The legal basis for the agreement is articulated in two linked texts. Council Regulation EC 3381/94 gives the general framework and the Joint Action (Council Decision 94/942/CFSP) contains a number of annexes which specify the common list of dual-use goods covered by the Regulation as well as a list of criteria by which authorizations will be granted or refused.[63]

As stated above, this division of competence represented a compromise between the role of the Commission under Article 113 of the Treaty of Rome (and a functionalist approach to integration) and that of member states under Article 223 (and the intergovernmental approach). In effect, dual-use goods were first considered to lie within the economic sphere, where the Commission has a major role, and the text of the Regulation reflects this position. It also meant that the Regulation could be modified by a simple qualified majority within the Council (because it fell under the first 'pillar' of the EU, setting up Community procedures for which unanimity is not always necessary). However, because of their strategic sensitivity, dual-use goods also fell within the political sphere, and this brought them under the second 'pillar'—the CFSP. In this sphere the procedures are intergovernmental and normally require unanimity. Although Article J.3 of the Maastricht Treaty allows the Council to

[61] 'Council Regulation (EC) no. 3381/94 of 19 Dec. 1994 setting up a Community regime for the control of exports of dual-use goods'; and 'Council Decision no. 94/942/CFSP of 19 Dec. 1994 on the joint action adopted by the Council on the basis of Article J.3 of the Treaty on European Union concerning the control of exports of dual-use goods', *Official Journal of the European Communities*, L367, vol. 37 (31 Dec. 1994).

[62] 'Council Regulation (EC) no. 837/95; Council Decision 95/127/CFSP; and Council Decision 95/128/CFSP of 10 Apr. 1995', *Official Journal of the European Communities*, L90 (21 Apr. 1995).

[63] See note 61.

take decisions involving joint actions by a qualified majority,[64] no such possibility was offered in the Joint Action on dual-use goods. This meant that any modification to the lists of goods and the export criteria in the annexes requires unanimity.[65]

The Regulation

Licensing

Article 3 of the Regulation states that a licence is necessary for the export and re-export to third countries (i.e., outside the EU) of those dual-use goods listed in Annex I of the Joint Action. One of the key elements to the proper functioning of this new export control system is the idea of a Community Licence introduced under Article 6. This means that any licence—individual, general or global—that is granted for the export of Annex I goods is valid throughout the Community. A harmonized individual licence has also been introduced and is available for use in all member states (in conjunction with existing national individual licences). However, the volume of goods covered by individual licensing is quite small. General and global licences account for somewhere between 80 and 90 per cent of the volume of trade in dual-use goods, and these licences remain different between the member states. Nevertheless, when any of these are now issued in respect of Annex I goods they must be treated as Community licences (although in practice mutual recognition of global and general licences has proved problematic, as discussed below).

Normally an individual licence is required for exports to third countries, but Article 6 allows simplified forms of licensing (i.e., general licences) to certain 'friendly' destinations, as listed in Annex II of the Joint Action. Individual licences are also still required in respect of *intra-EU trade* in: (*a*) the most sensitive dual-use goods (listed in Annex IV of the Joint Action); (*b*) items which one or more member state continue to treat as military products under their national legislation (listed in Annex V of the Joint action); and (*c*) certain nuclear materials (defined in Article 21).

Furthermore, Article 5, the 'safeguard clause', specifies that member states may apply more restrictive national regulations than those defined by the EU (i.e., impose a licence requirement on goods not in Annex I). These have to be declared and published in the *Official Journal*.[66]

Article 7 stipulates that export licences are to be issued in the member state where the exporter is established, and (under Article 6) these are valid throughout the EU, which means that goods may leave at any EU border. Article 7 also

[64] *Treaty on European Union* (Office for Official Publications of the European Communities: Luxembourg, 7 Feb. 1992), document no. 1759/60, available on the European Union Internet site at URL <http://europa.eu.int/abc/treaties_en.htm>.

[65] Adam (note 29), pp. 79–80.

[66] Only 2 governments have imposed additional licence requirements under Article 5. Germany listed 13 dual-use items not covered by Annex I and the UK listed 25 items (mainly supercomputers and cryptographic equipment). These lists appeared in the *Official Journal of the European Communities*, C334 (12 Dec. 1995).

allows for two types of consultation between member states when the goods are located in a different state from that from which the licence application is made. First, the member state of location must be consulted prior to the granting of the licence and may oppose it within 10 days, and such a decision is binding. Second, any other member state may 'oppose' the export (within 10 days) if the export threatens its vital interests, but the licensing state is not required to take this opposition into account. While both these consultation mechanisms are designed to prevent circumvention, the latter mechanism is also a safety net to protect the reputation of supplier states.[67]

Finally, although most of the intra-EU trade in dual-use goods is now licence-free, exporters are still obliged to register with their licensing authority within 30 days of an intra-EU transfer of goods listed in Annex I and to keep records of such transfers for at least three years.

The catch-all clause

There is a wide range of non-listed industrial goods and materials which are extensively traded for legitimate purposes but which may also be used, wholly or in part, in connection with a WMD programme. Including all these items in the control lists would have created a major burden on both industry and the licensing authorities. Thus, Article 4 of the Regulation introduces a catch-all clause for these non-listed dual-use goods in relation to NBC weapons. The article has three specific sub-clauses, which introduce end-use controls based in part on the awareness of the exporter. Member states are obliged to implement the first two sub-clauses, but the third is optional (and was largely incorporated for the benefit of the UK which had a similar clause in its national legislation).[68] In summary, the clause requires exporters to: (*a*) apply for a licence if told by the authorities that a particular export of non-listed dual-use goods is being or may be used in connection with a WMD programme—Article 4 (1); (*b*) inform the authorities (who will decide whether an export licence is required) if they are 'aware' that a particular export of non-listed dual-use goods is being or may be used in connection with a WMD programme—Article 4 (2); and (*c*) apply for a licence if they have 'grounds for suspecting' that the goods in question may be so used—Article 4(3).

This entire clause was a major source of disagreement during the negotiations, since only a few member states actually had such a clause in their existing national regulations. Indeed, it took Volker Hahn, a lawyer who represented Germany throughout the negotiations and was the principal architect of much of the draft Regulation, two and a half years to convince his counterparts in other

---

[67] E.g., British officials could challenge France if they discovered that a distinctive British commodity (such as a Rolls Royce engine) was being exported from France to a sensitive destination. Such a clause is deemed necessary because if such a commodity ended up with a known proliferator it would be likely that the UK rather than France came under international scrutiny.

[68] Only Austria, Belgium, Finland and the UK have incorporated Article 4(3) of the catch-all into their national regulations. *The EU Regulation on Dual-Use Goods After One Year: A Survey of Government and Industry* (Export Control Publications/ Deltac Ltd: Chertsey, 1996), p. 23.

national ministries of the benefits of the catch-all clause. In particular, many trilateral meetings took place during this time between France, Germany and the UK. France did not have a catch-all privision in its legislation and needed to be convinced that one was necessary, while both Germany and the UK were of the opinion that their own existing clause offered the best solution. The two main differences between the German and British provisions were, first, that the German catch-all clause also covered conventional weapons in addition to WMD (whereas the UK's only covered WMD) and, second, that the German provisions only referred to 'knowledge of' dual-use goods being used for military purposes, whereas the UK regulations added 'knows or suspects'. Such an addition was considered unnecessary in Germany because there was an expectation that German companies would attempt to discover this information for themselves, partly for cultural reasons and partly because of the potential consequences of failing to do so. As discussed in chapter 6, the German penalty regime is among the most severe in the EU.

Although the original catch-all clause in the Commission proposal of 31 August 1992 carried the German view, the final outcome was a compromise between the German and British positions. With the addition of Article 4(3), which allows for national variations, the UK was essentially allowed to keep its own catch-all clause. However, other aspects of the resulting compromise reduced both the severity and the scope of the clause. First, in the earlier version the exporter was automatically required to request export authorization, but the changes introduced a measure of discretion and shifted responsibility back on the regulators. Second, and more importantly in the context of this study, early in 1994 the German negotiators decided to drop their demand for the catch-all clause to mirror their own national legislation as regards the inclusion of conventional weapons. As discussed in chapter 2, there is a common export control philosophy or 'norm' surrounding controls on WMD which is largely absent in respect of conventional arms. It was this absence of a common normative base for the treatment of conventional weapons that forced the German negotiators to limit the scope of the catch-all to WMD. As a result, Germany is the only member state to have a national catch-all clause that covers conventional military projects (as discussed in chapter 6); in all other member states it is only applicable to WMD.

Customs procedures

Article 9 specifies that a licence may be refused, annulled, suspended or modified, in which case the other member states must be informed. Article 10 requires the exporter to provide evidence of the licence approval to the customs office when an item is exported. In addition, the article allows a member state to oppose the export if it considers that the conditions have changed since the issue of the licence (by another member state) and it believes that the export would be contrary to its essential foreign policy or security interests. A consultation is then organized between the two states within 10 days. If there is no agreement, the state from which the goods are being exported may deny the export and return the goods to the exporter. Article 11 allows member states the discretion to concentrate the export of dual-use goods at certain customs offices, and was designed for smaller states with weaker controls, such as Greece, Ireland and Portugal.

Administrative cooperation in the Co-ordinating Group

Following a recommendation by the Committee on Energy, Research and Technology within the European Parliament,[69] Article 16 introduces a Co-ordinating Group for overseeing the application of the Regulation, to be composed of representatives of each member state and chaired by a representative of the Commission. The European Parliament wanted to go much further and recommended the setting up of an 'operational system for mutual and obligatory' information exchange and greater cooperation between customs control methods.[70] The Regulation is silent on these two points, however.

End-use certification and penalties

Following another amendment by the European Parliament, end-use certification for exports of Annex I goods was made a discretionary requirement under Article 6(2). Article 17 stipulates that 'effective, proportionate and dissuasive' penalties must be introduced, but allows each member state to decide on the scope and nature of the penalties.[71]

The transition period

During the negotiations it was recognized that improvements were necessary in the export control practices of certain member states before licence-free intra-EU trade could take place. To reduce the risk of exporters exploiting weak links during this phase, Article 19 specifies a three-year transition period[72] for such improvements to be made during which time specific measures will apply for intra-EU trade. These measures include: the retention of commercial documents for Annex I goods which indicate clearly that the goods are subject to control if exported from the EU; individual licence authorizations for the most sensitive products (listed in Annex IV); and the maintenance of records for the above goods for a period of at least three years after the transaction has taken place.

At the end of the three-year transition period the Council was required to review the situation and consider whether an extension was required. The Commission made it known, however, that it was in favour of amending or repealing

---

[69] Amendment no. 3 in 'Opinion of the Committee on Energy, Research and Technology', European Parliament (note 59), p. 15.

[70] Amendments nos 5, 16 and 18 in European Parliament (note 59), pp. 9–10.

[71] The European Parliament had recommended that the penalties be the same in all member states.

[72] The time-limit for the transitional period was also the subject of disagreement during the negotiations. The Commission originally proposed a 1-year transition period, while the European Parliament recommended a 2-year period.

Table 3.1. The EU Dual-Use List

Category[a]	Item numbers[b]
0 Nuclear materials, facilities and equipment	0A001–0E001
1 Advanced materials, chemicals, micro-organisms and toxins	1A001–1E203
2 Material processing	2A001–2E201
3 Electronics	3A001–3E201
4 Computers	4A001–4E002
5 Part 1: Telecommunications	5A001–5E101
Part 2: Information security	5A002–5E002
6 Sensors and lasers	6A001–6E201
7 Avionics and navigation	7A001–7E104
8 Marine	8A001–8E002
9 Propulsion systems, space vehicles and related equipment	9A001–9E991

Notes:

[a] Each category has five sub-categories or 'product types': (*a*) equipment, assemblies and components; (*b*) test, inspection and production equipment; (*c*) materials; (*d*) software; and (*e*) technology.

[b] Each item in the list has a unique five-digit number which consists of three elements: the first digit denotes the category, the second digit denotes the product type (letters A–E) within each category, and the last three digits are the identification number (001–999) within the product type. Within the identification number, the first digit denotes the grounds for export control (the Wassenaar Arrangement, Missile Technology Control Regime, Nuclear Suppliers Group and so on) and the last two digits denote the type of control.

Source: Compiled by the author from 'Council Decision no. 94/942/CFSP of 19 Dec. 1994 on the Joint Action adopted by the Council on the basis of Article J.3 of the Treaty on European Union concerning the control of exports of dual-use goods', *Official Journal of the European Communities*, L367, vol. 37 (31 Dec. 1994).

Article 19 if there was consensus among the member states to do so.[73] The Commission is also required to present a report to the European Parliament and the Council on the application of the Regulation every two years.

The Joint Action

Controlled items

The five annexes are the most important part of the Joint Action. An extensive list of dual-use goods is contained in Annex I (and filled more than 140 pages of the *Official Journal*). The main element of the new regime, therefore, is that a licence is required for exports from the Community for all goods listed in Annex I and, once issued, is generally valid throughout the Community. The original Annex I list implemented internationally agreed controls of dual-use items by the member states in the MTCR, the Nuclear Suppliers Group, the

---

[73] Eavis, P., 'EC regulation', *Worldwide Guide to Export Controls 1996/97* (Export Control Publications/ Deltac Ltd: Chertsey, Feb. 1997), p. 4.

Australia Group and COCOM, but amendments were later necessary when COCOM was replaced by the Wassenaar Arrangement. The Annex I lists integrated all the items from these different international agreements and, as shown in table 3.1, followed the format and numbering scheme already used in Germany and the UK. Although COCOM ended on 31 March 1994, member states originally used the COCOM Industrial List as the basis for the Annex I list, with the higher control levels of the other regimes added on.

The introduction of Annex I specifies that the list is formally restricted to international agreements of member states (a de facto exclusion of goods which are controlled by member states outside of these international agreements) and to technology that is real and concrete. The latter limitation is a compromise between those states, such as France and the UK, which did not want to be very precise, and others such as Germany, which wanted a much more complete list in the intangible technology field (licences, process, plans and so on).[74]

Annex IV, which was proposed by France and the UK, lists the goods referred to in Article 19 of the Regulation and which, although already listed in Annex I, were considered to be so sensitive that for the duration of the transitional period they required licences even for intra-EU transfers. The goods listed include the most sensitive within several non-proliferation regimes and a number of highly advanced technologies such as stealth technology, cryptographic technology and supercomputers. Annex V is a compendium of national lists of goods in Annex I which individual member states, in accordance with Article 20 of the Regulation, regard as primarily military and wish to license on a national basis when traded within the Community. These national lists are quite small and only take up about three pages in the *Official Journal*.

Export criteria and country lists

Annex II contains the destinations for which simplified licensing procedures may be specified in accordance with Article 6 of the Regulation. This 'positive' list of countries includes the three countries which joined the EU on 1 January 1995 (Austria, Finland and Sweden) and six other industrialized 'friends' (Australia, Canada, Japan, Norway, Switzerland and the USA). A seventh country, New Zealand, was added on 10 April 1995[75] and other countries are likely to be added later. There is no negative or proscribed list of countries specified in the Joint Action, partly because France and the UK were opposed to such a list on the grounds that it would lead to diplomatic difficulties, and partly because of a clear lack of consensus on the scope of such a list.[76] Of course, the failure to agree a proscribed country list means that member states will continue to decide to whom they will or will not export the controlled goods listed in Annex I.

---

[74] Adam (note 29), p. 83.

[75] *Official Journal of the European Communities*, L90 (21 Apr. 1995), p. 4.

[76] Personal interview by the author with Brinly Salzmann, Manager, Market Information, DMA, Grayshott, 26 Aug. 1997.

Annex III is the Agreement of Member States on Guidelines and sets out four factors to be taken into account by member states in deciding whether to grant an export licence: (*a*) their commitments under international agreements on non-proliferation and control of sensitive goods; (*b*) their obligations under sanctions imposed by the UN Security Council or agreed in other international forums; (*c*) considerations of national and foreign security policy, including, where relevant, those covered by the criteria they agreed at the European Council meetings in Luxembourg in June 1991 and in Lisbon in June 1992 with regard to the export of conventional arms; and (*d*) considerations about intended end-use and the risk of diversion.

While these criteria included and went beyond the Luxembourg and Lisbon conventional arms export criteria (discussed in chapter 4), the additions were of a general nature and were always likely to suffer from the same difficulties regarding common interpretation as discussed in chapter 2. In any case, these criteria were effectively replaced with the introduction of the EU Code of Conduct on Arms Exports in June 1998 (which also covers dual-use exports).

Areas that remained outside the scope of the Regulation

Two main issues concerning dual-use goods and technologies remained outside the scope of the Regulation—intangible technologies and transit trade. As regards dual-use technologies, only blueprints and software were included in the Regulation and treated like goods. Intangible technology was left to the discretion of member states, with a declaration of intent to review the situation later. Dual-use goods in transit (i.e., coming from a non-EU state to another non-EU state via a member state) were also not covered by the Regulation, and each member state may adopt its own regulation in this area.

Both these issues were fiercely debated during the negotiations and it seemed likely that intangible technologies in particular would be included at a later date. Germany, for example, subsequently proposed several changes to the Regulation to bring it into line with its own national regulations, including measures to control intangible technologies, technical services and 'trafficking' services.[77] Although these proposals were put to the Commission, opposition from France and the UK within the Co-ordinating Group (which had already declared that these matters were not part of its mandate) meant that the German negotiators faced an uphill struggle to add these provisions to the Regulation.

---

[77] At that time only Germany sought to control technical services in relation to dual-use goods. According to German sources the risk is that, rather than import turnkey production, proliferators can import components in small pieces like a jigsaw puzzle and then import technicians to supply the technical services with which to put the puzzle together. Similar proliferation risks apply to trafficking in services. E.g., an Indian machine tool company could import a design from a member state and then re-export the goods manufactured from that design to Iran. In German legislation such trafficking services are covered by a legal contract that specifies onward shipment to 3rd countries, and such contracts require an export licence. Personal interviews with German officials, 1997.

The European Court of Justice and the legal structure of the Regulation

From the very beginning, the legal status of this agreement was contested. As stated above, there were disagreements during the negotiations as to whether the Community regime should be based solely on an Article 113 Regulation, or on an Article 113 Regulation combined with a Council Decision (i.e., a Joint Action under articles J2 and J3 of the Maastricht Treaty). Although the latter situation prevailed, the European Commission continued to contest the inclusion of the annexes in a Joint Action (and therefore by implication member state competence in this area). The European Court of Justice later confirmed the Commission's view in two rulings in 1995 and 1997. The first judgement, on 17 October 1995, was made in respect of two German cases (C-70/94 and C-83/94), while the second, on 14 January 1997, was in respect of a British case (C-124/95). In short, both judgements assert that under EC competition rules as set out within Article 113 of the Treaty of Rome, the annexes fall within Community competence and should thus be included in the Regulation rather than the Joint Action (and be subject to qualified majority voting rather than unanimity).

The court cases also reveal the extent to which national positions in this area are often rather fluid and reflect political expediencies which can change over time. During the original negotiations to agree the Regulation, for example, the British and French representatives always argued that Article 113 was irrelevant, and that articles J2 and J3 provided the appropriate legal framework. However, when the two German cases went to the European Court of Justice, France (and to a lesser extent the UK) adopted different positions. The German companies had applied to the Court on the basis that the additional German regulations (i.e., in addition to those contained in the EU Regulation) were illegal because they fell within the competence of Article 113. When the cases were submitted the other member states were invited to give comments. Rather surprisingly, the written submission from France suggested that this policy area did, after all, fall within the competence of Article 113, whereas the UK sat on the fence and suggested that the question be left open.[78]

However, despite the two rulings from the Court, initially at least, changes to the common lists in the annexes were still required to be made in accordance with the Joint Action. This is because the member states were unwilling to give up the Joint Action (and the Commission was unwilling to press the issue further at that time). Indeed, the new Regulation and Joint Action remained in force for nearly five years before the latter was eventually repealed in June 2000 (as discussed below).

---

[78] Personal interview with a German official in the Federal Ministry of Economics (BMWi), Sep. 1997.

VI. The EU dual-use export control regime in practice: achievements, limitations and changes

From 1 July 1995, the dual-use Regulation became directly applicable in law in all member states. However, most member states drafted new national legislation or modified existing laws in order to eliminate any potential for conflict or contradiction with the Regulation.[79]

Economic, security and harmonization objectives

Although there were clearly differences of opinion among NGOs, industrial groups and member state governments, and within the European institutions, on the *means* of achieving a common approach to export controls for dual-use goods, there was a strong measure of consensus that any solution had to achieve three main objectives:

1. *Economic objectives.* As a result of the SEM imperative, the Regulation was expected to remove the barriers to the free movement of dual-use goods (and especially the need for licensing) when traded within the Community, and thereby improve the international competitiveness of European industry.

2. *Security objectives.* A prerequisite for moving to licence-free trade in all dual-use goods within the Community was the setting up of a strong anti-proliferation 'fence' around the Community to prevent diversion and to protect the security interests of member states and the EU.

3. *Harmonization objectives.* The setting up of a common system for the control of exports of dual-use goods from the Community was expected to lead to progressive harmonization of existing national export control policies and procedures.

There was no clear time-scale for achieving these objectives and it was unlikely that they could be achieved before the end of the transition period. Indeed, in seeking to encompass complex technical aspects as well as the convergence of foreign, security and trade policy interests, the Regulation and Joint Action are unique in the history of multilateral export control regimes. They were undoubtedly an extremely useful first step, both in terms of the development of a comprehensive Community regime for the control of dual-use exports and as a guide towards any future convergence of arms export controls. For example, the common (Annex I) list of dual-use goods may allow a clearer interpretation of Article 223. From now on goods will be more clearly classified as civil, dual-use or military. If an item is not included in Annex I and is unaffected by the catch-all clause but has military use or potential, then by default it should be on a military list.

---

[79] See, e.g., the legislative changes made in the UK, Germany and Sweden and discussed in Part III.

However, the European Commission[80] and others[81] identified several areas of concern as to the effectiveness of this new control system at a very early stage in its existence. These concerns and the measures deemed necessary to improve the control regime are discussed below.

Economic objectives

The Regulation sustains the idea of the SEM. As a rule, most dual-use goods on an agreed common list (Annex I) are now allowed to circulate freely across EU territory without the necessity of normal export procedures—licensing, customs controls and so on. However, there are still some exceptions to this rule and many of the anticipated economic benefits ascribed to the Regulation appear to be illusory. Most of the industrialists surveyed after the first year of operation, for example, took the view that the Community Licence was not being fully utilized because of a lack of confidence in it. In the same survey, government officials stressed differences in member states' general and global licences as the major issue of concern. Although these concerns led the Co-ordinating Group to explore the development of common EU general and global licences, the survey concluded that until such matters were resolved there was unlikely to be widespread use of the Community Licence.[82] The Commission's first review report in 1998 confirmed that the problem of customs officers failing to recognize (and therefore accept) export licences, especially global licences, from other member states continued to discourage industry from using the Community Licence other than in exceptional circumstances.[83]

While the possibilities may not have been exploited to the full, earlier fears about the regulatory burden of the Regulation and Joint Action appear to have been largely unfounded. There is an increased onus on industry to engage in self-regulation, particularly with the advent of the catch-all clause, which requires industry to ensure that exports of dual-use goods are intended for legitimate purposes.[84] However, this seems to have been more than adequately compensated for by other articles in the Regulation that liberalize controls, such

[80] The Commission's first assessment of the control regime covering the first 2 years of its operation (up until July 1997) was published in Apr. 1998. European Commission, 'Report to the European Parliament and the Council on the application of Regulation (EC) 3381/94 setting up a Community system of export controls regarding dual-use', COM(98)258 (final), Brussels, Apr. 1998. The response of the European Parliament was published on 24 Mar. 1999. European Parliament, 'Report on the Commission report to the European Parliament and the Council on the application of Regulation (EC) no. 3381/94 setting up a Community system of export controls regarding dual-use goods, Committee on Economic and Monetary Affairs and Industrial Policy, Rapporteur, Werner Langen', DOC_EN\RR\374\374943, PE 229.137/fin, Strasbourg, 24 Mar. 1999.

[81] E.g., an independent survey of government officials and industrialists was carried out after the first year of the Regulation. *The EU Regulation on Dual-Use Goods After One Year* (note 68).

[82] *The EU Regulation on Dual-Use Goods After One Year* (note 68), pp. 29–30, 37–38 and 58–59.

[83] European Commission (note 80), pp. 8–11.

[84] Both the independent survey and the Commission report revealed difficulties in the implementation of the catch-all, especially in those member states (Austria, Denmark, Finland, Greece, Ireland, Luxembourg, Portugal and Sweden) which did not have prior experience of this kind of end-use control. European Commission (note 80), pp. 11–12; and *The EU Regulation on Dual-Use Goods After One Year* (note 68), pp. 22–24, 50–57 and 69–71.

as Article 6 which allows simplified licensing to friendly destinations. Indeed, in the case of the UK, for example, nearly everything on the Annex I list can be exported under a general licence to apprximately 90 per cent of the world.[85] Furthermore, the regulatory burden was described by a German industrialist as 'negligible' in comparison to some of Germany's additional national requirements (discussed in chapter 6) and the burden created by US extraterritorial jurisdiction.[86]

This said, however, much work still needs to be done to realize industries' aim of a complete LFZ within the EU for such goods. In addition, complaints still persist from within the ERT and UNICE that the EU Regulation is more restrictive for extra-EU exports than is equivalent legislation in Japan and the USA. As a result they have urged the Commission and member states to simplify the general and global licensing system, to provide information for sensitive end-users at an EU level, to restrict the scope of the catch-all clause, and to follow the USA in liberalizing trade in certain goods.[87]

The Commission clearly shared much of this assessment and proposed a number of measures to harmonize national export licence forms and simplify export procedures for dual-use goods in a new draft Regulation, which is discussed below.

Security objectives

As a quid pro quo for the free movement of dual-use goods, member states agreed a common set of rules for extra-EU exports. Of course, security objectives sometimes have to be balanced against, and implemented at the expense of, economic objectives. In this case, the Regulation and Joint Action permit the continuation of a range of national controls on extra-EU exports, in addition to the few remaining in place for intra-Community trade. The new system also gives individual member states some continuing say in what dual-use goods leave their territory by the inclusion of consultation and safeguard measures.

As was to be expected, the new Regulation encountered several teething problems in the first six months or so, mainly over the consultation procedures for export licences applied for in a member state other than the one where the goods were located. In addition to confusion over where consultation should take place, the actual consultation procedures often took longer than the stated maximum of 10 days. The Co-ordinating Group attempted to address these concerns by drawing up additional guidelines on how to interpret certain provisions of the Regulation (including the consultation procedures) in July

---

[85] Personal interview with independent UK consultant on export controls, 1997.

[86] Personal interview, 1997. Extraterritorial jurisdiction is the practice whereby US authorities demand the right to impose penalties on companies in allied countries which re-export or transfer US technologies to another user without the permission of the US Government.

[87] Quoted in European Commssion (note 80), p. 7. However, industrial lobby groups failed to come up with much evidence to substantiate their claims about the restrictive nature of the Regulation. Personal interview with a Commission official, 1997.

1997.[88] As a result, consultation is no longer required for temporary exports and follow-on exports (i.e., for the purposes of maintenance and repair) already licensed after consultation.[89]

Given the limited use being made of the Community Licence, it was no surprise that the independent survey found that these consultation procedures were being invoked very infrequently.[90] Nevertheless, the majority of government officials who responded to the survey said that no objections had been raised against any licence they had granted and that the consultation mechanisms had been effective in bridging the gaps in the export policies of member states.

There are other potential weaknesses. First, the Regulation may lead to a 'watering down' of controls in those states with a more restrictive approach to exports, such as Germany. Indeed, as discussed in chapter 6, there are indications that Germany has relaxed its rules (and may do so further) in order to fall in line with the emerging European standards. On the other hand, it is also clear that a number of member states have improved their export controls in line with these standards. Thus, for the EU as a whole, it could be argued that the perimeter fence is higher than it was before the advent of the Regulation.

Second, even if the height of the EU fence as a whole has been raised, there still appear to be a number of holes in it. For example, the fact that dual-use goods are now in free circulation throughout the EU presents potential difficulties for verifying and safeguarding end-use. This situation is exacerbated by the variations in end-use and end-user provisions within the Union.[91] In addition, although the Regulation places an increased onus on industry through the catch-all clause, the optional nature of the clause has resulted in considerable differences in its implementation and operation. For example, Austria, Belgium and Finland adopted all three sub-clauses into their national legislation; Denmark, Germany, Ireland, Spain and Sweden only incorporated clauses 4(1) and 4(2); Italy only incorporated clause 4(1); and the UK only incorporated clauses 4(2) and 4(3).[92] Penalties for violation of the catch-all clause also vary widely between member states: in Germany violation can result in a prison sentence of up to 15 years, while in Denmark, Finland, Greece and Ireland a similar violation might only result in a two-year sentence. Moreover, these national differences in the regulatory framework adopted for the catch-all are likely to be exacerbated by the differences in the practical application of the clause: some countries appear to be completely ignoring it, while others (such as Germany and the UK) implement it vigorously.[93]

---

[88] These informal guidelines ('Elements of consensus between member states') are published as Annex 1 to European Commission (note 80), pp. 14–17.

[89] Eavis (note 73), p. 4.

[90] This was also the view of the British Department of Trade and Industry (DTI) in its 1996 consultation document, *Strategic Export Controls: A Consultative Document*, Cm 3349 (Her Majesty's Stationery Office: London, July 1996), p. 21.

[91] British Department of Trade and Industry (note 90), pp. 27–29, 57–58 and 71.

[92] *The EU Regulation on Dual-Use Goods After One Year* (note 68), p. 21.

[93] Personal interviews with John Thurlow, Managing Director, Deltac Ltd, Chertsey, Surrey, 14 July 1997.

According to the Commission the main problems with the catch-all clause have been the different degrees to which governments inform their exporters about sensitive end-users. In addition, the lack of information exchange between member states on sensitive end-users not only distorts competition but also 'defeats the purpose of the catch-all'. To rectify this, the Commission recommended improved information sharing between member states on sensitive end-users with a view to greater convergence of national guidance to exporters.[94]

Similarly, the failure to agree a common approach to sensitive destinations means that member states will continue to implement differing export policies to countries of concern (although the proper implementation of the EU Code of Conduct should minimize such disparities in licensing policies). Even so, such disparities and other differences (such as in end-use provisions and penalties) offer the potential for diversion of trade to the member states with the weakest controls.[95]

Third, any delays in amending the annexes in the Joint Action might compromise security. Such amendments were originally discussed within the Council's Ad Hoc High Level Working Party,[96] whose main activity was to update the technology lists in accordance with developments within the multilateral supplier regimes. Some analysts expressed concern that difficulties in achieving the unanimity required to update the lists in the annexes might result in a lengthy time-lag between amendment of the control lists of a particular regime and the incorporation of that amendment in the EU legislation. According to research undertaken for the European Parliament, at least one chemical agent added to the Australia Group list in 1995 was still not under EU control well into 1997.[97] However, the situation concerning conventional weapons appears to be much healthier. When the Wassenaar Arrangement came into force in July 1996, the introduction of new control lists associated with this regime necessitated changes to Annex I in the Joint Action. This was done during the Italian presidency by way of a Council Decision (96/613 CFSP) which member states officially adopted on 15 November 1996.[98] Moreover, when the new Regulation entered into force in September 2000 (see below in this section), amendment of the lists came under Community competence and became subject to qualified majority voting (QMV).

---

[94] European Commission (note 80), pp. 11–12.

[95] While there is currently little or no evidence (at least in the public domain) to suggest that the external fence is being breached by diversions to its weakest points, the covert nature of such transfers makes it difficult to verify the situation with any certainty. Moreover, information about diversions often only comes to light several years after the goods have been exported.

[96] At the time of writing, the Working Party had a small technical secretariat located in the British DTI. The future of the Working Party under the new Regulation introduced in June 2000 is uncertain.

[97] Mollas-Gallart, J. and Perry Robinson, J., 'Assessment of dual technologies in the context of European security and defence', PE 166 819/Final, European Parliament, Directorate General for Research, Luxembourg, Oct. 1997, p. 50. The authors of this study also foresaw other potential conflicts between the EU Dual-Use Regulation and certain provisions of the Chemical Weapons Convention. Mollas-Gallart and Perry Robinson, pp. 47–50.

[98] *Official Journal of the European Communities*, L278 (30 Oct. 1996), pp. 1–215.

Finally, more needs to be done to improve the relationship between EU dual-use controls and the development of global and regional dual-use controls. In, particular, there needs to be better coordination and information exchange between the various working groups and a greater willingness to coordinate an EU position within some of the non-proliferation regimes. A closer relationship between the Wassenaar Arrangement and the Regulation may also need to be developed at some stage, but for the present the two regimes appear to have completely separate goals and agendas. Thus, there has been no attempt, for example, to reconcile the Sensitive and Very Sensitive Transfer Lists of technologies in the Wassenaar Arrangement with the Annex IV control list in the EU Regulation. In effect, this means that some items on the Wassenaar Sensitive and Very Sensitive Lists are eligible for both licence-free intra-EU trade and simplified licensing when exported from the Community. Only time will tell whether this situation proves to be problematic.

There can be no doubt, however, that the Regulation has had a knock-on effect beyond the EU. The USA, for example, has adopted the Annex I list as the basis for its own national product list, while a number of other states, including Japan, Russia and Switzerland, have introduced a similar catch-all clause.[99]

Harmonization objectives

The central achievement of the Regulation is the concept of a Community Licence: an export licence granted by any member state is now normally valid throughout the Community. In addition, export authorizations to non-EU destinations are now based on common lists of goods and criteria, and the national licensing authorities have been brought closer together. The latter is a very important change. Prior to 1995 very few of the licensing personnel in the different member states knew each other, but the Co-ordinating Group has now institutionalized regular contact between officials.[100] As the Commission's report concludes, the improved administrative cooperation between the member states and consultations on policy issues have led to the development of a 'network of national officials responsible for export controls'.[101] As a result, lessons are being learned all the time and attitudes are shifting in accordance with experience. For example, during the negotiations Germany pressed for a *deminimus* limit of 5000 DM for certain exports, but other member states

---

[99] Personal interviews with officials in the European Commission and the German export control bureaucracy, 1997. The Russian 'catch-all' was apparently introduced in Jan. 1998. Anthony, I. and Zanders, J. P., 'Multilateral security-related export controls', *SIPRI Yearbook 1998: Armaments, Disarmament and International Security* (Oxford University Press: Oxford, 1998), p. 398.

[100] The Co-ordinating Group has met about 5 or 6 times a year to discuss the practical application of the Regulation, and on at least one occasion (7 Feb. 1996) the discussions included representatives of UNICE. Information exchange at the Co-ordinating Group meetings usually takes the form of written papers which are presented by individual representatives and then discussed by the group. Prior to the setting up of the group some administrative cooperation between officials with policy responsibility for dual-use export controls was facilitated under a 5-year exchange programme (called Karolus) which was launched by the Commission in Feb. 1993. Eavis (note 73), p. 4.

[101] European Commission (note 80), p. 7.

argued that this would lead to disaggregation of exports in order to circumvent the provisions, and hence the proposal was rejected. Instead, Germany introduced a *deminimus* clause in its national legislation for Open General Export Licences (OGELs). Although under Article 6 of the Regulation all licences are valid in any member state, OGELs under 5000 DM are not necessary in Germany. However, because exporters are now being attracted to Germany for such exports, other member states are now accepting the idea of an EU-wide *deminimus* clause.[102] Over time, this type of cooperation allows the possibility for a further convergence of views and for reaching more common understandings.

Clearly, however, problems of administrative cooperation persist. In the meetings of both the Co-ordinating Group and the Ad Hoc Working Party, for example, some of the problems will be similar in nature to those discussed in chapter 2 in relation to COARM. These problems concern the usual rivalries between representatives from different member states, and can often be unrelated to the substantive matter under discussion. For example, the fact that all the product lists have to be translated into French prior to any discussion within the Working Party has more to do with French national pride and identity than with concerns over the contents of the lists. Moreover, according to one Commission insider, the language barrier has occasionally been used to hide true meanings or to allow many individual interpretations of a particular text. This situation is exacerbated by the fact that the EU translation service is unable to rewrite agreed texts into proper English (or whatever other language the text is being translated into), but instead is required to translate the document exactly as originally drafted. Not only does this account for the often poor phrasing and wording to be found in Community documents, but in this particular policy area it also hampers discussion of the creation of standardized forms and licences.[103]

The Commission report particularly highlights limitations in the information exchange mechanisms[104] and, as is the case for arms export controls, differing national constitutional, foreign policy and sovereignty perceptions are at the root of many of these difficulties.

As discussed in the context of economic objectives, there is also a clear need for further harmonization of licences and licence application procedures, particularly in regard to general and global licences, and in end-use certification. If the latter is taken as an example, it is not only a problem between the 15 member states, but also within some individual member states. As discussed in chapter 6, for example, Germany currently has 11 different forms for end-use certification. In comparison, the USA recently reduced its end-use requirement to a single form entitled 'Statement by Ultimate Consignee and Purchaser'.[105]

---

[102] Personal interview with a German government official, 1997.

[103] Personal interview with an official in the European Commission, 1997.

[104] European Commission (note 80), pp. 12–13.

[105] Personal communication with a German industrial representative, 1997.

The effectiveness of the Regulation also seems to be dependent on the implementation of appropriate cooperative enforcement practices by the licensing and customs authorities. While the EU does have substantial experience in harmonized customs policies, through such arrangements as Joint Customs Surveillance Operations (JSO),[106] the Single Administrative Document (SAD) and TARIC, in the short term at least qualitative differences continue to exist in these areas between member states. A major problem in the EU in general is the high level of customs fraud (from smuggling and so on), and some member states' customs regimes remain fairly primitive. The absence of a Community database of information on licences and sensitive end-users is a particular cause for concern. Although some intelligence dissemination does occur within the other non-proliferation regimes and between individual member states on an ad hoc basis, a more coordinated and systematic approach by member states will probably be necessary in the future to ensure an effective external fence. It also remains to be established what other agreements such as the Schengen Arrangement and existing cooperative structures between police forces, intelligence services and justice ministries can offer in terms of cooperation between customs and licensing authorities. These structures are mainly designed to prevent intra-Community movement of terrorists, drug traffickers and criminals, but there may be scope to adapt them to the control of dual-use exports.

Finally, both customs officials and company clerks alike have continually asked to be able to identify from the customs code whether an item is covered by an export control list. While the extensive work involved would appear to preclude such harmonization,[107] the future development of such a database should not be discounted. Indeed, at the very least, it should be possible to include the related customs codes in the text of Annex I throughout the Community (and not just in the Belgian export list as at present).[108]

Towards a new Regulation and repeal of the Joint Action

Overall, therefore, the Commission concluded that: 'the present system is too complex to be routinely managed by customs officials at the border, and is in any case judged by industry to be too cumbersome to be useful in practice . . . only a more harmonized export control regime, combining elements of

---

[106] Under a 1981 Council Regulation, any relevant authority can request information on customs or agricultural matters from an authority in another member state. One authority can also request another to keep watch on persons or places when they have reason to suspect illegal activities in these areas. 'Council Regulation (EEC) no. 1468/81 on mutual assistance between the administrative authorities of the member states and cooperation between the latter and the Commission to ensure the correct application of the law on customs or agricultural matters', *Official Journal of the European Communities*, L144/1 (2 June 1981), as amended by Regulation (EEC) no. 945/87, *Official Journal of the European Communities*, L90/3 (2 Apr. 1987).

[107] E.g., every time an export list was changed the voluminous books containing the customs codes would also have to be adapted. (Currently these are usually updated only annually in most member states.)

[108] Personal communication with a German industrial representative, 1997. In addition, work is in progress to design software which correlates customs codes with dual-use codes, and which will be added to the TARIC computer system. Personal interview with an official in the European Commission, 1997.

common policy with reinforced administrative cooperation will produce a system satisfactory to the practical need of exporters and public authorities'.[109] These conclusions led the Commission in 1998 to table a number of amendments to the Regulation, including proposals for: (*a*) the creation of a General Community Licence for non-sensitive exports to Annex II destinations and the extension of the provision to include the Czech Republic, Hungary and Poland; (*b*) the formal delegation of responsibility for updating the list of controlled goods to member states[110] and the establishment of a List Group (chaired by the member state exercising the presidency) for this purpose; (*c*) the extension of the catch-all clause to all military end-use where the destination country is subject to a UN embargo; (*d*) the extension of the Regulation to cover the transfer of technology by 'intangible' means (such as email, facsimile transmission and telephone); (*e*) the abolition of the majority of the licensing requirements for intra-Community trade in dual-use items (i.e., those currently listed in annexes IV and V), and their replacement with a notification procedure (Annex IV items only); and (*f*) reinforced administrative cooperation between member states regarding sensitive exports covered by the catch-all clause, including the introduction of non-binding 'no undercutting' consultations.[111]

During 1998 and 1999 these proposals were considered by a Council Working Group and by the European Parliament's Committee on Economic and Monetary Affairs and Industrial Policy. The latter reported in March 1999, largely agreeing with the Commission's analysis, and welcomed the proposal for a new Regulation.[112] Although the German Government announced in December 1998 that the adoption of the new Regulation was one of its objectives during its presidency of the European Council (in the first half of 1999),[113] agreement was not reached until the end of the Portuguese presidency (in the first half of 2000).

On 22 June 2000 the Council adopted a new Regulation setting up a Community regime for the control of exports of dual-use items and technology.[114] Two other complementary pieces of legislation were passed at the same time—

[109] European Commission (note 80), p. 14.

[110] The Commission continued to argue that, in line with European Court of Justice rulings, Article 113 is the appropriate legal basis for a Community export control regime for dual-use goods. However, the Commission also recognized that the technical expertise to update the control list resides with member states. European Commission, 'Proposal for a Council Regulation (EC) setting up a Community regime for the control of exports of dual-use goods and technology', COM(1998)257 (final), Brussels, Apr. 1998, p. 4.

[111] European Commission (note 110). The proposals were submitted simultaneously with the 'Report to the European Parliament and the Council on the application of Regulation (EC) 3381/94' (note 80). The annexes referred to (with Roman numerals) are the annexes to the Proposal.

[112] European Parliament, 'Report on the Commission report to the European Parliament and the Council on the application of Regulation (EC) no. 3381/94 setting up a Community system of export controls regarding dual-use goods (COM(98)0258–C4-0443/98), Committee on Economic and Monetary Affairs and Industrial Policy, Rapporteur: Werner Langen', A4-0145/99, 24 Mar. 1999.

[113] 'Objectives and priorities of the German presidency in the Council of the European Union', Press Release, Brussels, nr 5128/1/98 (Presse), 2 Dec. 1998, p. 2.

[114] 'Council Regulation (EC) no. 1334/2000 of 22 June 2000 setting up a Community regime for the control of exports of dual-use items and technology', *Official Journal of the European Communities*, L159, vol. 43 (30 June 2000), pp. 1–215. The full text of the Regulation is also available on the EU Internet site at URL <http://www.europa.eu.int/eur-lex/en/oj/2000/l_15920000630en.html>.

a Council Joint Action concerning the control of technical assistance related to certain military end-uses,[115] and a Council Decision repealing the 1994 Joint Action on Dual-Use Goods.[116] The new Regulation was due to enter into force 90 days after it was adopted (i.e., on 28 September 2000) and some parts required the introduction of new national legislation to give effect to enforcement and penalty powers.

The most significant change is that the new Regulation has a single legal base, namely, Article 133 (formerly Article 113) of the Treaty of Rome. This means that the common list of dual-use items subject to controls (Annex I of the Regulation) is no longer the subject of a CFSP decision ('third pillar') and instead competence is transferred to the Community ('first pillar'). The Regulation and the lists will also now be subject to qualified majority voting. The structure of the new Regulation is as follows:

1. Articles 1–24 set out the definitions, scope and procedures of the Regulation.

2. Annex I contains the list of dual-use items and technology whose export *from* the EU is controlled (nearly 200 pages in the *Official Journal*).

3. Annex II contains the Community General Export Authorisation (CGEA).

4. Annex III contains the 'model' format for Standard Individual Export Licences (SIELs)/Open Individual Export Licences (OIELs).

5. Annex IV contains the list of dual-use items whose transfer *within* the EU will continue to be controlled (including certain stealth technologies, items of 'strategic control' and MTCR technology).

All the Commission's proposals set out above have been realized by this new Regulation, albeit with some minor modifications. First, the introduction of a CGEA—the Community-wide equivalent to a UK OGEL—for non-sensitive exports to Annex II destinations will consolidate the substantial amount of de facto convergence and liberalization of member states' licensing policies to these 10 destinations[117] (which account for more than 70 per cent of exports of dual-use goods from the EU). Second, the catch-all clause has been extended to all military end-use exports where the destination country is subject to an EU, OSCE or UN arms embargo (rather than just a UN embargo as proposed by the Commission). In addition, it was considered appropriate to define the common standards required for the control of 'technical assistance related to certain end-uses' (especially when such assistance is given to countries subject to arms embargoes) in a new Joint Action rather than within the Regulation. Third, many of the licensing requirements for intra-Community trade have been

---

[115] 'Council Joint Action of 22 June 2000 concerning the control of technical assistance related to certain military end-uses, 2000/401/CFSP', *Official Journal of the European Communities*, L159, vol. 43 (30 June 2000), pp. 216–17.

[116] 'Council Decision of 22 June 2000 repealing Decision 94/942/CFSP on the Joint Action concerning the control of exports of dual-use goods, 2000/402/CFSP', *Official Journal of the European Communities*, L159, vol. 43 (30 June 2000), p. 218.

[117] The 10 countries are Australia, Canada, Japan, Norway, Switzerland, the USA, New Zealand, the Czech Republic, Hungary and Poland.

abolished: Annex V no longer exists and Annex IV has been heavily revised (and most cryptographic products removed) and split into two parts. Fourth, the Regulation closes the loophole with regard to intangible technologies. Finally, improvements in administrative cooperation include the introduction of a model format for licences. To facilitate recognition by enforcement authorities and to reduce the risk of abuse, all member states' SIELs and OIELs must be issued on forms 'consistent with' (Article 10) the model set out in Annex III. The Regulation also commits member states to: exchange information with each other and the Commission on denials, revocations, suspensions and so on; maintain a Co-ordinating Group chaired by the Commission; and inform other member states and the Commission 'where appropriate' when exercising the end-use controls set out in the Regulation.

Overall, therefore, this new Regulation is likely to lead to significant further harmonization and a strengthening of control procedures for dual-use items. However, for the foreseeable future there will continue to be elements of national discretion in the implementation of this new Community system of export controls. The extent of national discretion with regard to the application of the old Regulation and Joint Action will become clear in the national case studies in Part III of this book. In the next chapter, however, the discussion returns to the issue of convergence of arms export control policy within the EU.

4. Common European measures for controlling conventional weapons: the EU Code of Conduct on Arms Exports

I. Introduction

Chapter 3 outlined the historical development of common arms and dual-use export controls within the EU. It also explained why, in the early 1990s, the issue of dual-use goods and technologies became separated from the issue of conventional weapons in the debates about common export controls. This chapter takes up the story of the development of common EU export controls for conventional weapons, culminating in the establishment of an EU Code of Conduct on Arms Exports in June 1998.

Section II of this chapter explores the intergovernmental debates that led to a deepening of arms export control cooperation in the first half of the 1990s. This period saw the development of eight common criteria on arms export controls, the establishment of a group of experts (COARM) and the introduction of joint actions under the CFSP. Section III discusses developments in the latter half of the 1990s leading up to the EU Code of Conduct on Arms Exports. Finally, section IV discusses implementation of the code with particular reference to its operative provisions and guidelines, and the relationship with the six-nation Framework Agreement.

II. The deepening of cooperation on export controls in the early 1990s

The development of the Common Criteria

As discussed in chapter 3, although decisions on arms exports had been left for intergovernmental consideration, the legacy of the Gulf War and the expectation that more restrictive and coordinated controls would be necessary continued to influence policy makers. Thus, in March 1991 another group of experts was formed at the request of PoCo to examine issues related to conventional arms export controls. The first meeting of this new body—the Ad Hoc Working Group on Conventional Arms Exports, which was later that year reconstituted as the Committee Armament (or COARM, as it is known under its French acronym)—took place on 16 April 1991.

The Working Group's initial role was to compare national positions and investigate the possibility of further action. Despite differences between those member states (such as France and the UK) which sought to limit the process to a comparison of national lists of controlled military goods, and others (such as

Germany) which sought to harmonize national policies, this comparison of national practices soon resulted in two major policy announcements during the European Council meeting in Luxembourg on 28–29 June 1991. First, the member states proclaimed that, together with Japan, they would be presenting a draft resolution at the UN General Assembly in October later the same year creating a register on conventional weapons (see chapter 2). Second, and directly as a result of initiatives in the Ad Hoc Working Group, they adopted the Declaration on Non-Proliferation and the Export of Weapons, which specifies seven common criteria governing arms exports that were agreed by the heads of state:

– The respect for the international commitments of the member states of the Community, in particular the sanctions decreed by the Security Council of the United Nations and those decreed by the Community, agreements on non-proliferation and other subjects, as well as other international obligations.
– The respect of human rights in the country of final destination.
– The internal situation in the country of final destination as a function of the existence of tensions of internal armed conflicts.
– The preservation of regional peace, security and stability.
– The national security of the member states and of territories whose external relations are the responsibility of a member state, as well as that of friendly and allied countries.
– The behaviour of the buyer country with regard to the international community, as regards in particular its attitude to terrorism, the nature of its alliances, and respect for international law.
– The existence of a risk that the equipment will be diverted within the buyer country or re-exported under undesirable conditions.[1]

At the Lisbon European Council meeting on 26–27 June 1992 an eighth criterion was adopted: 'The compatibility of the arms exports with the technical and economic capacity of the recipient country, taking into account the desirability that states should achieve their legitimate needs of security and defence with the least diversion for armaments of human and economic resources'.[2]

Although the criteria were intended to provide the basis for a common political approach that might lead to harmonization of national export licensing policies for particular weapons and destinations, opinions continued to differ on their interpretation. 'For some they were merely a rather abstract lowest common denominator, while for others they represented a coherent policy framework. They were not mandatory and it was never made clear how exactly they should be applied.'[3]

---

[1] 'Declaration on non-proliferation and the export of weapons', appendix VII to the Communiqué of the Meeting of EC Heads of State, Luxembourg, 28–29 June 1991', EPC Press Release, 29 June 1991.

[2] 'Conclusions of the presidency of the European Council held in Lisbon on 26 and 27 June 1992', EPC Press Release, 27 June 1992. The complete list of 8 criteria is reproduced in appendix A.

[3] van Orden, G., 'European arms export controls', eds P. Cornish, P. van Ham and J. Krause, *Europe and the Challenge of Proliferation*, Chaillot Paper no. 24 (Western European Union, Institute for Security Studies: Paris, 24 May 1996), p. 66.

The criteria were used however, to provide guidelines for export control practices for dual-use goods (see chapter 3). In addition, discussions continued on the development of a common interpretation of the criteria for arms exports, both within COARM and in the context of the development of a code of conduct, as discussed below.

The Maastricht Treaty and the introduction of joint actions under the CFSP

The discussions leading up to the establishment of the eight Common Criteria took place within the larger framework of the IGC on political union. As outlined in chapter 3, during the second half of 1991 a consensus gradually emerged within the IGC that Article 223 should remain intact. It was no surprise, therefore, when the eventual Maastricht Treaty deferred any action on Article 223 until the start of the next IGC in March 1996 (as discussed below).

In essence, the Maastricht Treaty is structured around three 'pillars'—the three European Communities, the CFSP, and cooperation in the fields of justice and home affairs.[4] When the treaty entered into force on 1 November 1993, the EPC process was absorbed into the CFSP pillar of the EU. While the objectives of the CFSP are only defined in general terms, the Maastricht Treaty specifies that the common policy 'shall include all questions relating to the security of the Union, including the eventual framing of a common defence policy, which might in time lead to a common defence'.[5] In addition, the Western European Union (WEU) is asked to implement EU decisions taken under the CFSP which have defence implications.

Although the CFSP remains predominantly an intergovernmental process, such features as joint action carry it beyond the EPC and allow for the possible development of closer coordination of arms export control issues. The Maastricht Treaty provides that CFSP objectives shall be pursued by: (*a*) establishing 'systemic co-operation' (Article J.2) between member states in the conduct of policy—an agreement among the governments to 'inform and consult each other within the Council on any matter of foreign and security policy'; (*b*) assuming a 'common position' (Article J.2) within the Council to which national governments are 'politically' (as opposed to legally) obliged to adhere; and (*c*) gradually implementing joint action (Article J.3) in the areas in which the member states have important interests in common.

Although the scope of the joint action procedure is rather vague, member states are legally obliged to implement any such agreements (whereas the other two options are non-binding and effectively represent a continuation of the EPC

---

[4] For a discussion of the principal features of the 3 pillars see Nugent, N., *The Government and Politics of the European Union*, 3rd edn (Macmillan: London, 1994), pp. 64–81.

[5] *Treaty on European Union* (Office for Official Publications of the European Communities: Luxembourg, 7 Feb. 1992), document no. 1759/60, Article J.4.1, available on the European Union Internet site at URL <http://europa.eu.int/abc/treaties_en.htm>.

process[6]). Its second major advantage is the possibility of adopting decisions by QMV rather than by consensus or unanimity. In practice, however, this depends on the readiness of member states to use this potential to the full, particularly in relation to the definition of the issues to be covered by a joint action. In other words, member states reached agreement on the principle of joint action but left the Council with the authority to decide 'on the basis of general guidelines from the European Council' which matters joint action should cover. Although arms export matters were subsequently targeted for joint action, several analysts have suggested that this may have been done inadvertently, as a result of accident and confusion during the complex drafting of the Maastricht Treaty.[7] However, any mistakes in the initial drafting process are unlikely to have had a significant impact given that the declaration containing the revised list of joint actions (the Asolo List) was not published with the other treaty documents. Instead, governments were invited to reconsider potential subjects for the joint action procedure.

Six months after the Maastricht summit meeting, during the European Council meeting in Lisbon on 26–27 June 1992, the ministers for foreign affairs published a report on the likely development of the CFSP.[8] The aim was to specify objectives and determine possible joint actions arising from the treaty. Regarding security matters, one of the fields specified was 'the economic aspects of security, in particular control of the transfer of military technology to third countries and control of arms export' (i.e., a repetition of the commitment contained in the abortive declaration prepared for the Maastricht Treaty). The European Council also set up another ad hoc working group under the auspices of PoCo to prepare a more detailed report on possible areas for joint action for discussion at its next meeting in December 1992. The subsequent report, published at the Edinburgh European Council meeting (7–8 December 1992), noted that the development of a CFSP 'will be enhanced by practical co-operation on specific policies as from the entry into force of the Union Treaty', including the 'gradual implementation of joint action in areas in which the member states have important interests in common'. The report also contained a list of areas 'in which the Community and its member states are

---

[6] In the area of conventional non-proliferation, e.g., attempts have been made to reach a common position within the Wassenaar Arrangement. The EU arms embargo against Afghanistan in 1996 was a more successful initiative within the 'common position' framework. On the joint action procedure, see Anthony, I., 'European Union approaches to arms control, non-proliferation and disarmament', *SIPRI Yearbook 2001: Armaments, Disarmament and International Security* (Oxford University Press: Oxford, 2001), p. 601.

[7] Cornish, P., *The Arms Trade and Europe*, Chatham House Papers (Royal Institute of International Affairs and Pinter: London, 1995), pp. 22–23; and Taylor, T., 'European co-operation and conventional arms control', Paper for discussion at the International Institute for Strategic Studies Conference on Conventional Arms Proliferation at Barnet Hill, 5–7 May 1993, pp. 9–10 (unpublished).

[8] 'Annex to the Report to the European Council in Lisbon on the likely development of the Common Foreign and Security Policy with a view to identifying areas open to Joint Action vis-à-vis particular countries or groups of countries', quoted in Adam, B., *European Union and Arms Exports* (Groupe de Recherche et d'Information sur la Paix et la Sécurité (GRIP): Brussels, Dec. 1995), p. 69.

adopting a common approach, or which, based on the experience of [the EPC], seem to have the potential for such action'.[9]

Of the four main headings listed, only 'the economic aspects of security' heading included arms export-related matters. These were: (*a*) transparency in conventional arms transfers; (*b*) the 'transparency in armaments' item on the agenda of the UN Conference on Disarmament; (*c*) the follow-up to the UN Register of Conventional Arms; (*d*) the adoption by the CSCE of common arms export criteria similar to the EPC criteria; and (*e*) common licence revocation procedures and review of existing UN and European arms embargoes.

The scope for Union activity on arms export matters provided by these items appeared limited, however. First, the overriding focus was on greater transparency in arms exports, an exercise that was described with some justification as 'low-cost and low-impact in political terms'.[10] Moreover, with the exception of the EU's contribution to the adoption by the CSCE (as it then was) of a list of principles and guidelines governing conventional arms transfers in November 1993,[11] most of the other items simply represented a reworking of efforts already in progress under the EPC. Second, the list was effectively neutralized by Article J.4.3 of the Maastricht Treaty which specifies that issues which have 'defence implications' are not to be the subject of joint action. Given also that the overriding political atmosphere during 1992 changed from arms restraint to arms promotion,[12] it seemed likely, therefore, that certain member states (particularly France and the UK) would use this clause to resist joint actions in arms export matters, much as they had done with Article 223.[13]

This has not been the case, however. Since the Maastricht Treaty came into force three joint actions involving arms export issues have been agreed: (*a*) on dual-use goods (described in chapter 3); (*b*) on APMs adopted by the EU on 12 May 1995;[14] and (*c*) on small arms (discussed below).

---

[9] 'Edinburgh European Council list of areas for "Joint Action"', Dec. 1992, quoted by Cornish, P., *Weapons Proliferation and Control: A Summary*, NPRO 65 (Royal Institute of International Affairs: London, 1994), appendix X, p. 28.

[10] Cornish (note 7), p. 68.

[11] See chapter 2; and the CSCE Principles Governing Conventional Arms Transfers reproduced in appendix A.

[12] During 1992, e.g., the P5 talks collapsed; the USA concluded several large defence orders with the Gulf states; France had major arms export orders from the United Arab Emirates and South Korea; and the UK sought to finalize the 2nd phase of the Al Yamamah deal with Saudi Arabia, and completed major sales to Malaysia and South Korea.

[13] EU joint actions in the foreign policy area have been applied to a strange mix of ad hoc operations and more global undertakings. In addition to controls on exports, they include: observing elections (in Russia and South Africa); diplomatic involvement in wide-ranging and sensitive security issues (such as the Stability Pact for South Eastern Europe and the NPT Review and Extension Conference); and the mobilization of resources (for humanitarian aid to Bosnia, the administration of Mostar and the establishment of a Palestinian police force). Santer, J., 'The European Union's security and defence policy', *NATO Review* (Nov. 1995), pp. 6–7.

[14] 'Joint Action on anti-personnel mines: Council Decision of 12 May 1995', *Official Journal of the European Communities*, L115, vol. 38 (22 May 1995). Although this Joint Action was later overtaken by the complete ban on all APMs (see chapter 2), at the time it implemented a common EU moratorium on the export of non-detectable and non-self-destructing APMs to all destinations, and banned the export of all other types of APMs to those states which had not ratified the 1981 Inhumane Weapons Convention. It also committed the member states to strengthen the convention at the subsequent review conference in Vienna. van Orden (note 3), p. 70.

Overall, however, instead of looking to develop joint actions, most of the subsequent discussions within the COARM group of experts continued to focus on procedural matters.

The COARM group of experts

As stated above, COARM was formed in 1991 as an ad hoc working group to coordinate national policies on conventional arms exports and definitions of arms embargoes. It consists of one or two national representatives from each member state (usually, but not exclusively, from their ministry of foreign affairs), meets approximately six times each year and is chaired on rotation in the same six-monthly cycles as the Council presidency. At the start, COARM reflected the post-Gulf War optimism for the introduction of common controls on arms exports, and work began on drawing up a common Regulation for the 12 member states. As already noted, the lead-up to the Maastricht Treaty, the Maastricht summit meeting itself and the Lisbon Declaration all suggested that a joint action on arms exports could be adopted swiftly once the treaty came into force. With this aim in mind, during 1991–94 COARM undertook a number of initiatives.

First, it attempted to agree a common list of weapons and military items to which the eight Common Criteria could be applied. These discussions led to the drawing up of a Common Reference List, effectively an expanded version of the former COCOM International Munitions List.[15] However, the list was not acceptable to all member states.

Second, it completed a number of comparative studies of the arms export regulations, procedures and practices in each member state, including an examination of end-use certification (leading to a proposal in 1994 for a common end-use certificate); non-re-exportation clauses; and procedures for the revocation of export licences and the control of the production, storage and transport of conventional arms prior to export.

Third, arms embargo policies and practice within the EU were analysed. The EPC framework had previously been used to coordinate arms embargoes imposed by member governments against, for example, Argentina in 1982, Syria and Libya in 1985, South Africa in 1986 and Iraq in 1990. However, it was during the embargo on China after the 1989 uprising in Peking that discussions were held within COARM concerning the exact definition of products that fell under the embargo. These discussions led to agreement in 1991 on a four-level menu of options to ensure a common interpretation of the scope of UN and EU embargoes. This Common Embargo List[16] allows the EU greater flexibility in the potency of embargoes, as witnessed subsequently in the Yugoslav and Nigerian embargoes. In the menu of embargo options, the first level covers lethal weapons and related ammunition, the second (in addition) armed platforms, the third (in addition) non-armed platforms, and the fourth

---

[15] Personal interviews with EU officials, 1997.
[16] Reproduced in appendix B.

ancillary equipment. However, despite the success of the Common Embargo List, problems still remain with the implementation of EU embargoes.[17]

Finally, COARM also drew up and implemented in 1994 a 'standardised accompanying document' for arms transfers within the Union. The document is designed to prevent diversion of consignments during transit. When a consignment of weapons is transferred from one member state to another, the recipient state is required to validate the document and return it to the originating state.[18] However, the document has initially proved unpopular with industry, in part because of the absence of standard usage by all member states:

The Italians have gone overboard in using it, they almost use it as another export licence. Some other countries still haven't introduced it yet. [The UK] introduced it on the date we were meant to introduce it, and we do the minimum we are meant to do. But I think the Dutch introduced it eighteen months after it was meant to be introduced, and I think the French said after two years that they didn't think they could introduce it.[19]

During the German presidency in 1994, a review of the COARM mandate led to a change in direction, set out in a Council Decision of 29 December 1994. Rather than work towards a common Regulation, COARM's main objective now was to explore the harmonization of the (now 15) member states' export policies by seeking a common interpretation of the Common Criteria decided in Luxembourg and Lisbon. This was not the only objective set out in the Decision. Under the revised mandate COARM was asked to do: (*a*) (in terms of seeking a common interpretation), 'contribute to increasing transparency, by comparing national procedures on the authorisation or denial of licences and identifying common elements and differences in national regulations' and 'propose appropriate measures to attune national export controls of military goods where the differences would constitute a possible obstacle to a harmonisation of arms exports policy'; (*b*) examine 'elements relevant for the CFSP of the EU with regard to the export of conventional arms' and 'prepare and suggest common positions and joint actions'; (*c*) continue to compare national policies with a view to identifying potential further criteria for consent by the European Council; (*d*) identify 'further steps which could make possible a common approach by the member states leading to harmonisation of national policies on arms exports'; (*e*) determine the possible action of the EU at a multilateral level regarding transparency or restraint in exports of conventional arms; and (*f*) 'exchange information . . . concerning exports of conventional

---

[17] E.g., there is no standard mechanism for rigorous and speedy implementation of EU and other international embargoes by member states, particularly in relation to their dependent territories, and this has been used to circumvent EU embargoes in the past. MilTec, a company based in the Isle of Man, shipped arms to the former Rwandan Government before and during the genocide of 1994 because the EU embargo had not been introduced in this UK Crown Dependency.

[18] For detail on the Community transit regulations see section 11.3 in the UK chapter of *Worldwide Guide to Export Controls 1998/99* (Export Control Publications/Deltac Ltd: Chertsey, May 1999).

[19] Personal interview with an official of the British Defence Manufacturers Association (DMA), 1997.

arms in international organisations or conferences where not all the member states participate'.[20]

The difficulty in defining this role and the continuing preference for inter-governmentalism among key states are highlighted by the following caveat in the Council Decision that was inserted on the insistence of France: 'Exports of conventional arms touch upon important and legitimate national interests (foreign policy or other), and no mention in the mandate should be construed as curtailing national decision-making capability'.[21]

Thus, while the mandate held out the possibility of harmonization, it was not a goal that all signed up to. Some member states clearly wanted closer coopera-tion; others did not. Although both sides could take some satisfaction in the mandate, the weight of national sovereignty considerations, particularly among the French and the British at that time, prevented much follow-up work during 1995 and 1996. This situation began to change again, however, in the lead-up to the IGC in Amsterdam.[22] For the European Council meeting in Dublin in October 1996, for example, COARM produced a draft document setting out 'guidelines for interpretation and practical measures for application of the common criteria to be applied to arms exports'.[23]

III. Towards an EU Code of Conduct on Arms Exports: 1996 and beyond

The 1997 Treaty of Amsterdam and growing support for coordinated export controls

Many of the concerns that applied to the EPC system (see chapter 3) continued to hamper the effectiveness of the CFSP in its early years.[24] They included: slow and reactive foreign-policy decision making and frequent failure of member states to agree common positions; differing security objectives of member states; and institutional and functional weaknesses.[25]

There were broadly two areas on the IGC agenda concerning the CFSP. The first involved a range of proposals to improve the functioning of the CFSP, and the second addressed the relationship between the EU and the WEU.

Functional improvements in the CFSP

Many EU countries believe that the key obstacle to European cooperation on foreign policy issues is the unanimity requirement. Unanimity allows the EU to

---

[20] Quoted in Adam (note 8), p. 72.

[21] Adam (note 8), p. 72.

[22] The main aim of the 1996 IGC was to modernize and remodel the Union in readiness for EU enlargement. Accession negotiations were timed to begin after completion of the IGC process.

[23] Personal interviews with EU officials, 1997. This document has not been published.

[24] For a summary of these concerns see Gordon, P., 'Europe's uncommon foreign policy', *International Security*, vol. 2, no. 3 (winter 1997/98), pp. 74–100.

[25] Despite the introduction under Maastricht of QMV in pre-agreed areas of common actions, most foreign policy decisions still required unanimity at that time.

present a united front externally (at least in theory), although a single member state can block or hold up agreement.[26] Thus, the IGC looked at various changes in voting methods, including further use of QMV[27] and the introduction of other variants such as 'reinforced' or 'super' majority voting,[28] or 'constructive abstention'.[29] Belgium, Germany, Luxembourg, the Netherlands and a number of other member states—together with the European Commission—wanted to see some form of majority voting extended to foreign policy matters.[30] Constructive abstention, as proposed in a Franco-German statement early in 1996, appeared to be the front-runner leading up to the IGC (despite opposition from Greece, the UK and the neutral countries) and was part of a developing concept in the discussions known as 'flexibility'.[31]

Flexible integration was being promoted at the IGC in order to allow a federal 'core' of states to move ahead without being delayed by weaker or unwilling ones. The resulting agreement in the 1997 Treaty of Amsterdam for a limited form of flexibility gave the green light for much more differentiated EU options (in pillars I and III); occasional flexibility on the basis of unanimity (so that all member states approve a small number moving ahead); or more wide-ranging scope for flexibility on the basis of QMV.[32] However, the draft clauses in the Amsterdam Treaty on flexibility in the CFSP (pillar II) were dropped in favour of a form of 'constructive absenteeism'.

Thus, the final outcome is that key foreign policy decisions—'common strategies'[33]—will continue to be taken by the European Council (the heads of

---

[26] Often there is no attempt to forge an EU response to even the most pressing foreign policy crises, e.g., in the case of the British Government's unilateral declaration of support for the US air strikes on Iraq in 1998. Adonis, A., '"President" Blair takes EU bypass', *The Observer*, 15 Feb. 1998.

[27] Before the IGC, QMV applied to laws covering agriculture, health and safety, foreign trade, transport and most environmental matters. QMV was crucial to the development of the SEM, as it allowed common industrial and social standards to be set, thereby preventing member states from using national regulations to keep out goods from other EU states. Under QMV a proposal needs just over 70% of the total votes allocated to EU member states to become law. Although the large states have more votes than the smaller ones (France, Germany, Italy and the UK, e.g., have 10 votes each, while Luxembourg only has 2 votes), the voting system gives small countries more votes per head of population in order to ensure that the EU is not dominated by larger states.

[28] Reinforced majority voting would require a percentage of votes larger than the present 70% required under QMV or possibly another variant, such as unanimity minus one country.

[29] Under this Franco-German proposal, constructive abstention would allow an EU country to remain outside a foreign policy initiative, such as sending troops on a peacekeeping mission, but would not enable that country to block such a decision or avoid contributing funds.

[30] For a summary of all the member states' opening positions on all the proposals for strengthening the EU's capacity for taking external action see Centre for European Studies, *The Member States of the European Union and the Inter-Governmental Conference*, Briefing Paper (University of Leeds: Leeds, Feb. 1997), p. 46.

[31] Discussions about flexibility and different speeds of integration go back to at least the mid-1970s. Mayer, H., 'Early at the beach and claiming territory? The evolution of German ideas on a new European order', *International Affairs*, vol. 73, no. 4 (1997), pp. 734–35.

[32] Strict conditions must be met before flexibility can be 'triggered'. Duff, A., *The Treaty of Amsterdam: Text and Commentary* (Federal Trust: London, 1997), pp. 85–197.

[33] The Treaty of Amsterdam introduced a new policy instrument of 'common strategies'. Although such strategies are not defined in the treaty, the fact that they require agreement by the European Council suggests that they are intended to be more significant than common positions and joint actions. However, it remains to be seen whether this latest policy instrument will be put into practice more consistently than the previous 'general guidelines from the European Council' provided for in the Maastricht Treaty. See the discussion in Cottey, A., *The European Union and Conflict Prevention: The Role of the High*

state and government) acting unanimously, but subsequent decisions on the details of policy implementation—joint actions and common positions—may be taken by QMV. Countries unwilling to take part in a particular joint action will be able to operate 'constructive absenteeism', allowing the others to act in the name of the EU. However, if the constructive abstainers comprise more than one-third of the weighted votes the decision will be blocked (under Article J.13(1)). Decisions without military implications will be taken by 'super QMV', that is, 62 votes in favour cast by at least 10 member states, unless a national veto is invoked on grounds of 'important and stated reasons of national policy' (Article J.13(2)). The national veto clause was inserted at the insistence of the British Government and, if it is invoked, the Council—that is, foreign ministers—may vote by QMV to pass the matter up to the European Council for decision by unanimity.[34]

In addition to changes to the decision-making architecture, other new procedures agreed at Amsterdam included the establishment of a Policy Planning and Early Warning Unit in Brussels that will recommend new CFSP strategies and joint actions, and the appointment of a foreign policy figurehead (the High Representative for the CFSP) within the Council.[35] However, without any agreement on the policies and strategic perspectives that should govern European security and defence arrangements, the benefits from these improvements are likely to be negligible.

The discussion of common arms export controls during the IGC

In the first half of 1997 the Netherlands took over the presidency of the EU and it was responsible for bringing the IGC to a conclusion in June 1997. As this deadline approached there were increasing signs that a number of industrial and political actors wanted a European-level solution to the 'external political problem' concerning arms export controls. However, in keeping with the different objectives of the groups concerned, the proposed solutions sometimes differed considerably, particularly in relation to the question whether controls should be harmonized at the strictest level. While some actors saw harmonization as an opportunity for further liberalization of military and dual-use export controls, others saw it as an opportunity to strengthen them. At one end of this spectrum of views, for example, could be found the European Defence Industries Group (EDIG) and at the other end the European Parliament. The European Commission fell somewhere in between.

Representative and the Policy Planning and Early Warning Unit (Saferworld/International Alert: London, 1998), pp. 21–23.

[34] Duff (note 32), p. 196.

[35] Discussions on the exact nature of the unit and the role and appointment of the High Representative began during the British presidency of the EU in 1998 but were not concluded until the Cologne meeting of the European Council in June 1999 (at which former NATO Secretary General Javier Solana was appointed to the new post of Secretary-General of the European Council and High Representative for the CFSP).

The European Defence Industry Group

In its submission to the IGC, EDIG called for the development of a common European policy on defence exports which 'does not impede international cooperation and which takes into account the need to strengthen the European commercial position'.[36] Accordingly, EDIG makes a strong distinction between intra-EU and extra-EU transfers. Disparities between national export control policies within the EU are regarded by industry as a strong impediment for European cooperative programmes, as outlined in an earlier EDIG policy paper: 'It would be difficult, if not impossible, for a major company to contemplate collaboration with another company unless that company exists in a country where the Government has accepted common principles of exporting policy. An absence of national Government agreement could therefore, mean that its national industry would find itself effectively debarred from participation in collaborative projects'.[37]

Some German companies, for example, feared that they would be excluded from collaborative projects because of their more restrictive national export regulations.[38] EDIG was also concerned about the administrative costs of intra-EU licensing for defence components destined for collaborative projects. Ultimately, therefore, EDIG wanted a European authority to be given the responsibility for harmonizing export policies (including common criteria for re-export outside the EU, and common product and destination lists), but recognized that 'an intergovernmental agreement on this matter will take some time, since it is linked to the establishment of a CFSP'.[39] Thus, in the short term EDIG asked for bridging arrangements based on the removal of all restrictions on intra-EU trade of Article 223 goods (i.e., on the supply of defence equipment between member state governments, as well as the sale of components or subsystems between exporting companies) which would then be controlled by a new global licence. For companies that are part of an accepted European collaborative project this global licence would allow the free movement of defence goods and components within the Union. Control of this global licence would lie with the nation in which the prime contractor is based.[40] Indeed, this policy goal will shortly be realized in France, Germany, Italy, Spain, Sweden and the UK where Global Project Licences are expected to be introduced under the terms of the new Framework Agreement signed in July 2000 (see the discussion below).

---

[36] European Defence Industries Group, 'The European defence industry: an agenda item for the 1996 InterGovernmental Conference, Memorandum by EDIG', 30 May 1995, p. 11.

[37] European Defence Industries Group, 'EDIG policy paper on conventional defence equipment export', Reference EPP/94/07, 13 Jan. 1994, p. 1.

[38] Personal interviews in Germany in 1997. See chapter 7 for further details.

[39] European Defence Industries Group (note 36), p. 11.

[40] European Defence Industries Group (note 36), p. 12; and note 37, pp. 2–4. A report by the European Parliament's Committee on Foreign Affairs, Security and Defence Policy also suggested that 'the country of the prime supplier should be responsible for monitoring arms exports'. European Parliament, 'Working document on the challenges facing the European defence-related industry, COM (96) 0010, by rapporteur Mr Gary Titley', 5 Sep. 1996, p. 7.

Finally, EDIG also proposed measures to strengthen the European commercial position in the global arms market. This would be achieved by developing intergovernmental support for defence exports (in the same way that several member state governments currently assist their own defence industries[41]) and eventually forming a European Export Support Office.[42] In summary, therefore, EDIG regards harmonization of arms export controls as desirable but not at the level of the most restrictive national policies.[43]

The European Commission

The European Commission also recognized that differences in national export policies were impeding intra-EU industrial cooperation and called for the harmonization of national export policies and controls. Again, in recognition of the difficulties this entailed the Commission recommended a two-step approach—regular exchanges of information between member states (as was currently the case in COARM), to be followed later by the development of an operational system 'aimed at eliminating the distortions between the various national treatments'.[44] One of the Commission's main objectives is the preservation of a healthy and strong defence industry, and it initially responded to EDIG's overtures regarding intra-Community defence transfers, for example, by proposing a simplified licensing regime for such transfers.[45]

A basic problem for the Commission remains the transatlantic relationship, and whether the EU should do more to protect its own market from US competition. Within this general framework, the Commission's proposals on arms export controls tend to be limited to measures to achieve greater transparency.

The European Parliament

Although the intergovernmental voting processes tend to push the European Parliament to the periphery, it has consistently exerted pressure for a more restrictive arms export control policy within the EU. Both individually and collectively, MEPs tend to take a much more radical stance on this issue than their national counterparts. Whatever the motives and merits of this radicalism,[46] during the early and mid-1990s the European Parliament (prompted by

---

[41] See, e.g., the role of the DESO in the UK as described in chapter 5.

[42] European Defence Industries Group (note 36), p. 11.

[43] Indeed, this view was noted in a report of a meeting in Brussels on 9 Mar. 1995 between 2 European commissioners and representatives from the European defence industry. Personal interview, 1997.

[44] European Commission, 'The challenges facing the European defence-related industry: a contribution for action at European level', Communication from the Commission to the Council, the European Parliament, the Economic and Social Committee and the Committee of the Regions, Jan. 1996, pp. 25–26.

[45] European Commission, 'Implementing European Union strategy on defence-related industries', Communication from the Commission to the Council, the European Parliament, the Economic and Social Committee and the Committee of the Regions, COM(97) 583 final, Brussels, 4 Dec. 1997, Annex II, pp. 2–3.

[46] It may be attributable to the fact that MEPs are outside the 'real' centres of political power and hence do not receive the same level of lobbying from vested interests that occurs at the national level. Indeed, governments in some member states have been critical of the European Parliament's reports and recommendations for being unfocused, driven by the narrow interests of individual MEPs and unreflective

NGOs, especially the UK-based Saferworld[47]) published several reports[48] and passed a number of resolutions which sought to create a more restrictive framework for arms exports at the EU level. Three resolutions in September 1992, March 1994 and January 1995 are indicative of the European Parliament's stance on this issue. The first called for: an end to the promotion of arms exports by government agencies (including the use of export credits); the addition of the 'sufficiency principle' to the eight Common Criteria; the creation of a Community conversion programme; and the deletion of Article 223. It also welcomed proposals for a code of conduct 'based on the highest levels of existing controls'.[49] The second resolution, among other objectives, set out in greater detail some of the key requirements of a restrictive code of conduct.[50] With the 1996 IGC near at hand, the third resolution again called for the deletion of Article 223, together with a 'coherent and comprehensive arms control policy at the Union level'. This included working towards establishing an 'international code of conduct on the control of arms transfers and exports' and investigating the possibility of creating a 'European Agency for the control of arms exports'.[51]

However, the eventual Treaty of Amsterdam (1997)[52] disappointed industry, the Commission, the European Parliament and other supporters of a more coordinated approach. The repeal of Article 223 was again discussed, both in the Reflection Group and in the main IGC negotiations, but was again abruptly rejected.[53] Thus, despite agreeing adjustments to the CFSP and a Dutch initia-

of the EU as a whole. The British Labour government, e.g., clashed with dissident Labour MEPs over what it saw as 'negative' and 'wayward' European Parliament motions on human rights. 'Cook infuriates MEPs with softer human rights stance', *The Guardian*, 7 Oct. 1997.

[47] Saferworld has been investigating ways in which the EU could develop its own export control policy since the early 1990s. See, e.g., Anthony, I., Eavis, P. and Greene, O., *Regulating Arms Exports: A Programme for the European Community* (Saferworld: London, Sep. 1991): Eavis, P., *Arms and Dual-Use Exports from the EC: a Common Policy for Regulation and Control* (Saferworld: London, Dec. 1992); and Eavis, P. and Shannon, A., 'Arms and dual-use export controls: priorities for the European Union', Saferworld, London, June 1994.

[48] See, e.g., European Parliament, 'Report of the Committee on Foreign Affairs and Security on disarmament, arms export controls and non-proliferation of weapons of mass destruction, Rapporteur Glyn Ford', PE 206.753/def., Strasbourg, 23 Feb. 1994. This report also contains the first draft of the 'Resolution on disarmament, arms export controls and the non-proliferation of weapons of mass destruction', Resolution A3-0111/94, 24 Mar. 1994, *Official Journal of the European Communities*, C114 (25 Apr. 1994).

[49] European Parliament, 'Resolution on the Community's role in the supervision of arms exports and the armaments industry, Resolution A3-0260/92', 17 Sep. 1992, *Official Journal of the European Communities*, C284 (2 Nov. 1992), p. 138.

[50] European Parliament, 'Resolution on disarmament, arms export controls and the non-proliferation of weapons of mass destruction' (note 48), p. 56.

[51] European Parliament, 'Resolution on the need for European controls on the export or transfer of arms', PE 186.411, Strasbourg, 19 Jan. 1995, quoted by Cornish (note 7), p. 24; and *Official Journal of the European Communities*, C43 (20 Feb. 1995), pp. 89–91.

[52] The Treaty of Amsterdam amending the Treaty on European Union, the Treaties establishing the European Communities and Certain Related Acts was agreed in June 1997 and formally signed in Oct. 1997, and entered into force in May 1999 following ratification by all the member states. The treaty is available on the European Union Internet site at URL <http://www.europarl.eu.int/topics/treaty/pdf/amst-en.pdf>.

[53] EC/IGC/CONF.3956/96, quoted in Dodd, T., 'European defence and armaments co-operation', House of Commons Research Paper 97/15, House of Commons Library, London, 4 Feb. 1997, p. 19.

tive on controlling illegal exports of light weapons (discussed below), there were no other important issues raised in Amsterdam with implications for EU defence-related export controls. This revealed the continuing lack of consensus in this area.

The rise of small arms and light weapons on the EU political agenda

While the Amsterdam IGC was undoubtedly disappointing, some progress was made by the Dutch presidency on the difficult issue of combating and preventing illicit arms trafficking. COARM was tasked in January 1997 with producing a common text on a future joint policy statement. After several revisions of the proposed text, EU heads of state agreed a final draft of the EU Programme for Preventing and Combating Illicit Trafficking in Conventional Arms in June 1997.[54] While the programme covers all conventional arms, it is predominantly concerned with the proliferation of small arms and light weapons, and reflects the growing international concern with these weapons in the late 1990s. The extensive policy objectives are divided into three parts, which commit member states to: (*a*) strengthen their collective efforts to prevent and combat illicit trafficking in arms from and through the territories of the EU. These efforts are expected to include improved cross-border cooperation between national policy and intelligence and customs forces; enhanced information exchange (e.g., through the development of shared databases); and prompt investigation and prosecution of cases of illicit arms trafficking; (*b*) assist other countries in preventing and combating illicit arms trafficking; and (*c*) assist countries in regions affected by small arms proliferation and illicit trafficking, especially in post-conflict situations and in regions with only minimal security and stability.

Thus, although the EU Programme involves no new EU legislation or legally binding intergovernmental instrument, it does commit each member state to use existing national rules and procedures to achieve the above goals. Described initially by one senior official within the export control bureaucracy of a key member state as a 'goodwill paper' with little practical impact,[55] it has forced member states to think about concrete measures to implement the policy objectives. Indeed, while it is still mainly a framework for proposed future action, a number of policy initiatives have already been taken under the EU Programme to enhance national and EU-level coordination among regulatory and enforcement agencies, and to develop cooperative partnerships between the EU and regions severely affected by small arms proliferation.

In March 1997 the Belgian Government set up a national interdepartmental committee for combating illicit weapons transfers, and similar committees were established in the Netherlands and the UK in 1998. Cooperation at the EU level is also beginning to evolve (although it is more difficult because the issue of

---

[54] Council of the European Union, 'EU Programme for Preventing and Combating Illicit Trafficking in Conventional Arms', June 1997, reproduced in appendix B.
[55] Personal interview, 1997.

arms trafficking cuts across important institutional and organizational divisions in the EU). During the UK's presidency of the EU, for example, a European Conference on Arms Trafficking was held in London in February 1998 to discuss ways in which closer EU-level coordination of operational and enforcement procedures could be achieved. By the end of 1998, however, only one concrete measure had been agreed—a Council recommendation on arms trafficking and terrorism.[56] This included a 10-point agenda for cooperation and information exchange among national intelligence, police and customs agencies to combat arms trafficking, principally within the context of counter-terrorism operations.

In 1998 an important start was also made on developing EU assistance programmes. At a conference in South Africa in May 1998, for example, a Southern African Regional Action Plan on Light Arms and Illicit Arms Trafficking was agreed. The plan sets out a detailed agenda for tackling light arms proliferation in the region and identifies ways in which the EU and member states can most usefully assist in implementing that agenda.[57] The action plan was subsequently endorsed at the EU–Southern African Development Community (SADC) ministerial meeting in November 1998. Although Southern Africa has been the primary focus for developing such partnerships, the EU also engaged significantly with West Africa and Albania in 1998.

The EU Joint Action on Small Arms

At the end of 1998, the EU programme was supplemented in an important way by a Joint Action on Small Arms which was adopted by the Council on 17 December 1998.[58] This joint action provides a framework for EU financial and technical assistance for specific projects and programmes designed to combat the destabilizing accumulation and spread of small arms. Although no specific budget line was allocated at the time it was adopted, limited funding may be available through the CFSP budget line in the short term, while in the longer term it should provide a vehicle for significant funding for EU action in this area.

The Programme for Preventing and Combating Illicit Trafficking in Conventional Arms and the Joint Action on Small Arms are complemented by the EU Code of Conduct on Arms Exports.

---

[56] Council of the European Union, 'Council recommendation on arms trafficking', Brussels, 24 Nov. 1998, 12875/98.

[57] Saferworld and Institute for Security Studies (ISS), 'Southern Africa Regional Action Programme on Light Arms and Illicit Trafficking', London, May 1998. See also Greene, O. and Gamba, V., 'Responding to small arms and light weapons proliferation in Southern Africa: developing a regional action programme', *African Security Review*, no. 4 (1998).

[58] Council of the European Union, 'Joint Action adopted by the Council on the basis of Article J.3 of the Treaty on European Union on the European Union's contribution to combating the destabilising accumulation and spread of small arms and light weapons', Brussels, 17 Dec. 1998. The text was published in the *Official Journal of the European Communities*, L9 (15 Jan. 1999).

The development of an EU Code of Conduct on Arms Exports

As noted above, the idea of a European code of conduct for arms transfers was first proposed in 1992 by the European Parliament following lobbying by Saferworld. A code was deemed necessary to reinforce the Common Criteria, which were not binding on governments and lacked common interpretation. In particular, the room for manoeuvre in interpreting the criteria led to several ambiguities and discrepancies between the arms export policies of member states, as the following three examples illustrate.

First, the German Government refused to agree a warship contract with Taiwan in 1994, while France supplied Mirage fighters and frigates worth an estimated $6.1 billion.[59] Second, with regard to arms supplies to Indonesia, Portugal imposed a unilateral arms embargo because of Indonesia's invasion of East Timor (a former Portuguese colony), Sweden would not sign new contracts (although it was still prepared to supply follow-on equipment for a naval contract signed in the 1960s), while Germany and the UK continued to supply warships and aircraft, respectively.[60] Third, Belgium ceased arms exports to Rwanda in 1990 for regional and internal security reasons, while France continued to supply artillery, munitions and military advisers to Rwanda between 1990 and 1992.[61]

Thus, if the eight criteria were to be effective, the major exporting countries in Europe would need to start interpreting and implementing them in common. To help this process, three UK-based NGOs and a team of international lawyers drew up a model text for a European code of conduct in 1993. This document, which expanded the eight EU Common Criteria, was launched in Brussels on 11 May 1995 with the endorsement of 40 other European NGOs and the European Parliament.[62]

Yet any new criteria in the code, however clear and consistently drafted, were unlikely to be effective on their own, given that (on the basis of past experience with the Common Criteria) the 15 member states were still unlikely to interpret them in the same way. In 1997, Saferworld set up a UK Code Working Group to examine this problem and to consider what other measures would be necessary for a rigorous EU code. A briefing paper published by the working group towards the end of 1997 set out the essential features of the code.[63] In addition to the detailed criteria set out in the earlier document, the mechanisms for consultation and implementation seen as essential by the working group

[59] Eavis and Shannon (note 47), p. 5.

[60] Chalmers, M., *British Arms Export Policy and Indonesia* (Saferworld: London, May 1997), pp. 13–16.

[61] Eavis and Shannon (note 47), p. 6.

[62] 'A European code of conduct on the arms trade', 11 May 1995, a document developed by the British American Security Information Council (BASIC), Saferworld and the World Development Movement, in cooperation with Marc Weller (University of Cambridge) and Françoise Hampson (University of Essex).

[63] 'An EU code of conduct on the arms trade: essential standards', briefing prepared by the Code Working Group (consisting of Amnesty International, BASIC, Christian Aid, Oxfam, Saferworld and the World Development Movement) in late 1997 (undated).

included: provisions for notification of transfers and denials; 'no-undercutting' guidelines; a list of sensitive destinations; harmonized control lists; end-use provisions; arrangements for parliamentary scrutiny; more comprehensive arrangements for implementing embargoes; and controls on arms brokering.

Supporters argued that such a code would produce three main benefits. First, it would enable the terms of each criterion to be clearly defined, thereby providing firm guidelines (possibly set out in national legislation) against which the legitimacy of specific arms exports could be judged. Second, it would provide a public mechanism for monitoring government practice. Parliamentarians, journalists, NGOs and members of the public would be in a stronger position to hold their governments accountable for arms exports. Third, the EU code would be an essential building-block for the development of other regional codes or an international code of conduct.[64] As discussed in chapter 2, the Nobel laureates' code of conduct and a US code of conduct were also under discussion at this time. Alternatively, the P5 or the CSCE principles were thought by some commentators to have the potential to be transformed into a globally applicable code of conduct, possibly linked to future development of the UN Register.[65]

Opponents of the EU code fell into two very different groups—those who saw the code as not going far enough and those who saw it as a step too far. The first group, and by far the more marginal of the two, was made up of anti-arms-trade NGOs and peace groups who opposed the code on the grounds that it would still permit arms exports to a wide range of non-EU states, including some less-developed countries (LDCs). The German-based Kampagne gegen Rüstungsexport (Campaign against Arms Exports), for example, described the proposed code as 'insufficient' and 'counterproductive', and argued instead for new binding EU regulations that prevented extra-EU arms transfers in all but exceptional cases.[66]

The second, more influential, group consisted of elements within the defence industries, political parties and governments in some member states (mainly France and the UK). These influential stakeholders opposed the code because they saw it either as a threat to future export opportunities with major customer countries or as a threat to national competence in this area. One of the main consequences of removing the ambiguity from the criteria, for example, would be to reduce the room for manoeuvre by individual member states and open national arms export decisions to greater scrutiny.

In order to win over this latter constituency, Saferworld together with other European NGOs began canvassing support for the code across the EU. By the

---

[64] See, e.g., the speech by Wood, B. (Amnesty International), in *Report on the International Conference on European Arms Export Controls, 13–14 November 1997* (Swedish Fellowship of Reconciliation and Saferworld: Stockholm, 1998), pp. 27–29.

[65] For a brief discussion of the linkage between the UN Register of Conventional Arms and a global code of conduct see, e.g., Donowaki, M., 'Developing a code of conduct for conventional weapons', *Nonproliferation Review* (fall 1995), p. 64.

[66] Letter from the Board of the Kampagne gegen Rüstungsexport (Germany) to Saferworld dated 24 Jan. 1996. See also the statement by the London-based Campaign Against the Arms Trade in *Campaign Against Arms Trade News*, Mar. 1996.

spring of 1997, governments in Belgium, Germany, Ireland, the Netherlands and Sweden had all expressed support for a restrictive common arms export policy, and over 300 members of parliament (MPs) from eight member states had asserted their support for a code.[67] Crucially, the opposition Labour Party in the UK also endorsed the idea of a code in the 'Eight-point plan' of Robin Cook, MP, of February 1997.[68] Moreover, by the end of 1997, over 600 European NGOs, including major development charities, such as Oxfam, the Catholic Agency for Overseas Development (CAFOD), the Refugee Council and Save the Children, were also campaigning for a restrictive EU code. NGOs were also targeting interest groups in the USA with the aim of establishing a parallel US code of conduct.[69] While this growing support for the principle of a code was encouraging, many of those expressing support continued to avoid making any commitment as to the actual content of the code.[70]

The first real test of this commitment came, therefore, with the election of the New Labour government in the UK in May 1997. In July 1997, a new national framework for considering arms exports was announced (see chapter 5) which included the commitment to 'work for the introduction of a European Code of Conduct setting high common standards to govern arms exports from all European Union member states'.[71] With the UK taking over the presidency of the EU in January 1998, the new government had the ideal opportunity to put this commitment into practice.

Initiatives under the British presidency

When the UK assumed the presidency, very little was publicly known about the substance of its proposed code, except that its own new national guidelines were expected to be at its core.[72] Early indications were that some progress on the second pillar of the CFSP could be expected, with an eventual voluntary code of conduct on the basis of 'mutual confidence' between member states.[73] An early initiative on the part of the new British Government was to engage the French Government (which was expected to be the most intransigent) in dia-

---

[67] *Saferworld Update*, spring 1997, p. 6.

[68] British Labour Party, 'Labour's policy pledges for a responsible arms trade', 13 Feb. 1997.

[69] *Saferworld Update*, summer 1996, p. 7; and spring 1997, p. 6.

[70] E.g., in the UK during 1996 Tony Blair, then Leader of the Opposition, endorsed the principle of an EU code, and Prime Minister John Major expressed support for an international code. However, neither leader made any detailed commitments.

[71] 'The government's pledges for responsible arms exports', announcement by the Foreign Secretary in the House of Commons, 28 July 1997. The full statement is reproduced in British Foreign and Commonwealth Office, Department of Trade and Industry and Ministry of Defence, *Strategic Export Controls, Annual Report* (Foreign and Commonwealth Office: London, Mar. 1999), pp. 3–6.

[72] A first draft of a code of conduct was prepared by Foreign and Commonwealth Office (FCO) officials and agreed by other interested government departments in Sep. 1997. The draft drew on the British national criteria, the 8 EU Common Criteria and the OSCE Principles. British Foreign and Commonwealth Office, 'UK defence export criteria and EU code of conduct', memorandum of 19 Oct. 1998, submitted as evidence to the House of Commons Trade and Industry Committee, *Strategic Export Controls*, HC 1998/99 65 (Her Majesty's Stationery office: London, 2 Dec. 1998), p. 112.

[73] Personal interview with Commission official, Brussels, 1997.

logue over the code.[74] The aim was to agree an Anglo-French draft which could then be circulated to other EU partners. According to one insider's view of these discussions, Prime Minister Lionel Jospin was supportive but President Jacques Chirac and French civil servants remained hostile, and the overall impression was that, despite public utterances of support, in private the French were not very helpful.[75]

However, enough of the French Government's reservations were eventually assuaged to enable a joint British–French first draft of the code to be circulated to EU partners on 23 January 1998. COARM subsequently met several times over the next three months to draft and redraft the precise terms of the code. NGOs (the UK Code Working Group) also provided analysis and recommendations based on leaked copies of the drafts. Ultimately, however, agreement within COARM was not possible, largely because of French reluctance to accept a strong code. Instead, COARM produced a draft code containing a number of alternative options for consideration by the EU foreign ministers. Some of the more restrictive options (including tighter human rights and development criteria) had been inserted in the draft as a result of intensive NGO lobbying, including meetings with British Foreign Secretary Robin Cook and his advisers responsible for drafting the code.[76] As the EU summit meeting in Cardiff approached, therefore, the NGO coalition lobbied hard for the most restrictive options.[77] The code was finally agreed by foreign ministers at the EU General Affairs Committee at the end of May 1998, for formal adoption at the European Council meeting in June. However, in the face of threats by France to jeopardize the whole agreement, all the weaker options were chosen.

The EU Code of Conduct on Arms Exports was formally adopted by the Council as a legally non-binding Council Declaration on 8 June 1998.[78] It applies to legal transfers of all types of arms—light and heavy, small and large—as well as dual-use technologies destined for military end-users. Its significance lies partly in the elaboration of guiding principles to be taken into account when considering arms export licence applications and partly in the operative provisions it establishes for information exchange and consultation. It sets out minimum levels of restraint and allows member states to operate more restrictive national policies if they so wish.

[74] The code was part of a 3-pronged approach to arms export controls by the British Government during its presidency of the EU. The other 2 objectives were to get the UK's ban on exports of torture equipment agreed at the European level and to take forward the EU Programme on Illicit Arms Trafficking. Personal interview with FCO official, Aug. 1997. See also the speech by Tony Lloyd, Minister of State for the FCO, in *Report on the International Conference on European Arms Export Controls* (note 64), pp. 24–25.

[75] Personal interview with a British Labour Party MEP, 1997.

[76] *Saferworld Update*, no. 21 (summer 1998), pp. 1–2.

[77] E.g., Saferworld produced a press release and media briefing (based on a leaked copy of the final draft of the code) 5 days before the foreign ministers' meeting urging governments to choose the more restrictive options in a number of key areas. 'EU countries divided at crunch-time for arms trade code', Saferworld Press Release, 21 May 1998; and 'Key issues unresolved as code enters final stage', Saferworld Media Briefing, 21 May 1998.

[78] Council of the European Union, 'Code of Conduct on Arms Exports', adopted by the General Affairs Council, 8 June 1998, reproduced in appendix A.

IV. The EU Code guidelines and operative provisions

The guidelines in the EU Code of Conduct are an elaboration (based on the British national criteria announced in July 1997) of the eight common criteria agreed in 1991 and 1992. While not as detailed as NGOs and some governments had hoped,[79] the guidelines are nonetheless an improvement on the earlier criteria. Member states are required to take into account the effect of arms sales on *inter alia* human rights, regional stability, and economic and social development. One of the strongest commitments, for example, is that EU governments will not issue an export licence if there is a clear risk that a proposed export might be used for internal repression. The key will be how the member states implement the guidelines in practice. If they are implemented in full, they should lead to increased restraint and closer alignment of member states' arms export policies.

The Code's key operative provisions are the denial notification mechanism and the associated 'no undercutting without consultation' procedure. When a member state denies an export licence (on grounds relating to one or more of the eight Common Criteria) it must notify all other member states. If another member state is approached for the same transaction within three years, it first has to consult the country that denied it. After the consultation the export may proceed (there is no right of veto) but the exporting country must provide a detailed explanation of its rationale. It is hoped that these requirements will prevent or at least reduce undercutting. If they do, this will be a significant achievement. The P5, for example, were unable to agree on a consultation mechanism for planned sales, and the Wassenaar Arrangement, while it does have a consultation mechanism, was unable to agree a 'no-undercutting rule' (see the discussion in chapter 2).

Member states are also required to circulate to each other in confidence annual reports of their national arms exports and implementation of the Code. These are discussed, along with ways to strengthen the Code, at annual review meetings in the Council, which then produces a consolidated report. The first annual review took place towards the end of 1999 and the first annual report was published during the Finnish presidency in November 1999.[80] The second annual review was published in December 2000 and described a year spent consolidating the achievements of the Code.[81] Because the consolidated report represents the lowest common denominator of different levels of national reporting (although most arms-exporting member states now publish annual reports, there is no uniform standard for them), it only contains limited information on the operation of the Code. This includes basic information on

[79] 'Anger as arms code is diluted', *The Guardian*, 26 May 1998.

[80] Council of the European Union, General Affairs Committee, '1999 annual report on the implementation of the EU Code of Conduct on Arms Exports, 11384/99–C5-0021/2000', *Official Journal of the European Communities*, C315 (3 Nov. 1999), pp. 1–4.

[81] 'Second annual report according to Operative Provision 8 of the European Union Code of Conduct on Arms Exports', *Official Journal of the European Communities*, C379 (2000), item 1.

the number of licences granted, their total value and the number of bilateral consultations on undercutting.

Nevertheless, implementation of the Code appears to be successful, and the first two annual reviews of its operation did establish some good precedents. For example, a large number of denial notifications (193 in the 1998 reporting period) were circulated and there was active consultation between EU member states on specific export licences issued.

Two further positive developments need to be mentioned. First, the operation of the Code was strengthened in June 2000 with the adoption of a Common List of Military Equipment to be covered by the Code.[82] The development of such a list had been identified by member states as a priority in the course of the first annual review of the Code. It is based on the Wassenaar Arrangement's Munitions List and is expected to act as a reference point for member states' national military lists rather than to directly replace them. The agreed list does not include police and paramilitary equipment and a common list for those goods is being developed separately.

Second, one of the key commitments in the Code—the requirement that member states work to secure wider subscription to the principles of the Code among other arms-exporting states—began to be realized almost immediately. The 13 non-EU associate countries[83] formally aligned themselves to the Code in August 1998, which means that, in principle at least, it now covers all the European arms producers outside the former Soviet Union except Bosnia and Herzegovina, Croatia, Serbia and Switzerland. However, the associate countries are not included in the crucial information exchange and consultation mechanisms, and at this stage they have only made a political commitment to follow the Code's guidelines. In addition, a committee of the Council of Europe Parliamentary Assembly called on all Council of Europe member states to respect the criteria contained in the EU Code and to work towards a Europe-wide code of conduct.[84] Since then other states including Canada, Iceland and Norway have also agreed to align themselves with the principles of the EU Code.

These declarations of support for the principles of the EU Code (and, in the case of the associate countries, the Programme for Preventing and Combating Illicit Trafficking in Conventional Arms and the Joint Action on Small Arms as well) significantly increase the possibilities for the EU to coordinate arms export controls with partner countries, and a framework now exists for such cooperation to take place on many fronts.

---

[82] 'Council Declaration of 13 June 2000, issued on the occasion of the adoption of the common list of military equipment covered by the European Union Code of Conduct on Arms Exports', Notice no. 2000/C 191/01, *Official Journal of the European Communities*, C191, vol. 43 (8 July 2000). The list is available on the European Union Internet site at URL <http://europa.eu.int/eur-lex/en/dat/2000/c_191/c_19120000708en00010019.pdf>.

[83] The 13 countries are Bulgaria, Cyprus, the Czech Republic, Estonia, Hungary, Iceland, Latvia, Lithuania, Norway, Poland, Romania, Slovakia and Slovenia.

[84] Council of Europe, Parliamentary Assembly, Political Affairs Committee, 'Drawing up a European code of conduct on arms sales', Rapporteur Mr Borut Pahor, Slovenia, Socialist Group, doc. 8188, 10 Sep. 1998.

Despite such progress towards a coherent and consistent EU policy on arms exports, there are a number of potential weaknesses in both the guidelines and the operative provisions which still need to be considered. First, some of the guidelines remain imprecise or too lax, particularly those concerning the internal situation of the recipient country. It is thought that France, for example, was responsible for diluting the criteria on human rights (criterion two) and development (criterion eight).[85] The human rights criterion only requires 'special caution and vigilance' in issuing licences to countries where serious violations have been established by 'the competent bodies of the UN, Council of Europe', or by the EU. Several ministers, including the Irish Foreign Minister, David Andrews, were hoping that the agreement would include an unequivocal ban on arms sales to governments accused of serious human rights abuses.[86] Similarly, while the guidelines under criterion eight require consideration of 'the recipient country's relative levels of military and social expenditure', the lack of any precise standard for evaluating these may mean that the various national licensing authorities will interpret them differently.

While these serious flaws in the wording of the Code may need to be addressed at a later date, it will be even more important that member states reach a common understanding of what the guidelines actually mean in practice. Thus, discussions will need to take place within the EU with explicit reference to specific destinations and regions in order for a shared understanding and common practice to be achieved.[87]

Second, the acid test of the Code will be whether it deters 'undercutting'. Although the consolidated report confirmed that 193 denial notifications were circulated in 1998 and 221 in 1999, and of these only 18 in 1998 and 33 in 1999 resulted in bilateral consultations, it is impossible to independently assess the effectiveness of this mechanism because the annual report does not provide information on the result of the consultations. There have been no reports of undercutting, but it remains to be seen whether these private bilateral consultations will be effective in the long term.[88] If, for example, certain member states do not regard themselves as being bound by denials issued by other countries, and undercutting becomes commonplace, the effects of such action will be divisive and lead to a loss of confidence in the Code.[89]

---

[85] *BASIC Reports*, no. 64 (4 June 1998), pp. 1–2.

[86] *BASIC Reports*, no. 64 (4 June 1998), pp. 1–2.

[87] It is significant that there is a clause within the code's operative provisions that allows the member states to 'assess jointly through the CFSP framework the situation of potential or actual recipients of arms exports from EU Member States, in light of the principles and criteria of the Code'. Previously, COARM was mandated only to discuss recipient regions and not specific end-users. Under this new arrangement, however, it is possible that discussions within COARM may eventually lead to the development of common approaches to specific destinations.

[88] Again, it is thought to be on the insistence of the French Government that the 'no undercutting' rule will be applied in private between the 2 countries concerned rather than involving more detailed consultations between all 15 member states.

[89] Although the code does not specify a time-limit for issuing denial notifications, early issue will be essential to prevent another member state granting the same licence. Other regimes do specify time-limits for similar requirements. E.g., there is a 10-day time-limit under Article 7 of the EU Dual-Use Regulation

Third, although the achievement of greater transparency in European arms sales is one of the stated objectives of the Code, there are no mechanisms within the agreement to achieve this. Neither the consolidated report nor the national reports have to be published or put before national parliaments or the European Parliament. Nor is there any agreement as to what should be included in these confidential reports. Publication of the first two consolidated reports was a welcome move towards greater transparency, and the Netherlands and Sweden were already publishing national annual reports prior to the introduction of the EU Code. Since then Belgium, Denmark, Finland, France, Germany, Ireland, Italy and the UK have published annual reports.[90] Arguably, the UK annual reporting system (first introduced in March 1999 and improved early in 2000: see chapter 5) is the most detailed in Europe so far, and may set an important precedent which other member states will find hard to ignore.

Finally, the Code contains virtually no provisions to address a number of loopholes in most member states' arms control regimes, such as the failure to strictly regulate international arms brokering and licensed production agreements, or to adopt rigorous systems of certifying and monitoring end-use.

All these omissions will need to be addressed in the near future if the Code is to achieve its aim of high common standards in the management of and restraint in conventional arms transfers. In addition, the new Framework Agreement (signed in July 2000) between six of the member states has the potential to undermine some of the progress made since the introduction of the EU Code, while Article 223 remains a key stumbling block to deeper cooperation. These last two concerns are discussed below.

The relationship between the EU Code and the Framework Agreement

A major obstacle to European defence industrial restructuring is the absence of a reliable political and institutional frame of reference for defence policy (including procurement). As one analyst concluded: 'the reality is that fifty years of institutional huffing and puffing on the subject has resulted in only the most limited of moves away from the knee-jerk protectionism that has characterised European defence industrial policy'.[91] However, a potential turning point

for issuing notices of objection to the granting of specific export licences (see chapter 3), and there are 60- or 30-day denial notification time-limits under the Wassenaar Arrangement (see chapter 2).

[90] For a comparative survey of transparency and parliamentary oversight provisions within the EU see Mariani, B. and Urquhart, A., *Transparency and Accountability in European Arms Export Controls: Towards Common Standards and Best Practice* (Saferworld: London, Dec. 2000).

[91] Cooper, N., *The Business of Death: Britain's Arms Trade at Home and Abroad* (Tauris Academic Studies: London, 1997), p. 114. The Western European Armaments Group (WEAG) is tasked with developing the institutional framework out of which common European defence research, development and procurement policies might eventually emerge. At a meeting of the WEU Council of Ministers in Noordwijk on 14 Nov. 1994, however, it was agreed to postpone the creation of a centralized European Armaments Agency, although the green light was given for the development of an earlier Franco-German initiative. A number of other initiatives have sought to take the idea forward in recent years, with little tangible success. See, e.g., European Commission (note 45), p. 3; Hayward, K., *Towards a European Weapons Procurement Process: The Shaping of Common European Requirements for New Arms Programmes*, Chaillot Paper no. 27 (Western European Union, Institute for Security Studies: Paris, June

in the development of European defence equipment cooperation began in December 1997 with the issue of a 'rationalize or die' warning to Europe's aviation and defence electronics firms by the heads of state in France, Germany and the UK (supported by the Italian, Spanish and Swedish governments).[92] This was immediately followed by the publication of another Communication from the Commission on this matter.[93] A further breakthrough was the signing of a Letter of Intent (LoI) accord between the defence secretaries of France, Germany, Italy, Spain, Sweden and the UK in July 1998.[94] The main aim of the LoI was to seek to define a framework of cooperation that would facilitate the restructuring and operation of the European defence industry.

An Executive Committee composed of high-level representatives from each participating country and six working groups were tasked with examining one of the areas highlighted in the LoI—security and supply; export controls; security of information; research and technology; the treatment of technical information; and harmonization of military requirements. Each participating state chaired one working group: France headed the working group on export controls.

Under the terms of the LoI, participating states are required to: (*a*) 'reinforce their cooperation and promote convergence in the field of conventional arms exports'; (*b*) 'take the necessary measures to develop common rules about defence exports, including the harmonization of their control policies (procedures, lists and authorization levels), and examine the scope for establishing a standard procedure'; (*c*) 'seek the means of simplifying the circulation of Defence Articles and Defence Services between themselves . . . with the aspiration gradually to reduce and, where appropriate, remove control procedures for transfers between them'; (*d*) 'apply their existing national laws and regulations for defence exports to third parties in a spirit of cooperation and in a more efficient way'; and (*e*) 'deal with the issue of recognising the political responsibility of the final exporter, taking into account the need for prior consultation with the Participants involved, within the ambit of the EU Code of Conduct on Arms Exports'.[95]

After two years of secret negotiations the six defence secretaries finally adopted a legally binding Framework Agreement Concerning Measures to Facilitate the Restructuring and Operation of the European Defence Industry.[96] This treaty establishes practical measures for improved cooperation on security

1997), pp. 34–45; and International Institute for Strategic Studies, *The Military Balance 1998/99* (Oxford University Press: Oxford, 1998), pp. 276–79.

[92] *The Guardian*, 10 Dec. 1997.

[93] European Commission (note 45).

[94] 'Letter of Intent between six defence ministers on measures to facilitate the restructuring of the European defence industry, signed in London on 6 July 1998', available on the SIPRI Internet site at URL <http://projects.sipri.se/expcon/loi/loisign.htm>.

[95] 'Letter of Intent' (note 94), paras 1.6–1.11.

[96] Framework Agreement between the French Republic, the Federal Republic of Germany, the Italian Republic, the Kingdom of Spain, the Kingdom of Sweden and the United Kingdom of Great Britain and Northern Ireland concerning Measures to Facilitate the Restructuring and Operation of the European Defence Industry, signed at Farnborough on 27 July 2000. Excerpts are reproduced in appendix A and the text is available on the SIPRI Internet site at URL <http://projects.sipri.se/expcon/loi/indrest02.htm>.

of supply, export procedures, handling of classified information, treatment of technical information, research and technology, and harmonization of military requirements. It is subject to ratification by national parliaments and other European countries that share a commitment to its principles will be allowed to join in the future. Whether this latest initiative will put an end to 'knee-jerk protectionism' is difficult to predict. This is partly because of the almost total absence of any substantive public or parliamentary debate within the six countries concerned on the terms and scope of the agreement, and partly because detailed implementation arrangements to further broaden and deepen cooperation will be the subject of additional negotiations.

Given that simplified export licensing procedures are envisaged under the treaty, the new guidelines have important implications for the development of harmonized export controls in the EU, and especially the operation of the EU Code of Conduct on Arms Exports. Part 3 of the Framework Agreement (articles 12–18) refers to transfer and export procedures. The objective of the agreement in this area is to 'bring closer, simplify and reduce, where appropriate, national export control procedures for Transfers and Exports of military goods and technologies' (Article 1).[97] This will be achieved in two ways: (*a*) by simplifying and reducing export control procedures for transfers of defence components on all joint ventures between any of the six signatory countries; and (*b*) by ensuring that export licensing decisions are taken by collective agreement of all states participating in the joint venture.

Initially, export control procedures for transfers of components among the six will be simplified by the introduction of Global Project Licences (Article 12) and the replacement of government issued End-User Certificates with 'company certificates of use' (Article 16). Although other relevant regulations will continue to apply to such transfers (e.g., transit requirements and customs documentation requirements), the aim is simplify and reduce such requirements (Article 18). Indeed, it seems clear that the ultimate aim is to move to licence-free trade for defence goods within the EU (as is currently the case for the vast majority of dual-use goods: see chapter 3).

Under the agreement, participating countries will also agree in advance, by consensus, a list of permitted export destinations for exports of jointly produced weapon systems (Article 13). This confidential 'white list' of agreed destinations will replace existing case-by-case decision making on export licensing. This substitution of national responsibility with collective responsibility is a significant development. It is currently the case, for example, that any state contributing to the manufacture of a jointly produced weapon system can usually (in theory at least[98]) raise objections to a particular export destination.

---

[97] 'Exports' in this context refers to any movement of defence equipment from the 6 participating states to a 3rd party, and 'transfer' means any movement of such goods between the 6 participating states. Framework Agreement (note 96), Article 2 (h) and (n).

[98] The ability of a partner country to influence export policy on collaborative projects was often dependent on that country having a substantial stake in the manufacturing or procurement of the weapon system. It would also depend on the terms of any memorandum of understanding between the parties: see the

This will no longer be the case. The white lists are likely to vary in accordance with the type and sensitivity of the weapon system concerned, although all NATO countries (with the possible exception of Turkey) are almost certain to appear on the vast majority of such lists. Consultations on acceptable export destinations will take into account 'national export control policies, the fulfilment of international commitments, including the EU Code of Conduct criteria, and the protection of the Parties defence interests, including the preservation of a strong and competitive European defence industrial base' (Article 13, 2(a)), but there are no provisions for public or parliamentary scrutiny.

While operational details of the Framework Agreement are still emerging, and may well change during the ratification process, as currently designed they raise a number of arms control concerns.[99] First, the agreement seems likely to reduce the level of transparency surrounding EU arms exports and may undermine some of the progress made in this area in recent years. The introduction of secret lists of approved export destinations is a particular concern, which might be assuaged by the introduction of parliamentary oversight (to ensure that all the permitted export destinations listed fully satisfy the EU Code criteria). It is also unclear how swiftly it will be possible to modify the lists in cases where the political situation in a permitted destination has changed. Removal of a permitted destination is envisaged 'in the event of significant changes in its internal situation, for example, full-scale civil war or a serious deterioration of the human rights situation, or if its behaviour becomes a threat to regional or international peace, security and stability, for example as a result of aggression or the threat of aggression against other nations', but only after a lengthy consultation process among partners of up to three months. However, during the consultation period any of the participating states can apply for a moratorium on exports of the product to the permitted destination in question. At the end of the three-month period, if there is still no consensus on its retention, that destination is then automatically removed from the list (Article 13, 2(b)).

Second, the proposed free circulation of defence components and finished products among the six participating states raises the potential of technology leakage outside EU borders through the weakest points in their control regimes. However, similar fears concerning the free circulation of dual-use goods within the EU have not materialized (see chapter 3).

Third, pressure to meet the level of cooperation envisaged under the agreement and to widen export opportunities may also lead to pressure to lower export control standards to the lowest common denominator. The EU Code is only a minimum set of guidelines, and adoption of simplified procedures could exert pressure to dilute the EU Code criteria, and undermine states maintaining best practice or higher standards.

---

discussions in relation to British, German and Swedish involvement in collaborative projects in Part III of this volume.

[99] Miller, K. and Hitchens, T., *European Accord Threatens to Lower Export Controls,* BASIC Papers no. 33 (British American Security Information Council: London, 2000).

Finally, although the new agreement is designed to give each participating country a voice in the decision-making process, the reality may be somewhat different. For example, each country's influence over the contents of the white list may turn out to be largely proportional to its role in the joint venture. If such a de facto proportional veto system were to emerge, it could 'further weaken European export controls because the countries that are certain to be the biggest contributors to any joint venture—the UK and France—are the countries where the defence industrial base is larger and thus has greater political influence'.[100]

It will also be interesting to see how the EU Commission views the agreement. If it discriminates against defence industries in other EU countries that are excluded from the agreement there may be pressure for the arrangement to be brought within an EU-wide legal framework.

The continuing vitality of Article 223

This chapter began by outlining the obstacle of Article 223. The future of Article 223 remains central to further EU cooperation on export controls. Such cooperation (and the future of Article 223) will depend on what EU-wide structures and policies evolve in three key areas: the SEM (and whether it is extended to the defence market); the CFSP (and in particular the evolution of the European Security and Defence Identity, the ESDI within NATO); and the web of multilateral non-proliferation and trading regimes to which member states already subscribe.

Although any change on Article 223 appears unlikely without deeper integration within the CFSP, it may be that the armament question, including procurement and export control issues, will be the engine for achieving a CFSP in the same way as some analysts regard the euro as the engine for economic union. As a next step, for example, the Commission might want to modernize the 1958 list associated with Article 223, in order to clarify which items fall within the common policy framework of Article 113 and which remain within the framework of Article 223. In the short term, it is difficult to see any revision being made to Article 223. Reforms proposed by the Commission or the European Parliament, for example, have invariably produced protests from industrial groups (although less so now than in the past) and from governments with a strong defence industrial base to protect. As a consequence, certain member states (such as those which are parties to the Framework Agreement) will continue to favour the status quo with regard to Article 223.

However, despite this status quo, the policy-making framework for arms export controls has developed a distinct and growing European dimension in recent years. The extent of this policy convergence is examined in greater detail in chapter 8. In any event, the convergence of arms export control policy should be seen as a long progression, with the subjection of national competences to

---

[100] Miller and Hitchens (note 99), p. 5.

Community competence being the last stage in a long evolutionary process preceded by various transitional stages. The EU is clearly still in the early stages of that process, and anything remotely resembling a common regulatory system remains unlikely while disparities of national practice and attitude continue to exist.

The extent of these disparities and consideration of the question whether they have been lessened by the cooperation described here is the subject of Part III of this book, which will also reveal the difficulties of establishing even a national consensus in this area. EU-wide agreement is significantly more elusive but not impossible, as the previous chapter demonstrated in relation to dual-use goods and technologies.

Part III

Regulations in practice: national export controls in the UK, Germany and Sweden

5. The regulation of arms and dual-use exports in the United Kingdom: towards a self-regulatory model?

I. Introduction

Chapter 2 argued that governments apply export controls for a number of reasons, including commitments to national and collective security, foreign policy, non-proliferation policy and international treaties, as well as concerns about terrorism, internal repression and other human rights violations. In short, most states recognize the need to ensure effective regulation of arms exports and to monitor and supervise the movement of arms. Chapters 3 and 4 examined the extent to which those obligations have been harmonized at the EU level. The purpose of the next three chapters is to provide a detailed picture of how three EU governments carry out this responsibility. The regulatory regimes of the Federal Republic of Germany and Sweden are discussed in chapters 6 and 7, respectively. The UK is the focus of this chapter.

In the opening chapter it was argued that the dynamics and interactions which take place between public policies, policy stakeholders and policy environments are crucial to understanding the formulation of arms export control policy. In recognition of the importance of the interrelationship of those three elements, section II of this chapter examines the political framework for export controls in the UK, including the policy environment for British arms transfers, the role of domestic policy stakeholders, and the role of arms promotion and export financing by public agencies and high-level government officials.

Section III examines the policy-making and administrative structures for regulating arms exports, including the role of the main government departments. Section IV evaluates the impact and outcomes of British arms export control policy: how has arms export control policy impacted on the actual level of arms exported from the UK? Has it reduced proliferation to sensitive destinations? In other words, has the policy process enhanced the situation and resolved problems, had little or no impact, or made matters worse? This assessment is divided into three parts: the post-World War II period up until 1997, in which a policy of supply rather than restraint appeared to dominate British thinking in this area; the seminal arms export scandals from the early 1990s and the subsequent three-year (November 1992–December 1995) Scott Inquiry into defence-related exports to Iraq, which highlighted major shortcomings in the British regulatory regime; and the declaration of a 'new' approach by the incoming Labour government in May 1997.

II. The policy environment and stakeholders

The policy environment

From the late 19th century to the early 1960s, the UK was among the first-tier global arms suppliers. In the early 1950s, for example, large quantities of weapons were delivered to British colonies and ex-colonies and to Western Europe. In the late 1950s and early 1960s, however, British arms exports fell sharply because of competition from other suppliers (most notably France and the former Soviet Union) and because British weapons were proving too expensive. These developments led to a crisis in the British arms industry, the cancellation of many projects and the concentration of production on a narrower range of conventional weapons with a strong export potential.[1] Britain's economic and military decline was such that during the cold war it remained firmly in the shadow of US and Soviet technological dominance, and hence was relegated to second-tier status in the arms supply hierarchy.

Nonetheless, the UK was a major arms exporter and its arms exports during the cold war were therefore closely linked to trends in the international political, strategic and economic environment, with periods of high tension (in the 1960s and early 1980s) often accompanied by increases in British arms exports. This was partly due to increased national defence expenditure and the availability of funds for the development of new weapon systems, and partly due to the drive to recruit anti-communist allies.[2]

During periods when domestic defence expenditure was being cut, as in the late 1960s and early 1970s, the weapons exported were sometimes better than those deployed with the country's own armed forces. However, the vigorous export policy during this period did lead to a partial recovery of market share. This market share was held and even increased at some points in the 1970s and 1980s, mainly as a result of exports to the developing world. In the period 1973–76, for example, 76 per cent of British arms exports (deliveries) were to developing countries, and this had risen to nearly 82 per cent by 1981–84.[3] An even more aggressive approach to arms sales under the government of Prime Minister Margaret Thatcher in the 1980s entrenched the UK's position as a leading second-tier arms exporter and enabled the UK to continue to improve its share of a declining market in the 1990s. However, as discussed later, this improvement was almost totally dependent on one deal—the Al Yamamah contract with Saudi Arabia.

[1] Krause, K., *Arms and the State: Patterns of Military Production and Trade* (Cambridge University Press: Cambridge, 1992), p. 134.

[2] Macdonald, G., 'UK arms exports: government policy, procedures and practice', *RUSI Journal*, Oct. 1995, p. 47.

[3] Ohlson, T. (ed.), SIPRI, *Arms Transfer Limitations and Third World Security* (Oxford University Press: Oxford, 1988), table 8.1, p. 131.

Table 5.1. Exports of British defence equipment: deliveries and identified orders, 1975–98[a]

Figures are in £m., current prices.

	1975	1980	1985	1990	1994	1995	1996	1997	1998
Identified defence equipment deliveries[b]	198	537	813	1 980	1 798	2 076	3 402	4 598	3 527
Estimates of additional aerospace equipment[c]	279	1 000	940	2 487	1 148	2 647	2 775	2 087	..
Identified defence export orders	..	815	2 688	4 735	4 608	4 970	5 080	5 540	6 049

Notes:

[a] Changes in the coverage of the data which occurred in 1985 and 1992 cast doubt on the reliability of the figures as a guide to the trends in exports.

[b] These figures are derived from Customs tariff headings that can reasonably be allocated wholly to defence (and thus exclude all dual-use transfers).

[c] These figures are based on estimates provided by the Society of British Aerospace Companies (SBAC) and include dual-use transfers to defence customers.

.. = Figures not available or not applicable.

Source: British Ministry of Defence, *UK Defence Statistics 1999* (Stationery Office: London, 1999), table 1.13, p. 18.

Thus, although total world arms exports declined by nearly 50 per cent in real terms between 1986–88 and 1994–96,[4] British defence exports only fell by 6 per cent during the same period. Moreover, the UK's share of total world exports of armaments rose from 7.4 per cent in 1986–88 to 13.7 per cent in 1994–96.[5] Other statistical sources regularly place the UK among the top five arms exporters in the world during the 1990s. SIPRI data, for example, rank the UK as the fourth-largest supplier with approximately 6.6 per cent of the global share of deliveries of major conventional weapons during 1995–99.[6] Measuring in terms of defence equipment 'orders', domestic British sources often indicated an even higher share of the global market. With orders worth approximately £5 billion in 1995 (see table 5.1), the UK claimed to be the second-largest supplier after the USA, with approximately 20 per cent of global orders.[7]

Two key factors contributed to the UK's increased share of a declining global market in the 1990s—the structure of the decline in the international market and the cushioning effects of one major British contract.[8] First, the decline in the regional export markets to which the UK exports the bulk of its arms—the

---

[4] US Arms Control and Disarmament Agency (ACDA), *World Military Expenditures and Arms Transfers 1997* (ACDA: Washington, DC, 1998), table II.

[5] *World Military Expenditures and Arms Transfers 1997* (note 4), table II.

[6] Hagelin, B., Wezeman, P. D. and Wezeman, S. T., 'Transfers of major conventional weapons', *SIPRI Yearbook 2000: Armaments, Disarmament and International Security* (Oxford University Press: Oxford, 2000), table 7A.2, p. 372.

[7] British House of Commons, *Statement on the Defence Estimates 1996*, Cm 3233 (Her Majesty's Stationery Office: London, May 1996), p. 71.

[8] Cooper, N., *The Business of Death: Britain's Arms Trade at Home and Abroad* (Tauris Academic Studies: London, 1997), pp. 133–37.

Table 5.2. Major recipients of British arms exports, 1994–96 and 1997–99
Figures are in current prices. Figures in italic are percentages.

1994–96			1997–99		
Country	Arms purchases (US $m.)	%% of UK arms exports	Country	Arms purchases (£m.)	%% of UK arms exports
Saudi Arabia	11 200	*68.0*	Saudi Arabia	2 511	*39.8*
USA	950	*5.8*	France	767	*12.2*
Malaysia	950	*5.8*	Germany	516	*8.2*
Oman	750	*4.6*	UAE	328	*5.2*
Indonesia	725	*4.4*	Indonesia	287	*4.6*
Kuwait	675	*4.1*	Malaysia	241	*3.8*
UAE	260	*1.6*	USA	224	*3.5*

Note: UAE = United Arab Emirates.

Sources: **1994–96**: US Arms Control and Disarmament Agency (ACDA), *World Military Expenditures and Arms Transfers 1997* (ACDA: Washington, DC, 1998), table III; **1997–99**: British Ministry of Defence, Foreign and Commonwealth Office, and Department of Trade and Industry, *Annual Report on Strategic Export Controls*, 1997, 1998 and 1999.

Middle East, South-East Asia, North America and NATO Europe—was far less dramatic than that in the global arms market. Indeed, the largest declines occurred in regions where the UK has not traditionally been a major player, including the former Warsaw Pact region, North and Sub-Saharan Africa, and Central and South America. However, as a result of the economic crisis in South-East Asia in late 1997 and early 1998 a number of important orders were cancelled or postponed. Second, the worst effects of the declining global market were cushioned by just one contract, the Al Yamamah contract with Saudi Arabia. This reliance is reflected in the fact that during 1994–96 arms exports to Saudi Arabia made up 68 per cent of all British arms exports (as shown in table 5.2). By 1997–99 this had fallen to 39.8 per cent. In 1999 it was less than 15 per cent and Malaysia had replaced Saudi Arabia as the largest single recipient of British defence goods by value for that year.[9]

The UK's position as a major second-tier exporter in the conventional arms market is a reflection of its extensive product range. In the air sector, this product range includes the Hawk attack aircraft, the Tornado, and the Lynx and the EH-101 helicopters, and in future will include the Eurofighter 2000. In the land sector, it includes the Challenger II tank, the GKN Warrior armoured personnel carrier, the Alvis Scorpion light tank, air defence systems, guns and other military vehicles. In the naval sector, it includes Type 23 frigates, mine hunters, corvettes, fast patrol boats and surplus Royal Navy ships. Finally, in

[9] British Ministry of Defence, Foreign and Commonwealth Office, and Department of Trade and Industry, *Annual Report on Strategic Export Controls* (Foreign and Commonwealth Office: London, Nov. 1999), table 4, pp. 299–301.

the dual-use sector it includes image intensifiers, thermal imaging, avionics, radar, sonar, and communication and information systems.

British export control policy was also heavily influenced by external environmental factors in the early 1990s, particularly the end of the cold war and the conflict in the Persian Gulf. The end of the cold war led to a shift in the focus of Western export controls on dual-use technologies away from controls against the former Soviet bloc to non-proliferation objectives concerning WMD and 'rogue states'. Not only did this result in a reduction in the scope of the controls (i.e., shorter control lists), but in the UK this shift in concentration by the Ministry of Defence (MOD), the Foreign and Commonwealth Office (FCO) and the security services in particular was accompanied by a 'relative lack of concern' about conventional arms production and transfers.[10] Indeed, in respect of dual-use goods and technologies for conventional weapons, the British export control regime in the mid-1990s moved very much to a self-regulatory regime of open licences.[11]

The 1980–88 Iraq–Iran War and 1991 Persian Gulf War, and especially the public debate about the UK's role in arming Iraq, led to a great deal of soul-searching within the policy-making community, calls for a more balanced approach to the conventional arms trade, a number of administrative changes and an ongoing process of reform that has still to run its course (as discussed below). In addition, the enhanced role of UN and other sanctions in the post-cold war era (see chapter 2) and the process of EU harmonization discussed in chapters 3 and 4 became increasingly important determinants of the UK's national export control policy in the 1990s.

The role of domestic policy stakeholders

Proponents of arms transfer restraint

With a few notable exceptions, most recently during and since the 'Arms to Iraq' case (discussed below), all the major political parties, the British Parliament as a whole and the general public have traditionally displayed a distinct lack of interest in the issue of defence exports. In Parliament, opposition has been restricted to a small number of MPs across all parties, predominantly Labour or Liberal Democrat. During an eight-year period in the 1970s, for example, only 13 MPs 'demonstrated a continuing interest in one aspect or another of arms sales', even though 261 parliamentary questions were tabled

---

[10] British House of Commons, *The Right Honourable Sir Richard Scott, Report of the Inquiry into the Export of Defence Equipment and Dual-Use Goods to Iraq and Related Prosecutions: Return to an Address of the Honourable the House of Commons dated 15th February*, HC 1995/96 115 (Her Majesty's Stationery Office: London, 1996), 5 vols and index (hereafter the Scott Report), paras D5.32-35, pp. 539–40. In this respect see also British House of Commons, Foreign Affairs Committee, *Second Report, UK Policy on Weapons Proliferation and Arms Control in the Post-Cold War Era*, HC 1994/95 34-I and 34-II (Her Majesty's Stationery Office: London, 30 Mar. 1995), vols I and II.

[11] British Department of Trade and Industry (DTI), 'Controls eased on exports to former Eastern bloc', DTI press notice, P/94/314, 25 May 1994.

over the same period.[12] There is also a perception that the public is ambivalent about arms exports—'at once suspicious of the motives of the players involved, and yet pleased when new orders appear to secure employment'[13]—and that opponents of arms sales are not representative of the public as a whole. This opposition tends to be located in a number of well-organized NGOs, such as the Campaign Against Arms Trade (CAAT), Saferworld, Amnesty International UK and the World Development Movement, and among smaller political parties which are not represented at Westminster, such as the Green Party. Overall this is by no means a small constituency. Amnesty International UK, for example, has 130 000 members and 330 local groups,[14] while the CAAT claims that approximately 75–80 MPs broadly (and somewhat passively) support its tough stance on arms exports.[15]

However, there was a growing public and political constituency in favour of greater restraint in the late 1990s, precipitated by three main factors: (*a*) the post-Gulf War revelations, trials and public inquiry into Britain's role in arming Iraq; (*b*) the high-profile involvement of the late Princess of Wales in the search for a global ban on landmines; and (*c*) the higher profile given to the issue by the Labour Party in the 1990s, both while in opposition and after forming the government in 1997. Together these three factors provoked a vigorous debate about some of the assumptions that underlie the UK's approach to the control of arms and strategic exports. Indeed, an opinion poll carried out in May 1998 on behalf of a number of NGOs suggested that British arms exports to repressive regimes were opposed by 90 per cent of the British public, with 79 per cent backing stronger restrictions even if that led to redundancies.[16]

Opponents of arms transfer restraint

Broadly speaking, since the end of World War II and until quite recently there existed a cross-party and media consensus on the utility of arms exports.[17] Although the Conservative Party is the traditional ally of defence exporters, the Labour Party and the Liberal Democrats have been equally eager to promote the well-being of the defence manufacturing base through the maximization of exports. However, this cross-party consensus appears to have ended, with the Labour Party (and the Liberal Democrats) now committed to a policy of greater restraint, and with certain sections of the media now taking a much more critical approach in their reporting of arms sales.

[12] Edmonds, M., 'The domestic and international aspects of British arms sales', ed. C. Cannizzo, *The Gun Merchants: Politics and Policies of the Major Arms Suppliers* (Pergamon Press: Oxford, 1980), p. 80.

[13] Miller, D., *Export or Die* (Cassell: London, 1996), p. 30.

[14] Amnesty International UK Section, 'Response to the consultation document of the Department of Trade and Industry on strategic export controls', London, Nov. 1996, p. 3.

[15] Personal interviews with Will McMahon, CAAT, 8 July, 1997.

[16] 'Ban arms sales to pariah states, say 9 out of 10', *The Observer*, 24 May 1998.

[17] The uncritical praise of the 1988 arms sale to Saudi Arabia is illustrative. See, e.g., Urban, M. and Fagan, M., 'Britain wins £10bn Saudi arms order', *The Independent*, 9 July 1988; and Fairhall, D., 'Britain signs £6 billion Saudi arms contract', *The Guardian*, 9 July 1988.

It can be taken as a constant, of course, that the defence companies are pro-sales and that they will continue to mount a vigorous defence of the status quo—or continue to stress the need for further deregulation. An extract from the Defence Manufacturers Association's (DMA) submission to the 1996 consultation exercise by the Department of Trade and Industry (DTI) is illustrative:

The trend over the last five decades, as successive Governments have become confused between licensing criteria and genuine defence and security considerations, has clearly been towards a more all-embracing export control regime, covering increasing numbers of goods to all destinations, and this trend must be reversed . . . We believe that one of the most promising means of possible simplification would be through the further expansion of the Open Licensing System, which could remove a very high proportion of applications currently being submitted.[18]

While the demand for greater simplification of an undoubtedly complex regime is understandable, many in the defence industry also argue that the right to export strategic goods should not be subject to foreign policy constraints.[19] Instead of the 'blunt instrument' of strategic export controls, they argue that other controls and pressures (such as the threat of removal from the MOD's contract list) could be applied to deter companies from pursuing contracts with repressive regimes.[20]

It is also clear that the defence industries enjoy regular contact with policy makers, by lobbying government either individually (generally only the larger companies) or via trade associations such as the DMA or the Machine Tools Trade Association (MTTA). In addition, the defence manufacturers have several advocates of their interests within the government machinery itself, mainly within the MOD's Defence Export Services Organisation (DESO), but also inside the FCO, the DTI and other parts of the MOD. Within this intimate government–company relationship, every effort is made to stress (and sometimes inflate) the business and employment benefits of proposed exports.[21]

Government promotion of arms exports

The British Government has traditionally used senior officials to promote arms exports. Since the early 1980s, under pressure of export interests, such officials (including government ministers, ambassadors and even prime ministers) were increasingly willing to intervene to influence competitions in favour of British defence companies. The successful competition against France for the sale of Tornado aircraft to Saudi Arabia is the most prominent example.

---

[18] 'Response of the Defence Manufacturers Association to the issues raised in the Department of Trade and Industry's consultative document on strategic export controls', DMA (undated), pp. 10–11.

[19] Sir Richard Scott also questioned the use of export controls as an instrument of foreign policy. Scott Report (note 10), paras K2.17–20, pp. 1764–66.

[20] Personal interviews with British officials, 1997.

[21] The influence of defence companies on government decision making on defence exports is discussed by Miller (note 13), pp. 31–32. See also Cooper (note 8), pp. 178–79. A specific example of such insider influence (the proposed Hawk deal to Iraq) is discussed in the Scott Report (note 10), paras D6.29–54, pp. 572–86.

The Al Yamamah (Al Yamamah is a region of Saudi Arabia) project is the largest British defence export package in history and one of the most controversial.[22] As prime contractor, British Aerospace (BAe) is responsible for managing the project, although production is shared both with its partners in Germany and Italy and among hundreds of smaller subcontractors. The project 'began' in September 1985—although it has its roots in the sale of British military aircraft to the Kingdom of Saudi Arabia in the 1960s—with an initial agreement between the British and Saudi governments, followed by a formal Memorandum of Understanding (MOU) in February 1986. The primary contract value has been estimated at approximately $7.6 billion, but the value of the total package (phases I and II, plus life-cycle support) is thought to be nearer $20 billion.[23] The British Government purchased the aircraft from BAe and dispatched them, along with spare parts, missiles and trainers, to Riyadh in return for oil shipments.[24]

In addition to the oil-for-weapons barter arrangement, the Saudis also insisted on a 35 per cent offset arrangement. Given that BAe was clearly unable to make such a large investment in Saudi Arabia's limited defence industry, the British Government instead made a commitment to promote high-technology industrialization in Saudi Arabia through indirect offsets. Under this arrangement, the British Government (in conjunction with British companies) was required to achieve an investment target of $1 billion (25 per cent of the technical sales cost of phase I) over a 10-year period. This $1 billion target was expected to double as part of phase II.[25]

While the Al Yamamah project is the most spectacular example of the scale and complexity of the British Government's involvement in the arms trade, it is by no means unique. Although the prime responsibility for defence export sales lies with industry, it has long been government policy to 'actively support such

<hr>

[22] In 1989 the National Audit Office began an investigation into the Al Yamamah arms deals, but the 1992 report has never been published. Foot, P., *The Guardian*, 31 Jan. 1994.

[23] The initial phase of the project resulted in the sale and delivery of 102 military aircraft to Saudi Arabia—48 Tornado Interdictor Strike (IDS) aircraft, 24 Tornado Air Defence Variant (ADV) aircraft and 30 Hawk Mk.65 advanced jet trainers. This initial phase included a weapons package, infrastructural support programmes and—according to a Channel 4 television Dispatches programme broadcast on 11 Jan. 1995—the supply of 8000 German-made electro-shock batons. It also included a government commitment to buy older British aircraft back from Saudi Arabia and cover any financial shortfalls. In Jan. 1993, the 2nd contract for a further 48 Tornado IDS aircraft was agreed between Prime Minister John Major and King Fahd, ruler of Saudi Arabia. This 2nd phase, which was originally outlined in 1988, also includes military infrastructure, aircraft shelters, support, maintenance, spares and other weapon systems, including 60 more BAe Hawk jet trainers, 88 Black Hawk helicopters and several minehunting vessels. Shifrin, C., 'Saudi Tornado order activates BAe assembly line', *Aviation Week & Space Technology*, 8 Feb. 1993, p. 27; and Matthews, R. *et al.*, 'Offsets: taking a strategic view', *Jane's Defence Weekly*, 5 Feb. 1994, pp. 23–30.

[24] During the late 1980s and early 1990s, Saudi Arabia normally paid for the weapons by daily setting aside hundreds of thousands of barrels of crude oil at market prices. The level was as high as 600 000 barrels per day (b/d) when the price of crude oil fell, and this was supplemented by a cash payment of £1.5 billion in 1992 as part of the continuing contract. The fluctuations in oil prices and dollar-to-pound exchange rates have also caused delays in Saudi payments, in turn provoking BAe into obtaining up to $2 billion in bridging loans to ease its cash-flow problems.

[25] By 1994, however, only 3 offset investments had been made, and unless the pace of inward investment quickened Saudi Arabia was expected to demand that the offset commitments be treated as credits against the arms sales. Matthews *et al.* (note 23).

exports wherever this is compatible with the United Kingdom's wider strategic, political and security interests'.[26]

This section examines the origins and nature of that support, and in particular the roles of the DESO and the Export Credits Guarantee Department (ECGD).

The Defence Export Services Organisation

In the years immediately after World War II private industry (as opposed to the government) was responsible for finding arms export markets.[27] Compared with those of other European countries, the British arms industry emerged from the war relatively unscathed and initially enjoyed moderate success in exporting its arms. Sales went mostly to captive markets within colonial regimes and Commonwealth countries. By the mid-1950s, however, sales began to fall, mainly because of competition from the USA—Britain's changing and smaller role in the world meant that it could not afford to match the massive US military aid effort—and other new suppliers, such as the former Soviet Union and France. The erosion of Britain's traditional arms market was evidenced by its military aircraft sales to the Middle East and North Africa: between 1945 and 1955 the UK supplied 95 per cent of the aircraft to those regions, but in the following decade its share of the market fell to less than 10 per cent.[28]

In order to allow the country to compete successfully in what was expected to be a growing aerospace market, the then Labour Secretary of State for Defence, Denis Healey, appointed Raymond Brown, a businessman from the electronics sector, as the first head of the Defence Sales Organisation (DSO, located within the MOD) in January 1966.

Throughout the 1960s and 1970s the DSO was responsible for promoting the export of British defence equipment and for selling defence products manufactured by the government-owned Royal Ordnance Factories. In 1983 the Royal Ordnance Factories assumed responsibility for selling their own products and the Defence Sales Organisation concentrated solely on supporting industry. Its title was changed in 1985 to the Defence Export Services Organisation. Today, the DESO, which remains part of the Procurement Executive within the MOD, acts as a focal point for the various sources of government support to defence exporters. In particular, it advises the Minister for Defence Procurement and the Secretary of State for Defence on export strategy and actively assists industry through regional marketing, overseas offices, market research, exhibitions and military support facilities. It is also directly involved in the negotiation and administration of government-to-government transactions.[29]

---

[26] British National Audit Office, *Ministry of Defence: Support for Defence Exports*, HC 1988/99 303 (Her Majesty's Stationery Office: London, 10 Apr. 1989), p. 1.

[27] From 1945 to 1965, the 3 branches of the armed forces each had separate sales organizations which provided some assistance to industry in securing orders, but such assistance was insignificant compared with the vigorous marketing function adopted later by the DESO.

[28] Thayer, G., *The War Business: The International Trade in Armaments* (Simon & Schuster: New York, 1969), p. 259.

[29] See, e.g., Thomas, A., 'Attacked from all sides: the UK 20 per cent in the arms market?', *RUSI Journal*, Feb. 1994.

With a staff of approximately 350 and an annual operating budget of approximately £56 million (in 1997–98), the DESO is divided into several functional directorates. Four regional marketing directorates with individual marketing desks provide advice and assistance on specific markets and projects, coordinate British marketing efforts through overseas sales teams and negotiate with customer countries. The Marketing Services Directorate carries out worldwide market information research and surveys, collates data on overseas defence markets and trends, and maintains equipment inventories of potential customer countries. The Defence Exports Services Secretariat formulates policy, is the focal point for British obligations under multilateral control regimes, considers compliance with government policy and security implications, and coordinates MOD assessment of AWP[30] and export licence applications. The staff under the Military Deputy to the Head of Defence Export Services (HDES) arrange for the use of service personnel for equipment demonstrations and the training of military personnel from overseas countries buying British equipment, and organize equipment exhibitions in the UK and overseas.[31]

DESO staff are also based in 12 overseas capitals[32] and close contact is maintained with the defence attachés in other British embassies and high commissions around the world. Some key senior posts, including that of head of the organization, are normally filled by secondment from private industry.[33] Its marketing activities and much of its military support services are currently provided to industry free of charge, although charges are levied for navy and army equipment exhibitions, loans of equipment and demonstrations.[34] In 1995, the DESO coordinated the development of a five-point export strategy for the defence sector which involved: the identification and ranking of the top 20 countries likely to purchase British defence equipment in the next five years; the completion of a strategic marketing plan for each country identified; more proactive marketing with clear milestones in each plan; offering 'packages not products' that will benefit the armed forces, industry and economy of the customer country; and increased concentration on logistics and after-sales support.[35]

The DESO also works with the MOD Procurement Executive to ensure that overseas sales potential is considered in the procurement of equipment for the British Armed Forces. Thus, overall, the DESO is clearly associated with the interests of defence companies and, in particular, allows the defence manu-

---

[30] See section III in this chapter.

[31] British Ministry of Defence, 'The Defence Export Services Organisation', June 1997.

[32] Known as First Secretaries Defence Sales (FSDS), these specialist salesmen are located in the embassies in Ankara, Bangkok, Bonn, Canberra, Jakarta, Kuala Lumpur, Kuwait, New Delhi, Paris, Riyadh, Seoul and Washington, DC. British Ministry of Defence, 'Britain's defence procurement', Ministry of Defence, London, 1993, p. 45.

[33] E.g., the current head of the DESO, Tony Edwards, took up his appointment on 14 Dec. 1998 on secondment from TI Group plc.

[34] In addition, the sale by private contractors of equipment originally designed in MOD research and development (R&D) establishments brings in annual royalties of around £50–80 million. This Commercial Exploitation Levy was worth £53.9 million in 1997/98.

[35] *Jane's Defence Weekly*, 9 Sep. 1995. See also Masefield, C. (former Head of the DESO), 'Defence exports: the challenge ahead', *RUSI Journal*, Aug. 1995, pp. 15–18.

facturer to 'wave the flag *inside*'[36] the government bureaucracy (through the secondment of industrial personnel).[37]

The Export Credits Guarantee Department

The ECGD's role as the supplier of export credit guarantees is as important as the promotion function of the DESO.[38] The ECGD provides support for both military and civil exports, including insurance cover for exporters against non-payment by overseas customers (up to a maximum of 90 per cent of the total due, but usually 75–80 per cent in respect of defence sales); unconditional guarantees to British lending banks covering 100 per cent repayment of export finance; and interest-rate subsidies for certain export markets, mostly within developing countries. Without these provisions many arms exports would never take place: 'The willingness of United Kingdom exporters to bid for overseas defence contracts and of the lending banks to provide loan finance often depends on the availability of Export Credits Guarantee Department cover and fixed interest rates which can have the effect of providing a subsidy for sales to developing countries'.[39]

The decision to provide cover on large military contracts is taken by the Export Guarantee Committee (EGC), an interdepartmental committee chaired by the Treasury. The EGC also sets the credit limit for individual countries (covering both civil and defence exports) which are ranked in four lists according to their potential to default. List A, for example, contains those countries presenting least risk, such as most NATO countries and EU member states, while List D comprises past defaulters and a number of the poorer African states.[40] In exceptional circumstances—for example, for very large military sales to a marginally creditworthy country—the case is referred to ministers for a decision.[41] In June 1988 an additional facility of £1 billion was introduced to cover the larger military contracts that could not be accommodated within the normal country limits. Indeed, the proportion of export guarantees going to defence projects increased markedly in the late 1980s and early 1990s. In the first half of the 1980s, for example, export credits for defence projects accounted for approximately 10 per cent of the total on average. In the nine-year period to 1997–98 the figure had risen to 25 per cent and even went as high as 48 per cent in 1993–94 (see table 5.3). Moreover, it is not unusual for states to default on export credits. For example, by February 1996 the ECGD

---

[36] Pearson, F., 'The question of control in British defence sales policy', *International Affairs,* vol. 59, no. 2 (spring 1983), p. 215.

[37] For a detailed analysis of the influence of industrial secondees within the DESO see Miller (note 13), pp. 43–49.

[38] Export credit guarantees are a type of insurance cover for risk of loss as a result of such factors as exchange rate fluctuations or non-payment by the purchaser. They can allow access to financing for exporters extending credit to their customers and for overseas customers borrowing directly from banks.

[39] *Ministry of Defence: Support for Defence Exports* (note 26), p. 29.

[40] Phythian, M. and Little, W., 'Administering Britain's arms trade', *Public Administration,* vol. 71 (autumn 1993), p. 274.

[41] *Ministry of Defence: Support for Defence Exports* (note 26), pp. 29–30.

Table 5.3. ECGD support devoted to defence exports, 1989/90–1997/98

Figures are in £m., current prices. Figures in italics are percentages.

	Defence cover	Total cover	Defence as % of total cover
1989/90	378	1 959	*19*
1990/91	640	2 300	*28*
1991/92	276	2 095	*13*
1992/93	1 591	3 803	*42*
1993/94	1 973	4 086	*48*
1994/95	543	3 005	*18*
1995/96	841	4 062	*21*
1996/97	374	2 613	*14*
1997/98	763	3 166	*24*
Annual average	819	3 009	*25*

Source: British Export Credits Guarantee Department, *Annual Report,* various years.

had paid out £696 million on claims relating to Iraq, most of it since the Gulf War.[42]

Following a review of the aims, objectives, role and status of the ECGD by the new Labour government in July 1999, a new mission statement was agreed for the ECGD in July 2000. This requires the ECGD to 'benefit the UK economy by helping exporters of UK goods and services win business and UK firms to invest overseas, by providing guarantees, insurance and re-insurance against loss, taking into account the Government's international policies'. The ECGD will also be required to 'ensure its activities accord with other Government objectives, including those on sustainable development, human rights, good governance and trade'.[43] However, there is no change in the use of ECGD support to promote arms exports.

'Aid for arms'

Unlike some arms-exporting countries,[44] the UK has never had a policy of targeting aid towards countries that purchase British military equipment. In the 1980s, however, some linkage between British aid and British arms sales to developing countries did take place, although the scope and nature of that linkage are disputed.[45] The most notorious example was the linking of

[42] British House of Commons, *Parliamentary Debates: Official Report* (hereafter *Hansard)*, written answers, 26 Feb. 1996, col. 337. See also Norton-Taylor, R. and Leigh, D., 'For sale (credit available for Iraqis)', *The Guardian*, 17 Feb. 1998.

[43] British House of Commons, *International Development, Sixth Special Report: Government Response to the First Report from the Committee, Session 1999/2000: The Export Credits Guarantee Department—Development Issues*, HC 1999/2000 862 (Stationery Office: London, 2000), appendix, para. 2.

[44] In the USA, e.g., about 35% of the foreign aid budget—amounting to $5 billion in 1992—was devoted to direct grants or loans to foreign governments for the purchase of US military equipment. Hartung, W., 'Curbing the arms trade: from rhetoric to restraint', *World Policy Journal*, vol. 9, no. 3 (spring 1992), p. 239.

[45] For a sober assessment see Macdonald (note 2), pp. 51–53.

£1.3 billion of British defence contracts with £234 million of British aid to the Pergau hydroelectric dam project in Malaysia.[46] In many of the other suspected cases much of the evidence is circumstantial, although there is a strong correlation between arms contracts and disproportionate increases in aid to countries such as Indonesia, Jordan, Nigeria, Oman and Thailand.[47] Indonesia, for example, agreed to buy Hawk military jets from BAe in June 1993 at a total cost of £500 million only two months after Foreign Secretary Douglas Hurd had visited Indonesia to agree a £65 million 'soft loan' for a power station to be built by a British company.[48] A confidential report by the National Audit Office confirmed that £65 million given in aid to India in 1984 was used to purchase 21 Westland helicopters. The decision to support Westland in the Indian deal was described as 'catastrophic': the British Government lost £105 million (the DTI had already given Westland £41 million to develop the helicopter) and the helicopters were in service in India for less than two years before being mothballed after two fatal crashes.[49]

Other government actors

A number of other government actors and agencies are (or have been) prominently involved in arms export promotion in the UK. These include International Military Services (IMS, 1967–91),[50] the Disposal Sales Agency (DSA, 1990–), a subsidiary of the DESO which is responsible for the sale of British surplus equipment in the UK and in Germany,[51] and military or service

[46] British House of Commons, Public Accounts Committee, *Seventh Report, Pergau Hydro-Electric Project*, HC 1993/94 7 (Her Majesty's Stationery Office: London, 21 Mar. 1994); and Foreign Affairs Committee, *Public Expenditure: The Pergau Hydro-Electric Project, Malaysia, The Aid and Trade Provisions and Related Matters, Third Report*, HC 1993/94 271-I (Her Majesty's Stationery Office: London, 1994), vol. 1. See also *The Times*, 8 Feb. 1994; and *The Observer*, 30 Jan. 1994.

[47] World Development Movement (WDM), *Gunrunners Gold: How the Public's Money Finances Arms Sales* (WDM: London, 1995), p. 15.

[48] British National Audit Office, *Overseas Development: Aid to Indonesia*, HC 1996/97 101 (Her Majesty's Stationery Office: London, Nov. 1996).

[49] 'Government lost £105 m on aid deal', *The Guardian*, 3 Mar. 1998.

[50] Millbank Technical Services was established in 1967 to promote exports of defence services and dual-use equipment, mainly to the former Shah of Iran. In 1979, the company changed its name to IMS and effectively became a wholly-owned subsidiary of the MOD. Its basic function was to provide multiple contracts with foreign customers and arrange ECGD credit and other support services for them. IMS ceased trading on 31 July 1991 following the decline in government-to-government contracts. For a detailed discussion of the IMS see Phythian and Little (note 40), pp. 271–72; and Pearson (note 36), pp. 232–34.

[51] The Directorate of Sales (Disposals) was made responsible for the sale of surplus equipment in Apr. 1990 to centralize the disposal function, and in Aug. 1991 took responsibility for the disposal operation in Germany. The Directorate was given agency status in 1994 and became the DSA. With 101 staff (1994 figures), including 42 civilian and industrial staff in Germany, the DSA's remit is to maximize the returns from the sale of surplus equipment, including capital equipment, smaller weapons and stores. Commercial contracts with private-sector companies are used to maximize the sale of bulk stores, allowing the agency to concentrate its own resources on larger capital equipment sales to foreign governments. In the 8-year period 1987/88 to 1994/95 inclusive, receipts from surplus sales totalled £458.5 million. Overseas sales of major equipment, predominantly ex-Royal Navy warships, are the most financially rewarding. Over the 10 years to the start of 1992 the agency sold 35 warships to other governments, raising £135 million. For a detailed discussion of the role of the DSA see Davis, I. and Schofield, S., *Upgrades and Surplus Weapons: Lessons from the UK Disposal Sales Agency*, BICC Papers no. 11 (Bonn International Center for Conversion: Bonn, Aug. 1997).

attachés—officers of the armed forces posted to British embassies and high commissions around the world.[52]

All the structures and measures discussed so far have been designed to promote arms exports. In the following it will become clear that some of these agencies, especially the DESO, are also involved in the making of policy on and the administration of arms export controls.

III. The British arms export control regime

The policy-making structure

Principal legislation

Under the 1939 Import, Export and Customs Powers (Defence) Act—an emergency measure taken at the outbreak of World War II and later made permanent by the 1990 Import and Export Control Act—the British Government can prohibit or regulate the export or import of any goods or services.[53] A new Export Control Bill was introduced in Parliament on 26 June 2001. This followed publication of a draft bill on 29 March 2001 for public consultation.[54] Once it becomes law the Export Control Act will replace the 1939 Act and provide new powers that are expected to strengthen the UK export control regime while also providing greater accountability to Parliament.

However, this primary or enabling legislation only provides the government with the power to make and enforce export regulations. The main export control regulations are currently set out in a statutory instrument to the 1939 Act, namely the 1994 Export of Goods (Control) Orders (EGCO),[55] which lists the goods to be controlled, defines terms, and establishes offences and penalties for violation of the regulations. The EGCO has traditionally been the basis of British export controls and is amended periodically to take account of changes in military technology and political changes.[56] Britain's membership of several of the international regulatory regimes discussed in chapter 2 helps determine the composition of the EGCO.[57] Until July 1995 this statutory instrument

---

[52] There are some 140 service attachés in 109 countries. They provide market information for the DESO and direct assistance to defence exporters. Support for defence sales is only part of their work and the extent of their involvement varies from post to post. *Ministry of Defence: Support for Defence Exports* (note 26), pp. 3, 21–26. These figures were broadly confirmed during personal interviews, 1997.

[53] Prior to 1939, the statutory basis for export controls derived primarily from the 1879 Customs and Inland Revenue Act and a number of subsequent acts, although the power to grant licences was exercised by the Privy Council on a non-statutory basis at least as far back as the 18th century. On the current legislation and the pre-1939 background see Scott Report (note 10), part I, chapter C1, pp. 49–105.

[54] British Department of Trade and Industry, *Consultation on Draft Legislation, the Export Control and Non-Proliferation Bill*, Cm 5091 (Stationery Office: London, Mar. 2001).

[55] British Customs and Excise, Export of Goods (Control) Order 1994, Statutory Instrument no. 1991 (1994), *Statutory Instruments, 1994* (Her Majesty's Stationery Office: London, 1994). Amendments to statutory instruments can normally be introduced at any time without parliamentary procedure and thus relatively quickly. New secondary legislation is expected to be introduced after the Export Control Bill 2001 becomes law.

[56] As at May 2000, there had been 15 amendments to the 1994 EGCO.

[57] E.g., because the UK is a signatory of the MTCR, exports of items such as laser radar, analog-to-digital converters and wind tunnels are restricted.

contained all the UK's export licensing controls, but now it only covers controls on military equipment (following the removal of dual-use controls).

Since July 1995, there have been major changes in the legal basis of British export controls resulting from the introduction of the EC Regulation on Dual-Use Goods and Technologies (discussed in chapter 3). To bring the British system into line with the EC Regulation, which is directly applicable in UK law, new regulations—the Dual-Use and Related Goods (Export Control) Regulations (DUEC)—were introduced in July 1995.[58] From that date, the EGCO no longer applied to dual-use and nuclear goods, but it remains extant in respect of military or military-related exports. The DUEC directly refers to the Annexe I and Annexe IV EC control lists and includes additional national controls for certain dual-use goods not covered by the EC Regulation.[59] It also includes the EC Article 4 'catch-all' end-use control, and defines the violations and penalties associated with breaches of the regulations. The 1995 DUEC was replaced in November 1996 by a new DUEC (which has since been amended eight times). The 1996 DUEC will in turn be superseded by new legislation needed to implement the new EC Regulation on dual-use goods which was adopted in June 2000 (see chapter 3).

Few procedural changes were necessary to implement the EC dual-use regulation as most of its features were already to be found in the British regime. The main change has been that in most cases a licence issued for dual-use goods in one member state is valid for exporters from the other 14. Although most dual-use goods moving between member states no longer require a licence, exporters are still required to register with the DTI within 30 days of exporting such goods and to keep records of such movements for a minimum of three years.

The British regulations as at May 2000 thus comprised two statutory instruments: the Export of Goods (Control Order) 1994, as amended; and the Dual-Use and Related Goods (Export Control) Regulations 1996, as amended.

The legal basis for enforcing the regulations is the 1979 Customs and Excise Management Act. Evasion of British export controls is a criminal offence for which the penalty can be an unlimited fine and up to seven years' imprisonment. Under recent legislation there is an additional sanction of confiscation of the profit of a previously successful crime. Penalties for offences in connection with the falsification of export licences are less severe—either a fine or up to two years' imprisonment.

Trade sanctions and arms embargoes imposed in accordance with resolutions of the UN Security Council are implemented in the UK[60] by way of Orders in

---

[58] The DUEC was set up under the European Communities Act of 1972, which provides government with the power to execute EC agreements in UK law. Like the EGCO and its relationship to the 1939 Act, the DUEC is an instrument to the 1972 EC Act.

[59] The British Government imposed a licence requirement on 25 additional items (mainly supercomputers and cryptographic equipment). This list appeared in *Official Journal of the European Communities*, C334 (12 Dec. 1995).

[60] Some difficulties have arisen in the recent past regarding the implementation of arms embargoes in the 3 crown dependencies (Guernsey, Jersey and the Isle of Man) and the dependent territories (Anguilla; Bermuda; British Antarctic Territory; British Indian Ocean Territory; the British Virgin Islands; the Cayman Islands; the Falkland Islands; Gibraltar; Montserrat; the Pitcairn, Henderson, Ducie and Oeno

Council made under the United Nations Act 1946. As of late 1999, there were Orders in Council prohibiting the export of goods to Iraq (total embargo) and Angola, Ethiopia, Eritrea, Liberia, Rwanda, Sierra Leone, Somalia and Yugoslavia (arms embargo). Other embargoes of varying levels of complexity were also in place as a result of OSCE decisions (against Armenia and Azerbaijan); EU decisions (against Afghanistan, Bosnia and Herzegovina, Burma, China, Croatia, the Democratic Republic of the Congo, Indonesia, Libya and Sudan); and national decisions (against Argentina, Cyprus, ECOWAS member states, Hong Kong, India, Pakistan and Taiwan).[61]

Weapons, dual-use and country lists

Two classes of goods require export licences: military goods and dual-use goods.

The former are controlled under the Military List (sometimes described as the Munitions List) which is 10 pages long and forms part III of Schedule 1 of the EGCO. The list covers military, security and paramilitary goods and arms, ammunition and related material. A number of the Military List items refer to goods 'specially designed' for some specific military purpose (for example, ML4 refers to 'Bombs . . . mines, missiles . . . and specially designed components and software therefor'). Most of the equipment listed requires a licence for export to any country, but more restrictive licensing is applied to particular countries and for specific kinds of equipment. The majority of the items on the Military List derive from the current Military List in the Wassenaar Arrangement (discussed in chapter 2). The relatively few additional items in the UK's Military List cover such items as shotguns, anti-terrorist equipment, and security and paramilitary equipment.[62] The Common List of Military Equipment adopted by the EU in June 2000 (see chapter 4) will also now offer a baseline for the British Military List, but is unlikely to result in any new additions (or removals) of items to be controlled in the short term.

The dual-use control lists derive from the 1994 and 2000 EC regulations. The main list, Annex I, defines all the dual-use goods that are subject to common export control procedures for extra-EU exports. A second, shorter list, Annexe IV (which was substantially revised by the 2000 EC Regulation), covers a few very sensitive items which are still subject to intra-EU licensing.

Overall, the DTI estimates that only approximately 5 per cent of total British exports are affected by these military and dual-use control lists.[63] All the goods listed require a licence before they can be exported. In addition, non-listed dual-

islands; St Helena and its dependencies; South Georgia and the South Sandwich Islands; the Sovereign Base Areas of Akrotiri and Dhekelia; and the Turks and Caicos Islands) because of their different constitutional arrangements. British Interdepartmental Committee, 'Trafficking in arms: controls and procedures', Cabinet Office, 17 Dec. 1996.

[61] *Annual Report on Strategic Export Controls* (note 9), pp. 152–76.

[62] A British proposal to extend the Wassenaar List to include these additional items was resisted by a number of other participating states.

[63] British Department of Trade and Industry, Export Control Organisation, 'Code of practice for enforcement', DTI/Pub 1220/5K/2.94/AR, p. 2, London, Dec. 1993.

use goods also require an export licence if the exporter 'knows or suspects' that the supply will be used in WMD or the missiles to deliver them. Once the 2000 EC Regulation enters into force, this provision will also be extended to any military end-use where the destination country is subject to a UN, OSCE or EU embargo.[64] This type of end-use or 'catch-all' control was first introduced into legislation in 1990 but has since been superseded by similar provisions in the DUEC. Items deemed critical to WMD programmes are specifically controlled (and require an export licence), whereas for other more general dual-use items the onus is placed on the potential exporter to make 'reasonable enquiries to allay any suspicions' that the goods might be used for such purposes.[65]

From December 1991 until early 1998, the DTI published a list of destinations (in the form of a guide to exporters[66]) for which licence applications were subject to special procedures.[67] The list reflected strategic and proliferation concerns and other factors, such as the risk of diversion or a country's lack of effective export controls. Export licence applications for these destinations were still dealt with on a case-by-case basis (see below), and inclusion of a destination on the list did not in itself prevent the granting of an export licence. In practice, therefore, the sensitive country list was rather meaningless, and it was withdrawn in 1998 on the grounds that it might cause diplomatic offence to some of the countries listed on it. In practice, however, such lists continue to be compiled for internal use by the relevant government departments. Indeed, as discussed in the previous chapter, the UK (together with partner states in the Framework Agreement) is now drawing up 'white lists' of permitted destinations for the export of military products from joint ventures.

Who decides export control policy?

British arms export control policy is 'difficult to delineate', with only some elements well defined.[68] The above equipment lists are the means by which the UK meets its international obligations on arms export control, including UN mandatory arms embargoes, embargoes and other common measures agreed under the framework of the EU Council and other multilateral controls such as the MTCR and the Wassenaar Arrangement. While these international commitments, particularly those agreed within the EU, are significant determinants of British export control policy, a great deal of discretion remains at the national level. At ministerial level, the Cabinet Defence and Overseas Policy Committee (DOPC) lays down additional formal guidelines covering political and strategic

---

[64] The government was also thinking about extending the catch-all control for dual-use goods associated with conventional weapons to embargoed destinations. British Department of Trade and Industry, *Strategic Export Controls*, Cm 3989 (Her Majesty's Stationery Office: London, July 1998), section 5.

[65] British Department of Trade and Industry, 'The end-use control: a guide for exporters', DTI/Pub 1280/5K/4/94/NP, London, 1994.

[66] The last published guidance to include the list was British Department of Trade and Industry, 'Non-proliferation controls (revised July 1995): a guide for exporters', London, July 1995.

[67] Before 1991, similar lists of countries were used for the purpose of internal decision making within the export control bureaucracy.

[68] Miller, D., 'The Scott Report and the future of British defense sales', *Defense Analysis*, vol. 12, no. 3 (1996), pp. 359–60.

issues. Ministerial responsibility for arms export policy, including export licensing, has traditionally been allocated to the minister for defence procurement in the MOD. The same minister is also responsible for promoting defence exports—a state of affairs about which Lord Justice Scott had some doubts:

The combination of these two responsibilities in the same Minister made it inevitable that the maintaining of a proper balance between the two would be difficult, not only for the Minister but for the DESS [Defence Export Services Secretariat] officials advising him. Whether an enthusiasm for defence sales was allowed to detract from the due weight to be given to security and operational objections to particular exports is one of the matters that the Inquiry has had to consider.[69]

After the 1997 election the lead role in policy formulation shifted to the FCO—witness the new export criteria discussed below and the prominent role of the first two junior FCO ministers, Tony Lloyd and then Peter Hain. However, responsibility for the administration and integrity of the licensing system remains with the DTI.[70]

The interdepartmental Strategic Exports Working Party (SXWP) provides policy advice on strategically sensitive goods and has effectively formulated government policy on export controls on a working level since it was established in 1956. Reporting to the Cabinet Office, the SXWP has representatives from the DTI, the MOD and the FCO and is chaired by the head of the Defence Export Services Secretariat (DESS) in the MOD. The DTI's role is very narrow and is essentially concerned with administering the licensing system, while actual policy formulation is largely determined by the MOD and FCO. In turn, each government department with a responsibility for export controls has its own set of internal guidelines (based on the policy guidelines dictated from the centre[71]). In the DTI, for example, guidelines are contained in the Manual of Instructions of the Export Licence Unit, while the FCO has its own Guidelines for Desk Officers.[72] Similarly, the MOD and Customs and Excise both have a set of internal guidelines, which are generally classified.

Export control criteria

These internal departmental guidelines were traditionally the only source of criteria for deciding on individual licence applications. Until the publication of

---

[69] Scott Report (note 10), para. C2.27, p. 114.

[70] There still seems to be some confusion over ministerial roles and responsibilities. A recent select committee report, e.g., drew attention to the 'apparently unresolved conflict of interest which exists between three major departments of government' and recommended that 'the government state unequivocally that the FCO has lead responsibility for all matters of policy concerning the export of arms'. British House of Commons, Select Committee on Foreign Affairs, *Foreign Policy and Human Rights*, HC 1998/99 100-I (Her Majesty's Stationery Office: London, 10 Dec. 1998), para. 163, pp. lv–lvi.

[71] In her detailed study of arms exports to Iran and Iraq, Davina Miller concludes that 'there was not a single example of a decision taken by an official which did not cohere with the policy of the centre'. Miller (note 13), p. 27.

[72] British Department of Trade and Industry, Non-Proliferation Department, 'Export Licence and Arms Working Party (MOD Form 680) applications, guidance for desk officers', London, Mar. 1997. This edition was later updated to take account of the government's new export criteria introduced in July 1997.

the Scott Report in 1996, however, these criteria rarely appeared in the public domain. One notable exception was a memorandum from the FCO to the House of Commons Foreign Affairs Committee in 1981, which set out a number of criteria.[73] It stated that controls were imposed on countries 'which pose a direct threat to the safety of Britain or our NATO allies . . . [which are] covered by mandatory UN embargo; [and] to regimes to which special considerations apply, (for example, Taiwan and North Korea)'. In other applications, the 'basis of assessment' would include: (*a*) the stability of a region; (*b*) the safeguarding of British dependent territories; (*c*) multilateral arms control (for example with regard to 'inhumane' weapons); (*d*) the 'interests and attitudes' of allies and other friendly countries; and (*e*) the nature and potential uses of the equipment.

On the last point, the FCO sometimes differentiated between offensive and defensive equipment, and between items that could be used for 'internal repression' and those that could not be so used. Publication of the Scott Report brought the full FCO criteria into the public domain for the first time. More alarmingly, it also revealed that the criteria were solely for the assistance of FCO officials: the contents had not even been brought to the attention of the DTI officials dealing with export controls.[74]

Since the 1997 election, however, both the FCO criteria and the levels of public access to them have changed considerably. They are no longer just a framework for internal decision making but a clear statement of public policy. Foreign Secretary Robin Cook introduced the new guidelines in July 1997[75] and they also formed the basis of the EU Code of Conduct agreed nearly a year later (as discussed in chapter 4).[76]

The new British guidelines, which are reproduced in full in appendix A, begin by stating that: 'An export licence will not be issued if the arguments for doing so are outweighed by the need to comply with the UK's international obligations and commitments, or by concern that the goods might be used for internal repression or international aggression, or by the risks to regional stability, or other considerations as described in these criteria'. Although these considerations include the potential effect on Britain's commercial interests and its 'essential strategic industrial base', the guidelines also stress the importance of human rights ('the government will not issue an export licence if there is a clearly identifiable risk that the proposed export might be used for internal repression') and the need 'not to introduce into a region new capabilities which would be likely to lead to increased tension'. Thus, the new guidelines set out in

---

[73] British House of Commons, Select Committee on Foreign Affairs, *Overseas Arms Sales: Foreign Policy Aspects, Minutes of Evidence*, HC 1980/81 41 (Her Majesty's Stationery Office: London, Mar. 1981), Q187 (Douglas Hurd, FCO), p. vi.

[74] Scott Report (note 10), paras C.2.44–46, pp. 118–19.

[75] 'Statement by the Secretary of State for Foreign and Commonwealth Affairs', British House of Commons, *Hansard*, written answers, 28 July 1997, cols 27–29. The criteria are reproduced in appendix A.

[76] A memorandum from the FCO to the House of Commons Select Committee on Trade and Industry, 'UK defence export criteria and the EU Code on Arms Exports', 19 Oct. 1998, sets out some of the relatively minor differences between the EU Code and the UK's national criteria. British House of Commons, Select Committee on Trade and Industry, *Strategic Export Controls*, HC 1998/99 65 (Her Majesty's Stationery Office: London, 2 Dec. 1998), appendix 8, pp. 112–14.

greater detail the criteria to be taken into account when deciding on individual licence applications.[77]

However, there remain ambiguities and room for interpretation in each individual criterion and between the different criteria. The internal repression criterion, for example, is qualified by the need for 'clear evidence of recent use of equipment for internal repression'. Similarly, it is not clear under what circumstances the human rights record or the economic conditions of the recipient country would be deemed to be of secondary importance to the effects of the proposed sale on the UK's strategic industrial base or balance of payments.

In October 2000 the British Government announced the consolidation of the British national licensing criteria with those in the EU Code of Conduct.[78] The consolidation was carried out to clarify the situation for officials and exporters, and does not imply any change in policy.

Regulatory oversight: annual reporting and the role of parliamentary select committees

The British Parliament currently has no formal role in either the policy-making or the licence application authorization process. For example, although the EGCO is subject to oversight by the Joint Standing Committee on Statutory Instruments, amendments to it do not require prior parliamentary consent and are normally made by the Secretary of State for Trade and Industry or by an official from the DTI. However, new legislation (when introduced in 2001) is expected to provide for parliamentary scrutiny of EGCOs and there have also been discussions about introducing prior parliamentary scrutiny of individual licence applications.[79]

Even the right of MPs to ask questions on the arms trade has often been blocked in the past by the policy of restricting information on grounds of commercial and customer confidentiality.[80] Several select committees (including the foreign affairs, trade and industry, public accounts and defence committees) have been able to exert some (retrospective) influence over this aspect of government policy. Again, however, this has often been limited because of restricted access to ongoing export negotiations and the frequent refusal of officials to supply information. Although the MOD revised its policy on the provision of information to Parliament in July 1996, information will still be

---

[77] The main changes in the criteria from those applied previously are set out in an FCO memorandum to the Select Committee on Trade and Industry. *Strategic Export Controls* (note 76), pp. 110–12.

[78] British House of Commons, *Hansard*, written answers, 26 Oct. 2000, col. 200W. The full text of the consolidated criteria can be found on the Foreign and Commonwealth Office Internet site, URL <http://files.FCO.gov.uk>.

[79] British Department of Trade and Industry, *Strategic Export Controls* (note 64), section 2. See also Oxford Research Group (ORG), *Weapons Decisions: Proposals for an Informed Parliament*, Current Decisions Report no. 17 (ORG: Oxford, Oct. 1996); and Davis, I. (ed.), *An Independent Audit of the First UK Annual Report on Strategic Export Controls* (Saferworld: London, Sep. 1999), section 1.5, pp. 7–9.

[80] See, e.g., the reply by former Under-Secretary of State for Defence, Tim Sainsbury, to a parliamentary question in British House of Commons, *Hansard*, 7 Mar. 1989.

withheld on grounds of national security, the security interests of the purchasing government, commercial confidentiality and the UK's bilateral relations.[81]

Greater transparency was achieved in 1999 with the introduction of an annual reporting system. The first *Annual Report on Strategic Export Controls*, published in March 1999, was a significant improvement on previous practice, allowing increased scrutiny of licensing decisions and enhancing the quality of parliamentary oversight.[82] In addition, a Joint Select Committee was formed in order to review the annual report and undertake retrospective parliamentary scrutiny of licences granted and refused. The second *Annual Report on Strategic Export Controls* was published on 3 November 1999.[83] Although among the most detailed reports published by any European country, it was disappointing in that it failed to make good the shortcomings in the ground-breaking first report.[84] However, further improvements were made in the third and fourth annual reports, which were published in July 2000 and July 2001.[85]

In addition, on 20 April 1999 the four select committees principally concerned with strategic export controls (Defence, Foreign Affairs, International Development, and Trade and Industry) met as a joint select committee to discuss the annual report. The establishment of such a committee is unusual in British parliamentary practice, and thus indicates how seriously they recognized the issue. Having obtained written information from the government and heard oral evidence from a number of non-governmental and other sources, the joint select committee published two reports: a Special Report on 15 June 1999,[86] and a substantive report on 2 February 2000.[87] A second substantive report was published on 25 July 2000[88] after further evidence had been collected from ministers, officials, companies and other sources, and the government's response to the first substantive joint committee report had been published.[89]

The first joint committee report set a number of useful precedents (including, for example, the publication of an FCO memorandum setting out the general policy considerations that operated in respect of individual licence applications

---

[81] British Ministry of Defence, 'The release of information on defence related exports', July 1996.

[82] British Ministry of Defence, Foreign and Commonwealth Office, and Department of Trade and Industry, *Annual Report on Strategic Export Controls* (Foreign and Commonwealth Office: London, Mar. 1999). The report covers licences issued during May–Dec. 1997. Its publication was delayed by problems in compiling some of the statistical data. Since then 3 further annual reports have been published.

[83] British Ministry of Defence, Foreign and Commonwealth Office, and Department of Trade and Industry, *Annual Report on Strategic Export Controls* (note 9).

[84] Davis (note 79), pp. 3–5.

[85] British Ministry of Defence, Foreign and Commonwealth Office, and Department of Trade and Industry, *Annual Report on Strategic Export Controls* (Foreign and Commonwealth Office: London, July 2000): and British Ministry of Defence, Foreign and Commonwealth Office, and Department of Trade and Industry, *Strategic Export Controls: Annual Report 2000* (Stationery Office: London, July 2001).

[86] British House of Commons, *Committees' Inquiry into the 1997 and 1998 Annual Reports on Strategic Export Controls*, HC 1998/99 540 (Stationery Office: London, 15 June 1999).

[87] British House of Commons, *Committees' Inquiry into the 1997 and 1998 Annual Reports on Strategic Export Controls*, HC 1999/2000 225 (Stationery Office: London, 2 Feb. 2000).

[88] British House of Commons, *Strategic Export Controls: Further Report and Parliamentary Prior Scrutiny*, HC 1999/2000 467 (Stationery Office: London, 25 July 2000).

[89] British House of Commons, *Annual Reports for 1997 and 1998 on Strategic Export Controls: Response of the Secretaries of State for Defence, Foreign and Commonwealth Affairs, and Trade and Industry*, Cm 4799 (Stationery Office: London, 14 July 2000).

for exports to Indonesia, Morocco, Nigeria, Saudi Arabia, Sri Lanka and Turkey). Following the publication of the second annual report, the committee asked for and obtained further information on specific licences granted to a large number of sensitive destinations, including Algeria, Bahrain, Colombia, Indonesia, Morocco, Nigeria, Pakistan, Sri Lanka and Zimbabwe. Unfortunately, it did not publish this information for public scrutiny but merely commented on its implications in its first substantive report.[90] However, the committee did hear oral evidence from Foreign Secretary Cook, when NGOs and the media were allowed access and the policy considerations for exports to a number of the more sensitive destinations were discussed.[91] Similarly, in the second substantive report, the joint committee published the oral evidence from the then minister of state (Peter Hain, MP) in relation to licences to Pakistan and Zimbabwe, and further consideration of licences for China and Hong Kong.

Members of the joint committee are also examining the case for prior parliamentary scrutiny of arms export licence applications and have looked at the Swedish system (which is discussed in chapter 7).[92] Indeed, the committee's two reports of February and July 2000 contain a number of conclusions and recommendations about prior parliamentary scrutiny and how progress on transparency and accountability in the arms trade can be furthered more generally. The government in its response of 14 July 2000 accepted some of these recommendations, including the introduction of a parliamentary debate on strategic export controls in 2000, subject to the availability of parliamentary time, and improvements in the scope and coverage of future annual reports, including information on the total value of applications for which individual licences are issued for each destination (introduced with effect from the 1999 report), and information on the numbers of small arms and major conventional weapon systems which have been licensed, except in certain specified circumstances (with effect from the 2000 report).[93]

The government also made it clear, however, that it does not intend to make any further changes to the format and content of future reports for the next three years in order to 'see whether other arms exporting states are moving towards the level of transparency shown by the UK'.[94]

---

[90] *Committees' Inquiry into the 1997 and 1998 Annual Reports on Strategic Export Controls* (note 87), appendix 17, Memorandum submitted by the Department of Trade and Industry. The information was provided 'in confidence' to the committees in Confidential Annex E.

[91] Examination of Rt Hon Robin Cook, 3 Nov. 1999; for Minutes of Evidence see *Committees' Inquiry into the 1997 and 1998 Annual Reports on Strategic Export Controls* (note 87), pp. 1–18.

[92] *Committees' Inquiry into the 1997 and 1998 Annual Reports on Strategic Export Controls* (note 87), annex II, Clerk's note of visit to Sweden, 29 Nov. 1999.

[93] See the response to recommendations (1), (32) and (33) in *Annual Reports for 1997 and 1998 on Strategic Export Controls: Response of the Secretaries of State for Defence, Foreign and Commonwealth Affairs, and Trade and Industry* (note 89), pp. 1 and 11–12.

[94] *Annual Reports for 1997 and 1998 on Strategic Export Controls: Response of the Secretaries of State for Defence, Foreign and Commonwealth Affairs, and Trade and Industry* (note 89), p. 14.

The administrative (policy-execution) structure

The administration of export controls in the UK has been the responsibility of the DTI (or its predecessors) since World War I.

Publication of export guidelines

Although there is no single set of integrated guidelines covering exports, licensing and customs procedures, the available information has improved considerably in recent years. The DTI now publishes a number of booklets and software training packages, has developed an Internet site[95] and undertakes regular education seminars with the aim of increasing awareness of export control policies and procedures. By communicating guidelines to exporters in this way, the government can also apply more (or fewer) constraints than are contained in the legislative framework. In March 1994, for example, as part of the previous government's Citizen's Charter initiative, the DTI published a code of practice setting out general guidance to exporters on how its Export Control Organisation (ECO) seeks to carry out its responsibilities and what it expects from companies in return.[96] The code consists of eight main recommendations to help companies operate effectively within the law and, although it is not legally binding, the DTI considers that adherence to it is an important indicator of an exporter's commitment to high standards of compliance.

The decision-making process for licence applications[97]

Licences for the export of equipment listed in the annexes of the EGCO and the DUEC have to be obtained from the ECO, although other departments are often involved in the decision-making process in an advisory capacity on a case-by-case basis.[98] Companies can appeal against the refusal of a licence (although, as yet, there is no statutory appeals procedure) and have the right to request a judicial review of a licensing decision.[99]

There are three types of export licence: permanent, temporary and transhipment. Temporary licences are issued on the basis that the goods will eventually

[95] URL <http://www.dti.gov.uk/export.control>. The site includes export control guidance, lists of controlled goods, the texts of OGELs and latest news updates.

[96] British Department of Trade and Industry, Export Control Organisation, 'Code of practice for enforcement' (note 63).

[97] British Department of Trade and Industry, 'The licensing process', memorandum of 13 Oct. 1998 in *Strategic Export Controls* (note 76), pp. 62–76.

[98] An export licence is not required, however, for goods exported by, or on behalf of, a British government department or for goods exported by certain international organizations. These include, e.g., government-to-government transfers and transfers of surplus arms by the DSA. The UK currently has 3 major government-to-government sales agreements with Saudi Arabia (since 1985), Malaysia (since 1988) and Kuwait (since 1993).

[99] In 1997, a group of NGOs took the unusual step of seeking a judicial review of 2 decisions by the head of the DTI—the granting of export licences for the supply of armoured vehicles and water cannon to Indonesia in Dec. 1996; and the refusal in Mar. 1997 to revoke those licences following further disclosures of the human rights situation in Indonesia. At a preliminary hearing, however, the judgement was that such matters involved political (rather than legal) decisions and were therefore not subject to judicial review. High Court Judgement, CO/944/97, Royal Courts of Justice, London, 25 Mar. 1997.

return to the UK, while transhipment licences allow controlled goods to pass through the UK en route from one country to another. Permanent licences are divided into three categories:[100]

1. The *Standard Individual Export Licence (SIEL)*. This is the most common licence and permits shipments to a single consignee up to the quantity specified by the licence. It is normally valid for two years, and applicants are required to submit an End-User Undertaking (EUU) in all cases, except where the consignee is a government body.

2. The *Open Individual Export Licence (OIEL)*. This licence is specific to an individual exporter and covers the regular shipment of certain (non-sensitive) goods to a range of specified (usually non-sensitive) destinations. It is normally valid for either two years (military goods) or three years (dual-use goods). The exporter is required to demonstrate that the company has effective internal compliance procedures, so that end-use details are not normally required.

3. The *Open General Export Licence (OGEL)*. These licences remove the need for an exporter to apply for an individual licence and no specific application to the DTI is necessary, although Customs and Excise must be notified when the goods are shipped that they are covered by a specific OGEL. There are 24 different OGELs currently in force covering such items as military components, the export of military goods after exhibition or repair, military surplus vehicles, dual-use goods, technology for dual-use goods, low-value shipments, and Wassenaar-controlled goods. Certain OGELs require registration before or within 30 days of use.[101]

Although most major arms exports tend to require an SIEL (and suppliers of spare parts generally use an OIEL), exporters of dual-use goods and certain types of military equipment increasingly only need to register for an OGEL. This is in keeping with the general policy thrust of deregulation, in this case reducing the burden (on both the licensing authority and companies with a good record of compliance) of multiple individual licence applications by the wider use of open licences.[102] Of course, with open licences the responsibility for asking basic questions about the destination or the end-use of the goods is transferred from government to the company.

While this deregulation has done much to reduce the cumbersome nature of British export control procedures in recent years, it may eventually lead to a watering down of non-proliferation objectives in the longer term. In 1996, for

[100] British Department of Trade and Industry, 'A brief guide to export controls (revised March 1994)', DTI/Pub 1241/4K/3.94/AR; and 'United Kingdom', *Worldwide Guide to Export Controls 1996/97* (Export Control Publications: Chertsey, 1997), pp. 12–23.

[101] For brief details of current OGELs see *Worldwide Guide to Export Controls 1996/97* (note 100), pp. 20–23.

[102] In early 1994 it was understood that *c.* 400 companies had registered their use of open licences with the DTI. Thurlow, J., 'Export control policy', Paper presented at the Foreign Affairs Committee Seminar, Royal Institute of International Affairs, London, 10 Mar. 1994. By the end of 1995, however, there were almost 1000 registered OGEL users and about 500 holders of OIELs. British Department of Trade and Industry, *Export Control Organisation Annual Report 1995*, London, Oct. 1996, p. 6.

example, the Select Committee on Trade and Industry recommended that 'the availability of open licences be reviewed in the light of possible diversion whenever embargoes are imposed on particular countries'.[103] The continued expansion of open licensing since then—by the end of 1998, approximately 1000 OIELs were being granted each year—drew a further recommendation of caution from a later report of the Select Committee: 'It is obviously necessary to strike a balance between reducing the burden of unnecessary individual applications and retaining a degree of detailed control. We counsel caution in moving too rapidly towards yet greater use of open licences, and OIELs in particular'.[104]

Informal procedure

Prior to the formal application for an export licence it is possible to obtain an informal consultation in order to establish at the outset whether the goods or technology are licensable. This can be done either by submitting a Rating Request Form to the Technologies Unit at the DTI (in cases where the technology is the reason for the doubt), or by the MOD Form 680 procedure (if the potential destination and/or goods are in doubt). The Rating Request is the most straightforward form of prior assessment and involves a technical adviser assessing the equipment against the EGCO/DUEC and advising whether an export licence is required. In 1995 there were 1579 written rating requests.[105]

The MOD Form 680 procedure is more widely used. The DESO and DESS effectively consider applications—approximately 4000–5000 per annum[106]—on the company's behalf and seek prior clearance for the potential export through an interdepartmental committee known as the Arms Working Party (AWP), a process that normally takes approximately two months. Applications are sometimes first sent to the Export Guarantees Committee to 'test whether ECGD cover would be available'.[107] Within the AWP, which is chaired by the DESO and has operated since 1983 as a predominantly 'paper committee' (i.e., it works by correspondence), each department (the DTI, the MOD, the FCO and the Treasury) has a de facto veto.[108] In particular, the AWP review allows the MOD to consider the application against a key document called 'table X', an interdepartmental list of sensitive destinations which are graded by the

---

[103] British House of Commons, Select Committee on Trade and Industry, *Third Report, Export Licensing and BMARC*, HC 1995/96 87-I (Her Majesty's Stationery Office: London, 12 June 1996), para. 67, p. xxvi. BMARC is the British Manufacturing and Research Co., Ltd.

[104] *Strategic Export Controls* (note 76), para. 69, pp. xxx–xxxi. In a separate memorandum to the committee, the DTI confirmed that in the year ending 28 June 1998 the Compliance Unit had made 354 visits to exporters and audited 517 OIELs. Of these, 11 OIEL holders were found to have 'seriously breached one or more conditions of their licences'. *Strategic Export Controls*, p. 150.

[105] *Export Control Organisation Annual Report 1995* (note 102), p. 12.

[106] Personal interview with a British official, 1997. Note, however, that Miller (note 13, p. 35) quotes a figure of 10 000 per annum.

[107] Inquiry into Exports of Defence Equipment and Dual-Use Goods to Iraq, Hearings in the presence of the Rt Hon. Lord Justice Scott, Evidence of Sir Stephen Egerton, Day 11, p. 96. Quoted by Miller (note 13), p. 55.

[108] Miller (note 13), p. 34.

'classifications of equipment which Whitehall as a whole, thinks it fit for them to get'.[109] Although the MOD 680 procedure is distinct from and does not replace the formal export licence application procedure, it is only rarely that an approval under the former is subsequently overturned under the latter. Indeed, over a 10-year period, only five AWP approvals did not result in an export licence.[110]

Formal procedure

Applications for individual export licences for military and dual-use goods (i.e., those not covered by OGELs) are first assessed by the ECO, a branch of the Export Controls and Non-Proliferation Division of the DTI. The ECO, which was set up in 1988 following a major review within the DTI of export control arrangements, has itself been reorganized several times in the 1990s, most recently in April 1996 when it was reorganized into six major units in order 'to focus more sharply on the licensing process'.[111] Approximately 135 people are currently employed in the ECO.

A new computer system, the Export Control Licence Information Processing System (ECLIPS) was introduced in March 1995 to improve processing of licence applications, but by late 1997 it had become apparent that the system was 'seriously deficient'.[112] Efforts were therefore focused on a new project, Export Licence Applications Transmitted Electronically (ELATE), which would allow for electronic submission of licence applications and (in time) for electronic circulation of data between the DTI and the other two advisory departments (the FCO and the MOD). ELATE was introduced in March 1999.[113]

The ECO decides whether it is necessary to consult other departments about the application. If the product features on the EGCO Military List, or the MTCR Annex, the MOD and FCO are always consulted, but in the case of dual-use items on the DUEC Industrial List the ECO has a degree of discretion about which combination of product and destination merits referral. Thus, all arms export applications and some dual-use equipment applications (for example, all those to countries on the sensitive destination list) are passed to the MOD, the FCO—and since mid-1997, if appropriate, the Department for Inter-

---

[109] Inquiry into Exports of Defence Equipment and Dual-Use Goods to Iraq, Hearings in the presence of the Rt Hon. Lord Justice Scott, Evidence of Christopher Sandars, Day 3, pp. 7–8. Quoted by Miller (note 13), p. 34.

[110] Inquiry into Exports of Defence Equipment and Dual-Use Goods to Iraq, Hearings in the presence of the Rt Hon. Lord Justice Scott, Evidence of Ian McDonald, Day 28, p. 161. Quoted by Miller (note 13), p. 35.

[111] *Export Control Organisation Annual Report 1995* (note 102), p. 3. For an up-to-date organogram for the ECO see the DTI Internet site, URL <http://www.dti.gov.uk>.

[112] *Strategic Export Controls* (note 76), para. 70, p. .xxxi.

[113] *Strategic Export Controls* (note 76), paras 70–71 and 'Supplementary Memorandum submitted by the DTI on Computer Systems in the Export Licensing Process', 13 Oct. 1998, paras 75–76, p. xxxi. An earlier committee report had criticized the separate development of information systems and recommended 'that the three departments allow mutual access to their computerised information relating to export licensing and that the DTI's export licensing database be developed for the benefit of all three departments'. British House of Commons, Select Committee on Trade and Industry, *Third Report, Export Licensing and BMARC* (note 103), paras 77–81, pp. xxviii–xxix.

national Development (DFID)—for a ruling.[114] Each department uses its own internal criteria to form a judgement on the desirability of the sale.

Within the MOD, licence applications are circulated by the DESS for technical evaluation and security assessment, for instance, of what would be the impact of selling the equipment on a regional balance of power, whether it would be a threat to British or allied forces, what level of technology should be released, and whether there was a risk of the equipment being diverted. Teams of security advisers within the MOD provide the most exacting scrutiny of applications, but they appear to be 'somewhat outnumbered and out-manoeuvred by the sales promotion staff of the DESO'.[115] Indeed, the DESS is often required to provide intra-departmental arbitration between the security branches and the DESO's regional marketing desks (even though it remains a DESO secretariat).[116]

Within the FCO it is the Non-Proliferation Department that coordinates the evaluation (made by the relevant geographical departments) of the political and foreign policy impact of a proposed arms export. However, it is the impact on civil markets that often appears to be uppermost in the minds of the FCO:

The Foreign Office knows that 'Britain exports or dies' and this acts as both a constraint upon and a springboard for defence sales. Where the potential recipient is willing to link arms sales to access to the general market of the country, the FCO's concern for commerce inclines it to support sales. The FCO is thus disposed to seek restraint where commercial relationships with neighbours and/or adversaries of the potential recipient will be damaged. This is the Department's most important role in the export licensing process. It advises on the political, and thus the commercial, reaction of other states to particular sales.[117]

In addition, the intelligence services play an important role in assisting both the MOD and the FCO on specific export licensing matters, and the Treasury sometimes applies its own ratings of the prospective customer's credit-worthiness.

Most routine sales decisions are considered (and approved) on a case-by-case basis following acceptance of the licence application by the MOD and/or FCO. Where conflicting advice emerges from different departments, the issue is normally settled either through a further review by the Release of Military Information Policy Committee (RMIPC, an internal MOD committee of senior officials, usually including a representative from the FCO, which is also meant to handle appeals against refusals for exports)[118] or through ad hoc meetings of

---

[114] Formerly the FCO would consult with the Overseas Development Agency (ODA) over the development implications of a proposed military export, but following the general election in 1997 the ODA was transformed into an independent government department (the DFID), which is now an advisory department in its own right.

[115] Miller (note 13), p. 49.

[116] For a discussion of the DESS's role as intra-departmental arbiter see Miller (note 13), pp. 49–50.

[117] Miller (note 13), pp 54–55.

[118] Evidence at the Scott Inquiry, however, revealed that the RMIPC appeals procedure is sometimes ignored. Instead, the DESO applies pressure on opponents of the sale within the MOD to change their

Table 5.4. Export licence applications and refusals, late 1970s–1999

Figures in italics are percentages.

Period	Total no. of applications (per annum)	No. of applications relating to military equipment (per annum)	Total no. of applications refused (per annum)	%% of refusals	No. of military applications refused (per annum)	%% of refusals
late 1970s[1]	..	..	..	..	..	7
early 1980s[1]	..	6 500	..	..	195	3
1985[2]	83 863	10 284	..	..	..	..
1986[2]	89 705	10 415	..	..	..	..
1987[2]	97 842	11 644	200[3]	0.2	..	..
1988[2]	92 280	10 756	..	..	..	..
1987–88	..	16 643[a]	..	..	268[a]	1.6[4]
1989[2]	75 925	10 099	..	..	..	..
1989	..	14 601	..	..	1 017	7[4]
1990	46 000[3]	14 966[4]	..	..	393[4]	2.6[4]
1991[4]	..	3 313[b]	..	..	320[b]	9.7
early 1990s[3]	21 000	..	300	1.4	..	..
1994[5]	17 007	..	..	..	..	..
1995[5]	15 588	..	83	0.5	..	..
1997[6]	6 638[c]	..	52	0.8	..	..
1998[7]	10 576	..	124	1.2	..	..
1997–98[8]	..	11 900[d]	89	..	..	..
1999[9]	9 569	..	130	1.4	..	..

Notes:

[a] 1987 and 1988 have been aggregated because the DTI figure for 1988 includes some approvals carried over from 1987.

[b] Only includes the first quarter of 1991.

[c] Only covers the period between 2 May and 31 Dec. 1997 and refers to decisions on SIELs (6463 applications), Standard Individual Transhipment Licences (SITLs) (13 applications) and OIELs (162 applications).

[d] Covers the year from Aug. 1997 to Aug. 1998.

.. = Data not available or not applicable.

Sources:

[1] Pearson, F., 'The question of control in British defence sales policy', *International Affairs*, vol. 59, no. 2 (spring 1983), p. 214.

[2] British House of Commons, Trade and Industry Select Committee, *Third Report: Export Licensing and BMARC*, HC 1995/96 87-I (Her Majesty's Stationery Office: London, 12 June 1996), table 1, p. xxiv. BMARC is the British Manufacturing and Research Co., Ltd.

[3] Inquiry into Exports of Defence Equipment and Dual-Use Goods to Iraq, Evidence of Michael Coolican, Day 59, p. 9, quoted by Miller, D., *Export or Die* (Cassell: London, 1996), p. 35.

decision. Miller (note 13), pp. 34 and 48–49. The 1998 Government White Paper (DTI, *Strategic Export Controls* (note 64), section 4) confirmed that in the future the appeals committee will be made up of senior officials from the DTI, MOD, FCO and, where appropriate, DFID.

[4] Written reply to Parliament, quoted in *Defence Industry Digest*, June 1991, p. 19.

[5] British Department of Trade and Industry, *Export Control Organisation Annual Report 1995*, London, Oct. 1996, p. 3.

[6] British Ministry of Defence, Foreign and Commonwealth Office, and Department of Trade and Industry, *Annual Report on Strategic Export Controls* (Foreign and Commonwealth Office: London, Mar. 1999), p. 20.

[7] British Ministry of Defence, Foreign and Commonwealth Office, and Department of Trade and Industry, *Annual Report on Strategic Export Controls* (Foreign and Commonwealth Office: London, Nov. 1999), p. 8.

[8] British House of Commons, Trade and Industry Select Committee, *Strategic Export Controls*, HC 1998/99 65 (Her Majesty's Stationery Office: London, 2 Dec. 1998), p. 65.

[9] British Ministry of Defence, Foreign and Commonwealth Office, and Department of Trade and Industry, *Annual Report on Strategic Export Controls* (Foreign and Commonwealth Office: London, July 2000), p. 12.

either senior officials or ministers. More difficult applications are always referred to ministers,[119] while decisions on very sensitive applications are likely to be taken by a cabinet committee or even the full Cabinet and/or Prime Minister.

Sensitive applications may also be discussed at the fortnightly meetings of the Restricted Enforcement Unit (REU)—an interdepartmental committee of officials with non-proliferation responsibilities from the DTI, the MOD, the FCO, Customs and Excise and the intelligence services. Chaired by the head of the ECO, the REU was established in 1987 to 'provide a forum for identification and discussion of information on actual or suspected breaches of UK export controls'.[120] Hence, it is essentially a clearing house for information exchange rather than a decision-making or policy-making forum.[121]

Before 1992, information in the public domain on approval rates for licence applications was ad hoc, inconsistent and limited in scope and detail (as shown in table 5.4). After 1992 the situation improved when the DTI began placing a register of export licences granted and refused during the previous year (and later every six months) in the House of Commons Library. Of the 15 505 licences issued by the ECO in 1995, 66 per cent were issued by the Military Licensing Unit (of which 27 per cent were for small arms), 25 per cent were issued by the Sensitive Destinations Licensing Unit, and the remaining 9 per cent fell within the 'Industrial/Atomic' category.[122] However, not only did the register fail to distinguish between different categories of goods (one category ranges from aircraft to parachutes), but problems with the ECO's computer system led to an arranged parliamentary question in 1997 in reply to which the government admitted that the computer databases 'do not provide a fully accurate record' and that some previous parliamentary answers, using informa-

[119] According to evidence from Mrs Roche, Under-Secretary of State at the DTI, to the Select Committee on Trade and Industry, only about 3% of applications reach ministers and only a 'handful' of these lead to inter-ministerial discussions. *Strategic Export Controls* (note 76), para. 81, p. xxvi.

[120] Scott Report (note 10), para C.2.68, p. 124.

[121] The REU was criticized at the Scott Inquiry for failing to ensure proper dissemination of information back through the relevant departments. Miller (note 13), p. 35.

[122] *Export Control Organisation Annual Report 1995* (note 102), p. 10.

tion from the computer databases, 'could be proved wrong if recourse were made to the original paper records'.[123] These problems also delayed the publication of the first *Annual Report on Strategic Export Controls*. However, as discussed above, the annual reporting system does represent a much higher degree of transparency than was provided by the half-yearly register.

Despite these data problems, the figures in table 5.4 do suggest two clear trends. First, since the introduction of OGELs the number of licence applications has dropped dramatically, from over 97 000 in 1987 to less than 10 000 in 1999.[124] Second, over the last three decades the percentage of licence applications refused has remained low. The main reason for such a low refusal rate is that the control regime is well understood by exporters: companies are unlikely to apply for a licence if they know it will be refused. Alternative explanations are that the scope of the controls is too wide (the explanation preferred by industry) or that the controls are too lax (the explanation preferred by opponents of the arms trade). Of the 83 licence applications refused in 1995, three were for end-use (i.e., under the catch-all clause), 5 were for nuclear materials, 33 were for dual-use goods and 42 were for military goods. These licence refusals were spread between 28 different destinations, the destinations with the most refusals being Iran (22), and India and Pakistan (8 each).[125]

Compliance and enforcement procedures

End-user and end-use controls differ according to the type of export licence. For individual licences, an EUU is normally submitted with the export licence application. The DTI provides guidance and specimen wordings for end-use certification to suit particular circumstances. In the case of non-government end-users, for example, it normally includes information about the end-use of the goods[126] and assurances about re-export. In the past, the government has been unable (or unwilling) to enforce end-user assurances, and reliance is traditionally placed on intelligence information to track down harmful re-exports and the threat of future sales bans to discourage them.[127] Given also that the penalty for failing to provide an end-user certificate is only £2000, it is little surprise to find a minister in the former Conservative government, Alan Clark, describing them as 'not worth the paper they are written on'.[128]

[123] British House of Lords, *Parliamentary Debates, Official Report (Hansard)*, House of Lords, 30 Oct. 1997, cols WA 256–WA258.

[124] Similarly, the number of British companies that apply for export licences has gradually fallen by nearly 50% since 1987 (from 8239 to 4402 in 1993). Quoted in 'Response of the Defence Manufacturers Association to the issues raised in the Department of Trade and Industry's consultative document on strategic export controls' (note 18), pp. 26–27.

[125] *Export Control Organisation Annual Report 1995* (note 102), p. 12.

[126] During the COCOM era, e.g., the country receiving dual-use goods covered by the regime had to undertake not to use the goods for military purposes.

[127] Pearson, F., 'Problems and prospects of arms transfer limitations among second-tier suppliers: the cases of France, the United Kingdom and the Federal Republic of Germany', ed. Ohlson (note 3), p. 134. See also Scott Report (note 10), para E9.27, p. 906.

[128] Inquiry into Exports of Defence Equipment and Dual-Use Goods to Iraq, Hearings in the presence of the Lord Justice Scott, Evidence of Alan Clark, Day 49, pp. 14–15, quoted by Miller (note 13), p. 20.

However, there is an element of self-fulfilment in such a statement, given the reluctance of the Conservative government to discourage clear diversions of British arms transfers at that time. During the Iraq–Iran War, for example, end-user certificates were falsified by Jordanian officials to allow the re-export of British arms to Iraq. Despite being in possession of over 20 intelligence reports over a five-year period confirming that war materials for Iraq were being diverted through Jordan, the government failed to act.[129] In contrast, following the invasion of Kuwait, measures were taken almost immediately to prevent Jordanian diversions to Iraq.

British diplomatic posts overseas regularly carry out pre-export checks on the accuracy of information contained in end-user documentation. Post-export checks are rare, however, although defence attachés in British embassies have been known to undertake them occasionally.[130]

Although the British export licensing system has become 'essentially self-regulatory',[131] a number of mechanisms exist for monitoring and enforcing compliance. Customs and Excise is the 'policing and prosecuting authority' within the export control regime.[132] It attempts to prevent the export of unlicensed goods or goods which do not have the correct licences and to apply suitable enforcement measures. These vary from warning letters, through seizure of goods or compounding of proceedings for offences, to criminal proceedings in the most serious cases. In enforcing export restrictions, Customs and Excise has to balance the need to minimize interference with legitimate trade with the requirement to prevent illegal export, and largely does so by targeting checks on export consignments on the basis of intelligence and risk assessment. A team of investigators in the Customs Investigation Division carries out intelligence gathering and analysis. Only in the early 1990s was this team first provided with a computer system for information storage, retrieval and analysis.[133] There is no computer link between the investigation team and individual customs offices at ports and airports,[134] and the latter largely rely on building up 'local profiles' of possible offenders as the principal means of making informed risk evaluations.[135]

Measures to encourage compliance with the regulations are the responsibility of the DTI rather than Customs and Excise. Since its formation in August 1991 the Compliance Unit within the ECO has made approximately 300 visits to companies each year, with a particular focus on inspections of holders of

---

[129] Scott Report (note 10), part 2, chapter E2, pp. 819–51. See also the criticism of end-use controls in *Strategic Export Controls* (note 76), pp. xxiv–xxvi.

[130] Personal interviews, 1997.

[131] Michael Coolican, Head of the ECO, in British House of Commons, Select Committee on Trade and Industry, *Exports to Iraq: Minutes of Evidence, 26 November 1991*, HC 1990/91 86 (Her Majesty's Stationery Office: London, 1991), p. 4.

[132] Scott Report (note 10), para C.3.4, p. 130. The role of Customs and Excise in export control is discussed in part I, chapter C3, pp. 129–50.

[133] Scott Report (note 10), para G3.6, p. 1117.

[134] Although export licence details are fed into the customs computer system (known as CHIEF), this is only for the purpose of compiling trade statistics, and hence only the volume of exports is recorded.

[135] Personal interviews with .British government officials, 1997.

OIELs.[136] The visits provide the DTI with information on the companies' export activities and ensure that correct use is being made of the licensing system. However, according to one international trade consultant, 'publicity and training in targeted institutions is the single most important contribution to compliance and the weakest component of the current regime'.[137]

IV. Policy outcomes

Fifty years of supply rather than restraint, 1947–97

According to most analysts, a mixture of economic and foreign policy considerations have dominated British arms export policy in the post-World War II period.[138] First, export policy has been treated as a subsidiary function of defence policy, resulting in economic pressure to maximize financial returns in order to subsidize procurement for the British armed forces. As a former Minister for Defence Procurement, Sir Adam Butler, explained at the Scott Inquiry, 'if we could increase the sales of equipment which our own Armed Forces were using, it would clearly have an effect on the unit cost of that equipment'.[139] While the effect has been somewhat marginal (averaging some £400 million per year in the early 1990s, or nearly 6 per cent of the British procurement budget[140]), it nonetheless remains a key MOD and government objective.

Second, foreign policy considerations provide the main political context for sales. These considerations include the protection of the UK's wider commercial and trade interests (i.e., economic security) and concerns about arms falling into the 'wrong hands', be they terrorist organizations or unfriendly governments (i.e., military security).[141] As a result of this military concern about the horizontal proliferation of sensitive technologies, some weapon systems have been downgraded or modified prior to transfer and others have been subject to outright ban. The dominant foreign policy motive appears to be the linkage between defence and civil trade.[142] Although pursuit of this motive can serve to constrain sales (in cases where the export of weapons to one country may

---

[136] Personal interviews, 1997.

[137] Response of Alex McLoughlin to the DTI's consultative document, 29 Oct. 1996, in British Department of Trade and Industry, 'Responses to the Department of Trade and Industry's consultative document on strategic export controls', Ref. URN 97/752, London, 5 June 1997.

[138] See, e.g., Anthony, I. (ed.), SIPRI, *Arms Export Regulations* (Oxford University Press: Oxford, 1991), p. 180; Miller (note 13), pp. 61–63; and Spear, J., 'Britain and conventional arms transfer restraint', ed. M. Hoffman, *UK Arms Control in the 1990s* (Manchester University Press: Manchester, 1990), pp. 170–89.

[139] Inquiry into Exports of Defence Equipment and Dual-Use Goods to Iraq, Hearings in the presence of the Rt Hon. Lord Justice Scott, Evidence of Sir Adam Butler, Day 6, p. 3, Quoted by Miller (note 13), pp. 51–52.

[140] Freeman, R. (former Minister of State for Defence Procurement), 'Moving Britain forward: defence exports in the 1990s', *RUSI Journal*, Feb. 1995, p. 1.

[141] The use of British (and French) arms by Argentina to sink British warships in the Falklands War highlights the difficulty in predicting with any certainty the end-use of exported weapon systems.

[142] Miller (note 13), pp. 62, 96–104.

damage trading relationships with other countries[143]), on the whole it generally seems to have been associated with the promotion of arms sales. Two well-documented cases (which took place in the late 1980s, but only came to light in the early 1990s)—the Pergau 'aid for arms' scandal and the Arms to Iraq affair—illustrate this linkage and in particular the perception among officials and ministers that a refusal to sell defence equipment may have adverse implications for civil trade. Indeed, this perception, combined with the perceived importance of the defence sector within the country's manufacturing base, has made the UK particularly vulnerable to the phenomenon of 'reverse influence', as demonstrated in evidence before the Scott Inquiry and in the attempt by Saudi Arabia to have the dissident, Mohammed al-Mas'ari, deported from the UK in 1996.[144]

According to the Scott Report, the main criticisms of the British arms export regime concern questions of ministers' accountability to Parliament, failures in administrative systems and errors on the part of civil servants, but this is too simplistic and narrow an explanation. For the past 40 years or so, government thinking on the regulation of arms transfers has been dominated by somewhat contradictory economic, security and political motives. These contradictions have been played out through a largely reactive interdepartmental decision-making process, which considers individual applications as they are made. However, the shortcomings in this approach that have been demonstrated are clearly political rather than administrative in origin. Moreover, according to the Scott Report, the 1939 legislation has given successive governments 'an unfettered power to impose whatever export controls it wishes and to use those controls for any purposes it thinks fit'.[145] Or, to put it another way, 'departments manoeuvre *within* the framework of policy, not without'.[146]

It is equally clear that the political framework has generally been permissive rather than restrictive (i.e., favouring supply rather than restraint). In the immediate post-war period, the UK tried to retain its increasingly fragile military role in world politics in part through military sales, and in subsequent years (especially the 1960s and 1970s) arms sales were used to cement political ties with certain states (especially those in the Middle East with oil wealth) and to support the cost of retaining an 'independent' defence industrial base.

Under the Labour Party and up until 1979 a twin-track policy of control and simultaneous promotion of arms was followed, while under the Conservatives (from 1979 until May 1997) even fewer restrictions were applied and ministers were ready to 'travel in support of exports at the drop of a hat'.[147] In short, political or economic pressures to export have often undermined any objectivity in the control criteria discussed above. Chile, for example, was promoted from

---

[143] The UK, e.g., has been consistently inhibited in selling arms to Israel out of concern for economic ties with the Gulf (and other Arab) states in the Middle East. Stanley, J. and Pearton, M., *The International Trade in Arms* (Chatto & Windus: London, 1972), p. 17.

[144] Rose, D., 'The man they had to silence', *The Observer*, 7 Jan. 1996.

[145] Scott Report (note 10), para. K2.1, p. 1759.

[146] Miller (note 13), p. 61 (emphasis in the original).

[147] Masefield (note 35), pp. 1–8.

'unacceptable' status to counterbalance strategic concerns over Argentina (and to offset the loss of the Argentinean market) during and after the 1982 Falklands War. India, despite close links to the former Soviet Union during the cold war and domestic unrest, was a major market for British weapons during this period (and since). The oil-producing Nigerian Government received British weapons during the 1967–70 Biafran War and continued to receive 'non-lethal' military equipment following the imposition of an EU arms embargo in 1993.[148] In addition, British military, security and police equipment or services have been supplied to countries where serious human rights violations take place.[149]

During the 1980s in particular, the prime minister took a growing interest in defence sales, and with Prime Minister Thatcher as its de facto head the DESO became a powerful voice in arms export decision making. The human rights record of recipients was played down during this period: instead, the high-level government backing for arms exports resulted in a plethora of sales teams, overseas missions and public calls for more exportable designs. This level of influence also appeared to continue (but to a lesser extent) in the successor government led by John Major. After the Persian Gulf War, for example, the prime minister responded to the chorus of voices calling for arms trade restraint by endorsing the long-standing call for an arms register at the UN (see chapter 2) (although this was seen as a way of undermining a Dutch proposal that would have committed the EC to a policy of actually reducing weapon exports).[150]

Overall, therefore, it seems that in accordance with specific political intervention the economic-oriented arms regulatory bureaucracy instinctively takes the side of the applicant for a licence. Indeed, the Scott Inquiry seemed to confirm that the decision-making process favoured commercial interests even in borderline cases.

A great deal of media, political and judicial activity has been focused on export control procedures in the UK since the early 1990s, particularly in respect of dual-use goods and small arms. One case in particular, the Arms to Iraq affair, raised highly controversial issues which went to the very centre of British export control policy.[151] It not only revealed the extent to which domestic politics shaped 'official' policy, but also illustrated how political intervention can sometimes undermine or nullify the formal and written guidelines. Just over a year after the publication of the report of the inquiry into the Arms to Iraq affair, a new government was elected with a strong commitment to an ethical approach to arms export controls. As these two events mark a potential turning point in British export control policy they are discussed in greater detail below.

---

[148] 'Arms for Nigeria evade ban on exports', *The Guardian*, 21 May 1995.

[149] See, e.g., Amnesty International UK, *Made in Britain: How the UK Makes Torture and Death its Business* (Amnesty International: London, Nov. 1996).

[150] Hitchens, T., 'EC spurns tight arms control: leaders back British plan to have UN monitor exports', *Defense News*, 15 Apr. 1991.

[151] The popular usage of the term 'Arms to Iraq' is somewhat misleading as no arms were directly supplied to Iraq during the period in question: the case concerned chiefly dual-use exports.

Arms to Iraq and the Scott Inquiry

Early in the Iraq–Iran War, the UK adopted a rule that exports of 'lethal' weapons should be banned to both sides. The ambiguity of this definition, commercial pressures, strategic concerns (including pressure from the USA and major trading partners in the Middle East to cease supplying Iran), Iraqi battlefield reverses and questions of existing, paid contracts with Iran brought a policy reformulation in December 1984. Sir Geoffrey Howe, then Foreign Secretary, set out this policy change in a written parliamentary answer in October 1985.[152] Although the ban on lethal equipment to either side was upheld, the new wording suggested that future orders for other types of defence equipment would only be refused an export licence if they were to 'significantly enhance the capability of either side to prolong or exacerbate the conflict'.

This new criterion allowed the government even more room to manoeuvre either to disallow or, as was more frequently the case, to allow specific export licences.

The two key groups policing the guidelines—an MOD Working Group (MODWG) and an Interdepartmental Committee on Defence Sales to Iran and Iraq (IDC)—were both heavily biased in favour of the exporters.[153] Thus, among the 'non-lethal defence equipment' exported to Iraq during the late 1980s were fighter aircraft spares, body armour, ballistic jackets, laser range-finders, radar systems, radios, tank helmets, gun sound-ranging equipment and machine tools for the manufacture of artillery shells.[154] Four British companies were involved in the export of these machine tools to Iraq, and one or more of the directors from each of the companies were subsequently prosecuted or threatened with prosecution for export offences. Of these, however, only the Matrix Churchill prosecution reached the courts. The Matrix Churchill directors were arrested in October 1990 for the 'illegal' supply of machine tools and lathes to Iraq, and their trial began two years later.[155]

Also under investigation by Customs during 1990 was the 'Supergun' project, also known as Project Babylon. Supergun was the first case to gain a high public profile following reports that British companies were involved in supplying large steel tubes to Iraq. It was originally claimed that these tubes were destined for Iraq's petrochemicals industry but it eventually became clear that they were to be used to develop a long-range gun. Customs and Excise did attempt to prosecute some of the senior personnel in the main British supplier

---

[152] British House of Commons, *Hansard*, 29 Oct. 1985, col. 46. It should be noted, however, that these guidelines had been operating for nearly a year before this announcement. Scott Report (note 10), paras D1.145–65, pp. 202–11.

[153] The majority of MODWG members were from the DESO, while the IDC consisted of mainly pro-arms sales representatives from the MOD, DTI and FCO. Scott Report (note 10), paras D1.103–44, pp. 187–202; and Miller (note 13), pp. 72–79.

[154] A full list of export licence applications for Iraq during 1984–90 is contained in the Scott Report (note 10), appendix A, part A, pp. 1–107.

[155] For a detailed discussion of the Matrix Churchill case see the Scott Report (note 10), part 2, section G, pp. 1097–1538.

companies, but these prosecutions were dropped in November 1990.[156] During a subsequent investigation by the Trade and Industry Select Committee, several changes to British export control procedures were introduced, including: the establishment of a Sensitive Destinations Section in the ECO; the requirement that all licence applications be subject to comprehensive documentation, detailed technical assessments and full disclosure of end-use and end-user; and the introduction in December 1990 of a 'catch-all' clause for chemical and biological weapon programmes (later extended in June 1991 to include missile delivery systems and nuclear weapon programmes).[157] In addition, efforts were made to improve both data management and interdepartmental coordination.[158]

It was the collapse of the Matrix Churchill trial in November 1992 that set in motion the subsequent judicial inquiry, headed by a senior judge, Sir Richard Scott. After spending over two years receiving written and oral evidence from more than 200 witnesses, including former prime ministers John Major and Margaret Thatcher, and gathering some 200 000 pages of documents, Scott published a report of 1806 pages in February 1996.[159] The report revealed that further substantial changes in government policy had occurred following the end of the Iraq–Iran War in 1988. In particular, a key part of the guidelines was amended to: 'We should not, in future, approve orders for any defence equipment which, in our view, would be of direct and significant assistance in the conduct of offensive operations in breach of the ceasefire'.[160]

This slackening of the guidelines—which was agreed by three junior ministers of state, Lord Trefgarne (MOD), Alan Clark (DTI) and William Waldegrave (FCO), but remarkably not submitted for approval to any of their three secretaries of state or the Prime Minister[161]—meant that exports were banned only if they were held to affect 'offensive operations'. The report also revealed that the impartiality inherent in the 1984 guidelines was also secretly dropped early in 1989, when the guidelines in respect of Iran were tightened following the issue of a fatwa by the Iranian Government against the British

[156] For a detailed discussion of the Supergun case see the Scott Report (note 10), part 2, section F, pp. 945–1096.

[157] British House of Commons, Select Committee on Trade and Industry, *Second Report, Exports to Iraq: Project Babylon and Long Range Guns*, HC 1991/92 86 (Her Majesty's Stationery Office: London, 13 Mar. 1992), pp. xxxix and xl.

[158] 'Government's response to the Second Report of the Trade and Industry Select Committee', *Exports to Iraq: Project Babylon and Long Range Guns*, Cmnd 2019 (Her Majesty's Stationery Office: London, July 1992), p. 3. In addition, the practice of automatically destroying previous licence applications after 6 years was stopped in July 1991 as it was recognized that such material might be useful in future audits. British House of Commons, *Hansard*, 27 Oct. 1995; and personal interviews with British government officials.

[159] Scott Report (note 10).

[160] John Goulden, Assistant Under-Secretary of State at the FCO, in British House of Commons, Select Committee on Trade and Industry, *Exports to Iraq: Minutes of Evidence, 28 January 1992*, HC 1991/92 86 (Her Majesty's Stationery Office: London, 1992), viii, p. 281. Most ministers and senior officials who gave evidence to the Inquiry contended that government policy as formulated in the 1984 guidelines had not changed. Scott, however, concluded that they had. Scott Report (note 10), paras D3.122–25, pp. 426–28.

[161] This was Scott's conclusion based on the documentary evidence (Scott Report (note 10), paras D3.2, D3.102, pp. 372–415) but, having considered the circumstantial evidence, Davina Miller reaches a different conclusion. Miller (note 13), pp. 74–77.

novelist Salman Rushdie. The net result of these unpublished changes was an increase in sales of defence-related equipment to Iraq and the systematic deception of Parliament by ministers and officials. Indeed, for more than a year, ministers answered questions and letters from MPs without disclosing that the guidelines were different or that the policy of vetting export licences for defence-related equipment was not impartial as between Iran and Iraq.[162]

The evidence of Alan Clark, the former Minister for Trade at the DTI, to the Scott Inquiry (referring to the Howe guidelines) exemplifies the belief that policy declarations in this area rarely equate with actual policy outcomes: '[The guidelines] were high-sounding, combining it seemed both moral and practical considerations, and yet imprecise enough to allow real policy considerations an override in exceptional circumstances'.[163] Indeed, this case clearly shows the contradictions inherent in an official policy of restraint with regard to arms sales to Iraq and Iran and an unofficial one of supply. Moreover, the restraint of arms exports to the two countries was aimed at preserving relationships and trade with the Gulf as a whole, rather than a policy for bringing the war to its earliest conclusion. Between 1985 and 1990, the British Government admits exporting defence-related equipment worth $222 million to Iraq. While this was only a fraction of the arms sales supplied to Iraq by Chile, China, France, Russia and other Western governments,[164] these sales represent only a partial picture of the UK's involvement in arming Saddam Hussein. First, this figure does not include dual-use equipment, such as machine tools or industrial and scientific equipment, which were worth at least another $200 million. Second, and more significantly, the figure of $222 million takes no account of the supply of weapons diverted to Iraq via Jordan. Three large arms deals were signed by Prime Minister Thatcher with Jordan in 1979, 1985 and 1987, and it is now clear—despite ministerial protestations at the Scott Inquiry that this was not known at the time—that 'a lot' of this equipment ended up in Iraq.[165]

The Scott Report also made a number of wide-ranging recommendations, the scope of which included: (*a*) revision of the legislative framework so that parliament has more influence over the imposition of controls, and (preceded by an open debate) of the purposes of export controls in order to make them narrow and precise; (*b*) improvements in export licensing procedures, including the possible transfer of defence export controls from the DTI to the MOD; (*c*) better use and dissemination of intelligence relevant to export licensing decisions by and between government departments; and (*d*) improvements in

---

[162] Scott Report (note 10), part I, chapter D4, pp. 473–507.

[163] Scott Report (note 10), para. D2.22, p. 222.

[164] For a detailed account of how Western governments armed Iraq see Timmerman, K., *The Death Lobby: How the West Armed Iraq* (Fourth Estate: London, 1992).

[165] At the Scott Inquiry, Alan Clark (Junior Minister at the DTI) said that: 'More than half the material purchased by Iraq was actually consigned to Jordan'. While no figures were supplied to sustain this evidence, Clark confirmed that it was 'a kind of slang expression for "a lot" . . . There was a tendency for the trickier items to be consigned to Jordan'. Quoted by Foot, P. and Laxton, T., 'Not the Scott Report', A *Private Eye* Arms to Iraq Special, Nov. 1994, p. 23. See also Miller (note 13), pp. 110–14.

ministerial accountability, including the provision of more information to Parliament about arms sales.[166]

In response to the Scott Report and to further concerns about lax British export controls,[167] the Conservative government initiated a major review of export control legislation and procedures in July 1996, including an open invitation to 'people with an interest in strategic export controls to contribute to the improvement of policy in this area'.[168] More specifically, respondents were invited to offer comments on the desirability of: new primary legislation to replace the existing legislation on strategic exports; potential changes to the scope and coverage of controls; the introduction of a formal appeals procedure for exporters; new provisions for parliamentary scrutiny; and potential changes in the location of the export licensing authority. Although the then government envisaged continuing the consultation process at a more detailed level in late 1996 or early 1997, any further action was delayed pending the outcome of the 1997 general election.

The reforms of 'New Labour': towards greater restraint in the late 1990s?

In February 1997, on the anniversary of the Scott Report, the Labour Party committed itself, if elected, to tougher checks on arms exports as part of an ethical foreign policy. It pledged itself to: (a) refuse sales to regimes that 'might' use them for 'internal repression or international aggression' or in circumstances where the sale of weapons 'might intensify or prolong existing armed conflict' or 'might be used to abuse human rights'; (b) press for an EU code of conduct on arms transfers and strengthen the UN Register of Conventional Arms; (c) immediately ban the manufacture of, and trade in, landmines and torture equipment (such as electric-shock batons); and (d) publish an annual report on British strategic exports.[169]

Many of these commitments were implemented within months of the new administration taking office. First, on 12 May 1997, Foreign Secretary Cook, announcing a new mission statement for the FCO, stated that: 'Our foreign policy must have an ethical dimension and must support the demands of other

---

[166] Scott Report (note 10), part 4, chapter K2, pp. 1759–66, 1795–1806.

[167] Two incidents were of particular concern. First, 2 Channel 4 television programmes (Dispatches, 'The Torture Trail', 1 Jan. 1995 and Dispatches, 'Back on the Torture Trail', 13 Mar. 1996) revealed the involvement of British companies in the brokering of equipment that was used in torture and other human rights violations. Second, in late 1996 there were widespread newspaper allegations concerning the involvement of an Isle of Man-registered company, MilTec Corporation Ltd, in the provision of arms and ammunition to the former Rwandan Government during and after the 1994 genocide, and despite the imposition of a UN arms embargo. See, e.g., 'How the West fuelled genocide', *The Observer*, 24 Nov. 1996. The government set up an interdepartmental committee to investigate the allegations and agreed to implement its recommendations, including the setting up of an interdepartmental committee chaired by the Cabinet Office to coordinate the introduction, application, amendment and lifting of all arms embargoes. 'Trafficking in arms: controls and procedures' (note 60); and British House of Commons, *Hansard*, 21 Jan. 1997, cols 536–37.

[168] British Department of Trade and Industry, *Strategic Export Controls: A Consultative Document*, Cm 3349 (Her Majesty's Stationery Office: London, July 1996), p. 1.

[169] British Labour Party, 'Labour's policy pledges for a responsible arms trade', 13 Feb. 1997.

peoples for the democratic rights on which we insist for ourselves. The Labour Government will put human rights at the heart of our foreign policy'.[170]

Second, the government on 21 May 1997 announced a ban on the import, export, transfer and manufacture of all forms of anti-personnel landmines and imposed a moratorium on their operational use by British forces. Third, following a review of the criteria used to assess export licence applications, Robin Cook published the new criteria in July 1997 (as discussed above). Fourth, having already published the responses to the previous administration's consultation document on strategic export controls,[171] the government published its own White Paper on the issue in July 1998.[172] Among the main proposals in the White Paper, which sets out a new legislative framework for strategic export controls and improvements to export licensing procedures, are: the extension of the catch-all clause to intangible technology transfers (where used to promote or facilitate the development or production of WMD and long-range missiles); the imposition of controls on the brokering of and trafficking in certain strategic goods (including WMD, long-range missiles and torture equipment); and provision for parliamentary scrutiny of EGCOs. The government also concluded that the licensing authority should remain with the DTI. The responses to the White Paper were published in November 1998,[173] and a draft export control bill was published in March 2001. The first *Annual Report on Strategic Export Controls* was published in March 1999.[174]

Although the new export criteria introduced by Labour held out the promise of greater restraint, the scope for flexible interpretation still remained. While it is too early to determine whether or how often the new ethical criteria will outweigh trade considerations, the portents are not promising. First, in comparing the new criteria with their predecessors, the Trade and Industry Committee has already concluded that: 'The July 1997 criteria represent a rather less radical break with past policy than is sometimes represented to be the case. As before, Ministerial interpretation of the criteria in the difficult cases is the touchstone of their real significance'.[175]

Thus, the real test of an ethical foreign policy will be the hard cases, including the more powerful regimes with which the UK has substantial trading relationships. One such case is Indonesia, where the UK sold approximately £900 million worth of defence equipment over the decade 1987–96—approximately 15–20 per cent of total British exports to Indonesia and more than any other EU member state—despite the former Suharto regime having illegally

---

[170] British Foreign and Commonwealth Office, 'Press conference on the FCO mission statement, opening statement by the Foreign Secretary, Robin Cook', FCO Press Release, 12 May 1997.

[171] 'Responses to the Department of Trade and Industry's consultative document on strategic export controls' (note 137). There were 38 responses received by the DTI, of which just over one-half were from industry (either individual companies or trade associations) and the rest from NGOs concerned with human rights and arms trade issues, from church representatives and from private individuals.

[172] British Department of Trade and Industry, *Strategic Export Controls* (note 64).

[173] There were 54 responses. British House of Commons, *Hansard,* written answers, 30 Nov. 1998, col. 55 w.

[174] See note 82.

[175] *Strategic Export Controls* (note 76), para. 28, p. xviii.

occupied East Timor since 1975 and its long history of internal repression and serious violations of human rights.[176] The record of the new Labour government in dealing with licence applications for Indonesia has been mixed. It began by honouring the export licences to Indonesia granted by the previous administration (covering sales of Hawk jet aircraft, Scorpion armoured vehicles and water cannon, some of which had still to be delivered),[177] then refused to grant three licences for the sale of six adapted Land Rovers and two consignments of sniper rifles (worth up to £1 million).[178] The government subsequently turned down four more licence applications to Indonesia in 1997 and approved another 56 licences.[179] While the government's *Annual Report* later confirmed that the majority of these licences were for non-sensitive equipment transfers, those granted for 'aircraft machine-gun spares', 'body armour' and 'military helmets' continued to cause some concerns.[180] Moreover, several licences granted in 1998 (including 'components for combat aircraft', 'components for aircraft cannon', 'components for military utility helicopter', 'military utility vehicles', 'military electronics equipment' and 'communications equipment') had the potential to be associated with equipment used for internal repression.[181]

Licence approvals to Indonesia are not the only example of a potential breach of the new ethical guidelines. With the publication of the first four annual reports on strategic arms controls, a clearer picture has emerged of how the export criteria have been implemented so far. While the majority of licences granted during these periods were clearly to non-sensitive destinations (i.e., allies and other like-minded states), the annual reports reveal that significant numbers of licences were granted to sensitive destinations in Europe, Africa, the Middle East, South America and Asia.

An audit of the 1997 report carried out by the present author on behalf of Saferworld, for example, revealed that approximately 100 licences to 22 countries (out of a total of 142 recipient destinations that received at least one SIEL) still raised concerns when measured against the government's export criteria. Indeed, it is in respect of the interpretation and implementation of the human rights criterion that the most inconsistencies are to be found, particularly regarding the licensing of small arms, light weapons and ammunition. For example, despite raising serious human rights concerns, Bahrain, Colombia, India, Kenya, Lebanon, Pakistan, Sri Lanka, Turkey and Zambia were all recipients of licences for these categories of weapons.[182] The absence of information

---

[176] The case for a more restrictive approach in the British arms export policy towards Indonesia was made in Chalmers, M., *British Arms Export Policy and Indonesia* (Saferworld: London, May 1997).

[177] 'Cook says Indonesia arms sales go ahead', *The Guardian*, 29 July 1997. Although the government claimed that it would be liable for compensation if the licences were revoked, some analysts dispute this view. See, e.g., Pilger, J., 'Moral policy won't stop British bullets', *The Observer*, 20 July 1997.

[178] 'Cook lays down law on arms', *The Guardian*, 26 Sep. 1997.

[179] 'Ministers attacked over military export licences', *The Guardian*, 15 May 1998; and 'We train Suharto's killers', *The Observer*, 10 May 1998.

[180] Davis (note 79), section 5B.

[181] *Annual Report on Strategic Export Controls* (note 9), pp. 48–49; and Davis, I. and Heathershaw, J., *Some Early Reflections on the Second UK Annual Report on Strategic Export Controls* (Saferworld: London, Nov. 1999).

[182] Davis (note 79).

on the quantities of small arms exported and the end-users makes it difficult to confirm with any certainty whether or not these exports breached the British Government's export guidelines. However, the continuing high level of British licences issued for these weapons does not sit comfortably with the government's recent commitment at the UN to make increased regulation of small arms transfers a global priority.

Second, the role of the FCO in trade promotion is expanding under 'New Labour'. Commercial work is now the FCO's largest single activity and accounts for 25 per cent of its resources and 34 per cent of staff overseas. 'Everyone at the Foreign Office is more than happy to roll up their sleeves and get their hands dirty for British business' said the late FCO Minister of State, Derek Fatchett. He also restated the importance of the link between military and civil sales: 'I am particularly pleased that Leeds University, in my constituency, has won a large contract to teach Omani teachers English. Oman is a market more usually associated with British exports in the defence, construction and energy sectors, yet it is our reputation for quality in these sectors which helps us to export British skills, services and training to these very same markets'.[183]

Third, only limited measures have been taken to curtail the arms export promotion machinery within government. The Aid and Trade Provision (ATP), which helped British industry to win foreign (but mainly civil) contracts, has been cancelled, and the Treasury has announced that export credits will no longer be granted for 'unproductive projects' (including defence projects) to low-income countries.[184] However, the government continues to see a central role for the DESO in 'maintaining long term relationships with our traditional customers and of pursuing vigorously new export opportunities'.[185]

Fourth, a new export scandal, the 'Arms to Sierra Leone' affair, emerged to caste a shadow over Labour's ethical foreign policy. The main allegations were that FCO officials and ministers had prior knowledge of the activities of Sandline International, a London-based mercenary company, but withheld the information from Parliament. These activities concerned the overthrow of Sierra Leone's military junta in 1997–98 and the suspicion that Sandline supplied weapons to Sierra Leone in breach of a (British-drafted) UN arms embargo.

A Customs investigation concluded that there was insufficient evidence to warrant a prosecution against the company, and an internal Whitehall inquiry concluded that 'official misjudgement and systematic cultural failures' were responsible for the breach of the UN arms embargo.[186] A more wide-ranging

[183] Speech by the then FCO Minister of State, Derek Fatchett, to the Institute of Export's Partnership 2000 Conference, London, 13 Nov. 1997.

[184] 'Overseas aid paper focuses on morality', *The Guardian*, 6 Nov. 1997.

[185] British House of Commons, Select Committee on Defence, *Fourth Special Report: Government Response to the House of Commons Defence Committee Report on the Appointment of the New Head of Defence Export Services*, HC 1998/99 512 (Stationery Office: London, June 1999).

[186] British Foreign and Commonwealth Office, *Report of the Sierra Leone Arms Investigation*, HC 1997/98 1016 (Her Majesty's Stationery Office: London, 27 July 1998).

inquiry by the Foreign Affairs Select Committee reached similar conclusions, citing 'poor administration' within the FCO as a key concern.[187]

Although seemingly less damaging than the earlier arms scandals, the Sierra Leone affair provided the impetus for Robin Cook to propose a number of wide-ranging reforms of the FCO, including restoration of a sanctions enforcement unit to make sure that arms embargoes are fully observed, better procedures for handling intelligence reports and a ban on unauthorized contacts with private military firms.

Finally, the record of other reforming governments with strong arms lobbies (most notably, the USA under President Jimmy Carter in the 1970s, and more recently the Czech Republic under President Vaclav Havel and South Africa under President Nelson Mandela) suggests that unilateral restraint is always more difficult to sustain in practice than in rhetoric. Indeed, according to reports in one British newspaper, the government's ethical foreign policy was likely to be abandoned after the general election which took place in 2001 because it had become 'a millstone' around the neck of the foreign secretary.[188]

[187] British House of Commons, Select Committee on Foreign Affairs, *Second Report, Sierra Leone*, HC 1998/99 116-I & II (Her Majesty's Stationery Office: London, 3 Feb. 1999). This affair also received extensive media coverage. See, e.g., 'MPs probe for truth in Sandline murk', *The Observer*, 2 Aug. 1998; 'MPs turn wrath on Cook', *The Guardian*, 26 June 1998; 'FO delayed arms alert to Customs', *The Guardian*, 19 May 1998; 'Diamond dogs of war', *Sunday Times*, 10 May 1998; and 'The covert side of Cook's ethical foreign policy', *The Guardian*, 9 May 1998.

[188] 'Labour drops "ethical" tag', *The Guardian*, 4 Sep. 2000.

6. The regulation of arms and dual-use exports in Germany: the legalistic model

I. Introduction

This chapter examines how the Federal Republic of Germany (FRG) has carried out its arms export control responsibilities since the 1960s, with particular emphasis on the changes introduced in the period 1989–92 and since. In order to facilitate a comparative analysis of British, German and Swedish policy in chapter 8, its structure mirrors that used in the previous chapter.

Section II examines the political framework for export controls in Germany, including the policy environment for German arms transfers, the role of domestic policy stakeholders and the limited role of government-backed support mechanisms for arms exports. Section III examines the policy-making and administrative structures for regulating arms exports, including the role of the main government departments. Section IV evaluates the impact and outcomes of German arms export control policy.

II. The policy environment and stakeholders

The policy environment

Germany's involvement in the international arms market is particularly complicated and discriminating as a result of the experience of World War II. In the immediate post-war years, for example, the Allied powers imposed tight restrictions on the development, production and transport of and trade in weapons by the FRG. In addition to a prohibition on the production of NBC weapons, the 1954 Brussels Treaty of the WEU also prevented the FRG from producing a range of offensive conventional weapons. These included long-range aircraft and guided missiles, strategic bombers, fighting ships above 3000 tonnes and submarines above 350 tonnes. These restrictions were gradually lifted until the last restriction on the production of long-range guided missiles—except those equipped to carry weapons of mass destruction—was removed in 1984.[1]

In the 1950s and early 1960s, the Federal Republic slowly re-entered the arms production business, but its military research and development (R&D) was limited and the country was content to import (or produce under licence) most of its weapons from the USA. Until the mid-1960s, therefore, West German arms exports consisted mainly of surplus US-designed weapons exported through a military aid programme. During the early 1960s the West German

---

¹ Wulf, H., 'The Federal Republic of Germany', ed. I. Anthony, SIPRI, *Arms Export Regulations* (Oxford University Press: Oxford, 1991), pp. 73–74.

Table 6.1. Licensed exports of German weapons and dual-use goods 1990–98
Figures are in DM b., current prices. Figures in italics are percentages.

	1990	1991	1992	1993	1994	1995	1996	1997	1998
Weapons of war licensed under the Weapons of War Control Act (KWKG)	1.9	4.1	2.6	2.6	2.1	2.0	1.0	1.4	1.3
(as %% of total exports)	*0.3*	*0.6*	*0.4*	*0.4*	*0.3*	*0.3*	*0.1*	..	..
Licences issued under Foreign Trade Statutory Order (AWV)									
Section A:[a]									
Weapons, ammunition and other military material	20.7	16.0	9.0	12.9	27.0	12.7	11.3	..	..
(as %% of total exports)	*3.0*	*2.4*	*1.3*	*2.1*	*3.9*	*1.7*	*1.5*	..	..
Section C:									
Industrial dual-use goods that can be used for the production of weapons	27.4	20.2	17.3	22.2	63.8	12.7	..	..	..
Sub-total (A + C)	**48.1**	**36.2**	**26.3**	**35.1**	**90.8**	**25.4**	..	..	..
(as %% of total exports)	*7.1*	*5.4*	*3.9*	*5.6*	*13.1*	*3.5*	..	..	..
Total German exports	680.9	665.8	671.2	628.4	690.6	727.7	771.9	..	..

Notes:

.. = Data not available or not applicable.

[a] Includes 'weapons of war' under the Weapons of War Control Act of 20 April 1961 (Gesetz über die Kontrolle von Kriegswaffen, KWKG).

Sources: Written Parliamentary Answers, *Deutscher Bundestag, 13. Wahlperiode: Drucksache* [Printed papers of the German Parliament, 13th Parliament], 13/5680, 2 Oct. 1996 and *Drucksache*, 13/10104, 11 Mar. 1998; and Hagelin, B., Wezeman, P. D. and Wezeman, S. T., 'Transfers of major conventional weapons', *SIPRI Yearbook 2000: Armaments, Disarmament and International Security* (Oxford University Press: Oxford, 2000), table 7E, p. 437.

Government—along with many other NATO countries—operated a programme of military aid as an instrument of foreign policy. Most of this aid (and the resulting arms exports) went to newly independent African states, although India, Iran, Israel and Jordan were also significant recipients of German arms. As a result of domestic political unease with such a programme, the German Cabinet decided in 1965 to prohibit the delivery of arms into 'areas of tension', and by the end of the 1960s all major military aid programmes had been abandoned.[2] However, this rather vague principle was to become a central component in future German arms export control guidelines.

Partly as a result of a number of co-production agreements within the European NATO context and partly as a result of the development of a strong dual-use manufacturing base, the FRG was again a major producer of arms by the 1970s. This left it well placed to take advantage (alongside a number of other

---

[2] For a detailed description of the Federal Republic's military aid programme see Cowen, R., *Defense Procurement in the Federal Republic of Germany: Politics and Organisation* (Westview Press: Boulder, Colo., 1986), pp. 259–62.

Western suppliers) of the rapid expansion in the international arms market in the early 1970s. This expansion included new Third World markets and, despite the ban on the export of weapons to 'areas of tension', German arms companies were also successful in some of these emerging markets, especially in Africa, Asia and Latin America. Indeed, the ban was initially confined largely to the Middle East, but even there it excluded dual-use goods, large quantities of which were exported to the region.

For exports of major weapon systems, however, the declared preference was sales to NATO countries. While this continued to be the case throughout the 1970s, the accumulation of oil wealth in the Middle East subsequently drew the FRG into becoming a significant supplier of major conventional weapons to that region as well. In the period 1973–77, for example, some 46 per cent of West German arms and dual-use exports were to the Middle East (while Africa accounted for 27 per cent, Latin America 21 per cent and Asia 6 per cent). In sum, Third World destinations accounted for 70 per cent of German arms and dual-use exports during this period, with 30 per cent going to NATO countries.[3]

When considering the position in the 1980s and 1990s it is worth looking at the statistical evidence in greater detail. The international sources are complemented by national statistics showing the total value of all licences granted under the two main legislative provisions (which are described in more detail below). The value of licences issued for 'weapons of war' (roughly defined as major weapon systems) under the Weapons of War Control Act of 20 April 1961 (Gesetz über die Kontrolle von Kriegswaffen, KWKG) fluctuated between DM 0.6 and 2.2 billion over the 11-year period 1977–87, while those issued for dual-use goods and other weapons under the Foreign Trade and Payments Act (Aussenwirtschaftsgesetz, AWG) fluctuated between DM 0.9 and 7.1 billion. However, by 1989 the total value of the latter had increased to DM 13 billion, suggesting both the increased significance of dual-use and other types of weapon exports, and the increased scope of the controls.[4]

As table 6.1 shows, these trends continued into the first half of the 1990s. Licences issued for 'weapons of war' continued to account on average for less than 0.5 per cent of total German exports, and it is these figures that are usually provided in official government statements on German arms exports. These figures hugely underestimate the true involvement of German companies in the international arms trade. A more realistic view is provided by the export licence figures under the Foreign Trade Statutory Order (Aussenwirtschaftsverordnung, AWV).[5] Section A of the AWV includes not only the weapons licensable under the KWKG but also ammunition, small arms, weapon components, military electronics, manufacturing licences and other military-related goods and services. During the seven years 1990–96 the value of this category of export

<hr>

[3] ACDA figures quoted by Pearson, F., '"Necessary evil": perspectives on West German arms transfer policies', *Armed Forces and Society*, vol. 12, no. 4 (summer 1986), p. 529.

[4] Wulf (note 1), pp. 78–79.

[5] See section III in this chapter.

licences granted fluctuated between DM 9 and 27 billion in current prices or between 1.3 and 3.9 per cent of total German exports.

If the industrial dual-use equipment exported under section C of the AWV Export List (Ausfuhrliste, AL) is included in the picture (and these figures exclude dual-use goods and technologies exported for NBC purposes), then the fluctuations are even more dramatic, ranging from DM 90.8 billion (or 13.1 per cent of total exports) in 1994 to DM 25.4 billion (or 3.5 per cent of total exports) only one year later. However, inclusion of this category of exports would be equally misleading, as often they are not destined for military use. Moreover, 1994 was clearly an exceptional year, which may be partly explained by the ongoing relaxation of national rules for international joint ventures in arms production (see below) and/or by a surge in exports of surplus weapons and materials transferred under the NATO 'cascade' programme in 1992–94. Overall, however, the figures in table 6.1 clearly show the importance of dual-use and arms exports to the German economy.

SIPRI data on the supply of major conventional weapons confirm the mini-boom in German arms exports during the period 1990–96[6] (as does the UN Register[7]). This was largely due to exports of surplus equipment following German unification, which accounted for approximately one-half of all German equipment exported during this period.[8] For example, 39 former East German naval ships were supplied to Indonesia in 1993.[9] Although most of these surplus stocks were exhausted by 1997, Germany continued to account for a significant share of the world total of major conventional weapons in the latter half of the decade (5.5 per cent of the global total during the five years 1995–99, worth $6085 million at constant 1990 prices) and was ranked by SIPRI as the fifth-largest exporter of major conventional weapons in the world over that period.[10]

In terms of German export controls, two issues dominated the policy environment during the cold war—West European integration (both within NATO and within the EC) and the end of the division of Germany. Many politicians, particularly within the German Social Democratic Party (Sozialdemokratische Partei, SPD), believed that the maintenance and expansion of East–West trade

[6] See, e.g., Anthony, I., Wezeman, P. D. and Wezeman, S. T., 'The trade in major conventional weapons', *SIPRI Yearbook 1995: Armaments, Disarmament and International Security* (Oxford University Press: Oxford, 1995), p. 493; and Anthony, I., Wezeman, P. D. and Wezeman, S. T., 'The trade in major conventional weapons', *SIPRI Yearbook 1997: Armaments, Disarmament and International Security* (Oxford University Press: Oxford, 1997), p. 268.

[7] In 1994, e.g., the UN Register suggests that Germany exported far more conventional weapons than any other country, including the USA. United Nations, Register on Conventional Arms, UN document A/50/47, 1995.

[8] Wezeman, P. D. and Wezeman, S. T., 'Transfers of major conventional weapons', *SIPRI Yearbook 1998: Armaments, Disarmament and International Security* (Oxford University Press: Oxford, 1998), p. 298. It should be noted, however, that SIPRI values are not the same thing as actual prices received.

[9] Nassauer, O., 'An army's surplus: the NVA's heritage', eds E. J. Laurance and H. Wulf, *Coping with Surplus Weapons*, Brief no. 3 (Bonn International Center for Conversion: Bonn, 1995), pp. 45–46 and 58–59.

[10] Hagelin, B., Wezeman, P. D. and Wezeman, S. T., 'Transfers of major conventional weapons', *SIPRI Yearbook 2000: Armaments, Disarmament and International Security* (Oxford University Press: Oxford, 2000), table 7A.2, p. 372. The figures are SIPRI trend-indicator values and cannot be equated with prices paid or other economic indicators.

and liberalization of export controls would contribute to unification. Hence, traditionally Germany supported a less restrictive policy within the Western COCOM group as part of its Ostpolitik strategy. This strategy often placed Germany in opposition to the USA on export control matters and at times seriously affected NATO cohesiveness. With the end of the cold war export controls on East–West trade ceased to be a contentious issue. The newly unified Germany led the calls for a radical reduction of the COCOM Industrial List and readily embraced the post-COCOM reorientation of international export controls around WMD proliferation concerns.

While German foreign economic policy and the emphasis on export-led growth have remained largely unchanged by the seismic changes since 1989, the future orientation of German foreign and military policy is less clear. There has been and continues to be a wide-ranging debate on the issue, and differences of opinion exist between and within the national political parties.[11] Despite the absence of any political consensus on Germany's future international role, the German military has changed enormously in recent years.[12] The West German Bundeswehr absorbed the East German Army and manpower was cut from almost 600 000 to 340 000 (almost one-half of whom are conscripts). However, the shortage of recruits and high levels of conscientious objection to military service may in time lead to the creation of an elite force of professional soldiers who could take part in the WEU/NATO rapid reaction force.[13] Troops have already been sent abroad for the first time since 1945 in UN peacekeeping missions to Somalia, Albania, and Bosnia and Herzegovina, and, like other NATO members, Germany has begun to restructure its forces according to the ideas of power projection. The heavy budget burdens of rebuilding eastern Germany (including military clean-up costs) have constrained such military restructuring so far, but a future consequence of adopting a higher military profile is likely to be increased equipment expenditure. With increased arms procurement also comes the possibility of increased defence-related exports.

However, the situation remains fluid and the implications for German export controls are as yet unclear. The emphasis on multilateral diplomacy and integration in supranational institutions appear to remain core objectives of the present SPD–Green coalition government, elected in September 1998, and these would lock German export control policy to developments at the European level (as discussed in part II of the book). Again, however, this policy is not set in stone and may well change under the next (or a later) generation of political leaders,

---

[11] See, e.g., Mayer, H., 'Early at the beach and claiming territory? The evolution of German ideas on a new European order', *International Affairs*, vol. 73, no. 4 (1997), pp. 721–37; Janning, J., 'A German Europe—a European Germany? On the debate over Germany's foreign policy', *International Affairs*, vol. 72, no. 1 (1996), pp. 33–41; Young, T.-D., 'Nationalization or integration? The future direction of German defense policy', *Defense Analysis*, vol. 11, no. 2 (1995), pp. 109–20; Meiers, F.-J.,'Germany: the reluctant power', *Survival*, vol. 37, no. 3 (autumn 1995), pp. 82–103; and Gutjahr, L., *German Foreign and Defence Policy After Unification* (Pinter: London, 1994).

[12] For an overview see Schulte, H., '1995: a year of adjustment', *Jane's Defence 96: The World In Conflict* (Jane's Information Group: Coulsdon, 1996), pp. 44–45; and Schulte, H., 'Country briefing: Germany', *Jane's Defence Weekly*, 20 Mar. 1996, pp. 23–36.

[13] 'German angst at professional army', *The Observer*, 14 Feb. 1993.

particularly if European political integration becomes deadlocked. Indeed, if Germany at some later stage decides that it no longer wishes to 'punch below its weight' in foreign policy, then its post-war policy of self-limitation with regard to arms exports may also disappear.

The role of domestic policy stakeholders

Proponents of arms transfer restraint

Arms transfer restraint, particularly towards the Third World, has been an important issue of morality and political culture for a wide variety of groups and institutions in Germany. In the mid- and late 1960s, for example, the most vociferous opposition was provided by the West German SPD, which promised to forbid the export of arms to the Third World. Once it was in power, however, in coalition with the liberal Free Democratic Party (Freien Demokratischen Partei, FDP), for which arms transfers were less of a concern, the guidelines the SPD introduced in 1971 (see below) fell well short of this commitment. Moreover, despite continuing to advocate a strict control position, the SPD–FDP coalition oversaw a boom period in German arms exports during the 1970s.

In the conservative political parties which shaped arms transfer policy until 1969 and were the main governing parties from 1982 until 1998—the Christian Democrats (Christlich Demokratische Union, CDU) and Christian Social Union (Christlich Soziale Union, CSU)—opposition to arms transfers to the Third World was limited to a few individuals. Similarly, in the late 1970s and early 1980s the issue also became less relevant for the SPD leadership (although many individuals within the party continued to advocate a policy of restraint). Instead, the main party-political opposition to arms transfers during this period came from a new political force, the Green Party (Die Grünen), which placed the issue at the centre of its foreign policy.[14] During this period, the Greens became the focal point for many small Third World NGOs and peace groups, and for strong minorities in larger organizations, such as the Protestant and Catholic churches and the trade unions. A significant number of journalists and academics (both to the left and to the right of the political spectrum) favoured more restraint in arms transfers. While opposition to arms transfers to the Third World is based on a diverse range of reasons, arguably the two most important have been the desire to break with the German militarist past and the belief that arms transfers are inimical to development.[15]

Since the end of the 1991 Persian Gulf War political and public support for peace groups in general, and for those campaigning against the arms trade in

---

[14] See, e.g., the speech by E. Stratmann, a Green deputy in the Bundestag, *Verhandlungen des Deutschen Bundestages, 11.Wahlperiode, Stenographische Berichte* [Proceedings of the German Bundestag, 11th Parliament, Stenographic record], 11/153, p. 11585.

[15] Brzoska, M., 'The erosion of restraint in West German arms transfer policy', *Journal of Peace Research*, vol. 26, no. 2 (1989), pp. 166–67.

particular, has tailed off. This is largely attributed to a shift in attitudes and the domination of German politics since unification by the issue of employment.[16]

Opponents of arms transfer restraint

Supporters of a less strict control regime have generally fallen into three main categories—the arms industry; political parties on the right, namely the CDU and the CSU; and the foreign policy elite.[17] It was not until the early 1970s that the German arms industry began to lobby effectively for arms exports: until then there had been no need as domestic demand had largely outpaced domestic arms production. However, the emergence of new and lucrative export markets among the oil-exporting nations and an economic crisis in the FRG, particularly in shipbuilding, meant that the employment argument became a very effective instrument of arms trade expansion during the 1970s. The employment question also enabled the arms companies to elicit some support for a relaxation of the arms export rules among trade union representatives.

Over the years the political organization of the arms industry has grown more self-assured and demanding. It is now centred in the Federation of German Industries (Bundesverband der Deutschen Industrie, BDI) and other trade associations, such as of the machinery, electronics and aerospace industries. In the 1990s these associations became increasingly critical of the complexity of the licensing process and, in particular, the additional national controls on dual-use goods which go beyond the harmonized European arrangements.[18]

During the 1970s and 1980s the use of arms transfers as a foreign policy instrument was advocated by many career diplomats and conservative politicians, who believed that Germany's policy of restraint was damaging bilateral relations with many Third World leaders. More generally, the post-war period was marked by an almost continuous political consensus around the export orientation of the German economy, with export successes being seen as compensation for Germany's limited global political role. A temporary change in attitude occurred in the late 1980s. Under the political influence of Hans-Dietrich Genscher,[19] the German Foreign Ministry (Auswärtiges Amt) began to challenge the dominant policy role of the Ministry of Economics (Bundesministerium für Wirtschaft und Technologie, BMWi) and argued successfully for a tightening of export controls. However, this increased support among political and bureaucratic elites for strict export controls remains fragile and is certainly not universal. Indeed, in the difficult post-unification economic

---

[16] Personal interviews with NGO activists, 1997.

[17] For a discussion on elite opinion on arms control see Krell, G., *The Federal Republic of Germany and Arms Control*, PRIF reports no. 10 (Peace Research Institute Frankfurt: Frankfurt, Feb. 1990).

[18] For the BDI's reaction see, e.g., Kelle, A. and Müller, H., 'Germany', eds H. Müller and J. Prystrom, *Central European Countries and Non-Proliferation Regimes* (Polish Foundation of International Affairs and Peace Research Institute Frankfurt: Warsaw, 1996), pp. 148–50.

[19] Genscher, a member of the CDU's liberal coalition partner, the FDP, was German Foreign Minister from 1974 to 1992.

climate strict national export controls for both arms and dual-use exports have come under increasing scrutiny within the German polity.[20]

Government promotion of arms exports

Since the cessation of the military aid programme in the late 1960s, successive German governments have generally been reluctant to promote arms exports overtly. Indeed, because of the sensitivity of defence exports as an issue in domestic politics, German governments have generally avoided using high-level officials to promote them. (There have been notable exceptions. Advocacy by the German Chancellor and Minister of Defence in the early 1990s, for example, is thought to have contributed to Sweden's decision to buy the German Leopard 2 tank in preference to French or US tanks.) Neither does Germany have an organization that is responsible for identifying defence export opportunities: in the past this function has largely been left to industry, although the visit of a German delegation to the British DESO in 1997 may indicate a future change of policy.[21] Similarly, although it is official policy that German military attachés cannot promote arms sales, they are reported to have aided the negotiations for the sale of submarines to India in 1981–82. Nor is it usually the practice of the German Government to issue MOUs to guarantee the goods and terms of defence exporters (as is the case in the UK and elsewhere), although, again, in some cases it has done so.[22]

In the late 1990s, however, there was increasing pressure for the German Government to take a more active role in arms export promotion. Indeed, such activities are beginning to happen on a small scale, through, for example, the German Navy carrying out arms promotion tours (most recently to South Africa) and government representation at international arms fairs and exhibitions.

As regards export credits for arms sales, the German Government does provide loan guarantees for private banks that underwrite export deals through its Hermes credit guarantee agency. The agency is generally barred from assisting in defence sales, but important exceptions were made in the late 1970s and early 1980s, when Hermes-backed military exports were authorized to a number of regions of tension.[23] Generally, however, export credits for military exports are only provided for deliveries to EU and NATO countries and other like-minded countries, such as Australia and New Zealand. Data on the value of guarantees for defence exports are unavailable because the FRG only reports total export financing.[24]

---

[20] See, e.g., the discussion in Hofhansel, C., *Commercial Competition and National Security: Comparing US and German Export Control Policies* (Praeger: Westport, Conn., 1996), pp. 124–25.

[21] Personal interview with a DESO official, Sep. 1997.

[22] Pearson (note 3), pp. 536–37.

[23] Pearson, F., 'Of Leopards and Cheetahs: West Germany's role as a mid-sized arms supplier', *Orbis*, spring 1985, p. 171.

[24] US General Accounting Office, *Military Exports: A Comparison of Government Support in the United States and Three Major Competitors*, GAO/NSIAD-95-86 (GAO: Washington, DC, May 1995).

III. The German arms export control regime

The policy-making structure

Principal legislation

The Constitution of the FRG (Grundgesetz für die Bundesrepublik Deutschland) imposed by the Allied powers in May 1949 explicitly prohibits activities that might threaten peaceful cohabitation in Germany, including actions to prepare for or carry out offensive war. In particular, Article 26, paragraph 2 specifies that 'weapons intended to be used for war' can only be produced, transported and traded with the permission of the federal government.[25] In the mid-1950s, as a consequence of the constitutional restrictions (and the WEU restrictions mentioned above) and in response to West German rearmament, two laws to regulate the arms and dual-use exports of the FRG were prepared: (*a*) the Weapons of War Control Act (KWKG) of 20 April 1961; and (*b*) the Foreign Trade and Payments Act (Aussenwirtschaftsgesetz, AWG) of 28 April 1961.

The Weapons of War Control Act

The KWKG regulates exports of 'weapons of war' as defined by the contents of a detailed War Weapons List (Kriegswaffenliste). Under Article 2, paragraphs 1 and 2 of the KWKG a government permit is necessary to produce, obtain and allow others to have possession of weapons. The federal government is legally obliged to deny a permit in three sets of circumstances: if there is reason to believe that it would be detrimental to the international relations of the FRG (Article 6, paragraph 2); if there is a danger that the weapons will be used in a peace-threatening action, particularly an offensive war (Article 6, paragraph 3); or if there is reason to believe that the export would not be in accordance with the FRG's responsibilities under international law (Article 6, paragraph 3).[26]

If an arms export licence is refused the burden of proof is on the applicant to show that the refusal is unjustified, if necessary in court.

The Foreign Trade and Payments Act

The AWG regulates military-related technology and armaments, and was originally designed to enact the COCOM regulations. Although the focus is on dual-use goods, the AWG also extends to military weapons, in effect subjecting the export of weapons to a dual licensing requirement.[27] The rules governing AWG goods are less clear-cut than those stipulated under the KWKG, however. The right to trade freely is expressly guaranteed by the German Constitution. Thus, unless explicitly forbidden, foreign trade does not require a government

---

[25] Wulf (note 1), pp. 72–74.

[26] Wulf (note 1), p. 74.

[27] Weitbrecht, A., 'The control of arms exports in the Federal Republic of Germany', *Disarmament*, vol. 15, no. 1 (1992), p. 59.

licence. Restrictions are possible, however, under Article 5 in order to fulfil international agreements. Export licences can also be refused under Article 7, paragraph 1 of the AWG when an export might (*a*) endanger the security of the FRG, (*b*) threaten the peaceful coexistence of the peoples, or (*c*) disturb the external relations of the FRG. However, prior to a 1990 amendment to the AWG (discussed below), the burden of proof was on the government to prove that one or more of these three negative effects were likely to result from a sale, and in practice this was difficult to achieve.[28]

The regulations for the implementation of the AWG can be found primarily in the AWV,[29] the Export List (AL), and the Country Lists and circular directives on foreign trade[30] issued by the Ministry of Economics. The AWV lays down which goods, technologies, software and services are subject to export restrictions. In general it refers the exporter to the Export List and to specific Country Lists (discussed below).

The key reforms of 1989–93

Both laws and their associated lists have been amended several times since 1961, but some of the most notable amendments were passed between 1989 and 1993. In the 1980s there were several investigations into the violation of German export regulations, particularly with regard to exports of technology for the production of chemical weapons to Libya.[31] As a result of these investigations, new legislative initiatives were already in hand when further revelations surfaced about the role of German companies in the building up of Iraq's arms industry, including transfers of nuclear, chemical and missile technology.[32] Thus, as a result of increasing international and domestic pressures to tighten controls, a number of legislative amendments (and administrative improvements, which are discussed below) were made. The main changes to the federal laws were as follows.

1. *Burden of proof in AWG cases.* The AWG was amended in July 1990 and again in February 1992 in order to remove the burden of proof from the

---

[28] Wulf (note 1), p. 74. In short, the main difference between the KWKG and AWG provisions was that in cases of doubt the burden of proof required to deny a licence was much stronger in relation to the latter (and rested with the government rather than the applicant). The opposite was the case under the KWKG provisions.

[29] Key extracts are reproduced in the section on Germany in *Worldwide Guide to Export Controls 1996/1997* (Export Control Publications: Chertsey, 1997), pp. 2–9.

[30] Circular directives are official announcements on changes in the laws and the statutory orders concerning foreign trade, and explain important procedural regulations.

[31] Brzoska, M., 'Behind the German export scandals', *Bulletin of the Atomic Scientists*, July/Aug. 1989, pp. 32–35; and Kelle, A., 'German export controls on nuclear and dual-use goods, 1988–92', eds D. Carlton *et al.*, *Controlling the International Transfer of Weaponry and Related Technology* (Dartmouth: Aldershot, 1995), pp. 203–24.

[32] Of a list drawn up by US and British intelligence services of 110 German firms suspected of breaking the arms embargo on Iraq, the German authorities were investigating 11 cases in 1991. 'Top firms accused over sanctions', *The Guardian*, 30 Jan. 1991. For a discussion of the background leading up to the reforms see Müller, H. *et al.*, *From Black Sheep to White Angel? The New German Export Control Policy*, PRIF reports no. 32 (Peace Research Institute Frankfurt: Frankfurt, Jan. 1994), pp. 1–5.

government in respect of the three qualifying criteria. Under the new rules, all non-licensed exports of goods subject to licensing under both the AWG and the KWKG are treated as crimes and the three AWG criteria are now only used to define and judge the seriousness of individual breaches.

2. *The catch-all clause.* A catch-all clause (Article 5c of the AWV) was introduced in 1990 for exports under the AWV.[33] Although the catch-all in relation to NBC weapons (and the missiles capable of carrying such weapons) later became subject to Article 4 of the EC Regulation, the legislative provision for the catch-all in relation to conventional weapons remains unchanged and a unique feature of the German model: no other EU member state includes conventional arms in its catch-all to non-embargoed destinations. Under this provision, exports of goods not on the Export List require a licence when they are used as supplies for conventional weapons or armaments production plants in a country on Country List K (initially introduced as Country List H: see below) *and* the exporter has prior knowledge of this intended use. In effect, this requires companies to ensure that all proposed exports to these destinations are for civilian use only.

3. *Principles for examining the reliability of exporters.* Established in 1991,[34] these principles effectively make the granting of an export licence to certain destinations (32 specified countries as at March 2000[35]) dependent on the reliability of the exporter. Specific personnel and organizational requirements in the respective companies must be fulfilled as proof of reliability. Applicants under both the KWKG and the AWG regulations, for example, must appoint a 'Person Responsible for Exports' (Ausfuhrverantwortlicher) and obtain a certificate of reliability from the Federal Export Office (Bundesausfuhramt, BAFA). The named company official, who must be a person at executive board or managing director level, is also responsible for assessing end-use and can later be held accountable for any foreseeable diversion. Many individual German companies have responded by introducing their own internal guidelines and export controls which exceed the minimum requirements.[36]

4. *Penalties and sanctions.* Tougher penalties were introduced for violations of both the AWG and the KWKG. Amendments to the AWG in 1990 and 1992 changed the character of many of the categories of violations from a civil breach of administrative regulations to a criminal offence. Penalties were also considerably stiffened: illegal exports are now punishable by a prison sentence of up to five years or monetary fines (Article 34, paragraphs 1 and 2 of the AWG); serious cases of export violations are now subject to a minimum sentence of two years and a maximum sentence of 15 years' imprisonment

---

[33] *Worldwide Guide to Export Controls* (note 29), pp. 3–4 and 17–18.

[34] This legislative change was announced by the Federal Government on 29 Nov. 1990 (and came into effect on 1 Mar. 1991) in a Statutory Order entitled Basic Principles for the Assessment of the Reliability of Companies exporting War Weapons and Armament-relevant Goods. *Bundesanzeiger* [Federal gazette], no. 225 (1990), p. 6406.

[35] German Federal Export Office, 'BAFA export controls: brief outline', Eschborn, 15 Mar. 2000, p. 18.

[36] See, e.g., the corporate export control policies of Leybold AG and Daimler-Benz AG, discussed in Müller *et al.* (note 32), pp. 44–45.

(Article 34, paragraph 6); the violation of UN embargoes was created as a separate criminal offence with the same range of penalties (Article 34 (4)); and negligent or wilful violations of the export regulations can now be punished by up to three years' imprisonment or a fine (Article 34 (7)). Finally, further legal changes in 1992 also made it possible to confiscate the whole turnover from an illegal transfer (whereas previously only the net profit from any deal could be confiscated). As regards the KWKG, amendments to this legislation created a differential penalty structure for nuclear weapons (Article 19), chemical and biological weapons (Article 20) and all other weapons (Article 22a). Penalties for major violations now range from minimum prison sentences of 1–3 years to maximum prison sentences of 5–15 years. Minor violations carry lower prison sentences or a fine.[37]

5. *Surveillance of communications.* The February 1992 changes empowered the central office of the Customs Investigation Service (Zollkriminalinstitut, ZKI) to undertake intrusive surveillance measures (as discussed below).

6. *Intangible transfers.* In August 1993 the AWV was amended to include transfers of 'intangibles' in the scope of the controls.

Weapon, export and country lists

The War Weapons List is an appendix to the KWKG and is divided into two parts. Part A covers weapons that Germany has renounced (I: nuclear weapons; II: chemical weapons; and III: biological weapons) while part B covers weapons under national control.[38] Under Article 1, paragraph 2 of the KWKG the government is entitled (in agreement with the Bundesrat[39]) to amend the War Weapons List according to the latest scientific, technical and military knowledge.

While all the goods on the War Weapons List are subject to licensing requirements, most restrictions result from the Export List. The Export List, which is published as an annex to the AWV, is a more detailed and comprehensive list of controlled goods, including weapons, production technology, weapon-related materials and dual-use goods. It has undergone a number of changes since 1991, as table 6.2 shows. Many dual-use items no longer considered sensitive or sophisticated were removed from the list as part of the liberalization of the COCOM regime, while other items were added as a result of growing concerns about WMD procurement programmes by would-be proliferators.

The Export List was completely revised in July 1995 to reflect the new EC Regulation, and is currently divided into two parts. Only Part I is concerned with the AWG legislation.[40] It is subdivided into three sections: section A lists

---

[37] Müller *et al.* (note 32), pp. 31–34.

[38] Part B divides into: I: flight objects; II: aircraft and helicopters; III: fighting ships and auxiliaries; IV: fighting vehicles; V: artillery; VI: light anti-tank weapons, mortars, mine-laying and mine-throwing systems; VII: torpedoes, mines, bombs, independent munitions; VIII: other munition; IX: other significant components; and X: dispensers for submunitions.

[39] The Bundesrat is the 2nd chamber of the German Parliament.

[40] Part II regulates other civilian trade.

Table 6.2. The scope of the German Export List, 1961–99

	Sections of Export List
1961–30 June 1995	A. Weapons, ammunition and other military material
	B. Nuclear equipment
	C. Industrial dual-use equipment that can be used for the production of weapons
1984–30 June 1995	D. Chemical equipment
1989–30 June 1995	E. Biological equipment
1 July 1995 to date	A. Weapons, ammunition and other military material
	B. Other goods (at present this list only contains electric batons, electroshock devices, thumbscrews and shackles)
	C. Dual-use goods (this list is identical to Annex I of the EU Regulation, as extended by national items in the 900 numbering range)[a]

Note: [a] The German Government imposed a licence requirement on 13 dual-use items that do not appear on Annex I. This list is found in *Official Journal of the European Communities*, C334 (12 Dec. 1995).

Source: Compiled by the author on the basis of interviews and *Worldwide Guide to Export Controls 1996/1997* (Export Control Publications: Chertsey, 1997).

weapons, munitions and military equipment (the Munitions List), includes all items contained in the Weapons List, and was recently amended to reflect the Wassenaar Arrangement; section B is a short list of repressive technologies; and section C lists the dual-use goods subject to authorization for export from the EU (the common Annex I list, which replaced sections B, C, D and E in the previous German Export List). Section C is by far the longest list, covering pages 29–140 in the 1997 version of the Export List, while section A runs from page 1 to page 27.[41] (In contrast, the War Weapons List is only five pages long.) All goods, software and technology on the Export List are liable to export licence authorization for destinations outside the EU, but only those items within section A and a few particularly sensitive items in section C require a licence for intra-EU transfers. However, even non-listed goods may require a licence for certain destinations under the catch-all clause described above. Approximately 5 per cent of all German exports are covered by the licensing system.[42]

The German export control authorities have several listings of non-sensitive and sensitive countries. Following recent changes, there are now three non-sensitive lists: Country List A/B (predominantly 'free world' countries); Country List D (all countries which issue International Import Certificates before importing embargoed goods); and Country List L (all OECD countries).

Until very recently, there were also three separate 'sensitive country' lists.[43]

---

[41] The Export List was examined during personal interviews at BAFA, 1997.
[42] Personal interview with German government officials, Oct. 1997.
[43] For further details see *Worldwide Guide to Export Controls* (note 29), pp. 12–14.

1. *Country List C.* This covers 26 former COCOM-proscribed countries.

2. *Country List K* (formerly H). This list covers the most problematic and sensitive destinations which require a licence even for non-listed goods (i.e., for items which are not restricted under any of the proliferation control regimes) which are intended for use in conventional weapons. This is the list to which the German conventional weapon catch-all clause applies. The original H list contained 54 countries but this was reduced to 34 in January 1992.[44] In 1995 the H list was abolished and replaced with the much shorter K List (which at the end of 1999 contained 15 countries[45]). The reduction is intended to concentrate the controls on the most critical countries. At the same time, the scope of the list has been brought closer into line with similar lists in other exporting countries in order to simplify the necessary international harmonization of export controls.

3. *Country List N.* This list covers sensitive destinations (10 countries[46]) which require a licence for non-listed goods intended for use in nuclear programmes, whether civilian or military. This is the list to which the German nuclear catch-all clause applies.

Country List C was abolished in 1997, and Country List K (the only remaining list for conventional weapons) is acknowledged by officials as being only a partial list of sensitive destinations. Indeed, there are many destinations not included in the K List (most of the countries in Africa, for example) where licence applications for arms exports are likely to be denied.[47]

As at the end of 1999, Germany was implementing UN, OSCE and EU embargoes to the same destinations as the UK, as described in chapter 5. There are currently no German national embargoes in place.

Who decides export control policy?

Although the German Government is ultimately responsible for export control policy, with the exception of a few national regulations the items on the Export List are based on agreements concluded within international regimes. An Inter-Agency Foreign Trade Group (Ressortkreis Aussenwirtschaft) was created in 1989 for the ongoing review of proliferation issues and for the preparation of legal and regulatory amendments. Chaired by the Ministry of Economics, this group meets on a regular basis every six to eight weeks and includes representatives from the foreign, defence and finance ministries, the Office of the Chancellor and the intelligence services.[48] The Ministry of Economics is also the lead agency for managing the export control lists (although any proposed amendments are also discussed with the Foreign Ministry).

[44] Hofhansel (note 20), p. 42.

[45] Currently Afghanistan, Angola, Bosnia and Herzegovina, Croatia, Cuba, Iran, Iraq, North Korea, Lebanon, Libya, Mozambique, Myanmar (Burma), Somalia, Syria and the Federal Republic of Yugoslavia. 'BAFA export controls: brief outline' (note 35), p. 11.

[46] The 10 countries on Country List N in 1997 were Algeria, India, Iran, Iraq, Israel, Jordan, Libya, North Korea, Pakistan and Syria. *Worldwide Guide to Export Controls* (note 29), p. 20.

[47] Personal interview with German government officials, Sep. 1997.

[48] Müller *et al.* (note 32), p. 47.

The Federal Security Council (Bundessicherheitsrat, BSR) also provides political direction. It is a Cabinet committee for security policy matters, made up of senior ministers, headed by the Federal Chancellor and including the ministers for defence, economics, foreign affairs, finance and internal policies.[49] Individual licensing decisions are not normally part of its remit: for example, it might decide that Indonesia is a suitable recipient of German military goods in principle, but it would normally be the Ministry of Economics that decides whether or not to grant a licence for a specific weapon sale to that destination.

Export control criteria

Detailed guidelines for industry first appeared in 1971. They emerged from a domestic political conflict after the 1969 election which was both interdepartmental and between the two parties in the new coalition government.[50] The Ministry of Defence (Bundesministerium der Verteidigung), led by Helmut Schmidt of the SPD, preferred a complete ban on arms exports outside NATO, while other ministries (notably the Foreign Ministry under FDP leader Walter Scheel) favoured selective use of arms exports and military assistance as an instrument of foreign policy. In order to find a compromise route for future policy and to guide the administrative decision-making process, the Cabinet on 16 June 1971 established 'political principles for the export of weapons and other armaments goods' (Politische Grundsätze der Bundesregierung für den Export von Kriegswaffen und sonstigen Rüstungsgütern).[51]

The guidelines made a distinction between four groups of recipients: (*a*) NATO countries, to which, in principle, unrestricted exports of weapons and other armaments were permitted (although, in principle, these were not allowed to be re-exported outside NATO); (*b*) countries that fell under the COCOM regulations, to which no exports of weapons were permitted, and exports of dual-use goods were only permitted with the unanimous consent of COCOM member states; (*c*) countries in areas of tension (as defined by the Foreign Ministry), to which no exports of weapons were permitted, but exports of dual-use goods were allowed provided there were no grounds for denial under the AWG provisions; and (*d*) 'other countries', to which arms exports would only be allowed as a result of special political considerations and dual-use goods could be exported in accordance with existing laws.

These voluntary guidelines left several areas of ambiguity—most notably in the treatment of exports of weapons from co-production arrangements with other NATO countries, and the export of production licences and technology— and were sufficiently vague to allow the government to overrule many of the restrictions at its own discretion. The German Cabinet also made a decision later the same year which further eroded the policy of restraint. It was decided

---

[49] Wulf (note 1), pp. 78–79.

[50] Brzoska (note 15), p. 169.

[51] These guidelines, which had little legal force—they were neither law nor regulations, but simply internal Cabinet rules—were never officially published but were circulated to industry by an arms lobby newsletter. Wulf (note 1), p. 76.

that for exports from co-production projects between French and German companies the two governments would consult but there would be no German veto right on exports from France.[52]

By the beginning of the 1980s the integrity of the guidelines was being challenged by conflicting pressures and interests. On the one hand, there were growing pressures to export, even though Germany had captured a significant share of the expanding global arms market of the 1970s. On the other hand, there were continuing pressures for restraint, reinforced by a number of controversial export agreements in the early 1980s. As a result of these pressures, the coalition government of Schmidt and Genscher adopted new guidelines on 28 April 1982.[53]

The revised guidelines, which remained in force until January 2000, contained several important changes, the net result of which was to legitimize and extend the scope for sales of less controversial military equipment to Third World customers. First, the ban on exports of weapons to 'areas of tension' that characterized the 1971 guidelines was replaced by the arrangement (under Article 13) that 'the supply of weapons of war and war-related armaments goods must not heighten existing tensions'.

Second, the government was given even more room for manoeuvre by the adoption of a new broad principle (in Article 9) which states: 'Exports of weapons of war shall not be permitted unless exceptions of a general nature are made on the basis of special political considerations or, in individual cases, unless vital interests of the Federal Republic of Germany call for an exception to be made'. Such vital interests are the 'foreign and security policy interests of the Federal Republic of Germany, with due regard of Alliance interests'.[54]

Third, under Article 14 end-user certificates became necessary (rather than optional) for the export of weapons, but in respect of dual-use goods (covered by the AWG) the government only 'aims' to meet such a requirement. Over the years, however, the end-user system has been extended to dual-use goods (as discussed below).

Fourth, and most significantly, the problem of co-production programmes with other NATO countries was addressed (using the precedent set in 1972 in the agreement with France as the basis for the new policy). Because these government-to-government cooperation programmes were deemed to be in the interest of the NATO alliance, components supplied by German companies were now to be treated as an integrated part of the complete weapon system (under Article 4 of the guidelines). The legal effect was that the exporting country of the finished weapon system now became designated as the country

---

[52] Brzoska (note 15), pp. 170–71.

[53] This 2nd set of guidelines was published in the official government bulletin. 'Politische grundsätze der Bundesregierung für den export von kriegswaffen und sonstigen rüstungsgütern' [Political principles of the Federal Government for the export of weapons of war and other military equipment], *Presse- und Informationsamt der Bundesregierung*, no. 38 (5 May 1982). For a review of the public debate that preceded the new guidelines see Cowen (note 2), p. 269.

[54] Quoted in Wulf (note 1), p. 78. Interestingly, concern about employment is explicitly mentioned as not being a valid criterion. See also Brzoska (note 15), p. 171.

of origin of such components. Although the German Government tried to signify to foreign collaborators (through the wording of Article 3) that it would still seek to influence the export plans of the partners in a cooperative project, the reality was that it now appeared willing to allow such export decisions to be considered in accordance with the less severe guidelines operated by its partners.[55] In the ensuing years this increasingly became the norm, and by the early 1990s the balance between the desire to control partners' export behaviour and the need to work together in joint ventures had clearly shifted in favour of the latter. In 1993, for example, Germany approved the export of electronic parts for US-manufactured missiles destined for Taiwan (only two weeks after refusing to sell Taiwan 10 German-built submarines for fear of alienating China) and of tank engines for French vehicles destined for the United Arab Emirates (UAE) despite a long-standing unilateral ban on German tank sales to the Middle East.[56]

The situation was also exacerbated by the growing number of international cooperation agreements between private corporations (which were not covered by the 1982 guidelines). Thus, in April 1996 the Federal Security Council decided on a change in the interpretation of the 1982 guidelines. There was no public announcement about the change, but the BDI subsequently informed affected firms that there would now be a 'presumption of authorization' (i.e., a prior export licence was no longer required) for all private-sector deliveries of weapon components and spare parts for joint ventures with firms in the EU, NATO and 'NATO-equivalent' states (Switzerland and the ASEAN states, with the exception of Viet Nam) where the German share of the equipment was less than 20 per cent. This relaxation in the control regime also applies to other countries (excluding those on the K List) where the German components (excluding tank engines and gearboxes, and rocket components) amount to no more than 10 per cent of the total cost of the weapon.[57] In effect, this means that export licences for such supplies are now the responsibility of the government of the country in which the main contractor has its headquarters. The companies remain obliged to notify the German Federal Government of the identity of the end-user, and the export can still be blocked if the economics, defence and foreign ministries decide to do so unanimously.[58]

Three minor amendments were made to the 1982 guidelines on 21 May 1999: a note was added to the effect that the guidelines now operate in parallel to the export criteria contained in the 1998 EU Code of Conduct; the reference to Country List C was deleted; and a new commitment to submit an annual report on arms exports to the Bundestag was also added.

---

[55] Wulf (note 1), pp. 77–78; and Cowen (note 2), p. 270.

[56] 'Bonn attacked on arms exports', *Financial Times*, 16 Feb. 1993.

[57] 'Germany plans to ease defence exports', *Jane's Defence Weekly*, 5 June 1996; [Bonn makes arms deals easier], *Handelsblatt*, 10 July 1996; and [More German weapons for the flashpoints], *Süddeutsche Zeitung*, 12 July 1996.

[58] However, once the Framework Agreement (signed in July 2000) has been ratified, this will no longer be possible for collaborative projects with France, Italy, Spain, Sweden and the UK: see chapter 4.

The principles were further modified on 19 January 2000.[59] There are three major changes. First, a new set of five 'general principles' has been added which incorporate the key criteria from the EU Code of Conduct as an integral part of the guidelines, especially respect for human rights in the countries of destination and end-use. Licences will now be denied for war weapons and other military equipment where there 'are reasonable grounds to suspect they may be used for internal repression as defined in the EU Code of Conduct for Arms Exports or the sustained and systematic abuse of human rights'. This will require an overall assessment of the human rights situation in the recipient country to be made in each case.

Second, the less restrictive provisions in the 1982 guidelines which were said to apply to NATO countries only have been extended to EU member states and 'countries with NATO-equivalent status' (Australia, Japan, New Zealand and Switzerland). While this revision simply formalizes what was a de facto arrangement throughout the 1990s, it has been accompanied by some strengthening in the conditions for the transfer of German components to those countries within collaborative projects. The case against 'exports to countries involved in armed conflict', for example, has been revised to read 'exports to countries where an outbreak of armed conflict is imminent or where exports may stir up, perpetuate or exacerbate latent tensions and conflicts'. For countries outside this exclusive group a 'restrictive policy' will continue to be pursued under the terms set out previously, supplemented by the conditions laid down in the EU Code, including the impact of arms exports on sustainable development, regional stability and compliance with international obligations. In one important respect, however, the new principles go one step further than the EU Code. The German licensing authorities are also required to take into account 'the recipient country's conduct in terms of whether it . . . supports the UN Arms Register'.

Third, the provisions in relation to end-use have been strengthened and are elaborated in greater detail. The new guidelines state, for example, that arms cannot be re-exported without prior authorization by the German authorities and that 'stringent standards are to be applied in assessing whether the recipient country is capable of carrying out effective export controls'. Countries that breach re-export conditions will 'on principle, as long as such conditions persist, be excluded from receiving any further deliveries of war weapons or other military equipment related to war weapons'.

As with the EU Code, the relative weight given to these new principles in the licensing process will determine their overall effectiveness. Nonetheless on paper they represent a significant tightening. In addition to these national guidelines, the German export authorities also have to take cognizance of internationally agreed principles on arms transfers, such as the OSCE Principles.

---

[59] 'Politische grundsätze der Bundesregierung für den export von Kriegswaffen und sonstigen rüstungsgütern' [Political principles of the Federal Government for the export of weapons of war and other military equipment], available on the Internet site of the Ministry of Economics, URL <http://www. bmwi>. An unofficial translation of this latest version is reproduced in full in appendix A.

Regulatory oversight

While the legal framework for export controls requires the assent of the German Parliament, the formulation of the export guidelines and individual licence decisions have traditionally been undertaken within the federal bureaucracy, and without consulting parliament.[60] For, example, neither the Bundestag nor its Foreign Affairs Committee was informed, far less consulted, about the mid-1990s change in the interpretation of the 1982 guidelines discussed above.

Prior to the decision by the new German Government to make its annual report on strategic arms exports, as required under the EU Code of Conduct,[61] publicly available, the only oversight mechanism was provided by parliamentary questions on export control issues.[62] However, such questions could occasionally elicit a reply of such substance and scope that for all intents and purposes it took the form of an official parliamentary report. On 10 September 1997, for example, the SPD tabled a series of written questions (over 180 in total) which produced a 35-page written parliamentary reply in March 1998.[63] The reply includes information about the structure of, reasons for and purpose of German export controls, which agencies are involved and their budgetary and personnel details, the future of multilateral export controls, exports to specific destinations, illegal exports and prosecutions.

The administrative (policy-execution) structure

Publication of export guidelines

A systematic description of Germany's foreign trade legislation with guidance for exporting companies is contained in the Handbook of German Export Controls, known by its German acronym HADDEX (*Handbuch der Deutschen Exportkontrolle*) published by BAFA. Amendments to laws and announcements by BAFA are also published in the daily federal gazette (*Bundesanzeiger*). Since 1995 special courses in the field of export control and foreign trade have been offered by business, government and universities under a combined scheme known as FALEX (FAchLehrgänge Exportkontrolle/Auffenwirtschaft) with the aim of training export specialists and improving compliance with the regulations.

---

[60] For a discussion of the German Parliament's involvement in passing legislation relating to export controls and its role in legislative oversight see Hofhansel, C., 'German perspectives on export control policy', eds G. Bertsch, R. Cupitt and S. Elliott-Gower, *International Cooperation on Nonproliferation Export Controls: Prospects for the 1990s and Beyond* (University of Michigan Press: Ann Arbor, Mich., 1994), pp. 188–90.

[61] The first German annual report was approved by the German Cabinet and published on 20 Sep. 2000. It is available on the Internet site of the Ministry of Economics, URL <http://bmwi.de>.

[62] Although Müller *et al.* (note 32, p. 48) state that a system of reporting was introduced in Oct. 1992, personal interviews with civil servants in the key German ministries during 1997 confirmed that no such formal reporting system existed at that stage.

[63] 'Rüstungsexportkontrollen in der Bundesrepublik Deutschland: sachstand und perspecktiven' [Arms export control in the FGR: position and prospects], *Deutscher Bundestag, 13. Wahlperiode, Drucksache* [Printed papers of the German Bundestag, 13th Parliament], 13/10104, 11 Mar. 1998.

Of particular interest to industry is the regular 'warning list' issued to German trade associations by the foreign affairs and economics ministries since the mid-1990s. The list normally contains the names of approximately 50–60 foreign companies that have been identified by the two ministries, customs and intelligence agencies as being associated with the procurement network of 'sensitive countries'.[64]

The decision-making process for licence applications

From 1955 to 31 March 1992, the Federal Office of Economics (Bundesamt für Wirtschaft, BAW), an office of the Ministry of Economics, was in charge of licensing and controls. Following the 'Arms to Iraq' export scandal in the UK,[65] and simultaneously with the legislative changes discussed above, Germany separated its export control department from the Ministry of Economics and created a new independent federal control agency, BAFA. On 1 April 1992, BAFA, based in Eschborn, near Frankfurt, took over sole responsibility for export licensing and end-use controls. Although in practice this simply meant that the entire licensing division within the Federal Office of Economics moved to adjacent rooms in the same building, the number of staff employed was substantially increased. As part of the 1989/90 reforms, the Federal Office of Economics had already expanded from 6 to 22 divisions, with an increase in staff from approximately 70 to 170. The new agency, however, placed particular emphasis on the recruitment of its own technical experts, and staff numbers in BAFA quickly rose to approximately 430 (although by March 2000 this had been reduced to approximately 340). BAFA currently consists of three main divisions: Division I for internal administration; Division II for technical assessments on conventional armaments and export procedures; and Division III for international regimes and technical assessments of dual-use goods.[66] The 150 staff in Division III have two roles—the ongoing review of the export lists within international control regimes and technical evaluation of licence applications.

There are three main types of export licence, all of which are generally valid for two years (with the possibility of extensions) and must be retained by the exporter for a period of five years after they have lapsed:

1. *Individual export licences/maximum amount licences.* Individual licences authorize the export of one or several pieces of equipment to one recipient. The 'maximum amount' licence is a special type of individual licence which allows the export of equipment for several contracts up to a maximum amount.

2. *Collective export licences.* These permit the export of a group of equipment to several recipients.

<hr>

[64] Kelle and Müller (note 18), pp. 145–46.

[65] See chapter 5, section IV.

[66] The organizational structure of BAFA is available on its Internet site at URL <http://www.bundesausfuhramt.de>.

3. *General licences*. There are several types of general licence covering a range of specific goods for which no application by the exporter is necessary; instead he is required to make a post-export notification. The first general licence was issued in 1992 and several new general licences were introduced in June 1995 in response to the EC Dual-Use Regulation. There are currently 10 such licences in operation, and most dual-use goods under a DM 5000 threshold, for example, can now be exported under a general licence.[67]

Since the introduction of general licences the number of licence applications under the AWG has declined dramatically (see below), thereby allowing the licensing authority to concentrate resources on more sensitive cases. The ongoing liberalization of controls through greater use of general licences also has staffing implications: over the next 10 years, BAFA expects to lose approximately 80 staff through natural wastage.[68]

Pre-application advice for arms exports

Prior to the formal legal application for an export licence it is common practice in respect of weapon transfers for an informal consultation process to take place between industry and the Foreign Ministry. The Foreign Ministry usually consults the economic and defence ministries before reaching a decision. Occasionally such pre-application requests are forwarded direct to the Federal Security Council for decision. The resulting pre-application 'advice' then forms the basis of the negotiations between the exporting company and the customer. In the late 1970s and early 1980s up to 90 per cent of all decisions on exports of weapons made by the Federal Security Council related to these pre-applications. While there is no legal requirement for the government to follow the pre-application 'advice' when the formal application is eventually filed, in practice the legally required decision is more or less a formality. Indeed, because the actual licence is effectively decided in advance, applications that have no chance of success are not usually filed by industry.[69]

The export licence application procedure

A distinction is made between applications for exports of weapons of war in accordance with the KWKG and dual-use and other military-related exports under the AWG. Authority for licensing weapons of war rests with the Ministry of Economics, while authority for licensing under the AWG lies with BAFA. Companies wanting to export weapons of war under the KWKG must formally request an export licence from BAFA, which then forwards it to the Ministry of Economics. Approximately 1000 applications under the KWKG are received each year. In routine cases (i.e., if a precedent exists), the licence is granted by

---

[67] *Worldwide Guide to Export Controls* (note 29), pp. 20–22 and 29–35; and 'BAFA export controls: brief outline' (note 35), pp. 14–17.
[68] Personal interviews with BAFA officials, 1997.
[69] Wulf (note 1), p. 81.

Table 6.3. German export licence applications and refusals, Aussenwirtschaftsgesetz, early 1980s–1997

Figures in italics are percentages.

Year	Source	Total number of applications per annum	Total number of applications refused	Percentage of refusals per annum
1982	[a]	44 100	150	*0.34*
1983	[a]	48 150	106	*0.22*
1985 (estimate)	[b]	80 000	100	*0.13*
1991	[c]	33 455	1 016	*3.04*
1992	[b]	26 237	369	*1.40*
1993	[b]	27 501	168	*0.61*
1997 (estimate)	[d]	25 000	150	*0.60*

Sources:

[a] Pearson, F., '"Necessary evil": perspectives on West German arms transfer policies', *Armed Forces and Society,* vol. 12, no. 4 (summer 1986), p. 534.

[b] Hofhansel, C., *Commercial Competition and National Security: Comparing US and German Export Control Policies* (Praeger: Westport, Ct., 1996), pp. 46–47.

[c] Müller, H. *et al.*, *From Black Sheep to White Angel? The New German Export Control Policy*, PRIF reports no. 32 (Peace Research Institute Frankfurt: Frankfurt, Jan. 1994), p. 4.

[d] Personal interviews with BAFA officials, 1997.

civil servants at the ministry, whereas in non-routine cases the Foreign Ministry and Ministry of Defence are consulted. If none of the three ministries raises an objection, the export licence is granted. If disagreement exists or if the export is thought to be politically sensitive the case is referred to the Federal Security Council (as described above) for a decision.

Applications for exports of dual-use goods and other military equipment under the AWG are normally considered solely by BAFA, although it sometimes consults the Ministry of Economics and other departments. If the initial technical and legal review of the licence application results in the export transaction not being subject to licensing, BAFA issues a so-called Zero Notice.[70]

The number of export licence applications submitted under the AWG has risen and fallen over the past two decades in accordance with the changes in the scope of the regulations discussed above. Thus, in the early 1980s, approximately 45 000 applications were received each year and by the late 1980s this

[70] Until the end of 1997, if an exporter had doubts as to whether an export licence was required (because, e.g., the goods to be exported were not clearly specified in the Export List), or if the customs office dealing with the export required evidence of exemption from export licence authorization, the exporter could apply for a negative certificate (Negativbescheinigung, NB) from BAFA. The aim of this certificate was to provide the exporter with official proof that the export of a good was exempt from licence control. However, because some exporters were treating the negative certificate as an export licence, the documentation was changed in early 1998 to a Zero Notice. Since 1988 BAFA has also published an annual 'NB goods catalogue' which lists goods in the electrical engineering and electronics fields that are exempt from export licensing. Exports of goods appearing in the catalogue did not normally require a Zero Notice. *Worldwide Guide to Export Controls* (note 29), p. 37; and 'BAFA export controls: brief outline' (note 35), p. 21.

had risen to 80 000.[71] After the introduction of global licences in the early 1990s the number of applications fell to approximately 40 000 per year, a downward trend which has continued up to the present. In 1997, for example, BAFA received approximately 25 000 applications per year.[72]

The decision to approve or deny an export licence application depends on the type and quantity of the goods to be exported, their intended use, the country of destination, the final user and the information available about the exporter's reliability. The vast majority of applications are routinely approved by BAFA on this basis. Only in non-routine cases (less than 20 per cent) are cases referred to the Ministry of Economics for consultation with the Foreign Ministry. In particular, exports to non-NATO countries of weapons, munitions and weapon material in the AWG 'A List' often require the approval of these two ministries. Particularly sensitive AWG cases are decided by an inter-agency commission, which is headed by the Ministry of Economics and made up of representatives from all the interested ministries, BAFA and the security services.

The government does not publish statistics on the exact number and value of either type of export application, although occasionally the annual total value of all licences granted and denied is given upon request in Parliament. The former are shown in table 6.1. These official figures are supplemented by interview data collected by analysts over recent years, as summarized in table 6.3. A study carried out by Pearson in the early 1980s, for example, revealed that for 1982 and 1983, respectively, 150 and 106 AWG applications were rejected out of totals of 44 100 and 48 510.[73] In 1991, when the German export controls were arguably at their most restrictive, 1016 AWG applications out of a total of 33 455 for goods worth DM1.5 billion were refused (i.e., 5.5 per cent of all applications by value or 0.2 per cent of the value of all German exports for that year. Even for destinations in the then new Country List H, the approval rate was still above 80 per cent.[74] Of the current 25 000 AWG applications per year less than 1 per cent are refused.[75]

The fact that there are so few denials can be read as confirming that the regime is well understood by companies: they will not usually apply for a licence if they are reasonably sure that it will be refused. It is also clear that officials sometimes help companies to obtain a licence by negotiating modifications to the goods being exported so that the export criteria can be met. However, by the very nature of bureaucratic politics, similar licence applications may be denied to placate domestic political opposition: 'I have a feeling that sometimes they accept this one and deny the next one, so if they get complaints from the peace side, they can say, I didn't allow that one, but if they get complaints from the companies, they can say, but I allowed that one. So

---

[71] Brzoska (note 15), p. 33; and Pearson (note 3), p. 534.
[72] Personal interviews with BAFA officials, 1997.
[73] Pearson (note 3), p. 534.
[74] Müller *et al.* (note 32), p. 4.
[75] Personal interviews with BAFA officials, 1997.

officials have to have both types of cases in their portfolio, so they can answer all types of criticism'.[76]

Compliance and enforcement procedures

Compliance and enforcement procedures are mainly structured around four different mechanisms: end-use controls; border controls; company audits; and the work of the Customs Criminal Investigation Service (the Zollkriminalamt, ZKA).

The German system of end-use controls is based on a combination of government-issued international end-use certificates, private declarations made by importing firms and international import certificates.[77] In addition, as mentioned above, since 1990 exporting companies are themselves required to nominate an Ausfuhrverantwortlicher who is legally responsible for the assessment of end-use and can later be held accountable for any foreseeable diversion. End-use documents are normally required unless: (*a*) the export value is below certain lower limits (DM 10 000 for armaments and defence-related items listed in section A of the Export List and DM 20 000 for most dual-use goods listed in section C); (*b*) it is a temporary export; or (*c*) it is part of a government contract.

The end-use certificate contains a declaration by the consignee or end-user on the final destination and use of the goods. Standard texts are provided by BAFA and the declaration usually includes a commitment by the end-user not to re-export the goods without BAFA's prior written permission (although the exact content of each certificate will differ according to country of destination, end-user and type of goods). The validity of the end-use declaration may also be checked with the recipient country's embassy in Germany. In addition to these end-use documents, in certain cases BAFA also requires a delivery verification certificate (DVC) in order to prove the actual receipt of the goods in the importing state. Goods in sections A and B of the Export List valued above DM 20 000 traditionally required a DVC, as did goods in section C valued above DM 50 000.[78]

Supervision of cross-border goods traffic and the monitoring of compliance with the export regulations are the responsibility of the customs authorities. All German exports must be declared to and processed by customs officials. The export declaration is normally made in advance to a domestic customs office, and the resulting paperwork (including an export licence, if appropriate) is then checked by the border customs office when the goods leave the country. Although the border customs officers also have the right to inspect the freight

[76] Personal interview with an independent expert, 1997.

[77] Details regarding the various types of end-user document can be found in the BAFA Announcement referring to End-Use Certificates pursuant to Section 17 (2) of the Foreign Trade and Payments Regulation of 9 Dec. 1997, *Bundesanzeiger* [Federal gazette], no. 34a (19 Feb. 1998).

[78] From 1 Jan. 1993, as a result of the EU Dual-Use Regulation, a DVC is no longer required for goods in Section C that are exported to other EU member states. Simplified procedures also apply for intra-EU transfers of goods in Section A. *Worldwide Guide to Export Controls* (note 29), p. 28.

and compare it with the paperwork this is only done for a small percentage of the 18 million shipments that leave Germany each year. There are also simplified export declaration procedures for reliable exporters.

Both the customs authorities and BAFA carry out company audits which include oversight of export matters. At the regional level, for example, 'foreign trade inquiries' of exporting companies are undertaken on a random basis by company audit units of the Higher Financial Authorities (Oberfinanzdirektion, OFD), part of the Customs Service.[79] These inquiries are generally made with a great deal of caution, however. For example, they are only initiated if a well-founded suspicion of illegal exports already exists, and in undertaking them officers take the greatest possible care not to disrupt the company under investigation.

Prior to the early 1990s, surveillance of exports was primarily done by means of these foreign trade inquiries. While such audits continue to be an integral part of the compliance regime, the government strengthened its preventive monitoring options in a number of ways in the early 1990s. The most significant change was the transformation of the central office of the ZKI into the ZKA, by a law of 1 July 1992. The ZKI had been set up in 1952 as a criminological institute but over the years had developed an investigative role which included responsibility for detecting illegal exports, and investigating and prosecuting violations in conjunction with the intelligence services.

In the ZKA this export control function was substantially strengthened. In 1988, for example, it had employed 94 staff in total, whereas in 1994 it employed approximately 370, including 150 investigators on export controls. It also coordinates the activities of approximately 2500 customs investigation officers throughout Germany. One consequence of this expansion in resources was an increase in the number of investigations from 405 in 1989 to 1051 in 1991.[80] The status of the ZKA was also enhanced, as compared to the ZKI, which had the legal status of a local customs agency, to that of a central federal authority subordinated only to the Minister of Finance.[81]

The ZKA's export control function was further enhanced by the introduction of computer systems, better coordination with BAFA and the introduction of intrusive surveillance powers. Both BAFA and the ZKA have introduced computer systems to detect unlawful exports. BAFA operates two databases, one for information about licence applications and processing, the other containing intelligence information on illegal procurement activities. BAFA's database on sensitive foreign companies holds 'more than 1200 sentences' on Iranian companies alone.[82]

---

[79] Müller *et al.* (note 32), pp. 24–25.

[80] German Federal Ministry of Economics, 'Report by the Government of the Federal Republic of Germany on the tightening of export controls for goods with civilian and military applications (dual-use)', Ministry of Economics, Bonn, 11 Mar. 1992 , p. 6.

[81] *Zollkriminalamt, Development and Tasks* (ZKA: Cologne, Mar. 1996); and personal interviews with customs officials, 1997.

[82] Personal interviews with BAFA officials, 1997.

In addition, the ZKA introduced its own separate export data collection system called Kontrolle bei der Ausfuhr (KOBRA) on 1 April 1991. Based at the ZKA's headquarters in Cologne, it has many innovative computerized tracking and monitoring features. It is available on-line to most customs offices throughout Germany, centralizes in a single database all documents filed at individual offices and signals whether or not a stated end-user for a given product is known to be involved in weapon development.[83] It also compares export documents against checklists compiled by the ZKA of suspect end-users, countries and particular products associated with those countries' known weapon development programmes. The product coverage of KOBRA is extensive. In addition to arms and munitions it includes all chemical products, all related written materials and plans, all steel and metal products, machinery and transport equipment, electromechanical and electronic products, fine mechanics and optical devices. In 1990 these product categories amounted to 71.6 per cent of all German exports.[84]

There are problems with KOBRA. Because of the volume of export declarations these are entered into the system by means of a scanner. Sometimes the scanner is unable to read the information (because of the different types of forms used), or it fails to recognize that the importing company named on the export declaration is the same company listed in its database as a potential proliferator (because different writing styles and/or language translations have caused the computer to see two separate company names). One insider described this latter as a 'big, big problem with the warning system'. Also, where simplified licensing procedures apply, the export declaration is not delivered to the Customs House until weeks or months after the goods have crossed the frontier. It is thus relatively easy for licensable goods to be hidden among mass exports of non-licensable goods. Even the best data processing system is unable to neutralize such diversionary tactics.[85] Nonetheless, KOBRA is a useful tool for showing the larger proliferation picture and in particular for tracking the acquisition patterns of certain countries (although, of course, it is unable to track German technology acquired within the Single European Market and subsequently exported from the EU by another member state).

In addition to better computer resources, legislative changes introduced in 1989–92 removed some of the obstacles to cooperation between the various licensing and investigating authorities. In particular, changes to the AWG allowed BAFA to transfer information to the ZKA under special circumstances involving criminal investigations. Finally, as mentioned above, the ZKA was given new surveillance powers in February 1992, including the option of tele-

---

[83] KOBRA was initially designed and funded prior to unification with the intention of supplying 200 terminals to cover all the customs houses within the FRG. However, following unification the terminals were dispersed over a wider geographic area, and the intention of equipping every customs house was abandoned because of financial constraints. Personal interviews with customs officials, 1997.

[84] Reinicke, W., 'Cooperative security and the political economy of nonproliferation, ed. J. Nolan, *Global Engagement: Cooperation and Security in the 21st Century* (Brookings Institution: Washington, DC, 1994), p. 183.

[85] Personal interviews with customs officials, 1997.

phone taps and mail intercepts against companies suspected of breaking arms export laws.[86] Although these provisions are designed to deter illegal arms trafficking, they impinge on Germany's strict privacy laws and were vigorously contested by opposition parties during the bill's passage through Parliament.[87]

Approximately 100 personnel within the ZKA work on communications surveillance operations.[88] Between October 1992 and September 1997, 26 such operations were carried out. Approximately one-half of these resulted in formal investigations, and the first conviction was obtained in the spring of 1997 (five years after the initial surveillance operation).[89]

IV. Policy outcomes

Periods of restraint and periods of erosion

Ever since the re-establishment of the arms industry in the mid-1950s, the official arms export policy of the FRG has always been, on the surface at least, one of tight controls and restrictions. In practice, however, the restrictive policy was gradually eroded during the 1970s and 1980s and only began to be restored in the early 1990s following heavy international and internal political pressure.

The 1970s, in particular, were a boom period for weapon exports from the FRG, largely as a result of increased demand, particularly from oil-exporting countries. Iran, for example, received equipment for tank maintenance, ammunition plants, tank engines, tracks and guns, while Nigeria placed orders for a frigate, ground-attack aircraft and ground-to-air missiles. Other recipients of weapons, parts or arms production technologies from the FRG during this period were Brunei, Ethiopia, Sudan and Tanzania.[90] Not only was the West German arms industry now sufficiently developed to exploit this upturn in demand, but the economic crises in the shipyards and the threat to jobs led to a more generous treatment of licence applications at this time. In particular, exports of the less strictly regulated dual-use goods expanded to such an extent that some companies from the FRG became world leaders in the supply of certain arms production technologies.

The election of the Conservative–Liberal coalition government[91] in 1982 led to a further de facto liberalization of export policy without, however, requiring a change in the two relevant laws or the governmental guidelines. Several arms

---

[86] Article 39 of the AWG entitles the ZKA to intercept post and telecommunications outside a formal legal investigation. Prior approval has to be obtained from the ministry and then from a special court based in Cologne. If, however, the court decides that the ZKA already has enough information to proceed with a formal investigation, then such intercepts become possible under existing laws, namely, para. 108 of the Criminal Proceedings Law. Personal interviews with customs officials, 1997.

[87] For a summary of the political debates see Müller *et al.* (note 32), pp. 26–27.

[88] Müller *et al.* (note 32), p. 40.

[89] Personal interviews with customs officials, 1997.

[90] For further details of German weapon sales during this period see Cowen (note 2), p. 266.

[91] Headed by Chancellor Helmut Kohl, the coalition was between the 2 Christian Union parties (the CDU and CSU) and the Liberal Party (FDP). For further discussion of this period of German politics see Gutjahr, L., 'Continuity or change? Germany's foreign policy after the 1994 general elections', *Coexistence*, no. 32 (1995), pp. 102–103.

deals in the 1980s illustrate this trend. First, in 1983 the FRG signed a formal agreement for arms cooperation with Saudi Arabia, its first ever with a Third World country. At the same time, the government amended the weapon list and removed, for example, helicopters and aircraft without sophisticated electronics from the list. Second, in 1985 the government announced that the ASEAN countries would be treated as equal to NATO countries, giving geo-strategic reasons for the policy change. This meant that exports of weapons and dual-use goods to that region of the world were no longer restricted. Third, under pressure from the British Government, Germany agreed to partly finance the sale of co-produced Tornado fighter planes to Jordan. The credit financing was later withdrawn in response to public pressure, only to be re-offered in covert form by a bank owned by the state of Bavaria. Although the whole export later collapsed as a result of Jordanian financial difficulties, it clearly signified an increased willingness on the part of the government to take an active role in defence export promotion.[92]

The German policy on weapon sales outside NATO that emerged at the end of the 1980s had a number of distinct features. First, because economic policy in the FRG is based on constantly expanding exports of industrial products,[93] exports of dual-use goods under the AWG were more generously permitted than were exports of weapons under the KWKG. This overall economic priority resulted in a weak control framework for dual-use goods and facilitated a number of illegal or dubious dual-use exports. Second, there was a clear reluctance to permit the export of major weapon systems, with the exception of fighting ships (which formed the major share of German arms exports). German submarines and related technology have been transferred to Argentina, Chile and South Korea, while German-built fast-attack craft are in service with various Middle Eastern navies (Bahrain, Kuwait, Saudi Arabia and the UAE). Third, in addition to dual-use goods and fighting ships, the prospects of receiving export licences were positive for those exporters wanting to sell firearms and ammunition or smaller quantities of other weapons. Fourth, sales to Latin American and Asian states, and particularly the ASEAN countries, were more likely to be permitted than sales to the Middle East. Exports of weapons to countries fighting a war or to 'areas of tension' were unlikely to be permitted, although dual-use transfers were often granted in both cases. Finally, the desire to maintain certain industrial capacities and to protect employment in vulnerable industries (such as shipbuilding) also tended to enhance the prospect of a licence being granted.[94]

---

[92] Wulf (note 1), p. 83.

[93] Post-war Germany has always been an export-oriented economy, with exports contributing about one-third of GDP. Following unification, however, there is now a growing tension between Germany's domestic needs and its erstwhile role as a competitive exporter. Thus, many economic commentators expected Germany in the global economy of the 1990s to be characterized by internal and external imbalances. See, e.g., Gretschmann, K., 'Germany in the global economy of the 1990s: from player to pawn?', eds R. Stubbs and G. Underhill, *Political Economy and the Changing Global Order* (Macmillan: London, 1994). In 1992, however, some 18 million export consignments were still crossing the German borders annually. German Federal Ministry of Economics (note 80), p. 2.

[94] Wulf (note 1), p. 84.

Michael Brzoska offers several explanations for the erosion of restraint in West German arms transfer policy in the 1970s and 1980s.[95] They include the realist assumption that arms exports are a natural instrument of foreign policy and the arms economy; a parallel erosion of a German 'specialness' and the assumption of a less moralistic position in international relations; the political influence of the arms industry; an automatic expansionist trend within the arms export bureaucracy (the result of a reliance on precedence in decision making and contradictory signals from political leaders); and foreign policy interests of the government. Brzoska concludes, however, that none of the explanations is convincing by itself. Instead:

They have to be linked and expanded to capture the decisive interactive process of elements from all these explanations . . . The expansion of arms exports was a dynamic interactive process between politicians, the arms export bureaucracy, the foreign policy elite and the arms industry, with the last providing more and more of the momentum over time. Actual policy was determined mostly by arms exporting firms lobbying individual cases with bureaucrats and politicians and foreign policy elite groups. The erosion process proceeded step by step, from the licensing of items that were not defined as weapons of war, to items used in co-productions, to some types of weapons of war and on to almost all types of weapons of war.[96]

The net result was that by the end of the 1980s the German export control system was suffering from a number of weaknesses, including underfunded and understaffed export control agencies, ineffectual penalties for violations and serious loopholes in the scope of the regulations. These weaknesses were exacerbated by the attitude of the Ministry of Economics, which (given the political direction outlined above) viewed export promotion as a higher priority than export control. However, this leading political discourse on arms export controls that had existed since the 1970s began to change in the period 1989–92 following the fresh round of German export scandals discussed above. This led to a fundamental change of attitude both within the government of Chancellor Helmut Kohl and within Parliament.[97] Under Foreign Minister Genscher, non-proliferation became a much higher government priority and the executive branch generally became much more sensitive to criticism in this area.

In the early 1990s, for example, the most sensitive German arms transfers were to Turkey. Germany was well established as Turkey's second-biggest post-war arms supplier: between 1964 and 1994 German military aid to Turkey totalled some DM 908 billion.[98] However, in March 1992, Gerhard Stoltenberg was forced to resign as Defence Minister after widespread criticism of a transfer of 15 Leopard tanks to Turkey. Although it is a fellow NATO member state, Germany had applied a temporary arms embargo against Turkey in November

<hr>

[95] Brzoska (note 15), pp. 172–75.
[96] Brzoska (note 15), pp. 173–74.
[97] For a discussion of this change in mood on the part of the governing parties and within the Bundestag see Müller *et al.* (note 32), pp. 45–49.
[98] InterPress Service, 17 Apr. 1992.

1991 following reports of human rights abuses there. The tank transfers were revealed during a furious public debate triggered by the deployment of German-made armoured cars by the Turkish Government against Kurdish rebels. Another temporary arms embargo was applied against Turkey in 1994 following similar allegations.[99]

The Turkish example is symbolic of a reversal of the process of erosion which began in 1989 with the alterations to the legal and administrative frameworks for export controls. Between 1989 and 1992, as described above, new export limitations were placed on dual-use goods, communication between the different authorities concerned with export licences was improved, penalties for violators were increased, and BAFA and the ZKA were established as separate agencies with more administrative power and additional personnel. An analysis of these changes by the Peace Research Institute Frankfurt (PRIF) concluded that 'the export control system was transformed from one of the weakest within the group of supplier countries to one of the strongest'.[100] The revised policy principles agreed in January 2000 reinforce this trend.

However, these stricter controls may themselves begin to be eroded in the next decade under the possible twin pressures of a new global recession (exacerbated in Germany by continued economic difficulties associated with unification) and the failure to extend the new German levels of controls to the rest of the EU in the course of the harmonization process. Indeed, the reduction in the K List and the relaxation of controls for private cooperative ventures (culminating in Germany's participation in the Framework Agreement) are indicative that such erosion has already begun. Further liberalization of the dual-use area and a relaxation of weapon export criteria may occur in order to bring Germany into line with the rest of the EU.

On the other hand, Germany has continued to adopt a restrictive policy of arms exports to regions of tension, and this is unlikely to change in the short or medium term. Indeed, Germany still remains willing on occasion to intervene to block exports of German-made weapons by other countries. In 1996, for example, Germany successfully blocked the sale of 54 surplus Royal Netherlands Army Leopard tanks to Botswana.[101] Preliminary enquiries early in March 2000 by arms manufacturer Krauss-Maffei Wegmann to allow the export of up to 1000 tanks to Turkey were likely to be a stronger test of the vigour of the new policy guidelines.[102]

[99] *Jane's Defence Weekly*, 16 Apr. 1994.
[100] Müller *et al.* (note 32), p. I.
[101] 'Germany vetoes Dutch tank sale to Botswana', *Jane's Defence Weekly*, 31 July 1996.
[102] Reuters, 16 Mar. 2000.

7. The regulation of arms and dual-use exports in Sweden: the cooperative model

I. Introduction

Sweden has a long and interesting arms export control history which began in 1935 with the establishment of one of Europe's first national arms export control regimes under the guidance of the Military Equipment Inspectorate (Krigsmaterielinspektionen, KMI). In the 1940s, however, Sweden's major export control preoccupation was with nuclear technologies, and it was only during the 1960s that this preoccupation extended to international efforts to curb the conventional arms race. These efforts received new impetus in the early 1990s as a result of three more or less simultaneous events—the ending of the cold war, the conflict in the Persian Gulf and membership of the EU. This chapter explores how Sweden has carried out its arms export control responsibilities since the 1960s, with particular emphasis on the changes introduced since it joined the EU on 1 January 1995.

The structure of this chapter mirrors that of chapters 5 and 6. Section II examines the political framework for export controls in Sweden, including the policy environment for arms transfers and especially the consequences of EU membership, the role of domestic policy stakeholders and the role of government-backed support mechanisms for arms exports. Section III examines the policy-making and administrative structures for regulating arms exports, including the role of the national licensing authority, now the National Inspectorate of Strategic Products (Inspektionen för Strategiska Produkter, ISP, the successor to the KMI), and the industry–government cooperative process that lies at the heart of the Swedish system. Section IV evaluates the impact and outcomes of Swedish arms export control policy.

II. The policy environment and stakeholders

The policy environment

Sweden (along with three other EU member states, Austria, Finland and Ireland) has long been associated with the concept of armed neutrality.[1] It is a concept that is fully compatible with the right of states to possess conventional weapons for the purpose of national defence and hence would seem to add very little to the existing norms and principles concerning the transfer of arms dis-

---

[1] It is apparent, however, that Sweden arms itself very heavily, while the other EU neutral states get by with relatively much smaller military capabilities. Viotti, P. R., 'Comparative neutrality in Europe', *Defense Analysis,* vol. 6, no. 1 (1990), pp. 3–15.

cussed in chapter 2. Indeed, Sweden's arms and dual-use transfers have on occasions in the past sullied the positive image of Swedish neutrality. During World War II, for example, Swedish companies provided important financial services, raw materials and finished goods for the German war effort. Towards the end of the war this included meeting 70 per cent of Germany's demand for specialized ball bearings.[2] More recently, Sweden suffered a number of arms export scandals in the late 1970s and early 1980s which led to significant policy changes.[3]

The policy of non-alignment and armed neutrality kept Sweden out of two world wars and was also thought to have guided the country's foreign policy during the cold war.[4] Instead of participating in military alliances, Sweden sought to secure its independence with a 'total defence' posture that could generate a 500 000-strong conscript army on mobilization. Equipping these forces required a large defence industry. Of the three new member states which joined the EU in 1995, for example, Sweden has the most significant defence industry (with 4 per cent of the turnover of the other 12 member states in 1992, compared to 0.2 per cent in Austria and 0.5 per cent in Finland). In relation to the size of the country, Sweden's defence industry is extensive, with a weapons portfolio that can only be matched by some of the larger supplier states.[5]

However, Sweden is too small for such an industry to survive on national procurement alone, and thus, throughout the cold war period and since, it has been a significant second-tier exporter of arms. In the five-year period 1992–96, for example, one-third of Sweden's defence industrial production was exported.[6] According to SIPRI figures, this was the equivalent of 0.56 per cent of total

[2] Cesarani, D., 'Bearings of betrayal', *The Guardian*, 3 Dec. 1997.

[3] In the early 1980s several arms deals resulted in high-profile prosecutions under the 1960 Penalties for Smuggling Goods Act. Most of these prosecutions followed the publication of a report by a Citizens' Commission for the Examination of Certain Arms Exports in May 1988. In Dec. 1989, e.g., the Stockholm City Court convicted 3 former Bofors directors of illegal exports of RBS-70 anti-aircraft missile systems to Bahrain and Dubai in 1980. In another case the same year, however, which involved suspected illegal exports of powder and explosives from Sweden in the late 1970s and early 1980s, the representatives from 2 Malmö-based companies were acquitted by the District Court in Karlskoga. Hirdman, S., 'Sweden's policy on arms exports', Ministry for Foreign Affairs, Stockholm, 1989 (unofficial translation), pp. 27–28.

[4] Some analysts argue that Sweden's policy of neutrality was abandoned or modified during the cold war in response to the prevailing security conditions—a claim confirmed by the findings of a commission established in 1992 to reconsider Sweden's military cooperation with the West from 1949 to 1969. Archer, C., 'Nordic perspectives on European security' in *Visions of European Security: Focal Point Sweden and Northern Europe* (Olof Palme International Centre: Stockholm, 1996), p. 24.

[5] Sweden is a small country of less than 9 million inhabitants and it is the only country of its size, with the exceptions of Israel and South Africa, to produce most of the major conventional weapon systems. In 1992, about 70% of the equipment procured for Sweden's armed forces was manufactured in Sweden. The remaining 30% was imported, with about 45% of such imports coming from the USA and *c.* 55% from Western Europe. Swedish Ministry for Foreign Affairs, *Sweden's Policy on Arms Exports*, SOU 1993:1 (Stockholm, 1993), p. 8. The 70% figure does not reflect the growing number of imported subsystems and components or the importance of foreign skills and knowledge in Swedish military equipment, but even where there is heavy dependence on external supplies of spares and components, Swedish industry is skilled in repair and maintenance as a safety net against any cut-off in supply. Hagelin, B., 'Sweden's search for military technology', eds M. Brzoska and P. Lock, SIPRI, *Restructuring of Arms Production in Western Europe* (Oxford University Press: Oxford, 1992), p. 179.

[6] Swedish Ministry for Foreign Affairs, Strategic Export Control Division, *Swedish Arms Exports in 1996: A Government Report*, Swedish Government Report to Parliament 1996/97:138 (Ministry for Foreign Affairs: Stockholm, June 1997), p. 4.

world deliveries of major conventional weapons in the same period (placing Sweden in 15th position among the supplier states).[7] The most important categories of military equipment exported by Swedish manufacturers in the early 1990s were 155-mm field howitzers, 40-mm and 57-mm guns, plus ammunition; ground-to-air, anti-ship and anti-tank missiles; light anti-tank weapons and mines; naval command, radar and control and communications (C^3) equipment; other military electronics; submarines, mine hunters and minesweeping equipment; and explosives.[8]

Since the early 1970s Sweden has also adopted a policy of international military–industrial cooperation.[9] Together with the need to export, this economic and technical cooperation with other countries in military projects has continued to grow in importance. Today the scope and nature of that cooperation, as elsewhere in Europe, have become more complex. Several indicators reveal the increasing internationalization of Swedish military production, including increases in the number of joint ventures,[10] in Swedish firms' shares in foreign companies (and vice versa[11]) and in foreign sourcing of components for Swedish weapon systems. Moreover, Swedish participation in the Framework Agreement (discussed in chapter 4) fortifies this trend.

Indeed, the consolidation of the European arms industry has already resulted in considerable restructuring of the Swedish defence industry in recent years. Military production was already concentrated in a small number of major producers, but the formation of the Celsius Group in 1993 significantly increased Swedish military–industrial concentration. Celsius and Saab are now the largest defence groups in Sweden.[12] As shown by table 7.1, the companies in the Celsius Group accounted for well over one-half of Sweden's exports of military equipment in 1997.

Turning to the statistical evidence on Swedish transfers, in addition to the international data sources discussed in chapter 1, date on Swedish arms exports are published by three sources within Sweden: (*a*) the national licensing authority, the ISP, which publishes a range of statistics in an annual report (see below); (*b*) the national statistical office, Statistics Sweden (Statistiska Centralbyrån), which reports exports of 'weapons and ammunition' in accordance with the Standard Industrial Trade Classification (SITC) 891;[13] and (*c*) the Associa-

---

[7] Anthony, I., Wezeman, P. D. and Wezeman, S. T., 'The trade in major conventional weapons', *SIPRI Yearbook 1997: Armaments, Disarmament and International Security* (Oxford University Press: Oxford, 1997), p. 268. Of course, Sweden's share of global arms exports varies depending on the type of statistics used, but in recent years it has never exceeded 3% of world trade whatever the data source.

[8] *Sweden's Policy on Arms Exports* (note 5), pp. 17–18.

[9] For a discussion of this policy of international see Hagelin (note 5), pp. 178–94.

[10] For the period 1950–85 there were 42 new Swedish joint military–industrial ventures, compared with 56 in the 4-year period 1986–89. Hagelin (note 5), p. 184.

[11] In Apr. 1998, e.g., British Aerospace (BAe, now BAE Systems) paid £269 million for a 35% stake in Saab. *The Guardian*, 1 May 1998.

[12] Most of Sweden's defence companies are privately owned, although there is significant government ownership in the Celsius group of companies.

[13] As is the case in other countries, Swedish foreign trade statistics collected by the customs authorities do not normally distinguish between military and civilian products. While SITC 891 within the customs

Table 7.1. The major Swedish defence companies and their exports of military equipment in 1997

Company	Exports 1997 (SEK m., current prices)	Products
Bofors	500–1000	Artillery systems, anti-aircraft and anti-aircraft and anti-tank missiles, ammunition, electronics
Saab Training Systems	200–500	Simulators and other training equipment
Saab	200–500	Missiles, defence electronics, helicopter sights, submarine navigation systems and other electronics
CelsiusTech Systems	200–500	C^3 and fire control systems, other military electronics
Kockums Submarine	100–200	Submarines, minehunter vessels and other naval systems
Ericsson Microwave Systems	100–200	Radar systems and fire control, surveillance and communications equipment
Bofors Explosives	100–200	Powder and explosives
Hägglunds Vehicle AB	100–200	Tracked and combat vehicles
Celsius Tech Electronics	100–200	Defence electronics
Saab Dynamics	50–100	Defence electronics
Bofors Underwater Systems	50–100	Naval and submarine systems
Volvo Aero	50–100	Military aircraft engines
Norma Precision	50–100	Ammunition for sporting and hunting weapons

Source: Swedish Ministry for Foreign Affairs, Strategic Export Control Division, *Swedish Arms Exports in 1997: A Government Report*, Swedish Government Report to Parliament 1997/98:147 (Ministry for Foreign Affairs: Stockholm, May 1998), p. 28.

tion of Swedish Defence Industries (Försvarsindustriföreningen), which reports total annual sales by member companies.[14]

Of these three national sources, the ISP's export statistics, which are based on information supplied by the exporting companies regarding the value of equipment delivered, are the only figures that are directly related to Swedish legislation on military equipment. Table 7.2 shows the value of Swedish exports of military equipment over the past 26 years according to ISP data. The table also shows the proportion of military equipment in Sweden's total exports of manufactured goods. Although the defence sector is clearly dependent on arms exports for its survival, the overall Swedish economy is much less dependent. During the past 30 years the share of total exports accounted for by military

tariff does cover 4 distinct groups of military goods, its coverage is only partial and excludes, e.g., aircraft, missiles and electronics. *Swedish Arms Exports in 1996* (note 6), pp. 32–33.

[14] Founded in 1986: its member companies are responsible for the majority of exports of military equipment. They report invoiced deliveries abroad of 'military equipment and non-military goods to military customers'. In 1996, these exports were worth SEK 3942 million. *Swedish Arms Exports in 1996* (note 6), pp. 33 and 36.

Table 7.2. Swedish exports of military equipment, 1970–98

Figures in italics are percentages.

Year	Swedish exports of manufact'd goods (SEK m., current prices)	Swedish arms exports (SEK m., current prices	Total	MEC	OME	Share of arms in total exports (%%)	Total value (SEK m., constant 1968*/1990 prices)	%% change in constant prices on previous year
1970		322				*0.91*	299*	
1975		536				*0.74*	315*	
1980		2 078				*1.59*	775*	*+ 14.5*
1981		1 697				*1.17*	577*	*− 25.5*
1982		1 588				*0.95*	481*	*− 16.6*
1983		1 658				*0.79*	444*	*− 7.7*
1984		2 178				*0.90*	454*	*+ 24.8*
1985		2 137				*0.82*	511*	*− 7.8*
1986		3 243				*1.22*	796*	*+ 46.0*
1987	281 433	4 427				*1.57*	981*	*+ 31.5*
1988	304 782	6 155				*2.02*	1 313*	*+ 34.0*
1989	332 580	6 005				*1.81*	1 206*	*− 8.1*
1990	339 850	3 327				*0.98*	3 327	
1991	332 779	2 705				*0.81*	2 606	*− 21.6*
1992	326 031	2 753				*0.84*	2 647	*+ 1.6*
1993	388 290	2 863	1 216	1 647 ·	*0.74*	2 494	
1994	471 602	3 181	1 347	1 834	*0.68*	2 687	*+ 7.7*
1995	567 836	3 313	1 148	2 165	*0.58*	2 733	*+ 1.6*
1996	569 167	3 087	1 136	1 951	*0.54*	2 564	*− 6.2*
1997	632 709	3 101	939	2 162	*0.49*		
1998	673 091	3 514	1 662	1 852	*0.52*		

Notes:

* = 1968 prices; other prices in this column are 1990 prices.

MEC = 'military equipment for combat purposes'. OME = 'other military equipment'. The classifications were introduced in 1993: see section III below.

Sources: Swedish Ministry for Foreign Affairs, Strategic Export Control Division, *Swedish Arms Exports in 1996: A Government Report*, Swedish Government Report to Parliament 1996/97:138 (Ministry for Foreign Affairs: Stockholm, June 1997); *Swedish Arms Exports in 1997: A Government Report*, Swedish Government Report to Parliament 1997/98:147 (Ministry for Foreign Affairs: Stockholm, May 1998); and *Swedish Arms Exports in 1998: A Government Report*, Swedish Government Report to Parliament 1998/99:128 (Ministry for Foreign Affairs: Stockholm, May 1999); and Hirdman, S., 'Sweden's policy on arms exports', Ministry for Foreign Affairs, Stockholm, 1989 (unofficial translation), p. 14.

equipment has never exceeded 2.02 per cent, and in the three years 1996–98 it hovered around 0.5 per cent.

The geographical distribution of Swedish arms exports remained relatively stable throughout the cold-war period. This was largely due to long-standing norms of restraint and the promotion of humanitarian assistance, which were integral to Sweden's policy of neutrality (as discussed in more detail below and in chapter 8). This meant that Western Europe, and particularly the Nordic and other neutral countries, was the main recipient region, taking upwards of 50 per cent of total arms exports in any given year during this period, with a further 10–15 per cent normally going to North America and approximately 30 per cent to Asia. Similarly, Swedish military equipment was (and continues to be) only exported to a limited number of developing countries—a fact reflected in the small number of recipient countries in Latin America and Africa (although in Asia both India and Pakistan have been major markets for Swedish military equipment). There were practically no exports to the Middle East and Eastern Europe during this time.

This pattern continued in the post-cold war era. During the period 1994–97, for example, Sweden exported military equipment to 49 different countries, mainly OECD and 'like-minded' states, and to the UN. Over this four-year period exports to the Nordic countries and other West European countries averaged 43 per cent of the total value of military equipment exported, while Asia (with 31 per cent) and North America (18 per cent) were the other major recipient regions.[15] According to the Ministry for Foreign Affairs (Utrikes-departementet), since the 1980s approximately 70 per cent of Sweden's arms exports have gone to six countries—Denmark, Norway, Finland, Austria, the USA and India.[16]

In 1986, India was the recipient of what was then the largest export contract ever won by a Swedish company—a deal between Bofors and the Indian Government for the FH-77 155-mm howitzer. The agreement was thought to be worth approximately SEK 8 billion (in 1990 prices) and is the reason for the very large growth in total Swedish arms exports between 1986 and 1988 (see table 7.2). Indeed, over this three-year period, military equipment exports to India accounted for approximately 40 per cent of total military equipment exports. It was little surprise, therefore, that this was one of the very few contracts where the Swedish Government felt it necessary to back the sale with a government-to-government MOU. However, the contract caused a great deal of embarrassment to both Bofors and the Swedish Government when alleged financial improprieties came to light in 1987, when a disaffected employee at Bofors divulged the story on national radio.[17]

---

[15] *Swedish Arms Exports in 1996* (note 6), table 4, p. 28; and Swedish Ministry for Foreign Affairs, Strategic Export Control Division, *Swedish Arms Exports in 1997: A Government Report*, Swedish Government Report to Parliament 1997/98:147 (Ministry for Foreign Affairs: Stockholm, May 1998), table 4, p. 24.

[16] *Sweden's Policy on Arms Exports* (note 5), p. 16.

[17] There have been several investigations, both in Sweden and in India, in connection with the supply of howitzers by Bofors. A preliminary investigation in Sweden was closed in 1988, but early in 1990 the Indian Government opened its own inquiry and sought help from international law experts in Sweden to ascertain whether bribes were involved in the contract.

More recently, exports of military equipment to EU countries have become important, amounting to SEK 1299.2 million in 1997 (41.9 per cent of the total military equipment exported) and SEK 822.4 million in 1998 (23.4 per cent of the total). In the five years 1994–98, the USA was the largest single recipient, importing military equipment from Sweden to a value of SEK 2247.5 million, followed by Singapore (SEK 2156.6 million), Norway (SEK 2005 million), Germany (SEK 1349.4 million), Austria (SEK 992.3 million), the UK (SEK 820.6 million) and Denmark (SEK 793.7 million).[18] Future export orders are likely to centre around the JAS-39 Gripen, a multi-role fighter aircraft currently being promoted by Saab and its joint venture partner, BAE Systems, in five European countries (Austria, the Czech Republic, Hungary, Poland and Slovenia), one South-East Asian country (the Philippines) and two South American countries (Brazil and Chile). All these countries are thought to be looking to acquire new fighters, but the Gripen faces stiff competition from US and French contenders in the form of Lockheed Martin's F-16, Boeing's F-18 (which has already won the competition in Finland and Switzerland) and Dassault's Mirage 2000.[19]

The 1990s: a period of change

In the early 1990s, however, Swedish arms export controls underwent major changes as a result of at least four 'external' political factors which challenged the foundations of the policy of restraint.[20] First, the clandestine build-up of a nuclear weapons infrastructure in Iraq led in Sweden (as elsewhere) to rethink controls on dual-use goods that were applicable to WMD programmes. Second, with the end of the cold war and membership of the various international control regimes opening up to countries in both East and West, Swedish membership of such regimes was no longer considered to conflict with the nation's concept of neutrality. Thus, Sweden also joined many of these regimes at this time.[21] Third, Swedish membership of this increasing number of export control regimes led to a proliferation in the number of control lists and goods. In turn this forced Sweden to look to create a more transparent and efficient system for the benefit of its business community. Fourth, membership of the EU necessitated adaptation to EU export control regulations.

The impact of EU harmonization on Swedish export controls requires further elaboration.

---

[18] *Swedish Arms Exports in 1996* (note 6); *Swedish Arms Exports in 1997* (note 15); and Swedish Ministry for Foreign Affairs, Strategic Export Control Division, *Swedish Arms Exports in 1998: A Government Report*, Swedish Government Report to Parliament 1998/99:128 (Ministry for Foreign Affairs: Stockholm, May 1999), table 5 in each report.

[19] The Gripen has now been sold to South Africa. Hagelin, B. *et al.*, 'Register of the transfers and licensed production of major conventional weapons, 2000', *SIPRI Yearbook 2001: Armaments, Disarmament and International Security* (Oxford University Press: Oxford, 2001), p. 388.

[20] These reasons are quoted by van Dassen, L., 'Sweden', ed. H. Müller, *Nuclear Export Controls in Europe* (European InterUniversity Press: Brussels, 1995), pp. 198–99.

[21] See section III below for examples.

The decision to initiate EU membership negotiations in the early 1990s coincided with a process of reconsideration of the country's security priorities.[22] Several official reports and studies were published on the potential foreign policy and security repercussions of both joining and remaining outside the EU. One such report, for example, written by two former ambassadors on behalf of the Ministry for Foreign Affairs (and published in January 1994) concluded that there were no obstacles to full Swedish participation in the CFSP.[23]

The small majority in Sweden who voted for EU membership in the referendum are generally thought to have supported it more for social and economic reasons rather than out of concern for Swedish security, and if Sweden's security was not a major factor in the decision to join the EU, the question of arms export controls is likely to have been an even more peripheral issue. The issue of arms exports was not completely ignored during the EU membership negotiations, however. The broadening of the concept of military equipment in the arms export guidelines in 1993, for example, was done partly to bring Sweden into line with other EU member states. However, the official assessment seems to have been that there would be no radical change in Sweden's restrictive arms export policy. This largely appears to have been borne out by events so far. While EU membership has necessitated some additional changes, they relate almost entirely to the introduction of the EU Regulation on Dual-Use Goods and, more recently, the EU Code of Conduct on Arms Exports. For example, prior to the introduction of the common Regulation on Dual-Use Goods there was no catch-all clause within the Swedish export control regime. Despite opposition from some agencies and politicians,[24] Sweden now applies the catch-all provision of articles 4(1) and 4(2) of the EU Regulation. This means that a licence is required for an export regardless of goods classification when the Swedish authorities inform the exporter that goods may be used in WMD. In addition, where exporters 'know' that the goods may be used for such a purpose, they are required to ask the Swedish authorities whether an export licence is needed.

Sweden also had a problem in preparing the legislation for the EU Dual-Use Regulation. This concerned the difficulties in reconciling Article 7 (consultation prior to licensing) with the Swedish legal system.[25] Overall, however, given that Sweden has been at the forefront of developments to foster transparency in arms transfers at the international level, the exchange of information mechanisms associated with the EU Regulation (and now the EU Code) and the national enforcement of penalties are unproblematic.

---

[22] See the discussion in Hagelin (note 5), pp. 188–94.

[23] Quoted by Archer (note 4), pp. 24–25.

[24] Personal interviews with Swedish officials, 1997.

[25] *The EU Regulation on Dual-Use Goods After One Year: A Survey of Government and Industry* (Export Control Publications/Deltac Ltd: Chertsey, 1996), p. 17.

The role of domestic policy stakeholders

As a result of a long-standing belief in national unity in matters relating to external security, Swedish political parties and interest groups are not easily categorized as either proponents or opponents of arms transfer restraint. Instead, throughout the cold-war period there was a large measure of consensus among the major political parties—principal among them the Social Democrats (Socialdemokratiska Arbetarepartiet, the Conservatives (Moderata Samlingspartiet), the Centre Party (Centerpartiet) and the Liberals (Folkpartiet Liberalerna)[26]—and industry on an agreed agenda based around a strong, independent national defence policy. This being the case, there were only a small minority of voices calling for either greater or less restraint. Among the former were peace groups and the Communist Party, while the latter included some elements from the defence industry.

In the post-cold war era, as the policy focus has shifted from a strong and independent national defence policy to cooperation with partner states in the EU, this general security consensus, which was already showing signs of strain in the 1980s, is gradually dissolving. A step-by-step approach to European security integration initially held the consensus together. In recent years, however, both the former Supreme Commander of the Swedish Armed Forces, General Owe Wiktorin, and the Conservative and Liberal parties have publicly criticized the Social Democratic government over the scale of defence cuts and contradictions surrounding future policy.[27] The political debate about changing Sweden's traditional security stance has so far been rather limited, and hence the nature of any cooperation and its impact on Sweden's non-aligned and neutral status are as yet unclear. Nonetheless, the post-cold war environment for the 'function' of the Swedish variant of neutrality has clearly vanished and has been superseded by a different, multipolar environment. Several commentators have suggested that the legal status of neutrality is unlikely to survive membership of the EU.[28] In addition, Sweden having joined NATO's Partnership for Peace (PFP) in 1994, there is pressure from some quarters for it to become a full member of NATO. The mass-circulation liberal newspaper, *Expressen*, for example, started a campaign in 1995 to get Sweden into NATO on the grounds that membership would increase security and reduce defence costs. The political debate on future security options is likely to become polarized between the adherents of neutrality and those who would like to join NATO. Moreover, the likely redefinition (or abandonment) of neutrality in the context of EU (and

---

[26] The Left has dominated Swedish politics in the post-war period: the Social Democrats formed the government in the periods 1947–76, 1982–91 and 1994 to date. The Conservative Party formed the most recent non-socialist government (1991–94).

[27] Since the end of the cold war the number of army brigades has been cut from 29 to 16, and it is expected to be reduced to 13 by the year 2001. Despite these cuts, Sweden is still seeking to maintain the capability to rearm quickly. This is a key policy objective that is unlikely to change in the near future. *Jane's Defence Weekly*, 19 Aug. 1995, pp. 34–35; 13 Mar. 1996, p. 10; and 19 June 1996, p. 4.

[28] See, e.g., Lysen, G., 'Some views on neutrality and membership of the European Communities: the case of Sweden', *Common Market Law Review*, vol. 29 (1992), pp. 229–55.

possibly NATO) membership may well provide the green light for expansion of defence production and trade in Sweden.[29]

The current Social Democratic government certainly favours restructuring of the defence industry along European lines (as does industry, which is now represented at the European Defence Industry Group, EDIG[30]) but, as elsewhere in the EU until recently, there has been little political direction or clear thinking as to how this should proceed. However, as a contributor to the 1998 Letter of Intent and subsequent Framework Agreement on European defence restructuring signed in July 2000 (see chapter 4), the Swedish Government sent a clear signal to industry that it is no longer willing to subsidize production across the board and is seeking greater value for money in procurement. This means that future procurement may not necessarily favour Swedish companies. In short, domestic arms manufacturers are being told to seek partners in Europe, and as a result existing international and bilateral cooperation between Swedish firms and other defence manufacturers in Europe (such as the joint venture between Saab and BAE Systems, and the cooperation between Bofors and GIAT) is likely to grow: indeed, according to a 1996/97 bill on the Renewal of Swedish Defence, such cooperation is thought to be a precondition for the survival of the Swedish defence industry.[31]

The major complaint from industry in the past has been the lack of government support for marketing. As discussed below, this is now changing. With the greater emphasis on market and cooperative solutions, however, it seems clear that industry will be pushing for less restrictive arms export controls in the future so that the national guidelines fall into line with those of the rest of Europe (to create the so-called level playing field). The response from the government (at least in public) is that greater European cooperation should not be at the expense of Sweden's strict controls.

What of other dissenting voices in the domestic arena? The Left Party/ Communists (Vänsterpartiet) continues to remain outside this political consensus and has been joined by the Green Party (Miljöpartiet de Gröna) in recent years. In the parliamentary Export Control Council (discussed below), for example, the inclusion of these two parties in 1996 ended almost a decade of consensus within the Council. Although a 'solid majority' within the Council remain loyal to the present policy and the role of the Inspector-General of the ISP, the Green Party representative in particular voiced concerns during 1997 both in and outside the Council over Swedish military exports to India and Pakistan. This led to a number of critical newspaper articles demanding the resignation of the Inspector-General. However, continued support from a

---

[29] Unlike the cases of Austria and Switzerland, Sweden's neutrality is not grounded in any legal document such as the constitution or an international agreement. It is a policy choice that can be changed by government. However, no government would do so without being very clear about public support, probably via a referendum.

[30] Swedish industry was not a full member of EDIG until 2000 because EDIG members are the defence industrial associations of the members of the Western European Armaments Group (WEAG) and the Swedish Government did not become a full WEAG member until the autumn of 2000.

[31] Quoted in *Swedish Arms Exports in 1996* (note 6), p. 17.

number of 'heavyweight' politicians and the other nine Council members meant that this was never a serious proposition.[32]

Another proponent of a more restrictive policy is the Swedish Peace and Arbitration Society (Svenska Freds- och Skiljedomsföreningen), which follows the debates and writes articles for the national press in order to 'keep alive public scepticism'. However, with the exception of the controversial arms deals in the 1980s, which made headlines in the media and brought the issue to the attention of the general public, politicians and government officials, arms export controls have not been a major political issue in Sweden. Indeed, the majority of Swedish parliamentarians are usually untroubled by constituency interest in arms exports, and the only contact they have is with the industrial lobby.[33]

Government promotion of arms exports

Traditionally, Swedish defence companies have been responsible for marketing their own products. During the cold war, for example, the Swedish armed forces were not permitted to market weapons and there was no official government bureaucracy involved in marketing and advertising arms on a regular basis (although ministers occasionally undertook some limited promotional work for major projects).

However, the much tougher, competitive arms export markets in the post-cold war era led to a rethink. The bill on the Renewal of Swedish Defence instructed the government and Swedish authorities to 'actively and in a structured way' support the export endeavours of the defence sector, provided that those endeavours are in keeping with the guidelines for exports of military equipment. As a result, a number of measures have been taken. First, a group for defence industry matters and exports of military equipment was formed at state secretary level in 1996 with the aim of promoting exports of military equipment to approved countries.[34] Second, an ambassador was appointed within the Ministry of Trade (Handelsdepartementet) as a 'marketing supremo' for major systems such as the Gripen and submarines. However, the ambassador only has one secretary by way of support staff. Third, although Swedish embassies were specifically told in the past not to play a marketing role, following the appointment of the marketing supremo they have now been asked to play a support role and, more specifically, have been told to go out and find partners for Swedish projects.[35]

In many respects the Gripen project is an illustration of this change of thinking. Although the Saab–BAe partnership, formed in 1995 to market, adapt and manufacture the Gripen and support it in export markets, lies at the heart of the marketing effort, the companies also benefit from the marketing support of the two governments, through the DESO in the UK and the Defence Matériel

<hr>

[32] Personal interviews with Swedish government officials, 1997.
[33] Personal interviews with a Swedish government official, 1997.
[34] Quoted in *Swedish Arms Exports in 1996* (note 6), p. 18.
[35] Personal interviews with a Swedish government official, 1997.

Administration (Försvarets Materielverk, FMV)[36] in Sweden. In addition, since the early 1990s the Swedish Export Credits Guarantee Board (Exportkredit-nämnden, EKN) has been willing to offer credit terms for arms exports—an arrangement that has been described as a 'Nordic FMS'[37]—and in 1997 signed an agreement with the UK's ECGD to help facilitate joint financing of Gripen exports to third countries.[38]

III. The Swedish arms export control regime

The policy-making structure

Principal legislation

Swedish legislation on military equipment is governed by three basic norms:

1. The government decides what is to be considered military equipment.
2. The manufacture of military equipment requires a government licence.
3. The export of military equipment is prohibited unless the government allows such an export.[39]

Thus, the national regulations have several elements that reflect those norms, including provisions governing the definition of military equipment, guidelines for its manufacture and export, and associated obligations to notify and report. There is also separate national legislation governing the export of dual-use goods and technologies, enforcement and penalties, and the establishment of parliamentary oversight mechanisms.

The manufacture, supply and export of arms are governed by the Military Equipment Act of 1992 and associated Ordinance, both of which entered into force on 1 January 1993.[40] These replaced and consolidated two separate acts and accompanying ordinances, the Act concerning Control of the Manufacture of Military Equipment and Related Matters (1983) and the Act concerning Prohibition of Exports of Military Equipment and Related Matters (1988).[41] Although the 1992 act is based on a comprehensive review of arms export issues undertaken in the late 1980s,[42] it largely reflects previous legislation and

---

[36] The FMV's main task is that of a procurement agency for Sweden's armed forces.

[37] Quoted in *Armed Forces Journal International*, Sep. 1993, p. 30. Foreign Military Sales (FMS) is a US military assistance programme.

[38] *Aviation Week & Space Technology*, 16 June 1997, p. 186.

[39] *Sweden's Policy on Arms Exports* (note 5), p. 18.

[40] *Svensk Författningssamling* (*SFS*) [Swedish code of statutes] 1992:1300 and 1992:1303. Unofficial translations are available on the SIPRI Internet site at URL <http://projects.sipri.se/expcon/natexpcon/Sweden/krigmlag.htm>.

[41] *SFS* 1983:1034 and 1988:558. See also *Swedish Arms Exports in 1998* (note 18), p. 7.

[42] The groundwork for the new act was the findings of the 1987–88 Citizens' Commission set up to investigate the circumstances surrounding a number of controversial exports (see note 3) and the reports of 2 other commissions set up in the summer of 1988. The first, a parliamentary commission, the Military Equipment Exports Commission (Utredningnen om Krigsmaterielexporten), examined the financial consequences of further restrictions, drafted proposed guidelines for international cooperative programmes involving Swedish manufacturers and reviewed the guidelines for exports of military equipment in the light of the report of the Citizens' Commission. The 2nd, an independent commission, the Commission on

practice. For example, it sets out government guidelines for the export of military equipment which remain essentially the same as those originally formulated in 1971. These guidelines are reproduced in full in appendix A and are discussed further below. However, some of the provisions in the act concerning the overall control of the manufacture and supply of military equipment were simplified, clarified or modernized, and the concept of military equipment was broadened into two categories: (*a*) military equipment for combat purposes (MEC)—items which can be employed in a military context and which have a destructive effect in combat, such as artillery, fighter aircraft, missiles, warships and combat vehicles; and (*b*) other military equipment (OME)—items which have been designed or modified for military applications but which have no destructive effect, such as reconnaissance and measuring equipment, patrol vessels and specially designed vehicles.[43]

Detailed regulations concerning the division of items between the two categories are contained in the Military Equipment Ordinance. The main areas covered by these two categories are identified in table 7.3, which shows that the demarcation is based on whether or not the equipment is of a destructive nature. Most of the products falling within the 'other military equipment' category were not subject to controls prior to the introduction of the 1992 act. This broadening of the definition meant that a large number of previously unregulated exports began to be reported and made visible. The changes were also a reflection of technological developments and the desire to achieve a greater degree of conformity with corresponding definitions in other Western countries.

Under the 1992 act a licence is required from the ISP for the manufacture and/or export of both categories of military equipment. Another important new feature of the act was that a licence became necessary for any defence industry 'cooperation' with other countries and for the provision of most types of military training.[44] Whether a licence is granted for such cooperation largely depends on whether it is in keeping with Swedish defence policy requirements (as outlined in the guidelines below).

The export of dual-use goods and technologies

During the cold war Sweden sought to balance three competing concerns in its export control policy towards dual-use goods—neutrality, non-proliferation of

---

Classification (Utredningen om krigsmaterielbegreppet), was mandated to redefine the concept of military equipment. Both commissions submitted their reports in late 1989, and government proposals for new legislation appeared soon after. The subsequent report of the Committee on Foreign Affairs (Utrikesutskottet) on the government's proposed legislation was adopted by the Swedish Parliament almost unanimously. *Sweden's Policy on Arms Exports* (note 5), p. 20; and Hirdman, S., 'Sweden's policy on arms exports', *Military Technology*, Nov. 1990, pp. 54–55.

[43] *Sweden's Policy on Arms Exports* (note 5), pp. 20–21.

[44] Industrial cooperation is defined as 'the export, or other forms of supply, of military equipment, the allocation or transfer of manufacturing rights, agreements with another party on developing military equipment or methods of producing such equipment jointly with or on behalf of such a party, or the joint manufacture of military equipment with a party from abroad'. *Swedish Arms Exports in 1996* (note 6), p. 7.

Table 7.3. Swedish exports of military equipment in 1996–98 (in accordance with the military equipment classifications)
Values are in current prices.

Military equipment for combat purposes (MEC)		SEK m. 1996–98	Other military equipment (OME)		SEK m. 1996–98
MEC1	Small-calibre barrel weapons	0	OME21	Small-calibre barrel weapons, parts, etc.	10
MEC2	Cannons, anti-tank guns	514	OME22	Cannons, anti-tank guns, parts, etc.	183
MEC3	Ammunition	643	OME23	Ammunition for training purposes, etc.	896
MEC4	Missiles, rockets, torpedoes, bombs	945	OME24	Training rockets, sweeping equipment, etc.	339
MEC5	Firing control equipment	727	OME25	Reconnaissance and measurement equipment	820
MEC6	ABC weapons	1	OME26	Protective equipment, etc.	41
MEC7	Gunpowder and explosives	322	OME27	Gunpowder and explosives components	0
MEC8	Warships	114	OME28	Surveillance vessels, etc.	904
MEC9	Combat aircraft	0	OME29	Aircraft designed for military use, etc.	597
MEC10	Combat vehicles	471	OME30	Vehicles designed for military use, etc.	500
MEC11	Directed energy weapon systems	0	OME31	Directed energy weapon systems	0
			OME32	Fortifications	0
			OME33	Electronic equipment for military use	349
			OME34	Photographic and electro-optical equipment	15
			OME35	Training equipment	1 103
			OME36	Manufacturing equipment	182
			OME37	Software	25
Totals		**3 737**			**5 964**

Sources: Swedish Ministry for Foreign Affairs, Strategic Export Control Division, *Swedish Arms Exports in 1997: A Government Report*, Swedish Government Report to Parliament 1997/98:147 (Ministry for Foreign Affairs: Stockholm, May 1998); and *Swedish Arms Exports in 1998: A Government Report*, Swedish Government Report to Parliament 1998/99:128 (Ministry for Foreign Affairs: Stockholm, May 1999), table 3.

WMD and free trade. With the exception of international efforts to limit the spread of dual-use goods associated with the production of nuclear weapons,[45] Sweden tended to avoid membership of the international non-proliferation supplier regimes because membership would have encroached upon its neutrality. Thus, Sweden never joined COCOM (it abolished technology transfer controls

[45] E.g., Sweden has been a member of the NSG and the NPT since the 1970s.

in 1968 because of its disagreement with US policy in Viet Nam[46]) and did not join the MTCR and the Australia Group until 1991 (although cooperation with both the latter began in the mid-1980s). Today, however, in addition to participating in all the major non-proliferation regimes associated with WMD, Sweden is a member of the successor organization to COCOM, the Wassenaar Arrangement—indeed, it was one of the founder members (see chapter 2).

In the post-war period, however, Swedish companies faced the possibility of being blacklisted for exporting dual-use goods controlled by COCOM countries. To safeguard against this situation, most Swedish companies operated a policy of self-restraint with respect to exporting such goods. However, a number of high-profile re-exports of US technology from Sweden to the Soviet Union in the late 1970s and early 1980s led to pressure from the USA for reform. Faced with the prospect of being denied US technology crucial to its industrial and military programmes, the Swedish Government duly embarked on a number of confidence-restoring measures, including closer supervision of Swedish companies.[47]

Finally, as US pressure increased, Sweden passed its own dual-use export control regulation, the Ordinance on High Technology, in February 1986. The new regulation had two specific aims. First, it sought to prevent Sweden from becoming a transit route for exports from countries in export control regimes in which Sweden did not participate to third countries. Second, it sought to ensure that Swedish companies could import high-technology goods without any restrictions that might arise from other countries' fears that they would be re-exported. Thus, under the terms of the Ordinance, all imports to Sweden that had required a licence in the country of origin (because of COCOM, MTCR or Australia Group membership) also needed a Swedish licence, and sometimes the prior consent from the country of origin, if the goods were re-exported.[48]

In 1991 a Law on Weapons of Mass Destruction was introduced to implement the Swedish non-proliferation efforts with respect to missile technology and chemical and biological weapons (CBW).[49] This regulation also covered the dual-use lists of those regimes, and later the Nuclear Suppliers Group (NSG) list when it was established in April 1992.[50]

In November 1994 Sweden held a referendum on EU membership and two months later was a full member of the Union.[51] This necessitated further change in the national legislation for dual-use export controls to bring them into line with the emerging EU Regulation and Joint Action discussed in chapter 3. New national legislation was approved by the Swedish Parliament in June 1994,

---

[46] Stankovsky, J. and Roodbeen, H., 'Export controls outside CoCom', eds G. Bertsch, H. Vogel and J. Zielonka, *After the Revolutions: East–West Trade and Technology Transfer in the 1990s* (Westview Press: Boulder, Colo., 1991), p. 85.

[47] Stankovsky and Roodbeen (note 46).

[48] van Dassen (note 20), pp. 190–91; and Hagelin (note 5), pp. 182–83.

[49] Lagen om Strategiska Produkter, 16 May 1991, *SFS* 1991:341.

[50] van Dassen (note 20), p. 196.

[51] For background on the accession process see Miles, L., *Sweden and European Integration* (Ashgate: Aldershot, 1997), especially chapter 8.

which entered into force on 1 January 1995 and was implemented over the succeeding months (to coincide with the conclusion of the reorganization of the administrative structure—see below). The legal changes consolidated all the export control regulations, including the Ordinance on High Technology and special provisions on nuclear export controls, within the Law on Weapons of Mass Destruction. As the regulation had begun to encompass dual-use products which were not necessarily related to WMD, shortly thereafter the name of the regulation was changed to the Strategic Products Act.[52]

The Strategic Products Act (which is complementary to the EU Regulation) contains regulations relating to exports of dual-use nuclear materials, missile equipment, equipment for the production of CBW and 'sensitive' chemicals. A related ordinance on strategic products contains detailed regulations for different types of licences, export applications and obligatory notification, including a catch-all clause for dual-use goods intended for use in WMD programmes. The ordinance also contains six appendices which list the goods and chemical substances subject to export controls (including two control lists, in appendices 1 and 4, which are identical to the EU Annex I and Annex IV lists).

Enforcement and penalties

The administration and enforcement of Swedish export controls are the responsibility of the Swedish Customs and the ISP. The legal basis for enforcing export controls is the Customs Administration Act of 1987 which authorizes Customs to detain and seize shipments and inspect premises and company books. Offences and sanctions are governed by the Penalties for Smuggling Goods Act of 1960. In addition, both the Military Equipment Act and the Strategic Products Act have penalty provisions which stipulate fines and imprisonment for offences of misrepresentation, false reporting and the transfer of listed goods without an appropriate licence. Offences concerning illegal exports are in general punishable by fines or, in the case of a serious offence, by imprisonment for a maximum of two years.

Weapon and country lists

There are two weapon lists, one for military equipment and the other for dual-use goods and technologies. As mentioned above, the list of military equipment governed by the 1992 Military Equipment Act is contained in a special ordinance. The list defines 17 different groups of equipment, 11 of which are subdivided between MEC and OME (as shown in table 7.3). The Ordinance on Strategic Products contains a list of dual-use goods and technologies which is exactly the same as the Annex I list from the EU Regulation.

---

[52] Lag (1998:397) om Strategiska Produkter, 4 June 1998, *SFS* 1998:397. An unofficial translation is available on the SIPRI Internet site at URL <http://projects.sipri.se/expcon/dualuse/swedu.htm>. The law was updated in 2000 by Lagen om Kontoll av Produkter med Dubbla Användningsområden [Law on the control of dual-use products], *SFS* 2000:1064.

With the exception of the 'positive' country list established through the EU Regulation and Joint Action on Dual-Use Goods, none of the other Swedish export control regulations has either a positive or a negative country list. There are two reasons for this.[53] First, such lists were thought to be discriminatory and liable to cause diplomatic difficulties if revealed. Second, the Swedish procedure was traditionally based on individual treatment of cases using the criteria discussed below, and consideration of the country of destination was thus not regarded as a significant addition to the procedure. In practice, however, as the earlier discussion showed in relation to the policy environment, while there may not be any overt country list, it is clear that Sweden (like its counterparts) has to make a judgement about the country of destination within its export control criteria. Indeed, some discriminatory rules in favour of Nordic countries, the traditional neutral countries in Europe and EU member states are outlined in the guidelines for arms exports discussed below. In addition, one specialist journal has suggested the existence of 'red and green lists' that specify the destinations to which export sales of particular items of military equipment are either permitted or denied.[54]

Who decides export control policy?

Although the Swedish Government is ultimately responsible for arms export control policy, the actual policy is a reflection of the exceptionally strong norms of consultation in Swedish domestic politics and the international agreements to which Sweden is a party. National policy making, for example, takes place through discussion and compromise between political representatives and defence industrial groups, with a large role for parliamentary committees. The inclusion of most of the items on the Strategic Products List, on the other hand, is based on agreements concluded within international regimes.

Under Swedish law (the Instrument of Government, Regeringsformen) the government is required to consult the Advisory Council on Foreign Affairs (Utrikesnämnden, a special parliamentary subcommittee) before taking a major foreign policy decision, including decisions on important arms export matters such as significant international cooperation agreements. In the government, the Ministry for Foreign Affairs is the lead department on this issue.

Export control criteria

Successive post-war Swedish governments applied certain principles and practices to the control of arms exports and these were subsequently formalized as guidelines. Since the early 1970s the guidelines have been codified in laws which require the approval of Parliament. The overall purpose of the guidelines is to 'provide a stable and general base for assessing permit applications',

---

[53] van Dassen (note 20), p. 196.
[54] *Armed Forces Journal International*, Sep. 1993, p. 30.

although each export transaction is assessed individually.[55] The notion of producing government guidelines for arms exports was first conceived by Prime Minister Tage Erlander during a parliamentary debate on 25 April 1956 when he articulated a number of export principles, including 'that licences should on the whole be refused to states that at the time are involved in acute international conflicts or civil war, or to states where the international or internal situation is so threatening that there is a danger of disturbance or war'.[56]

It was not until a bill in 1971 that these ideas were set out in detail and became codified in law. Although the 1971 legislation has since been replaced by the 1992 Military Equipment Act, the guidelines are essentially the same. They refer to two kinds of obstacles to exports—unconditional and conditional.

The unconditional obstacles prevent the government from issuing a licence if: (*a*) the export is prohibited by an international agreement to which Sweden is a party; (*b*) there is a UN Security Council resolution prohibiting arms exports to a particular country; or (*c*) the export would be in contravention of the rules of international law concerning exports from neutral states in time of war[57] in accordance with the 1907 Hague Convention.[58]

The major changes between the 1971 and 1992 versions of the guidelines are in respect of the conditional obstacles and the treatment of international cooperation programmes (discussed below). The conditional obstacles now differ in accordance with the classification of the goods as either MEC or OME. The criteria are generally much more restrictive for the former than for the latter. In assessing cases involving exports of MEC, the guidelines state that the government should not issue an export licence to 'a state which is involved in armed conflict with another state, a state involved in an international conflict that is feared may lead to armed conflict, a state in which internal armed disturbances are taking place or a state in which extensive and serious violations of human rights occur'. These restrictive criteria are also applied to all cases involving the transfer of manufacturing rights and cooperation with foreign partners irrespective of the type of export. This is because such agreements often result in longer-term commitments than ordinary exports of finished products. In cases involving OME, the guidelines state that an export permit should be granted to countries 'not engaged in armed conflict with another state, [which] are not subject to internal armed disturbances or where there are no extensive and serious violations of human rights'.[59]

Thus, for MEC there is a de facto export ban to which exceptions can be made, but only where there is a direct link to Swedish national security. In other

---

[55] *Swedish Arms Exports in 1996* (note 6), p. 7.

[56] Quoted in *Sweden's Policy on Arms Exports* (note 5), p. 23.

[57] The export restrictions that must be observed as a result of Sweden's neutrality only apply during a state of war, as it is only under such circumstances—the outbreak of war or the threat of war in its vicinity—that Sweden would make a formal declaration of neutrality. *Sweden's Policy on Arms Exports* (note 5), p. 24.

[58] Hague Convention XII respecting the Rights and Duties of Neutral Powers in Naval War, signed on 18 Oct. 1907.

[59] *Swedish Arms Exports in 1996* (note 6), p. 8.

words, there has to be a clear reason to sell that would override the general ban. For OME (and dual-use products) the opposite is true. The principle is that exports are permitted (encouraged in fact) and there has to be a good reason to stop the export—which means that a larger number of countries may be considered as potential recipients of OME.

It can be seen that respect for human rights in the recipient country is a core criterion in both categories, even in cases where the goods being exported could not be used to violate human rights. This was not previously the case. Under the 1971 guidelines arms exports were prohibited to states which were 'assumed to be likely to use the military equipment for the suppression of human rights in breach of the UN Charter and the UN declarations and conventions relating to such matters'.[60] However, while the new wording is more restrictive in that respect (i.e., there is no longer a requirement for the equipment to be directly linked to acts of suppression of human rights), it is clearly more liberal in two other respects. First, the *assumption* that violations may take place is no longer sufficient cause for prohibition. Instead, actual violations must have taken place. Second, these violations must be both *extensive* and *serious*. The net effect would therefore seem to be a liberalization of this human rights provision.

The guidelines also set out certain rules concerning the level of restrictiveness as determined by the country of destination and the conditions for cooperative projects. For example, less restrictive conditions are applied in the case of exports of military equipment to the other Nordic and neutral countries in Europe. Foreign policy considerations are not normally applied to such states, and in peacetime export licences for these destinations will normally be issued as a matter of course. A proposal in the draft guidelines to treat EC countries in the same way as the Nordic bloc was rejected by the Swedish Parliament in 1992, and it was only when Sweden joined the EU three years later that EU member states gained similar treatment. On the other hand, Sweden generally applies a restrictive policy to all other states, particularly those for which licences have not been granted in the past. In addition, the guidelines also stipulate that an export licence may only be issued if the recipient is a state, a government authority or an entity authorized by the government (which includes agreements between Swedish companies and their international partners concerning the joint development or manufacture of military equipment).[61] This implies, for example, that export to a guerrilla movement or to a province trying to obtain independence is not allowed.

In the late 1980s a special commission[62] studied the implications of a growing number of international cooperative military programmes for Sweden's export policy in order to determine the rules that should apply to the export to third

---

[60] Gullikstad, E., 'Sweden', ed. I. Anthony, SIPRI, *Arms Export Regulations* (Oxford University Press: Oxford, 1991), p. 151.

[61] However, licences may also be issued for exports of 'other military equipment' if the recipient is a 'reputable' company and it can be demonstrated that such equipment is required for that company's normal civil operations. *Sweden's Policy on Arms Exports* (note 5), p. 25.

[62] See note 42.

countries of jointly developed systems. The new legislation set out a number of principles based around the 'identity' of such a system. Thus, if the cooperation agreement with a foreign partner stipulates exports to a third country, assessment of such exports is undertaken in accordance with the dominant national identity of the final product. If the final product has a predominantly Swedish identity, then the question of such exports is assessed in accordance with the Swedish guidelines. If, however, it has a predominantly foreign identity (or if one of the prerequisites for a particular cooperation agreement is that certain third country exports be permitted, and Sweden has a strong defence policy interest in such an agreement), exports to a third country are allowed within the framework of the cooperation partner's national export regulations. Under the guidelines, the more important international cooperative agreements also require an intergovernmental MOU. The Advisory Council on Foreign Affairs has to be consulted prior to such an agreement being entered into.[63]

In practice, however, the guidelines proved to be inadequate because many of the industrial relationships turned out to be much deeper than originally anticipated, resulting in military products of 'mixed' identity. During 1997, for example, because there was no clear guidance on these cases for industry, a backlog of cases began to build up, with the danger that prospective cooperative ventures would be lost. It was anticipated, however, that the situation would be resolved on the basis of accepting the guidelines of the country of export (along the lines of the German approach).[64] Although less restrictive export guidelines have been applied to Swedish firms in international cooperative ventures since the early 1970s (because such arrangements were seen as necessary to the survival of domestic military production within important industrial sectors),[65] this new approach represents a considerable relaxation in the Swedish guidelines. It is also in keeping with the new arrangements anticipated under the Framework Agreement (chapter 4) for collaborative projects involving France, Germany, Italy, Spain and the UK.

Sweden also takes account in its guidelines of the need to be known as a credible supplier. Thus, if a foreign state has been allowed to purchase military equipment from Sweden in the past it is usually allowed to make the 'follow-on' purchases (such as spare parts, ammunition and other equipment) necessary to keep the equipment operational, unless new unconditional obstacles or other strong foreign policy considerations have arisen since. However, according to a

---

[63] *Sweden's Policy on Arms Exports* (note 5), p. 26. The actual wording in the 1992 legislation appears to have been watered down from what was originally proposed. In an earlier article, the former head of the KMI stated that the following principles had been established: 'If it has a Swedish identity—meaning that Sweden has supplied, say, 70 per cent or more of the inputs—we think we should have control over export. If, on the other hand, Swedish input is 10 per cent or lower, then we recognise that we are not entitled to much say. If the input is some figure in between, then our position is that there should be a joint decision, also involving government authorities on both sides'. Hirdman, S., 'Sweden's defence export policy', *Military Technology,* July 1990, p. 56. It would seem, therefore, that the Swedish Government rather belatedly recognized that its own regulations and guidelines were only likely to be acceptable to foreign partners if the project had a clear Swedish identity.

[64] Personal interviews with a Swedish government official, 1997.

[65] Hagelin (note 5), p. 181.

former head of Sweden's licensing authority, this follow-on rule applies 'even if by the time the customer asks for spares or ammunition, the political situation in the region or in the country itself has taken a turn for the worse'.[66] This would explain the 1996 controversy in Sweden concerning certain follow-on exports to Indonesia, which were criticized for taking place when the situation in East Timor was deteriorating. These exports of Bofors guns were considered by some to be new arms and by others to be a follow-on delivery. As a result, the government appointed a 'special expert' in 1997 to review the regulations for follow-on orders. The expert reported to the government on 31 March 1999 and the report was circulated for consideration, as is customary practice in Sweden.[67] However, as at April 2001, no changes to the guidelines were considered necessary.

A government-to-government MOU is also sometimes used to cement important military export agreements. In such bilateral MOUs the Swedish Government normally declares that it will fulfil the contract under any circumstances, the only conceivable obstacle being a mandatory UN or EU embargo. The large Bofors howitzer deal with India in the mid-1980s is the best-known example of this type of agreement.

Finally, the guidelines also indicate that diversion of Swedish exports to third countries will not be tolerated. In particular, governments which allow or neglect to prevent 'the unauthorized re-exportation of Swedish military equipment, shall not in principle be eligible to receive further equipment from Sweden as long as these circumstances remain'.[68]

The criteria applied to the export of dual-use and other strategic goods (covered by the Strategic Products Act) are broadly similar to those used for OME, that is, there is a strong presumption of approval. For nuclear substances and products that may be used in missiles, missile systems or CBW, for example, the absence of either a credible end-use or a controlling regime in the recipient country may be good reasons for stopping the export. Similarly, exports of high-technology dual-use products for conventional weapons are only likely to be stopped if they are at odds with some of the foreign policy considerations outlined above.[69]

Finally, the formal policy guidelines are supplemented by the internal guidelines of the various licensing authorities, which flesh out the legal guidelines and enable decisions to be reached on individual cases. With the exception of a few general principles, these administrative guidelines are not normally in the public domain, although given the close relationship between the licensing authorities and defence manufacturers they are likely to be shared with some of the latter.

---

[66] Hirdman (note 63), p. 56.

[67] Ericsson, D., 'The Swedish model of scrutiny in theory and in practice' in *Report on the International Conference on European Arms Export Controls, 13–14 November 1997* (Swedish Fellowship of Reconciliation and Saferworld: Stockholm, 1998), p. 34; and *Swedish Arms Exports in 1998* (note 18), p. 9.

[68] *Sweden's Policy on Arms Exports* (note 5), p. 38.

[69] 'National Inspectorate of Strategic Products: presentation in brief', Stockholm, 1996, p. 9.

Regulatory oversight and the Export Control Council

Although some arms export decisions fall within the remit of the Advisory Council on Foreign Affairs (as discussed above), it was decided in the early 1980s that a broader basis for considering export transactions was necessary. Thus, in 1984 a bill was passed by the Swedish Parliament setting up an Advisory Board on Military Equipment Export Issues (Rådgivande Nämnden för Krigsmaterielexportfrågor) with responsibility for advising on specific questions concerning arms exports. It consisted of six representatives from the political parties represented in the Advisory Council on Foreign Affairs (i.e., three Social Democrats and one representative each from the Conservative Party, the Liberal Party and the Centre Party) and was convened and chaired by the head of the KMI, the Inspector-General of Military Equipment. Although not exactly proportional to the party political situation in the Parliament, the membership of the Advisory Board was an approximation of that political reality. At that time the Green Party was not represented in Parliament and the Communists (who were represented in Parliament) were deliberately excluded.

By 1990, however, the feeling was that all political parties with parliamentary representation should be included in the process. Thus, following the recommendations of a Royal Commission, in February 1996 the structure of the Board was reformed and broadened, and it was re-named the Export Control Council (Exportkontrollrådet) to coincide with the formation of the ISP. The Council now has 10 political appointees with representation from all the major political parties, and continues to be convened by the Inspector-General of Military Equipment (the head of the ISP). Both the Ministry for Foreign Affairs and the Ministry of Defence (Försvarsdepartementet) also participate at the regular monthly meetings, with the former presenting assessments of the recipient countries and the latter providing a defence policy viewpoint. In addition to these regular meetings, council members also receive continual reports on all export decisions.[70]

Since 1985 the Swedish Government has also submitted annual reports to Parliament on arms exports, and since the May 1997 report this has included a summary of the activities of the ISP.[71] The Foreign Affairs Committee writes its own report (based on the government's annual report) which is then voted on in the Parliament. Taken together, therefore, the Export Control Council and the annual reporting system ensure that the Swedish Parliament is well briefed on arms export control matters and the work of the ISP.

[70] *Swedish Arms Exports in 1996* (note 6), p. 11. For a description by a Swedish parliamentarian (from the Christian Democrats) and current member of the Export Control Council see Ericsson (note 67), pp. 34–35.

[71] This requirement to submit an annual report was introduced by legislation in 1984/85 (Bill Concerning Greater Insight and Consultation in Questions Involving the Export of Military Equipment).

The administrative (policy-execution) structure

Publication of export guidelines

The Swedish Government publishes guidelines for exporters (and other interested parties) in a number of different media and formats, with different levels of access. First, following the recommendation of a government study in the early 1990s, the ISP now publishes official handbooks which contain guidance for the defence industry and government authorities on the manufacture and export of defence equipment.[72] The handbook describes the current legislation and the regulatory structure and procedures for obtaining a licence, including information for exporters on the catch-all clause. Second, the ISP holds regular seminars and information meetings about its activities. Third, the Ministry for Foreign Affairs publishes a periodic summary of Sweden's arms export policy, which also appears in English, French and German in order to improve awareness of this policy outside Sweden.[73] Fourth, as discussed above, since 1985 the government has published an annual report to parliament on its arms export policy.[74] Finally, since the autumn of 1996, the text of both the annual report and the summary document published by the Ministry for Foreign Affairs can be found on the Internet, together with English translations.[75]

The decision-making process for licence applications

As stated in the introduction, Sweden has a cooperative arms export control regime, consisting of a policy-making framework (i.e., the legislation and political guidelines discussed above), coupled with an administrative process of industry–government negotiation. While this latter process is not mentioned in the legislation or political guidelines it is a central feature of the Swedish system. It is also said to create a common interest in the responsible handling of cases and allows the government to object to a potential export early on in the process. From an industry perspective, for example, the close relationship with the government enhances companies' competitiveness because of the quick reaction time for licence applications. It also compensates for the perception in some quarters that Swedish industry is uncompetitive because of the highly regulated nature of the economy as a whole. Indeed, the ISP meets regularly with industry—more than 100 meetings per year with individual companies—on a 'commercial in confidence' basis. In turn, because the companies see the benefits of this approach, they tend to provide more information than is

---

[72] *KM handbok* [Military equipment handbook] and *Handbok strategiska produkter* [Handbook of strategic products]. See the ISP's Internet site at URL <http://www.isp.se>.

[73] *Sweden's Policy on Arms Exports* (note 5). A revised edition was published in 1998. *Swedish Arms Exports in 1998* (note 18), p. 12.

[74] The most recent version of this annual report is Swedish Ministry for Foreign Affairs, *Report on Sweden's Export Control Policy and Exports of Military Equipment in 2000*, Swedish Government Report to Parliament 2000/01:114 (Ministry for Foreign Affairs: Stockholm, Apr. 2001), available on the Swedish Government's Internet site at URL <http://www.regeringen.se>.

[75] URL <http://www.regeringen.se/info rosenbad/departement/utrikes/vapenexport>.

required by law. One consequence of this cooperative approach is that there are never any negative decisions, that is to say, there are no denials of formal licence applications in respect of military equipment.[76] To fully appreciate the significance of this situation it is necessary to examine the negotiating framework for licence applications in greater detail.

In the Swedish system a licence is required not only for the export of military equipment but also for the manufacture of that equipment. The ISP is responsible for issuing these licenses for military equipment, as well as the licensing of exports of dual-use goods. The ISP was formed on 1 February 1996 following the merger of the KMI and the Export Control Unit of the Ministry for Foreign Affairs (Enheten för Strategisk Exportkontroll, ESEK). The KMI was established in 1935 and was part of the Foreign Trade Department of the Ministry for Foreign Affairs. In addition to providing advice for government decisions on exports of military equipment, it was also responsible for drafting legislation in such matters. The ESEK was previously the primary licensing authority for all dual-use goods, but since 1 February 1996 it only handles sensitive licence applications that are referred from the ISP for decision by the Cabinet.

Since 1 February 1996, authority to take licensing decisions has rested solely with the head of the ISP, the Inspector-General (rather than with the government).[77] However, individual cases involving matters of principle or of particular importance are discussed by either (or both) of two official committees, the Export Control Council and the Advisory Council on Foreign Affairs (see above). In addition, licence applications that may have an impact on future policy are submitted to the government for a decision. Prior to 1996 virtually all decisions about export licences were taken solely by the government. The Minister for Foreign Trade considered routine cases (approximately 85 per cent of an annual total of 2300 applications), and the Cabinet dealt with the remainder of applications concerning major export deals. In 1995 and 1996, for example, government decisions accounted for 98 per cent of the total value of export licences granted.[78]

In its first year of operation, officials from the ISP and the Ministry for Foreign Affairs met regularly twice a month to exchange information and to organize the division of labour for participation in international and bilateral conferences. In short, a small unit (currently five people, with the most senior at ambassador level) within the Ministry for Foreign Affairs is responsible for policy making and international negotiation in multilateral working groups,

---

[76] Hence, Sweden failed to notify any licence denials to other EU member states during the first reporting year (1998) under the EU Code of Conduct. Council of the European Union, General Affairs Committee, '1999 annual report on the implementation of the EU Code of Conduct on Arms Exports', 11384/99–C5-0021/2000, *Official Journal of the European Communities,* C315 (3 Nov. 1999).

[77] This change is in keeping with the Swedish administrative and political philosophy of having small ministries mainly concerned with high policy underpinned by large independent authorities (*myndigheter*) mainly concerned with practical, day-to-day concerns. The current Inspector-General of the ISP is a civil appointment at ambassador level, and under the Swedish Constitution the post is independent from any government ministry. Personal interviews with Swedish government officials, 1997.

[78] *Swedish Arms Exports in 1996* (note 6), p. 21.

while the ISP is responsible for licensing. The ISP is organized into three special licensing departments which deal with military equipment, dual-use goods and the 1993 Chemical Weapons Convention. Like its predecessor, the ISP is self-financing—an annual fee is charged to companies manufacturing both strategic goods and military equipment if the invoice value of such products sold during the year is in excess of SEK 2.5 million)—which enables a staff of 17 to be employed.[79]

In 1998 approximately 200 companies were licensed to conduct activities in the military equipment area, of which 40 exported such equipment. These companies are obliged to submit reports to the ISP in various contexts, as discussed below.

Manufacturing and ownership

Swedish companies are obliged to apply to the ISP for a licence that permits them to manufacture and supply military equipment. Companies which have a manufacturing licence must also report their ownership structures to the ISP on an annual basis, and the manufacturing licence may be withdrawn if foreign influences gain a decisive say in a company.[80]

Marketing

The marketing of military equipment is not a restricted activity in Sweden (in contrast to France, for example, where a licence is required). However, Swedish companies are required to provide quarterly reports to the ISP on their marketing activities abroad regarding military equipment and on any measures undertaken to enter cooperative agreements with foreign entities. These compulsory reports must give details of the country, the type of military equipment and the target of their marketing activities. This information is later used as the basis for regular meetings between the ISP and the individual companies.

Transfers of manufacturing rights abroad, cooperation with foreign partners

Before granting a licence to companies that either want to transfer manufacturing rights or are looking to become partners in a cooperative international development programme, the ISP undertakes a detailed examination of the scope, duration and conditions (such as re-export clauses) of such agreements. This examination is conducted within the context of the more restrictive criteria

---

[79] Earmarking of funding/taxation is unusual in Sweden. In this case, the ISP determines the fee following an equitable scale based on the percentage of a company's total turnover. Following the introduction of the EU Regulation on Dual-Use Goods, dual-use companies also now contribute. Thus, the ISP costs are now split between dual-use and military manufacturers. With a *deminimus* limit in operation this means that for dual-use goods companies like Ericsson pay the most. *Swedish Arms Exports in 1996* (note 6), pp. 9–10; and personal interviews with Swedish government officials, 1997.

[80] In 1997, the British company Alvis plc was granted permission to acquire Hägglunds Vehicles AB. This was the first time 'in a very long time' that a foreign company was granted permission to acquire a Swedish defence manufacturer. *Swedish Arms Exports in 1997* (note 15), p. 16.

discussed above. In 1998, 5 new licences were granted (7 had been granted in the previous two years combined) for the transfer of manufacturing rights abroad to the UK, the USA (2 licences) and Japan (2 licences), and 1 licence was granted to extend a previous transfer of manufacturing rights (to Spain). In addition, 14 new cooperation agreements were examined and approved (as compared to 19 in the previous two years combined) for joint development or production with France (3 licences), Poland, Switzerland, Norway, the UK (4 licences) and the USA (4 licences). Once a licence has been granted, the company is obliged under the Military Equipment Act to report annually to the ISP with an update of the information supplied with the original application. In 1998, 11 companies reported a total of 196 transfers of licences and cooperation agreements in 8 countries.[81] For some cooperative projects the export conditions are stated in special bilateral government-to-government agreements.

Ownership of foreign defence manufacturing capacity

Companies which are licensed to manufacture or supply military equipment in Sweden are also obliged to report annually to the ISP if they have ownership in any foreign legal entities which pursue the development, manufacture, marketing or sales of military equipment. In 1997, 7 companies reported ownership in 26 foreign legal entities in 15 countries. A year later, the figures had risen to 10 companies reporting ownership in 41 foreign companies in 19 countries.[82]

Training services

Under the Military Equipment Act, foreign subjects can usually only be given military training (in or outside Sweden) with the consent of the government. There were no licences issued for military training services during the three-year period 1996–98.

Exports of military equipment and dual-use goods

All exports of controlled goods are subject to export licensing. For dual-use goods some special types of general and individual licences are available. For the export of military equipment only individual licences can be used, and both companies and government bodies must apply for a licence for each individual export order. There are four main types of licence:

1. *The Open General Licence (OGL) (EU).* Although most intra-EU transfers of dual-use goods are now licence-free, Swedish companies wishing to export to other member states are still required to register with the ISP. This type of OGL registration stipulates a text that has to be added to invoices notifying the importer of export control requirements for re-export outside the EU.

---

[81] *Swedish Arms Exports in 1998* (note 18), p. 28.
[82] *Swedish Arms Exports in 1998* (note 18), p. 28.

2. *The Open General Licence (regime countries).* There is an OGL for exports of dual-use goods to countries outside the EU which adhere to all four of the MTCR, the Wassenaar Arrangement, the Australia Group and the NSG. These countries are Australia, Canada, Japan, Norway, New Zealand, Switzerland and the USA—the same as are listed in Annex II of the EU Regulation on Dual-Use Goods. Applications for these licences are normally approved as a matter of routine.

3. *The Individual Open Licence (IOL).* Companies that regularly export high-technology goods may be granted this licence (introduced in 1995) which is valid for exports to all civilian consignees in a number of countries. It is granted only when the exporter can demonstrate a clear understanding of the regulations and has an internal compliance programme. Applications for an IOL go to the ISP in the first instance and are then referred to Customs for a pre-licence check on the company's internal control procedures. In addition, the exporter must obtain an end-user certificate from the consignee within 30 days of the first shipment. Approximately 40–50 companies currently use IOLs.

4. *Individual Licence.* When no open licence is available an individual licence is required. In most cases an end-user certificate is required.[83]

The stages through which an application for an export licence for military equipment normally goes are as follows.[84]

Stage 1. The company applies to the ISP for classification of a given product as MEC, OME or non-military equipment. The ISP consults its Technical–Scientific Council as appropriate and reports back to the company.[85] This stage normally only applies in doubtful cases, because companies are responsible for classifying their own products on the basis of the lists in the Military Equipment Ordinance.

Stage 2. Periodic meetings take place between the company and the ISP to discuss the market situation and current government assessments of potential recipient countries. These meetings provide an opportunity for early, open and informal discussion about individual cases while at the same time clarifying the export control system for companies.

Stage 3. The company supplies the ISP with *post factum* quarterly marketing reports and periodic meetings continue.

Stage 4. In certain difficult cases, the company makes a written preliminary inquiry as to whether an export licence is likely to be granted. The ISP

---

[83] See the section on Sweden in *Worldwide Guide to Export Controls 1996/1997* (Export Control Publications: Chertsey, 1997), p. 3.

[84] This account of the administrative procedures is mainly drawn from *Sweden's Policy on Arms Export* (note 5), pp. 29–31, but is supplemented by personal interviews with Swedish government officials, 1997.

[85] The Tekniskt-Vetenskapligt Råd was set up in 1984 and usually meets about 3 or 4 times each year. It includes experts from the Swedish Defence Research Agency (Totalförsvarets Forskningsinstitutionen (FOI) and the Royal Swedish Academy of Engineering Sciences (Ingenjörsvetenskapsakademin, IVA). Assistance with the classification of dual-use industrial goods is also available to companies through the Stockholm Chamber of Commerce, the Board of Customs and independent export control consultants. See the section on Sweden in *Worldwide Guide to Export Controls 1996/1997* (Export Control Publications: Chertsey, 1997), p. 4.

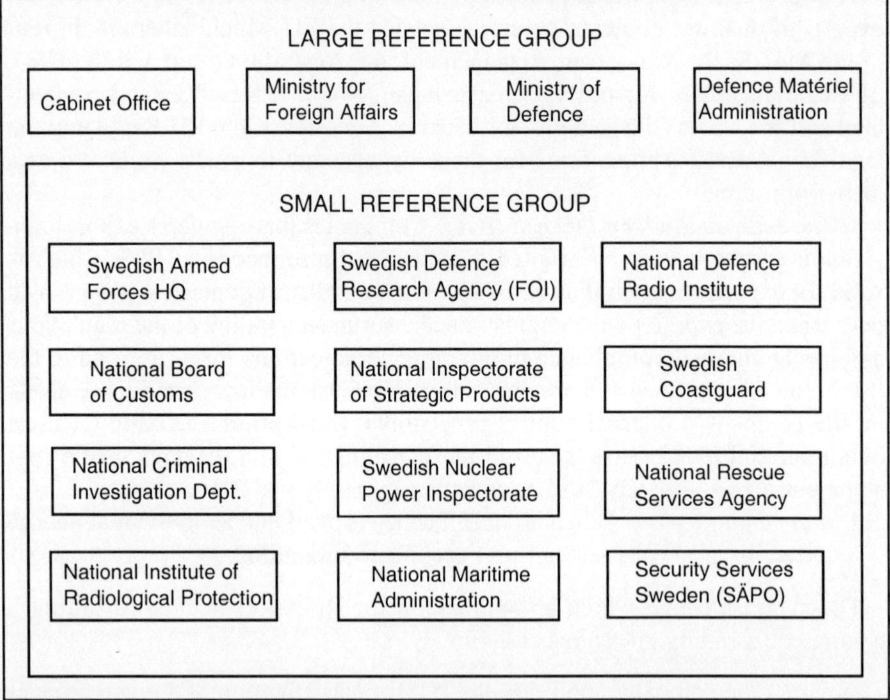

Figure 7.1. Sweden's interdepartmental cooperation on non-proliferation

coordinates the political examination of this advance notification, which might involve referral to the Political Department of the Ministry for Foreign Affairs and other bodies, consultation with the Export Control Council, presentation to the Minister for Foreign Trade and/or the Cabinet, and possibly consultation within the Advisory Council on Foreign Affairs. The ISP communicates the resulting preliminary assessment to the company, with a proviso that a final decision will be made when the export application is formally considered. There is, however, an unwritten 'gentlemen's agreement' that a positive ruling will be allowed to stand unless circumstances change, although in practice only approximately 25 per cent of such rulings result in an export. There are a number of reasons for this, such as market competition, changes in the technical specifications and so on.[86]

Stage 5. At least four weeks prior to the offer of a tender or of entering into an export agreement or other overseas cooperation concerning military equipment, the company notifies the ISP. The ISP assesses whether the tender or contract is so obviously inappropriate that it should be prohibited outright. Otherwise, no definite decision is made at this stage. This notification of tender is a legal obligation in all cases and is meant to avoid situations in which com-

---

[86] Personal interviews with Swedish government officials, 1997.

panies commit themselves to an export deal or cooperation agreement which is later prohibited by the government at the export licence stage.

Stage 6. The company enters into commercial negotiations and a Swedish Declaration by End-User (DEU) is presented to the recipient.

Stage 7. The DEU is signed by the recipient and submitted to the ISP via a Swedish embassy (which performs certain checks in the local context to ensure its authenticity and validity).

Stage 8. The company submits an application for an export licence which is examined by the ISP and a decision is taken by the Inspector-General. If the case is of special significance it is forwarded to the government with comments and the decision is taken either by the Minister for Foreign Trade or by the Cabinet. However, since the introduction of the ISP in February 1996 only one decision has been sent to the Swedish Government for advice.[87]

Stage 9. The ISP issues an export licence which may or may not contain specific conditions and control procedures.

Stage 10. At least one week prior to the date of the intended export the company submits a notification of exportation to the Board of Customs (Tullverket), which will consult with the ISP as necessary.

Stage 11. The company delivers the goods and, if appropriate, obtains an acknowledgement of receipt from the purchasing country and forwards this to the ISP.

Stage 12. The company may apply to the ISP for permission to export spare parts or other supplementary equipment. This is normally granted as a matter of routine, although the ISP will normally require a further DEU for such exports.

Stage 13. The company provides quarterly reports to the ISP on actual deliveries completed. These and other compulsory reports referred to above form the basis of the ISP's statistics and the government's annual report to the Parliament.

In contrast, the decision-making procedure for an export licence for dual-use goods is relatively straightforward. A formal application is made to the ISP and the decision whether or not to grant the licence is taken by the Inspector-General.[88] Cases of special significance are discussed within the Export Control Council and may also be submitted to the government for a decision.

The ISP aims to complete the assessment of export licence applications for both dual-use goods and military equipment (i.e., stages 8 and 9 in the latter case) within a month of receipt. However, there does appear to be a fast-track application process in operation for larger military projects. An interdepartmental cooperation group known as the Large Reference Group was established in late 1992 and meets twice a year to discuss some of the broad issues to do with strategic export controls.[89] A second interdepartmental cooperation group known as the Small Reference Group meets on a more regular basis to discuss

[87] Personal interviews, 1997 with Swedish government officials.
[88] Applications to export nuclear materials are submitted to the Nuclear Power Inspectorate.
[89] Personal interviews, 1997.

Table 7.4. Export licences granted by Sweden for sales of military equipment, 1989–98

Figures in italics are percentages.

Year	Total value SEK m. (current prices.)			Total value (SEK m., constant 1990 prices)			%% change in constant prices compared with previous year		
1989	7 245								
1990	2 869			2 869					
1991	2 487			2 396			*– 16*		
1992	2 992			2 877			*+ 20*		
	Total	MEC	OME	Total	MEC	OME	Total	MEC	OME
1993	6 106	1 942	4 164	5 319	1 692	3 627			
1994	4 268	1 991	2 277	3 604	1 682	1 923	*– 32*	*– 1*	*– 47*
1995	6 543	2 011	4 532	5 399	1 659	3 739	*+ 50*	*– 1*	*+ 94*
1996	2 859	662	2 197	2 374	550	1 825	*– 56*	*– 67*	*– 51*
1997	5 061	2 481	2 580						
1998	3 273	1 449	1 824						

Note: MEC = military equipment for combat purposes; OME = other military equipment.

Source: Swedish Ministry for Foreign Affairs, Strategic Export Control Division, *Swedish Arms Exports in 1996: A Government Report*, Swedish Government Report to Parliament 1996/97:138 (Ministry for Foreign Affairs: Stockholm, June 1997); *Swedish Arms Exports in 1997: A Government Report*, Swedish Government Report to Parliament 1997/98:147 (Ministry for Foreign Affairs: Stockholm, May 1998); and *Swedish Arms Exports in 1998: A Government Report*, Swedish Government Report to Parliament 1998/99:128 (Ministry for Foreign Affairs: Stockholm, May 1999), table 1 in each report.

more specific issues to do with non-proliferation. The membership of these two groups is shown in figure 7.1. The Large Reference Group, which includes representatives from the Ministry of Defence, the FMV, the Ministry for Foreign Affairs and the Cabinet Office, was set up with the aim of facilitating export applications for the JAS-39 Gripen. Indeed, Jan Hammerström, marketing director for the Gripen, is quoted as saying: 'You reach every institution through this group: you can get decisions overnight'. He also suggested that the activities of this group might be expanded in the future to the extent that it would 'act as an arbiter for all potential export destinations'. In turn this might lead to an expansion in the number of countries (particularly in the Middle East) to which Swedish firms are able to export military equipment.[90]

To date, this does not appear to have happened. Although the ISP does take advice from the government about specific countries (and receives a background 'country assessment' prepared by the foreign ministry), for the time being at least the ISP retains responsibility for deciding which countries are cleared to receive which equipment (within the context of existing guidelines).

[90] *Armed Forces Journal International*, Sep. 1993, p. 30.

In recent years the number of applications for export licences has been approximately 1600 per year, and most of these have been for reasons other than sale, such as export prior to or following repair, for demonstration purposes or for testing. In 1993, which was the first year the Military Equipment Act was in force, a large number of applications were initially received for export licences for OME (for which licences had not been previously required).[91] Table 7.4 shows the total *value* of export licences granted for sales of military equipment in the 10-year period 1989–98. The value of export licences granted often differs quite markedly from the value of actual deliveries (table 7.2) in the same year. This is because many of the licences relate to deliveries spread over several years, or because sometimes the licences are not fully utilized. The decrease in the value of export licences granted in 1996, for example, should thus be reflected in the export statistics in later years.

In 1998 the total number of export licences issued was 2040 (in 1997 the figure was 2235 and in 1996 it was 1923), of which 447 involved dual-use goods (compared with 403 in 1997 and 549 in 1996).[92] There are no statistics for negative decisions because, as stated above, such cases are weeded out at an earlier, pre-licence stage.

Compliance and enforcement procedures

For all exports of military equipment, Sweden requires a DEU signed and stamped by the purchaser (usually a responsible person in the procurement agency of the recipient country) stating that the equipment purchased will only be used by its national defence forces and will not be re-exported to a third country. Several types of DEUs are used (there are at least five standard DEUs plus ad hoc arrangements) according to the type of goods being exported and their end-use. For example, the categories of certificates required for exports of small products (no exact definition) and OME are different from those required for exports of MEC. In addition, different end-use certificates were introduced for Annex I goods exported under the EU Dual-Use Regulation.

The ISP uses a number of sources such as specialist journals, newspapers, intelligence reports and discussion within international regimes to keep abreast of proliferation trends, but post-DEU checks on individual countries are not undertaken as a rule. However, violation of a re-export clause would affect future arms deliveries to the country in question.

The Board of Customs is responsible for control policy and has an Export Control Division located in Stockholm which coordinates and advises field offices and also assists companies in regulatory questions. The Export Control Division has almost daily contact with the ISP and it receives all licences for exports of dual-use goods and military equipment. There are two officers within this division with specific responsibility for export control policy for dual-use and military equipment. Intelligence information on end-use and end-users is

---

[91] *Swedish Arms Exports in 1996* (note 6), pp. 20–21.
[92] *Swedish Arms Exports in 1998* (note 18), p. 11.

obtained from the various multilateral control regimes, national intelligence services and national companies. Approximately 2500 personnel in 12 regional customs offices undertake operational enforcement of the regulations. The customs authorities monitor the export of all controlled goods, for which an export declaration has to be made one week before the actual export takes place (i.e., stage 10 above). They also carry out post-export checks on a small number of suspect companies but where illegal activities are suspected, regional criminal investigation units take over responsibility for the inquiry.

Sweden has also developed a Customs Information System (known by its Swedish acronym, TDS—Tulldatasystemet), a computer system used to support customs clearance in connection with the export and import of goods. One of the main reasons for introducing the system was to move away from paper documentation and the associated problems of document retrieval and archive storage. For example, export declarations are now taken directly from the TDS, whereas previously they had to be obtained from microfiche archives. More importantly from a control perspective, the TDS (among other things) can alert officers to potential illegal exports and identify known proliferators. It cost approximately SEK 500 million to introduce and was phased in over a number of years, beginning with exports in 1992 (each exporting company has a unique registration number), imports in 1993–94 and a post-export control system in 1995. Work is currently in progress to build risk profiles within the system. There are 35 customs officers who act as contact points and specialists for the TDS within the customs regions.[93]

IV. Policy outcomes

A strict control regime: compromised by EU membership?

Prior to EU membership the principal policy influences for Sweden's post-war arms export policy were the country's non-aligned and neutral status, and the exceptionally strong norms of consultation in Swedish politics. Given Sweden's role as a neutral state, international mediator, proponent of disarmament and advocate of the UN, it is an apparent paradox that the country is an active exporter of conventional weapons. However, the paradox is easily explained. On the one hand, this desire to avoid reliance on foreign political or military support necessitated the development of an independent national defence industry, which in turn had to export in order to survive. Thus, the primary rationale for such exports was national security, rather than economic concerns, as outlined by Ambassador Sven Hirdman, former Inspector-General of Military Equipment:

The basic motive for permitting arms exports is that they are necessary for our own national security policy. We do not have as other countries may have, a strong economic need to allow arms exports in order to improve the balance of trade . . . What we

<hr>

[93] Personal interviews with an official of the Swedish Board of Customs, 1997.

look at when preparing the government's decision on a given export application is the extent to which the relevant technology is important to the Swedish Armed Forces. For instance, missile technology is important—this is an area we definitely want to preserve in Sweden, and where we have some advantage thanks to Bofors and other companies. Export applications on such items are, thus, looked upon favourably.[94]

Thus, it was normal practice in Sweden to offer on the export market the same weapons that were developed for the Swedish armed forces, while design and manufacture of export-oriented defence products were discouraged.

On the other hand, Sweden's policy of neutrality also led to a high degree of restrictiveness in the choice of recipient states. The basic principle was that exports of military equipment were not permitted unless they furthered Swedish security and foreign policy. Throughout the 1970s and 1980s, for example, Sweden usually only granted exported licences for military equipment to approximately 40 countries every year (i.e., approximately one-quarter of the total number of independent states in existence). Moreover, although Sweden never adhered to COCOM and did not join the MTCR and the Australia Group until 1991, throughout the cold war Swedish companies generally maintained a policy of self-restraint with respect to exporting goods listed in other countries. This protected Swedish business against being blacklisted and may be one reason why major exporting companies are today so familiar with and accept export controls.

The Swedish arms export control regime also reflected the exceptionally strong norms of consultation and consensus in Swedish politics. Not only does the policy-making structure involve discussion and compromise between political representatives and defence industrial groups, with a strong oversight role for parliamentary committees; individual licensing decisions also follow a similar process. In keeping with this distinctive Swedish model of political economy, the unique policy-execution structure involves a very close and informal working relationship between officials and agencies on the one hand, and exporters on the other. It is an approach that has a number of advantages. It enables problems to be easily communicated and resolved, it is quick and efficient, and it is easy for companies to get information and advice from the relevant authorities.

Of course, such a corporatist approach to policy execution also has the potential for officials to become too closely involved with the interests of exporters. Former heads of the KMI, for example, were taken from the military, and there was a 'revolving door' between military people and industry. Indeed, it was not always clear whether the KMI, which was too close to industry, was controlling or promoting equipment sales. Thus, as a result of the arms scandals in the 1980s, both the policy-making and the policy-execution frameworks were considerably tightened. First, the KMI was replaced by the ISP in 1996, and although the successor organization continues to adopt a strong cooperative approach to licensing it now has a measure of independence from government

---

[94] Hirdman (note 63), pp. 55–56.

interference. Second, the laws, regulations and guidelines were tightened in 1983, 1988 and most recently 1992 to form a more comprehensive package of control measures. Since then, the only difficulties with illegal activity have been with arms-trading 'middlemen' seeking to exploit loopholes.

Sweden's restrictive policy is now under threat. The central foundation of neutrality is gradually being replaced by the twin demands of European integration and the need to compete in a highly competitive international arms export market. In turn, these external dynamics are leading to less consensual domestic politics. Among Sweden's political elite groups in particular there seems to be growing pressure for Sweden to develop a less stringent export control regime. Even among the Social Democrats, for example, Swedish Defence Minister Björn von Sydow is thought to be keen to relax the rules, and government officials were talking to their counterparts in the UK with this aim in mind during 1997.[95] Although the net result for Sweden's arms export policy is as yet unclear, there are fears that a common EU position may in time lead to a watering down of the national control regime. In particular, there is a risk that in areas where Sweden applies a more restrictive approach (such as intangible knowledge, conditions on end-use and re-export), companies may be tempted to export from other EU member states where these restrictions do not exist.

Publicly, at least, the government continues to support a restrictive policy, and the basic laws and regulations have remained generally unchanged since 1992. However, the interpretation of the guidelines appears to be changing dramatically. In particular, the recently appointed Large Reference Group seems to be overseeing a liberalization of the guidelines for the Gripen project. Indeed, several sources suggested that a generous interpretation of the export guidelines is often applied to major manufacturers, such as Saab.[96] Thus, in the past, it may have been lack of market opportunity (in addition to the restrictive guidelines) that kept Saab out of some of the more sensitive destinations. The government's encouragement of military–industrial cooperation between its own military producers and European counterparts should therefore be seen as a way of breaking into new markets (the Saab/BAE Systems marketing arrangement being a case in point). In this respect, Sweden may be moving closer to the British model, where the largest manufacturers set the export control agenda based on market opportunity.

It is to the issues of convergence and divergence within the control regimes outlined in the three case studies that the next chapter turns.

[95] Personal interview with a MEP, British Labour Party, Oct. 1997.
[96] Personal interviews with industrial representatives and independent experts, Stockholm, Oct. 1997.

8. A comparative analysis of the regulatory regimes in the UK, Germany and Sweden: the convergence–divergence mix explained

I. Introduction

Since the UK, Germany and Sweden all belong to the same multilateral control regimes for conventional arms and dual-use technologies—the Wassenaar Arrangement and the EU common measures discussed in chapters 3 and 4—and share many other traits and concerns—all are industrial liberal democracies and EU member states—it is hardly surprising to find that they implement similar export control policies. All three have sophisticated regimes for controlling their respective arms and dual-use trades, and all operate export controls that are grounded in national law. The basic structures of their legislation are broadly consistent in that in all three countries it requires lists of weapons and dual-use goods to define what is to be regulated and criteria according to which export licences are granted or denied. All three countries follow the tradition of dividing responsibility between government departments. However, both quantitative and qualitative differences can be found in the scope and structure of the respective national control mechanisms. This chapter explores these similarities and differences in greater detail. In short, it seeks to explain the mixture of convergence and continuing divergence that characterizes the three control regimes.

Section II summarizes the main areas of and reasons for the continuing divergence between the three countries. In particular, two broad reasons are advanced in explanation: the different state strategies adopted towards arms production and exports, including systemic and international normative constraints, and the role of domestic policy stakeholders; and the different administrative norms associated with policy implementation. Finally, differences in policy outcomes are explored, including the impact of the different state strategies on licensing decisions and patterns of arms exports.

Section III summarizes the progress towards policy convergence within the EU as a whole on the basis of the evidence provided in chapters 2, 3 and 4, and outlines the main causes of the movement towards greater convergence. Section IV analyses the convergence–divergence mix in the three countries in focus and the extent to which it has changed in the post-cold war era. It does this by conceptualizing the idea of convergence as a continuum along which a range of policy responses is feasible. These policy responses are then used as analytical benchmarks to measure the progress towards policy convergence.

II. Explaining divergence

It is clear from the discussions in chapters 5, 6 and 7 that there are large areas of continuing divergence between the British, German and Swedish control regimes. For example, all three countries have adopted procedures for authorizing export licences but differences can be found in the export criteria, in the specific bodies with responsibility for decision making and the execution of those decisions, and in the compliance and enforcement procedures.

This study argues that these persistent differences are rooted in the different policy environments that shape policy formulation and execution. As discussed in chapter 1, the policy environment contains a number of overlapping 'policy-shaping' elements, namely, the state strategies adopted towards arms production and exports, systemic and international normative constraints, and the influence of domestic policy stakeholders. These explanations are discussed in the next subsection. An additional (but linked) explanation is provided by the different administrative norms associated with policy implementation, and these are explored in the subsequent subsection.

Differences in state strategies towards arms production and exports

In the post-war period, British, German and Swedish export controls rested on a reasonably clear normative foundation, although the substances of these foundations differed, largely as a result of the different positions the three countries occupied in the post-World War II international political and economic system and of the normative legacies associated with their past foreign policy and economic choices.

Foreign policy and export policy

The UK emerged from World War II on the winning side only to suffer an ongoing decline in its status and a retreat from empire. Although the cold war years were a period of relative economic, political and military decline for the UK, successive political leaders sought to maintain the capacity for power projection both in the context of the East–West conflict and as a means of acting independently on the international stage. To achieve this overriding objective, the government provided subsidies and support for domestic defence manufacturers and engaged in vigorous promotion of arms exports. Two subsidiary aims were to ensure a supply of cheap weapons for Britain's own armed forces and to use arms as a means of influencing and cementing relationships with allies. There was also a strong linkage between defence and civil trade. The relatively benign historical legacy of empire also left the UK in a strong position to exploit a number of key ex-colonial markets around the world.

Also by virtue of its immediate post-war gains (such as permanent membership of the UN Security Council) the UK tended to have a high profile in certain multilateral forums connected with arms export issues. For example, as a member of the P5, the UK was a member of both the 1992 and the 1994 UN groups of experts that were established to implement and further develop the UN Register of Conventional Arms.[1]

In contrast, the defeated Germany was divided into East and West, with the western half only emerging as an independent actor on the international scene in the mid-1960s. Indeed, throughout the entire cold war period this half-nation status and the legacy of the Nazi period severely restricted West German foreign policy and was the root of the restrictive approach to arms exports. During the early post-war years restrictions on the development, production and export of weapons were imposed on the FRG by the Allied powers in order to prevent a re-emergence of German power projection. In turn, this meant that Germany was initially required to import most of its weapons.

As these imposed restrictions were gradually lifted in the 1950s and 1960s and the FRG began to rearm and develop its own indigenous military capabilities, the country continued to adhere to a minimalist foreign policy and tight restrictions on arms exports. Although this policy of restraint has wavered at times, its durability can largely be attributable to the deep-seated commitment among most of Germany's domestic policy stakeholders not to repeat the foreign policy mistakes of the past. Thus, despite becoming an economic giant in the 1970s, the FRG by choice remained a 'political dwarf' until full sovereignty was obtained in 1991 after the Soviet Union ratified the 'Two-plus-Four' treaty.[2]

Neutrality has been the principal policy framework for Sweden's post-war arms export policy. On the one hand, this desire to avoid reliance on foreign political or military support has led Sweden to develop an independent national defence industry which, given its relatively small procurement budget, is forced to export in order to survive. On the other hand, the policy of neutrality has also led to a high degree of restrictivity in the choice of recipient countries. There were no alliance or 'bloc' partners for Sweden to sell to, for example, and the basic principle that exports of military equipment were only permitted if they furthered Sweden's national security also meant that arms were not normally exported for the purpose of generating political influence abroad. Indeed, Sweden's enlightened approach to international affairs (in terms of the high priority it gives to the provision of humanitarian assistance, the promotion of good governance and so on) also meant that the export of arms was generally prohibited to regions of tension and to countries involved in armed conflict.

Thus, as a result of these different historical normative frameworks—broadly speaking, the UK's retreat from empire, German war guilt and dependent status, and Swedish neutrality—there have been and continue to be differences

---

[1] In contrast, Germany was only represented on the larger 1994 Group of Experts, while Sweden was not represented on either. Chalmers, M. *et al.*, *Developing the UN Register of Conventional Arms* (University of Bradford: Bradford, 1994), pp. 5–8.

[2] The Treaty on the Final Settlement with Respect to Germany, signed in Moscow on 12 Sep. 1990 by France, the United States, the Federal Republic of Germany, the German Democratic Republic, the UK and the USSR. The treaty is reproduced in Rotfeld, A. D. and Stützle, W., SIPRI, *Germany and Europe in Transition* (Oxford University Press: Oxford, 1991), pp. 183–86.

between the three countries' foreign policies and in the relative importance of their respective defence industrial bases. It is not surprising, therefore, that these differences are reflected in their respective arms export control policies, especially given the high level of political symbolism attached to major contracts for arms exports.

In the past, such contracts were regarded as the 'currency of foreign policy'[3] and, although the currency may have been somewhat devalued by the end of the cold war, arms exports continue to have a foreign policy dimension in all three countries. Foreign policy goals, including the deterrence of aggression, the enhancement of regional stability and the maintenance of friendships with strategically crucial allies, have played and continue to play a role in determining arms transfer policy. However, the selection of allies and the means of supporting them differ markedly.

During the cold war the UK clearly saw some foreign policy benefits in arms transfers, partly in support of the wider East–West contest and partly as a means of enhancing the security of allies, both within and beyond the boundaries of NATO. The UK's residual imperial possessions or ties in the South Atlantic, the Indian Ocean, North America, the Persian Gulf,[4] the South Pacific and the Caribbean, together with a range of security commitments such as the bilateral arrangement with Oman and the Five Power Defence Arrangements in South-East Asia,[5] meant that the UK pursued a vigorous arms export policy in which foreign policy goals were a crucial determining factor.

Sweden and (to a lesser extent) Germany, on the other hand, tended to distance themselves from using arms exports as instruments of foreign policy in this way. Instead, they often opted to use export restraint as an important foreign policy instrument, frequently linked with securing human rights goals in recipient countries. Of course, the UK also had to exercise a degree of restraint, but usually for very different reasons. During the cold war it regularly deployed its military forces beyond Europe in pursuit of its own foreign or national security policy. Thus, in evaluating arms exports or sales of military-related technologies, the UK had to consider the possibility that sales might increase the military capabilities of a potential future adversary. Similarly, Sweden regularly contributed its armed forces to peacekeeping operations and was faced with similar concerns. During this period, however, there was no prospect of German military deployments beyond national borders, so this concern did not apply.

---

[3] Kapstein, E., *The Political Economy of National Security: A Global Perspective* (McGraw-Hill: New York, 1992), p. 141.

[4] E.g., British forces were stationed in the Persian Gulf until the 1970s and the UK has strong military and political relationships with a number of Gulf states, including Kuwait and the UAE. It has also cultivated strong military and export links with other states in the Middle East, most notably Saudi Arabia and at different times in the past both Iran and Iraq (all 3 were UK protectorates during the interwar period).

[5] The Five Power Defence Arrangements were signed in 1971. The members are Australia, Malaysia, New Zealand, Singapore and the UK. Chin Kin Wah, 'The Five Powers Defence Arrangements: twenty years after', *Pacific Review*, vol. 4, no. 3 (1991), pp. 193–203.

Finally, there were also differences in the respective strategic industrial motivations for arms exports by the three countries. Arms exports can play a role in providing the means for a state to sustain a defence industrial capability by helping to sustain production, after satisfying initial domestic demand, until a successor system is either ready or affordable. Sweden and the UK have had greater concerns with notions of military self-reliance and have therefore been the more reluctant to give up export opportunities.[6]

However, while both Sweden and the UK seek policy autonomy as a result of a high degree of arms autarky, the UK does so primarily for reasons of power projection while Sweden's policy objective is armed neutrality. The 'military–industrial complex' is also stronger in the UK. This is the result partly of size—the UK's military expenditure is 6–8 times that of Sweden, for example, as table 8.1 shows—and partly of the special pleading of bureaucratic, elite or 'establishment' and industrial interests in support of the specific foreign policy goals discussed above.

Although Germany's total military expenditure is comparable to that of the UK, its very different foreign policy preoccupations and much lower levels of equipment spending have resulted in a much weaker military–industrial complex. For example, German government expenditure on military R&D as a percentage of total government R&D expenditure is roughly half that of Sweden, which in turn is roughly one-half that of the UK (table 8.1). There is also a higher degree of diversification in German industry compared with the UK.

Economic policy and export policy

Although the wider foreign policy concerns of the three countries, including the historical position each occupied in the international system of states, have been crucial in shaping their respective arms export control regimes—and are a strong explanation for the continuing differences between them—this does not mean that commercial interests were unimportant in shaping the policy process. Some analysts argue that West European arms-exporting countries participate in the trade primarily for economic reasons, and that political and strategic concerns are only of secondary importance.[7] While economic factors are clearly growing in significance for each of the three countries, it is doubtful even now whether they are of primary importance for any of them. This argument is the least persuasive in the case of Sweden, where national security concerns have been and remain paramount. In Germany and the UK the situation is less certain. Economic factors are more significant for Germany (as compared with Sweden), especially for particular sectors such as shipbuilding, but the foreign

---

[6] However, all 3 states see arms sales abroad as a way of keeping design teams together and developing a national weapon technological capability.

[7] See, e.g., Krause, K., *Arms and the State: Patterns of Military Production and Trade* (Cambridge University Press: Cambridge, 1992); and the discussion in chapter 2. There is little agreement in the literature, however, on the extent of the economic benefits, nor is there usually any attempt to disaggregate and compare the economic significance of arms exports for individual European suppliers.

Table 8.1. Select military expenditure statistics for Germany, Sweden and the UK, 1988–98

Figures in italics are percentages.

	1988	1989	1990	1991	1992	1993	1994	1995	1996	1997	1998
Germany[a]											
1.	54 022	53 840	56 760	52 533	49 951	44 930	41 906	41 160	40 343	39 106	..
2.	*2.9*	*2.8*	*2.8*	*2.3*	*2.1*	*2.0*	*1.8*	*1.7*	*1.6*	*1.6*	*1.5*
3.	..	3 100	..	..	2 400	1 900	1 900	2 000	2 220	..	..
4.	..	*12.8*	..	..	*10.0*	*8.5*	*8.6*	*9.1*	*9.8*	..	..
Sweden											
1.	5 687	5 881	6 031	5 654	5 435	5 351	5 404	5 595	5 744	5 885	..
2.	*2.5*	*2.5*	*2.6*	*2.5*	*2.5*	*2.6*	*2.4*	*2.0*	*1.7*	*2.2*	*2.2*
3.	..	680	..	..	690	650	500	570	..	..	..
4.	..	*24.7*	..	..	*24.3*	*23.5*	*18.9*	*20.9*	..	..	..
UK											
1.	42 560	42 714	41 649	43 022	38 890	38 022	36 771	33 896	34 096	32 837	..
2.	*4.2*	*4.1*	*4.0*	*4.2*	*3.8*	*3.6*	*3.4*	*3.0*	*3.0*	*2.7*	*2.7*
3.	..	4 100	..	..	3 500	3 800	3 300	3 500	3 200	..	..
4.	..	*43.6*	..	..	*40.7*	*42.0*	*38.9*	*40.8*	*37.0*	..	..

Notes:

[a] Figures for Germany up to and including 1990 refer to the former Federal Republic of Germany (West Germany).

. . Data not available or not applicable.

1. Military expenditure in constant US $m. (1995 prices and exchange rates).

2. Military expenditure as a percentage of gross domestic product.

3. Government expenditure on military R&D, in constant US$ (1995 prices and exchange rates).

4. Government expenditure on military R&D as a percentage of total government R&D expenditure.

Sources: Sköns, E. *et al.*, 'Military expenditure', *SIPRI Yearbook 1998: Armaments, Disarmament and International Security* (Oxford University Press: Oxford, 1998), tables 6A.3 and 6A.4; Arnett, E., 'Military research and development', *SIPRI Yearbook 1998,* tables 7.2 and 7.3, pp. 269 and 273; and Sköns, E. *et al.*, 'Military expenditure', *SIPRI Yearbook 2000: Armaments, Disarmament and International Security* (Oxford University Press: Oxford, 2000), table 5A.4.

policy restraints discussed above have probably been at least equally important. Similarly, a mixture of economic and foreign policy considerations have shaped British policy. Again, however, even though economic motives are probably stronger in the UK than in Germany because defence manufacturing is more important to the UK's overall manufacturing base, the UK's past export-oriented foreign policy goals have probably had the most influence on policy.

While foreign policy offers a stronger explanation than economic policy for Germany's and Sweden's restraint (in comparison with the UK), the broader economic strategies adopted by each of the three countries and the historical position each occupies in the international economy have nonetheless had a similar shaping effect. It is therefore worth reviewing briefly the extent to which any significant differences in the three countries' economic policies are reflected, or help to explain, differences in their arms export control policies.

Despite a strong 'trading state' strategy,[8] at the macroeconomic level Germany appears to be no more dependent on foreign trade than the UK, and less so than Sweden.[9] However, Germany does have a larger number of small and medium-sized dual-use manufacturers (in areas such as machine tools) which produce for the world market.[10] Although the evidence is inconclusive, a much higher proportion of the controlled goods exported from Germany to military customers is likely to be dual-use than is the case in Sweden and the UK.[11] Moreover, for dual-use goods, Germany's export orientation has tended to outweigh foreign policy concerns, resulting in a much more relaxed control environment for such goods as compared with arms exports.

A broad indicator of the economic importance of arms (including dual-use) exports is the share of these exports as a percentage of total exports. According to US Bureau of Arms Control (ACDA)[12] figures for 1997, German arms

---

[8] Rosecrance, R., *The Rise of the Trading State: Commerce and Conquest in the Modern World* (Basic Books: New York, 1986), p. 16.

[9] Total exports as a percentage of gross national product (GNP) during the period 1993–96 were 21.2% for Germany, 19.8% for the UK and 30.5% for Sweden. Calculated from US Arms Control and Disarmament Agency (ACDA), *World Military Expenditures and Arms Transfers 1996–97* (ACDA: Washington, DC, 1998), tables I and II.

[10] E.g., in 1990 Germany accounted for 25.3% of world exports in both 'machinery tools for special industries' (SITC 7281) and 'metalworking machinery tools' (SITC 736). United Nations, *1990 International Trade Statistics Yearbook* (UN: New York, 1992), vol. I, p. 343 and vol. II, pp. 175 and 623.

[11] There are no statistics available for the UK's dual-use trade. However, the comparison in table 8.2 between US Bureau of Arms Control figures (which include dual-use transfers for military customers) and SIPRI figures (which only cover transfers of major conventional weapons) suggests that there might be a strong dual-use component in the UK's total arms export profile: Bureau of Arms Control figures are twice or sometimes 3 times the value of SIPRI data. On the other hand, a similar reading of the data for Germany in the same table would vastly understate the scope and extent of its dual-use trade because SIPRI figures for German arms exports are close to and sometimes exceed those of the Bureau of Arms Control. See the discussion in chapter 1 on the problems and discrepancies in comparing these 2 sources. Problems of comparing like with like also hinder comparison of total licence applications, although here at least there is a clearer indication of the difference in composition of the controlled trade. In the mid-1990s, e.g., Germany was issuing about 1000 licences per year under its 'weapons of war' legislation and 27 000 annual licences under its 'dual-use and other military equipment' legislation. Sweden, in contrast, was issuing about 2000 licences per annum, only one-quarter of which were for dual-use goods.

[12] ACDA became the Bureau of Arms Control, a part of the US State Department, in Apr. 1999.

Table 8.2. The value of arms deliveries and market share for Germany, Sweden and the UK: US Bureau of Arms Control[a] and SIPRI data compared, 1987–99

Figures in italics are percentages.

		1987	1988	1989	1990	1991	1992	1993	1994	1995	1996	1997	1998	1999
Germany	1.	1 960	2 149	1 460	1 874	2 832	1 330	1 836	1 692	1 760	1 322	750	..	..
	2.	*2.4*	*2.7*	*2.1*	*2.9*	*5.2*	*2.7*	*4.0*	*4.0*	*4.0*	*3.0*	*1.4*	..	..
	3.	824	1 147	961	1 640	2 507	1 527	1 562	2 392	1 465	1 413	682	1 191	1 334
	4.	*1.9*	*3.0*	*2.6*	*5.3*	*9.5*	*6.1*	*6.5*	*11.8*	*7.3*	*6.6*	*2.7*	*5.0*	*6.5*
Sweden	1.	980	1 011	913	849	736	942	918	899	1 010	1 220	900	..	..
	2.	*1.2*	*1.3*	*1.4*	*1.3*	*1.3*	*1.9*	*2.0*	*2.1*	*2.3*	*2.7*	*1.6*	..	..
	3.	320	533	508	364	117	123	58	59	186	150	42	117	157
	4.	*0.7*	*1.4*	*1.4*	*1.2*	*0.4*	*0.5*	*0.2*	*0.3*	*0.9*	*0.7*	*0.2*	*0.5*	*0.8*
UK	1.	6 141	5 561	6 085	5 387	5 550	6 873	4 967	5 499	5 488	6 303	6 600	..	..
	2.	*7.5*	*7.1*	*8.9*	*8.3*	*10.2*	*14.2*	*10.8*	*13.0*	*12.4*	*14.2*	*12.1*	..	..
	3.	2 246	1 203	2 371	1 573	1 366	1 315	1 585	1 506	1 206	1 520	2 460	1 079	1 078
	4.	*5.1*	*3.2*	*6.3*	*5.1*	*5.2*	*5.3*	*6.6*	*7.4*	*6.0*	*7.1*	*9.6*	*4.6*	*5.2*

Notes:

[a] The US Arms Control and Disarmament Agency (ACDA) became the Bureau of Arms Control, a part of the US State Department, in Apr. 1999.

.. = Figures not available or not applicable.

1. US Bureau of Arms Control estimates of arms transfer deliveries in US $m. (constant 1997 prices).

2. US Bureau of Arms Control figures, percentage market share.

3. SIPRI trend-indicator values for deliveries of major conventional weapons in US $m. (constant 1990 prices). SIPRI trend-indicator values do not correspond to prices paid or to other economic indicators such as gross domestic product (GDP).

4. SIPRI figures, percentage market share.

Sources: US Arms Control and Disarmament Agency, *World Military Expenditures and Arms Transfers 1998* (ACDA: Washington, DC, 2000); Anthony, I., Wezeman, P. D. and Wezeman, S. T., 'The trade in major conventional weapons', *SIPRI Yearbook 1997: Armaments, Disarmament and International Security* (Oxford University Press: Oxford, 1997), p. 268; Hagelin, B., Wezeman, P. D. and Wezeman, S. T., 'Transfers of major conventional weapons', *SIPRI Yearbook 2000: Armaments, Disarmament and International Security* (Oxford University Press: Oxford, 2000), table 7A.2, p. 372; and SIPRI arms transfers database.

exports represented only 0.1 per cent of total exports (in the previous 10-year period, the highest share for any given year was 0.6 per cent); in Sweden the figure was 1.1 per cent (with a 10-year high of 1.7 per cent in 1987 and 1993); and in the UK the figure was 2.3 per cent (down from a high point of 3.6 per cent in 1987).[13] These crude figures together with those in table 8.2 showing the value of weapons transferred suggest that the UK benefits the most in terms of foreign exchange from arms exports.[14]

According to SIPRI the total aggregate value of global exports of major conventional arms to the leading recipients during the five years 1995–99 was $111.3 billion (in 1990 prices and SIPRI trend-indicator values).[15] Of this Germany, Sweden and the UK accounted for $14.1 billion, representing approximately 12.7 per cent of the global market. The UK ($7.3 billion) accounted for the largest share in a direct comparison between the three countries, closely followed by Germany ($6.1 billion). Other trend indicators (see table 8.2) suggest an even more dominant position for the UK in relation to Germany and Sweden. The Bureau of Arms Control figures, for example, when aggregated for the five-year period 1993–97, show the value of British arms deliveries as $28.9 billion (or 70 per cent of the three-nation total), while Germany accounted for $7.4 billion (18 per cent) and Sweden only $4.9 billion (12 per cent) in constant 1997 prices. These differences in relative market share appear to have remained fairly constant over the past 10 years or so, and there are few signs of any emerging convergence. According to the aggregate Bureau of Arms Control figures for the period 1987–91, the UK had 66 per cent ($28.7 billion) of the total value of arms delivered by the three countries, Germany 24 per cent ($10.3 billion) and Sweden 10 per cent ($4.5 billion). The one clear exception was the temporary surge in German arms exports in the first half of the 1990s, which was largely a result of exports of surplus cold war-era equipment (in particular, surplus major conventional weapons, as reflected in the comparison of SIPRI and Bureau of Arms Control figures for this period).

Another important economic indicator is the level of employment generated by arms exports. In the mid-1990s, total defence employment in the UK, Germany and Sweden was approximately 350 000, 210 000 and 15 000, respectively.[16] However, the share of total defence employment provided by exports (as opposed to domestic production) is difficult to estimate and changes from year to year. In 1996/97, for example, the British MOD stated that approximately 35 per cent (or 150 000 jobs) were directly or indirectly dependent on

[13] US Bureau of Arms Control, *World Military Expenditures and Arms Transfers 1998* (Bureau of Arms Control: Washington, DC, 2000), table II.

[14] The foreign exchange benefits may be overstated, however, given the high levels of state subsidy for arms exports. For a discussion of arms export subsidies see Smith, R., 'Is Europe pricing itself out of the market ?', *RUSI Journal*, Feb. 1994.

[15] Hagelin, B., Wezeman, P. D. and Wezeman, S. T., 'Transfers of major conventional weapons', *SIPRI Yearbook 2000: Armaments, Disarmament and International Security* (Oxford University Press: Oxford, 2000), p. 341. SIPRI trend-indicator values do not correspond to prices paid or to other economic indicators such as GDP.

[16] International Institute for Strategic Studies (IISS), *The Military Balance 1996/97* (Oxford University Press: Oxford, 1996), table 10, p. 283.

arms exports.[17] In comparison, as noted below, the percentage of total arms production attributable to exports is thought to be higher for Sweden but lower for Germany. Despite the many possible sources of inaccuracy in these figures, and on the assumption that these percentages can be directly equated with the share of defence employment provided by exports), approximately 42 000 German defence jobs and 4500 Swedish defence jobs are likely to be dependent on arms exports.[18]

Again, the UK appears to 'benefit' most in terms of employment from arms exports. Alternatively, this can be read as meaning that the UK is the most dependent of the three countries on employment from arms exports, especially given the decline in defence employment over the 1990s. In the mid-1980s, for example, total defence employment in the UK, Germany and Sweden was approximately 625 000, 350 000 and 27 000, respectively. Compared with the employment figures in the mid-1990s, defence employment had declined by approximately 45 per cent in the UK and Sweden, and by 30 per cent in Germany.[19] This trend preceded the end of the cold war and reflects cuts in defence expenditure, the global decline in arms exports and other corporate trends, all of which led to plant rationalization and redundancies. Not surprisingly, these factors also resulted in a sharp decrease in the number of jobs directly related to arms exports.

Another way to analyse the economic significance of arms exports would be to compare the budget savings that accrue to the respective countries. It is generally recognized that arms exports enable the state to pay a lower price for the domestically produced equipment purchased for its own forces. Reductions in the cost of domestic weapon procurement can be achieved through economies of scale in production and/or by recouping R&D expenditures. Although there is some (albeit dated) evidence for such savings in the USA,[20] there are no empirical studies comparing the extent of these savings for the major European suppliers. Any differences between the UK, Germany and Sweden in terms of the percentage of export value that can be attributed to unit cost and R&D savings are likely to be marginal, and will occur largely as a result of the different weapon mixes in their export portfolios. It might be expected, for example, that savings would be lower in Germany as a result of its large number of exports of naval craft (as shown in table 8.4).[21]

---

[17] British Ministry of Defence, *MOD Performance Report 1997/98*, Cm 4170 (Her Majesty's Stationery Office: London, 1998), p. 33.

[18] Author's estimates, based on the assumption that 20% of German arms production and 33% of Swedish arms production was being exported in the mid-1990s.

[19] *The Military Balance 1996/97* (note 16).

[20] A 1976 study by the US Congressional Budget Office suggested that package deals and price cuts offered in contracts reduced the possible savings in R&D and unit costs to an average of $70 million for every $1000 in exports. However, the savings vary in accordance with the length of the production run. Krause (note 7), p. 107.

[21] The US study also suggested that savings would vary depending on the mix of weapons, construction and support services within the sales programme: for high-technology production sectors such as aircraft, aircraft engines, electronics, helicopters or missiles (without support services) the savings are high, but for a mix of ships, ammunition, construction and services, the savings are negligible or non-existent. Krause (note 7), p. 141.

An indicator of the economic significance of arms exports at the industrial level is the percentage of arms produced for export. Between 1984 and 1989, Germany exported approximately 10 per cent of its arms production, compared to 33 per cent for the UK.[22] Sweden was estimated to be exporting approximately 50 per cent of its arms production in the mid-1980s.[23] In the mid-1990s, however, the UK was exporting approximately 20–30 per cent of its arms production, Germany 15–20 per cent and Sweden 30–40 per cent.[24] More recently, data from several British sources suggest an even higher share of exports in the total arms sales for the UK, with an estimated 48 per cent of production exported in 1998.[25]

However, these very rough averages hide substantial intra-industry variations. In Sweden, for example, the weapon systems (which includes armoured and tracked vehicles) and electronics sectors export roughly 50 per cent of their production.[26] Similarly, in Germany, the percentage of production exported in respect of naval vessels is likely to be 60 per cent or higher.[27] The main reason for Germany's different treatment of, for instance, tanks and warships is political rather than economic: tanks are generally perceived as offensive weapons and can be used for internal repression, while warships are more politically acceptable.[28]

Overall, therefore, economic issues have had the most influence in the way in which policy makers weigh commercial and strategic industrial interests in their conception of the national interest. Both Germany and the UK place greater weight on the value of exports to the economy, although in the case of Germany the focus is dual-use exports, whereas for the UK it is arms exports. In Sweden, on the other hand, the greatest weight is in strategic industrial interests.

The role of policy stakeholders

Arms export policy is generally formulated by executive agencies within government in consultation with industry. It would, however, be wrong to characterize it as a closed political system because, as discussed in chapter 1, the involvement or non-involvement of other policy stakeholders (including political parties, policy analysts and NGOs) is often a crucial factor in shaping policy. Indeed, it has tended to be political parties (both government and opposition) and NGOs that have articulated the main policy alternatives in the wake of arms scandals. Hence, although government–industry relations play the major role in shaping the political debate on export control issues in the three

<hr>

[22] Brittleson, M., International Institute for Strategic Studies, *Co-operation or Competition? Defence Procurement Options for the 1990s*, Adelphi Papers 250 (IISS: London, 1990), p. 25.

[23] Krause (note 7), table 10, p. 93.

[24] Estimates based on personal interviews with EU and national officials, 1997.

[25] *SIPRI Yearbook 2000* (note 15), table 6.8, p. 319.

[26] Swedish Ministry for Foreign Affairs, *Sweden's Policy on Arms Exports*, SOU 1993:1 (Stockholm, 1993), p. 13.

[27] Hofhansel, C., *Commercial Competition and National Security: Comparing US and German Export Control Policies* (Praeger: Westport, Conn., 1996), p. 105.

[28] Hofhansel (note 27), p. 107.

countries, the role of other stakeholders, particularly those advocating greater restraint, has been influential at crucial times. Indeed, there remain qualitative differences in the roles each of the policy stakeholders play in the three countries, and the roles themselves differ in significance over time.

Government–industry relations

Through its vociferous lobbying for particular exports—the recent BAE-Saab arms contracts with South Africa, based around the heavily promoted JAS-39 Gripen fighter aircraft, being a good example[29]—the defence industry is clearly an important influence on export policy and on decision making for individual export licence applications. Like their counterparts in the civilian sector, the largest defence contractors are multinational in nature and can therefore wield considerable economic power, including the threat of diverting private capital (and jobs) abroad as a lever to extract favourable decisions. In the UK, for example, the close relationship between defence companies, the military and former MOD employees—known as the 'revolving door' syndrome—has been a particular cause for concern.[30]

In none of the three case studies did industry appear to dominate policy making on or the execution of export controls. Nonetheless, the relationship between government and industry is another area in which marked differences between the three regimes can be found. Sweden, for example, as a result of its particular model of social democracy operates an intimate corporatist model in which government and industry cooperate very closely and companies are directly involved in the evolution and implementation of the regulations. While this was also formerly the case in the German economic model (which still reflects elements of corporatism), government–industry relations in the defence sector there are now closer to the British rather than the Swedish model.

In both Germany and the UK the relationship between industry and government is rather mixed, containing elements of both 'top-down' (i.e., government-led) and joint shaping of the regulatory environment. On the one hand, guidance on export matters (including proliferation concerns) comes from government and is passed down to defence companies and trade associations through various government agencies. In turn, most companies are required to appoint a responsible manager to ensure corporate compliance with this guidance. On the other hand, defence industry organizations and major defence companies are

---

[29] Coalition for Defence Alternatives, 'South Africa's R30 billion weapons procurement programme: OFFSETS, an invitation to corruption in a country desperate for socio-economic development', available on the Internet site of the Quaker Peace Centre, Cape Town, at URL <http://www.quaker.org/capetown/cda/cda0500.htm>.

[30] More than 2000 British MOD civil servants and armed forces personnel joined British and foreign defence companies and management consultants during the 11 years 1985–95. These included 2 former heads of the DESO, Sir James Blyth (1981–85), who went on to become Managing Director of Plessey and a director of BAe, and Sir Colin Chandler (1985–89), who came from BAe and went on to become chairman of Vickers. The biggest recruiters are BAE Systems and its subsidiaries, which took on 33 former civil servants and forces personnel in the 2 years 1993–94, including an air vice-marshal, a vice-admiral, 2 wing commanders, a Royal Navy commander, a group captain, 1 major, 1 squadron leader and 1 under-secretary. *The Guardian*, 25 Jan. 1995.

involved in joint government–industry review panels for export control practices and contribute significantly to the drafting of legislation. While in some respects this situation mirrors the intimacy of the Swedish model, in others (such as the consideration of licence applications) it does not.

In any case, such intimacy can be problematic. In Germany, for example, the relatively smooth cooperation between the state export control agencies and industry made the Rabta and Iraq scandals possible.[31] In addition, the erosion of political restraint on arms export controls in Germany in the 1970s and 1980s was largely a result of increased economic pressure by industry. The current concerns of German industry may result in a similar outcome in the future (although the tightening of export controls during 1989–92 did take place with the agreement of industry). In the UK, on the other hand, the recent policy changes are mainly attributable to domestic pressures for reform following the 'Arms to Iraq' scandal, with industry a rather reluctant participant in the reform process (and generally doing its best to slow down and mitigate the scope and pace of the changes). This slowing down of reform in the UK is assisted by those civil servants and ministers advocating industry's interests within the government machinery itself, mainly within the DESO, but also inside 10 Downing Street, the FCO, the DTI and the rest of the MOD.

Proponents of greater restraint

In all three countries there have at times been groundswells of domestic opposition to particular aspects of the arms trade or specific contracts, but such opposition has waxed and waned over time. In Germany, political parties (or factions within political parties) and business interests are the major actors, and in the past there has been considerable domestic opposition to German arms exports. German interest groups which want a restrictive approach to exports include the political parties on the left, particularly elements of the SPD and the Greens, some trade unionists,[32] the peace movement and religious groups.

In Sweden, most of the political parties and interest groups are not easily categorized into either proponents or opponents of arms export restraint. Because of the large measure of consensus among the major political parties and industry favouring the foreign policy agenda outlined above, which takes as its starting point a more restrictive approach than the UK's, traditionally only a small minority have called for either greater or less restraint. As discussed above, this consensus is now dissolving but there are few clear signs as to

---

[31] In 1989 it was revealed that a small German chemical company had supplied Libya with a turnkey chemical weapons plant at Rabta. After the Iraqi invasion of Kuwait in 1990 it also became known that German companies had supplied militarily-relevant equipment and dual-use technology to Iraq. Müller, H., *After the Scandals: West German Non-Proliferation Policy*, PRIF Reports no. 9 (Peace Research Institute Frankfurt: Frankfurt, Feb. 1990).

[32] The position of German trade unions is mixed. On the one hand, they often oppose arms exports on ideological grounds; on the other hand, they represent workers employed in the industries. Most German defence workers are centred in the metalworkers union (IG Metall), which has long favoured a restrictive policy of arms exports. However, individual union representatives have often ignored this official policy and argued for increased arms exports.

whether this will lead to more or less domestic opposition to Swedish arms exports.

In the UK the major political parties and the general public have traditionally displayed a distinct lack of interest in the issue of arms exports. Apart from a small number of political and trade union activists, opposition to the trade has tended to be located in a number of peace, human rights and development NGOs. However, in the early 1990s a growing public and political mood for greater restraint became evident as a result of the Arms to Iraq scandal and was an important ingredient in the electoral success of 'New Labour' in 1997. Whether this change of mood is sustainable or whether the general public will revert to its traditional indifference is uncertain.

Differences in administrative norms

While policy decisions on arms exports are politically determined, the execution of policy and the implementation of the law are undertaken by civil servants. Although all three countries operate within parliamentary systems, there are structural differences between the three systems—for instance, in the roles played by the legislative and executive arms of government, and in civil service practice or structures. If, as a result of disparate administrative norms, there are marked differences in the ways in which the three countries reach policy decisions generally, such differences are also likely to be reflected in the specific field of arms export control policy. These cultural and political differences in policy making can be found at various levels of the policy process.

Three examples illustrate this point: the different levels of discretion within each policy regime; the different levels of secrecy; and the ways in which governments have responded to policy inadequacies.

Discretion

There are clearly different levels of discretion in the decision-making process for licence applications.[33] While almost all delegated tasks involve some degree of discretion—the notion of total political control in any organization is unrealistic—in the context of the complex regulation of armaments it becomes of salient importance. If the balance between rules and discretion in complex organizational situations is not right, it can, as Ham and Hill point out, lead to the emergence of gaps between intentions and outcomes.[34] (Such an analysis lends itself, for example, to the Sandline controversy in the UK, which was discussed in chapter 5.) Indeed, officials in all three countries face situations in which the export criteria either conflict or are ambiguous, and hence choices have to be made between the criteria or about the spirit in which they are to be considered. Just as politicians (when providing the broader political direction)

---

[33] For a discussion of the concept of 'discretion' in the policy process see Ham, C. and Hill, M., *The Policy Process in the Modern Capitalist State*, 2nd edn (Harvester Wheatsheaf: Brighton, 1984), pp. 151–73.

[34] Ham and Hill (note 33), p. 153.

are troubled by unresolved value issues surrounding the balance between export restraint and economic or political advantage, so are the officials who implement the policy.

When deciding on individual licence applications, for example, officials have a measure of discretion as to the application of 'special procedures' for the export of arms and sensitive technology to listed or 'sensitive' destinations. A particular country may, for example, be refused access to some or all sensitive technologies, or exports may be permitted with extreme caution. The designation of what is a sensitive destination is also sometimes a discretionary decision, as is the decision to apply end-use restrictions. Nor is discretion limited to decision making for licence applications. The areas in which discretion is used by officials in the administrative framework are extensive. For example, there is discretion in departmental decision making about the deployment of personnel and resources (in licensing, enforcement and so on); in decisions on the extent to which reported breaches of the regulations should be investigated; in decisions on whether to prosecute violations of the regulations; and in the extent to which information is made available to the public.

Overall it appears that the most discretionary licence decision-making process is to be found in the UK. There certainly appears to be less discretion in the German and Swedish models, particularly following the administrative changes in the early 1990s, as compared to the current British model in which responsibility remains more diffuse and implementation problems seem to be more acute. The creation of new and enhanced agencies in Germany and Sweden in the early 1990s also indicated a greater political will to resolve some of the policy problems.

It is also realistic to expect that, as a general rule, the policy problems associated with export controls would initially be tackled by loosely framed laws and guidelines but that those laws and guidelines would then evolve from the general to the specific.[35] This happened in both Germany and Sweden, where, since the formulation of export guidelines in the 1970s, the traditional approach has been to try to control discretion through ever-tighter rules and procedures. Such evolution has been slower to take place in the UK, where the evidence suggests that, in the past at least, the guidelines were often fudged because of the involvement of powerful economic and political interests. It could be argued, of course, that the higher level of discretion within the British model (and the preference for political flexibility over legal rigidity) is necessary in order to regulate the arms trade effectively. Alternatively, advocates of a more restrictive policy are more likely to see it as a consequence of regulator

---

[35] E.g., sensitive destination lists could be harmonized on a broad multilateral basis to include guidelines on the type of restrictions that would be applied to different categories of military equipment and sensitive technologies. One category might specify the sensitive destinations to which the export of the controlled technologies would be embargoed, the 2nd category could specify the countries which would be subject to special procedures (e.g., where end-use was monitored and where a 'no undercutting without consultation' rule would operate), and a 3rd category would include all other countries where export licensing would be subject to national discretion. Such an approach would remove discretion from officials in all but the 3rd, less sensitive, category of countries.

co-option by powerful interests within the defence sector. Of course, whether discretion is a 'good thing' or a 'bad thing' is partly a question of fact and partly a value judgement.

Nonetheless, in the British model, discretion was undoubtedly more of a conscious ingredient in the formal design of the regime, whereas it appears to be a reluctant concession to organizational realities in the other two countries. Thus, in the UK in particular it is necessary to see discretion in the context of the flexibility it gives officials to pursue the foreign policy and political goals outlined above.

Secrecy

In both Germany and the UK in the past it has generally been the practice only to provide information on arms exports on an unofficial and selective basis, and opposition parliamentarians were kept well away from any of the policy and decision-making processes. A number of examples are illustrative of British secrecy in this area. A 1989 National Audit Office report on commission payments associated with the Al Yamamah deal with Saudi Arabia was suppressed and has never been published,[36] and information has never been made available on the use of a £1 billion special fund set up in 1991 by the ECGD to support large contracts for defence equipment. The Scott Report also challenged the British Government on the secrecy surrounding the arms trade: 'Is it any longer satisfactory that Parliament and the British public are not entitled to be told to which countries and in what quantities goods such as artillery shells, land mines and cluster bombs have been licensed for export?'[37]

Sweden, on the other hand, has led the recent trend in Europe towards greater transparency. Since the mid-1980s, information has not only been provided to the Swedish Parliament on a regular and official basis, but potential opponents (from whichever political party) have been included in the information flow (as discussed in chapter 7). Nonetheless all three regimes can be characterized as having some degree of secrecy.

The traditional explanation for secrecy in this area is commercial confidentiality.[38] Both state and company actors adopt this widely as a reason for withholding information on specific arms exports from the general public and from other governments. States are motivated by concerns about the national interest and hence one of the main objectives of such secrecy is to deny important information about potential export opportunities to competitor govern-

<hr>

[36] Foot, P., *The Guardian*, 31 Jan. 1994 .

[37] British House of Commons, *The Right Honourable Sir Richard Scott, Report of the Inquiry into the Export of Defence Equipment and Dual-Use Goods to Iraq and Related Prosecutions: Return to an Address of the Honourable the House of Commons dated 15th February*, HC 1995/96 115 (Her Majesty's Stationery Office: London, 1996) (the Scott Report), para K8.13.

[38] A British review of the convention relating to the disclosure of information to Parliament on the export of defence equipment concluded that commercial confidentiality is only one of 4 main reasons for non-disclosure, the others being national security, the security concerns of recipient states and the adverse effect disclosure might have on bilateral relations. British Ministry of Defence, 'The release of information on defence related exports', July 1996, p. 7.

ments, particularly details of government-to-government defence trade negotiations. Similarly, corporations deem it necessary to withhold certain types of information that might be useful to their commercial competitors, both domestic and foreign.

While this is undoubtedly part of the reason for government information policy on export controls, another explanation is that government officials—and sometimes politicians—hide information from or mislead the public in order to ensure elite control over policy. In particular, this 'internal threat'[39] perspective argues that special efforts are made to conceal information on potentially controversial actions or activities that could generate public opposition. In the UK, for example, where there have been a number of newspaper exposés of arms scandals and where there is a small but effective grassroots opposition to the arms trade, it is easy to see how officials and politicians might see a conflict between the maximization of exports and the preferences of public opinion. Indeed, the use of secrecy and the selective dissemination of partial, distorted or one-sided information were strong features of the Arms to Iraq scandal, where the conduct of policy was 'accompanied by consistent endeavours on the part of officials and ministers to prevent being made public information that might lead to a critical public debate about export licensing decisions'.[40]

While the merits of secrecy and public deception in this area are a matter of much debate—proponents see such tools as being vital for effective foreign and military policy, while opponents challenge such views as undemocratic and elitist—it is interesting to speculate about what motivates officials and government ministers to act in this way. Gibbs offers a number of potential explanations in his overview of secrecy in international relations, from the realist premise that officials generally act to further the 'national interest', to the 'rational-action' perspective which assumes that they often act to further their own interests.[41] In the foreign policy sub-field of arms export controls the answers have to be even more tentative, given the lack of explicit research on this issue. Nonetheless, all three countries in focus here have had arms export scandals in which individual ministers and officials appear to have been motivated by a mixture of personal greed and highly selective notions of the national interest. In the UK in particular, the open promotion of arms sales at the highest level of government led to the secrecy and corruption associated

---

[39] Gibbs, D., 'Secrecy and international relations', *Journal of Peace Research,* vol. 32, no. 2 (1995), pp. 213–28. Gibbs advances 3 reasons for secrecy—external threat, bureaucratic politics and internal threat. The 1st is broadly similar to the commercial confidentiality approach described in this study. The main difference is that the external threat approach is used solely to explain state secrecy, whereas the concept of commercial confidentiality also explains corporate secrecy in this area. The bureaucratic politics explanation is quite different from questions of public disclosure and suggests that information is withheld from other government departments because of bureaucratic rivalry.

[40] Scott Report (note 37), paras D2.31–36, 226–228. Indeed, there are frequent references in the Scott evidence to the idea that if the policy became public knowledge this would jeopardize contracts, with knock-on effects for civil contracts.

[41] Gibbs (note 39), pp. 216–18.

with the arms trade becoming deeply implanted in government practice in the late 1980s.[42]

While there was movement towards greater transparency in all three countries in the late 1990s, largely as a result of pressure from NGOs and the reforms being introduced as part of the EU Code of Conduct, the most significant advances were made in the UK. The introduction of an annual reporting system in 1999 and stronger parliamentary oversight through a Joint Select Committee have transformed the UK from being one of the least transparent countries in Europe to being one of the champions for greater openness on this issue in the EU as a whole. In conclusion, therefore, although there remain differences in the degree of secrecy practised within each of the regimes, these are largely rooted in the different political traditions of each of the three countries.

Responding to policy inadequacies

Arms export control policy is inevitably subject to many conflicting pressures for the government authorities charged with ensuring the regime's effectiveness. There will be times, therefore, when the policy or administrative framework will be deemed inadequate to meet the tasks demanded of it, and changes will become necessary.[43] Such inadequacies have generally arisen either as a result of changes in the wider international system (such as the end of the cold war) or following exposés of alleged wrongdoing in relation to specific categories of exports (such as the Arms to Iraq controversy in the UK, the Rabta case in Germany and the Bofors howitzer sales to India in the case of Sweden). In the early 1990s, a combination of these factors was troubling each of the three regimes, but there were significant differences between their responses, both in terms of the type of debate which precipitated the changes and in the extent of the changes themselves.

In the UK, although the debate took place under the glare of the public spotlight, the long-drawn-out Scott Inquiry and subsequent departmental review reflected the UK's inclination to go for consultation, especially with entrenched interests. Rather than take the opportunity to appoint a Royal Commission to engage in a careful study of the policy problem, the UK's pre-1997 policy review and proposals for change were conducted primarily within government circles and with trusted stakeholders, such as defence companies. Numerous minor policy changes were made but the basic structures underlying British export control policy remained largely untouched (until the more radical changes since 1997, which have largely come about as a result of the change of government and common measures introduced within the EU).

---

[42] Although the Labour government elected in 1997 was said to eschew such practices, it has chosen to supply information on arms sales for reasons of political expediency. E.g., it released details of 3 export licences refused to Indonesia at a time when it was being heavily criticized for continuing arms sales to that country and only weeks before its first annual party conference after gaining power. The release of information at this time could be seen as an attempt to take the heat out of a potentially difficult debate on arms to Indonesia at the party conference.

[43] Inadequacies in the administrative structures may well reflect desired policy priorities, as was largely the case with the Arms to Iraq scandal in the UK.

Sweden also consulted widely but as part of a more consensual search for solutions to the problems, whereas in the UK, with its predilection for secrecy, the tendency was to impose policy rather than seek consensus. Also in contrast to the UK, Sweden was able to implement substantive changes to its export control regime very rapidly, even though the consultation and review process was a much more open process and even included citizen groups.

In Germany, the debate which precipitated the changes was conducted almost entirely within government circles (and was even more narrowly focused than in the UK), but, as in Sweden, it did result in the rapid implementation of substantive changes. Indeed, the 1989–92 changes to the German control regime were arguably the most dramatic since the 1950s.[44] As one analyst described it: 'This change was not meant to be window-dressing; it was serious, put a tangible and much undesired burden on industry, and risked even some competitive disadvantages for German companies at the margin. Moreover, it costs money: the decision to invest in new staff and equipment is not taken easily at a time of heavy strain on all public budgets caused by the exigencies of unification'.[45]

Overall, therefore, the different administrative traditions that influence policy implementation generally in the three countries clearly do have an influence on the structures that govern arms export controls. However, as an explanation for the continuing depth and scope of some of the main policy differences between the three export control regimes, they are at best a marginal explanation. As the previous section showed, most of the differences between the three regimes have political (and economic) rather than administrative origins. As a result there are major differences in the volume and types of weapons exported and in the recipient markets. The next section highlights the extent of those differences during the late 1980s and 1990s.

Differences in policy outcomes: the impact on post-cold war licensing decisions

To recap, during the cold war, the UK, Germany and Sweden developed three different approaches to export control policy, which have continued to impact on licensing decisions in the decade following its demise.

In the UK, the regulation of arms transfers has been dominated by contradictory economic, security and political motives which were largely framed by the retreat from empire, a strong commitment to the ideological fight against communism and a declining manufacturing base (within which the defence sector was regarded as the 'jewel in the crown'). On the one hand, this resulted in the screening of arms recipients to prevent arms and sensitive technologies

---

[44] German export control policy and institutions went through a period of rapid change during the 1950s until new legislation was passed in 1961 which replaced military occupation law. Although export criteria were introduced in 1971 and refined in 1982, these were not dramatic changes and merely reflected a public pronouncement of government policy.

[45] Müller, H. *et al., From Black Sheep to White Angel? The New German Export Control Policy*, PRIF Reports no. 32 (Peace Research Institute Frankfurt: Frankfurt, Jan. 1994), p. 57.

falling into the 'wrong hands', and military concern about the horizontal proliferation of sensitive technologies did lead to some weapon systems being downgraded or modified prior to transfer and others being subject to outright ban. On the other hand, any underlying desire to exercise restraint was progressively eroded under the pressures of defence producers faced with irregular procurement cycles, the desire to retain an advanced defence industrial base and the support for allies.

Germany's choice of a trading state strategy—the emphasis on multilateral institutions in German foreign policy and restrictions on arms exports (and the use of German armed forces)—is largely a moral response to past German militarism and the Nazi experience. In particular, the export orientation of the German economy was not only an economic strategy but also represented an attempt to escape from the autarkic traditions of the 1930s. Thus, Germany's integration into the world markets called for few restrictions on the export of dual-use goods. On the other hand, the experience of militarism in two world wars resulted in tight restrictions on German military statecraft, including controls on arms exports. However, this restrictive policy on arms exports has been increasingly compromised by co-production with countries that have more lenient export regulations.

In Sweden, the armed neutrality concept was a major factor in the country's historical and cultural development. In terms of foreign policy, this is reflected in the high priority that Swedes place on confidence-building measures, the peaceful settlement of conflicts and human rights. It is no surprise, therefore, to find that these concerns are also central to the criteria that govern their arms export control regime. However, the conclusion that Sweden's foreign, economic and security interests would be better served by a more restrictive arms export control policy has been balanced by the desire to retain a high degree of self-sufficiency in defence production (which traditionally necessitated a vigorous export market).

In turn, these normative differences were played out in individual licensing decisions to specific sensitive destinations. Generally speaking, all three governments licensed the export of dual-use goods unless there were compelling reasons not to do so. The granting of a licence depended on two overall factors—the nature of the recipient and the level of sensitivity of the goods or technologies to be exported. However, throughout the 1980s Germany was arguably more lax than the UK in licensing such exports because of the size and economic importance of its dual-use sector. Sweden, on the other hand, did not begin to licence dual-use goods associated with conventional weapons until 1993 (although there were some COCOM-related restrictions on re-exports of dual-use goods imported by Swedish firms from 1986 onwards, as discussed in chapter 7).

For arms exports the differences in policy were often (but not always) far more pronounced. The British Government generally encouraged the sale of defence equipment unless there were compelling reasons not to do so. Thus, all licences for the export of arms were reviewed on a case-by-case basis. In

Germany and Sweden the situation was different. While exports of German arms to NATO countries were likely to be permitted, this was not necessarily the case for destinations outside the NATO area. In particular, exports of arms to regions of tension were proscribed and for many destinations in the developing world a restrictive policy was applied (especially for land and air equipment, less so for naval equipment). In Sweden, the basic principle was that exports of military equipment were not permitted unless they furthered Swedish security and foreign policy (including strategic industrial concerns). Thus, Swedish controls were generally prohibitive but with a number of exemptions which allowed some exports to the developing world.

As in the case of dual-use transfers, the granting of an export licence was ultimately largely dependent in each of the three countries on the nature of the recipient and the level of sensitivity of the arms to be exported. However, unlike the case of dual-use goods (which had been subject to some early convergence through COCOM), the criteria and the interpretation of these criteria often differed greatly between the three countries, particularly in relation to sensitive destinations. In Germany, for example, the application of the criteria tended to vary across different weapon types, with fewer restrictions on the export of naval weapons as compared to tanks. Similarly, all three countries included the nature of the equipment to be sold in their evaluation of the human rights criterion, thus permitting transfers of items, particularly naval equipment, unlikely to be used for the repression of domestic political opposition. A brief survey of the recipient regional markets is illustrative of these differences.

Africa

Africa has been a marginal market for all three countries. According to table 8.3 (which shows the value of arms transfer deliveries by Germany and the UK by recipient region) and table 8.4 (which shows the number of major weapons delivered by the UK and Germany by type of weapon),[46] the UK delivered military equipment to the region worth $300 million in the three years 1986–88 and $100 million in the three years 1994–96 (in current prices), including significant supplies of land armaments. However, these deliveries represented less than 3 per cent and 1 per cent, respectively, of the total value of British deliveries in those two periods. The figures for Germany were $100 million in 1986–88 and less than $50 million in 1994–96, or less than 2 per cent of German deliveries in both periods. An alternative data source shows that Sweden's proportion of military equipment exported to Africa was also less than 1 per cent for 1995–97.[47]

---

[46] The US Bureau of Arms Control (formerly ACDA) does not include figures for Sweden.

[47] Swedish Ministry for Foreign Affairs, Strategic Export Control Division, *Swedish Arms Exports in 1997: A Government Report*, Government Report to Parliament 1997/98:147 (Ministry for Foreign Affairs: Stockholm, May 1998), table 4, p. 24.

Table 8.3. The value of arms deliveries by France, Germany and the UK, 1986–88 and 1994–96 compared, by recipient region

Figures are in current US $b. Figures in italics are percentages.

Recipient		France	Germany	UK	Total for France, Germany and UK	World total	France, Germany as and UK as %% of world total
World	1986–88	9.3	4.6	13.6	27.5	183.3	*15.0*
	1994–96	6.7	3.1	16.4	26.2	119.5	*21.9*
Developing	1986–88	7.2	2.6	10.7	20.5	124.8	*16.4*
countries	1994–96	4.5	1.0	15.0	20.5	67.4	*30.4*
Africa	1986–88	0.6	0.1	0.3	1.0	18.4	*5.4*
	1994–96	0.3	..	0.1	0.4	3.5	*11.4*
North America	1986–88	1.0	0.6	1.8	3.4	8.2	*41.5*
(NAFTA)	1994–96	0.3	0.3	1.0	1.6	4.5	*35.6*
Central and South	1986–88	0.6	0.8	0.1	1.5	11.0	*13.6*
America and the	1994–96	0.2	0.1	0.2	0.5	3.7	*13.5*
Caribbean							
East Asia	1986–88	0.2	0.2	0.6	1.0	21.8	*4.6*
	1994–96	0.9	1.3	1.8	4.0	25.6	*15.6*
South Asia	1986–88	1.3	0.2	0.2	1.7	16.1	*10.6*
	1994–96	0.4	–	0.1	0.5	2.6	*19.2*
Middle East	1986–88	4.2	0.5	9.1	13.8	64.4	*21.4*
	1994–96	3.2	0.2	12.9	16.3	44.5	*36.6*
Europe (East and	1986–88	1.2	2.2	1.2	4.6	39.0	*11.8*
West)	1994–96	1.2	1.6	0.2	3.0	26.9	*11.2*

Notes:

  . . = Figures not available or not applicable.

  – = Nil or a negligible figure.

Source: US Arms Control and Disarmament Agency, *World Military Expenditures and Arms Transfers 1997* (ACDA: Washington, DC, 1998).

North America

North America (and mainly the USA) has been a significant market for all three countries, but especially Sweden (which exported approximately 20 per cent of its military equipment to the region in the three years 1995–97). Approximately 10 per cent of total British and German arms deliveries were exported to North America in the two periods covered by table 8.3, but these included only a few major weapon systems (as shown by table 8.4). This indicates that both the UK and Germany export large quantities of dual-use goods, subsystems and/or light weapons to the USA.

Central and South America

This region as a whole has not been a significant market for any of the three countries, although particular countries (especially Argentina, Brazil and Chile) have at times provided major markets for each of them. Germany has generally had the largest presence, with deliveries to the region worth $800 million in 1986–88 and $100 million in 1994–96, including significant supplies of helicopters. Again, however, as a percentage of total German deliveries, the figures are relatively low: approximately 17 per cent and 3 per cent, respectively, for these two periods. The figures for the same periods were smaller still for the UK, despite supplies of armoured cars and surface-to-air missiles to the region. The proportion of Sweden's military equipment exports that went to Latin America was less than 5 per cent for the three years 1995–97.

East Asia

While it is an important market for all three countries, East Asia is one of four regions (the others being South Asia, the Middle East and Europe) where the differences between German and Swedish policy on the one hand, and British policy on the other, are most marked. At the aggregate regional level, the figures for Germany and the UK are quite similar: British deliveries to the region were worth $600 million in 1986–88 (less than 5 per cent of total British deliveries) and $1800 million in 1994–96 (approximately 10 per cent of the total), while the equivalent figures for Germany over these two periods were $200 million (less than 5 per cent of total German deliveries) and $1300 million (approximately 40 per cent of the total), respectively. In the case of Sweden, approximately 30 per cent of its military exports are normally exported to Asia as a whole (the figures are not disaggregated between East and South).

However, these figures mask wide variations between the three countries in the types and quantities of weapons exported to specific countries. In the case of Indonesia, for example, over the past three decades, the UK has supplied a wide range and substantial quantities of military equipment, including Hawk jets and armoured vehicles, and has only recently begun to reflect concerns

Table 8.4. The number of major conventional weapons delivered by Germany and the UK, 1985–96, by recipient region

	World		North America		South America		Western Europe		Eastern Europe		East and Central Asia		South Asia		Middle East		Africa	
	Ger.	UK	Ger.	UK	Ger.	UK	Ger.	UK	Ger.	UK	Ger.	UK	Ger.	UK	Ger.	UK	Ger.	UK
Land armaments																		
Tanks	1 260	160	10	–	–	–	1 230	–	–	–	–	–	–	–	20	20	–	140
Artillery, field and anti-air	1 130	250	–	–	10	40	1 120	140	–	–	–	20	–	–	–	40	–	20
APCs and armoured cars	1 990	460	–	–	10	90	1 950	20	–	–	10	110	–	20	–	190	20	60
Naval craft																		
Major surface combatants	47	26	–	–	4	10	11	–	–	–	32	1	–	14	–	1	–	–
Other surface combatants	78	53	–	–	6	–	19	7	4	–	15	2	–	11	23	25	11	8
Submarines	13	1	–	1	2	–	8	–	–	–	1	–	2	–	–	–	–	–
Missile attack boats	7	–	–	–	–	–	–	–	3	–	–	–	–	–	4	–	–	–
Aircraft																		
Combat aircraft, supersonic	200	90	–	–	–	–	200	10	–	–	–	–	–	–	–	70	–	10
Combat aircraft, subsonic	50	210	–	–	–	10	50	30	–	–	–	50	–	20	–	80	–	20
Other aircraft	150	90	–	–	10	–	20	20	30	–	10	20	10	–	–	40	60	10
Helicopters	160	60	10	–	40	–	30	10	40	–	–	30	–	10	30	10	–	–
Missiles																		
Surface-to-air	540	2 570	–	–	–	90	540	1 250	–	–	–	870	–	–	–	300	–	10
Surface-to-surface	–	–	–	–	–	–	–	–	–	–	–	–	–	–	–	–	–	–
Anti-ship	–	180	–	–	–	–	–	140	–	–	–	–	–	20	–	20	–	–

Note: APC = Armoured personnel carrier. – = Nil or a negligible figure.

Source: US Arms Control and Disarmament Agency, *World Military Expenditures and Arms Transfers 1997* (ACDA: Washington, DC, 1998), table V.

about human rights and internal repression in its licensing decisions to that destination. German policy, on the other hand, has consistently included a presumption of denial of the export of certain types of weapons, such as light weapons, that could be used in internal repression. Thus, Germany has supplied a more limited range of military equipment to Indonesia, but nonetheless remains a major supplier of naval equipment.[48] Finally, Sweden, in keeping with its greater emphasis on humanitarian concerns, applied a limited arms embargo on Indonesia under which arms exports to Indonesia were only allowed if they could be designated as follow-on deliveries to previous orders.

South Asia

It is in the South Asian market that the biggest difference can be found between German and Swedish policy. Germany has tended to treat South Asia as a 'region of tension' and has been reluctant to export major weapons to either of the two main protagonists, India and Pakistan. Sweden, on the other hand, has had strong arms export links with both countries in the past (and India in particular, with regard to exports of artillery), but following the Bofors arms scandal in the late 1980s has tended to export mainly non-combat-related military equipment (as defined in Swedish national legislation). India and Pakistan have also been important markets for British exports of major weapons.

The Middle East

The Middle East is the most crucial market for British arms exports, especially land armaments, aircraft and missiles, as shown in table 8.4. British deliveries to the region were worth $9100 million in 1986–88 (or 67 per cent of total British deliveries) and $12 900 million in 1994–96 (or 79 per cent of the total). In particular, Oman and Saudi Arabia are two of the largest recipients of British arms, and the Al Yamamah contract (discussed in chapter 5) was the largest British arms contract ever. The Middle East market generally is much less important to Germany and Sweden. The equivalent figures for Germany were $500 million (approximately 10 per cent of total German deliveries) and $200 million (approximately 6 per cent of the total). Moreover, Germany is unlikely to sanction arms exports to Oman or Saudi Arabia because, with the exception of small arms, arms production technology and other dual-use items,[49] and co-production items with other European companies,[50] it generally denies exports to Arab states in the Middle East out of concern for its relation-

[48] SIPRI data on exports of major conventional weapons to Indonesia show that between 1987 and 1996 Germany exported more than the UK—$1983 million as opposed to $685 million (in 1990 prices). Quoted by Chalmers, M., *British Arms Export Policy and Indonesia* (Saferworld: London, May 1997).

[49] E.g., German machine tool manufacturers have traditionally occupied a strong position in the Middle East and were to be found in large numbers in the arming of Iraq in the 1980s. Müller *et al.* (note 45), pp. 2–3.

[50] The effectiveness of this policy is questionable given the extent of German involvement in collaborative projects (see chapter 6). E.g., Germany is a partner in the 3-nation Tornado project and has incorporated engines into French Leclerc tanks exported to the UAE. The same applies to Sweden.

ship with Israel. Sweden's official figures do not show an aggregate percentage for the Middle East. Small quantities of military equipment were exported to Oman and the UAE in 1995–97,[51] but in general Sweden has traditionally applied a very restrictive policy to arms exports to the Gulf.

Europe

Both Germany and Sweden export the bulk of their major weapons to Western Europe. For Sweden the Nordic and other neutral countries are a particularly important component of this regional market, which accounts for upwards of 50 per cent of total arms exports in any given year. In the case of Germany, over 98 per cent of its exports of land armaments and all its exports of combat aircraft went to Western Europe during the 12-year period 1985–96, and it was a significant supplier of other aircraft and helicopters to Eastern Europe. Neither Sweden nor the UK has penetrated the East European market to any similar extent.

Total German deliveries to Europe as a whole were worth $2200 million in the three years 1986–88 (or 48 per cent of total German deliveries) and $1600 million in 1994–96 (or 52 per cent of the total). While it is also an important market for the UK, particularly for artillery and missiles, Europe accounted for less than 10 per cent of total British deliveries in 1986–88 and less than 2 per cent in 1994–96.

III. Explaining convergence

While there are clearly still large areas of persistent divergence in the three national export control regimes, chapters 2, 3 and 4 have already shown that there has also been significant progress towards policy convergence within the EU. The theoretical basis for that convergence is reviewed in chapter 9. Here the main instruments of convergence (namely, past and present multilateral control regimes and the process of European integration) are briefly reviewed before the detailed examination of the convergence–divergence mix contained in section IV this chapter.

Instruments of convergence

Multilateral control regimes

The ability of the UK, Germany and Sweden to pursue purely national export control policies for arms and dual-use goods is constrained by membership of multilateral control regimes. However, unlike the situation for WMD (where controls in all three countries operate as part of an array of interlocking and overlapping multilateral regimes, under the auspices of groups of like-minded supplier states, such as the MTCR and the Australia Group), multilateral

---

[51] *Swedish Arms Exports in 1997* (note 47), table 5, pp. 25–26.

controls for arms and dual-use goods have tended to have a much more limited effect on national decision making. As discussed in chapter 2, COCOM and, to a lesser extent, the OSCE and UN guiding principles for exports and embargoes were the main instruments of convergence during the cold war. However, while the successor regime to COCOM (the Wassenaar Arrangement) continues to be important, the most significant instrument of convergence in the 1990s has been the EU.

European integration

During the first 30 years of the European Communities there was little effort on the part of member states to collectively coordinate, control or restrain the arms trade. Member states were able to block progress in this area because of a restrictive interpretation of Article 223 of the Treaty of Rome, which presents arms exports as the prerogative of national decision making. From 1970 until entry into force of the Maastricht Treaty in 1993, it was the EPC forum that provided the focus of EC action on conventional arms trade matters. The Maastricht Treaty replaced the EPC process with the CFSP (or 'second pillar' of the Union), but differs only in so far as it makes intergovernmental cooperation a more formal affair. Indeed, both the Maastricht and the Amsterdam treaties upheld the intergovernmental approach to this issue. Within this intergovernmental framework, the CFSP does have the potential for effective cooperation on defence-related trade matters through information exchange, common positions and joint actions. At the start of 1997, however, this potential remained largely untapped and, according to one insider in the British export control bureaucracy, the EU was 'not remotely close to a conventional arms control regime'.[52]

While this is still undoubtedly the case, the process of integration in this policy area clearly accelerated and deepened during 1997 and thereafter.

Of the seven most significant achievements to date, four were initiated during the last few years of the 1990s. The seven are: the eight Common Criteria; the ongoing information exchanges within EU working groups; the EU Regulation on Dual-Use Goods; the EU Programme for Preventing and Combating Illicit Trafficking in Conventional Arms; the EU Code of Conduct on Arms Exports; the EU Joint Action on Small Arms; and the Framework Agreement Concerning Measures to Facilitate the Restructuring and Operation of the European Defence Industry. In each case, significant advances were made but with continuing limitations.

1. The *common export criteria* that were agreed in 1991 and 1992 were the first notable advance towards a common European arms export control policy. They emphasized that decisions on arms exports should take account of the internal and regional situation of recipients, as well as their human rights record, attitude towards terrorism and economic capacity to purchase arms, but

[52] Personal interview, 1997.

they remained an integral part of 'hard-core' national sovereignties. Thus major differences remained in the contents of military product lists and in the definition of criteria for the granting of export licences and of embargoes and sensitive destinations. In essence, the criteria were no more than a 'statement of intent' and it is doubtful whether they made any significant difference to the arms export behaviour of member states.

2. The benefits from regular discussions within *EU-level working groups*, such as COARM, should not be underestimated. In addition to the rare successes, such as the agreement of a common embargo list and more recently the agreement of a common control list for use with the EU Code of Conduct, these sessions have also helped to build intra-EU confidence between officials: 'At a time when there is no agreed European political strategy or common policy underlying the development of arms export control measures, the very fact that EU member states are regularly and intensively discussing aspects of the arms export question is itself a contribution to the political coherence of the EU'.[53]

However, just as the benefits should not be underestimated, neither should the problems. Discussions within the working groups, particularly in the crucial area of policy interpretation, are often disjointed and hampered by national rivalries. Several representatives on COARM indicated, for example, that both the British and the French delegations have in the past avoided any discussion of their own national export policy towards particular destinations. Without a real exchange of information on these national policies there will be no real harmonization. Although this negative attitude now appears to be changing, particularly with the change of government in the UK, structural deficiencies with COARM and other EU working groups continue to be problematic. For example, the infrequency of meetings and the size factor (which will become even more problematic with EU enlargement) tend to prevent the building up of good working relationships within COARM. Indeed, better discussions are often had outside the formal meetings within smaller groups (such as those put together by NGOs like Saferworld) or on a bilateral basis.[54]

3. The *EU Regulation on Dual-Use Goods* agreed in July 1995 and revised in June 2000 is a significant advance towards the establishment of a complete and consistent Community regime for the control of exports of dual-use goods. Although it started out as a Commission initiative, as a result of the SEM imperative, it was later commandeered by national governments and turned into a partial foreign policy and defence issue. Thus, the 1995 Regulation was a compromise between Community competence in trade matters and national sovereignty in the areas of foreign, security and defence policies. As one commentator said, 'it is a hybrid system, half-community, half-intergovernmental which in addition leaves the States to decide on its implementation'.[55] While the

[53] van Orden, G., DGIA, European Commission, 'European arms export controls', eds P. Cornish, P. van Ham and J. Krause, *Europe and the Challenge of Proliferation*, Chaillot Papers no. 24 (Western European Union, Institute for Security Studies: Paris, 24 May 1996), p. 64.

[54] Personal interviews, 1997.

[55] Adam, B. (ed.), *European Union and Arms Exports* (Groupe de Recherche et d'Information sur la Paix et la Sécurité (GRIP): Brussels, Dec. 1995), p. 75.

2000 Regulation tips the balance back towards Community competence, decisions on individual licence applications still rest with member states.

Within this new dual-use framework there is a common list of goods, a common Community licence and increased administrative cooperation, but the core policy decisions regarding the issue of licences for difficult destinations remain a national prerogative. While this is also the case for arms exports, there are two main distinctions between the treatment of dual-use goods and the treatment of arms. First, almost all dual-use goods can circulate freely within the EU, whereas intra-EU arms transfers still face some restrictions (although this may change if the Framework Agreement proves successful). Second, export licences issued for dual-use goods are recognized throughout the Community, which implies that there is a mutual recognition of, and confidence in, the underlying policy towards such goods. This is not the case for arms exports (despite the Code of Conduct) where it is still clearly the case that the French attitude to arms exports, for example, is not shared by London or Berlin.

It seems likely, therefore, that the role of the European Commission will remain subordinate to that of member states in this area. The Commission does not have the expertise or the resources to draw up and police the product lists, and there appears to be little enthusiasm on its part to undertake such a role in the future (although there is a desire within the Commission to get involved in reducing and simplifying the lists). Thus, even in the medium-to-long term there are no prospects for a transfer of sovereignty in this area to a centralized export control agency. This means that there will continue to be elements of national discretion irrespective of any further harmonization and strengthening of control procedures.

4 and 5. The 1997 *EU Programme for Preventing and Combating Illicit Arms Trafficking* and the 1998 *EU Joint Action on Small Arms* both focus on ways in which the EU can support other countries and regions in tackling small arms proliferation, as well as addressing illicit trafficking from or through the EU itself. While still at an early stage of development, these two initiatives (coupled with the EU Code of Conduct on legal transfers) provide a comprehensive framework for the development of future action in this area.

6. The 1998 *EU Code of Conduct on Arms Export* is an intermediate solution somewhere between the two options of no common policy at all and a model common legal framework. Nonetheless, it is no exaggeration to state that in terms of multilateral efforts to place concerns of conflict prevention, human rights, regional security and development at the centre of decisions on arms exports the Code is the most comprehensive agreement to date. Indeed, serious application of the Code's criteria should increase restraint in arms exports. However, regular information exchange and consultation will be necessary to minimize differences in the way the criteria are applied in particular cases or in relation to individual destinations. If the Code works well, the annual review process on its implementation should identify areas for further development, although progress is likely to be slow and gradual.

7. The *Framework Agreement Concerning Measures to Facilitate the Restructuring and Operation of the European Defence Industry*, agreed in July 2000, while only partially concerned with export controls, has the potential to significantly enhance coordination between the six signatory countries, as discussed in chapter 4.

Summarizing, it is clear that following nearly a decade of working towards common standards within the EU, and even longer within other multilateral control regimes, significant levels of convergence have occurred. In particular, the period since 1997 has seen a number of measures agreed that not only caused an immediate deepening of convergence, but will undoubtedly lead to a spillover effect and further convergence in member states' arms export control policies in the medium and long term.

IV. Progress towards convergence: an assessment

Having reviewed the instruments of convergence and discussed the reasons for continuing divergence and how these differences impact on policy outcomes, the final section of this chapter explores the extent to which the process of European integration is leading to convergence in the post-cold war era.

The convergence–divergence mix for the UK, Germany and Sweden

Convergence can be conceptualized as a continuum along which a range of policy responses is feasible. In a study by the Brookings Institution, for example, five such responses were identified:

1. *National autonomy*. This is the end of the continuum at which national sovereignty is at its strongest and national governments make decisions with little or no EU involvement, consultation or cooperation.
2. *Mutual recognition*. This entails exchanges of information and consultation among governments which constrain the formation of national regulations and policies.
3. *Coordination*. This involves jointly designated mutual adjustments of national policies, in which explicit bargaining occurs and governments agree to promote intergovernmental agreements.
4. *Explicit harmonization*. This involves even higher levels of inter-governmental cooperation and agreement, including the strengthening of, and possibly transfers of responsibilities to, EU institutions.
5. *Federalist mutual governance*. This is the far end of the spectrum and implies joint centralized decision making within strengthened EU institutions.[56]

---

[56] Aaron, H. *et al.*, 'Preface to the studies on integrating national economies', ed. M. Kahler, *International Institutions and the Political Economy of Integration* (Brookings Institution: Washington, DC, 1995), pp. xxi–xxiii. For an alternative 'hierarchy of cooperation' see Molle, W., *The Economics of European Integration: Theory, Practice, Policy* (Dartmouth: Aldershot, 1994), pp. 20–23.

Table 8.5. Synoptic view of the degree of convergence in British, German and Swedish arms and dual-use export controls, 1985–2005

Policy field	Mid-1980s[a]	Mid-1990s	Mid-2000s
The policy environment and stakeholders[b]			
Foreign policy	1–2	2–3	3
Strategic industrial policy	3	3	3–4
Policy stakeholders	2	2	1–3
Promotion of arms exports	1	1–2	2–3
Arms export control regime			
1. The policy-making structure			
Legislation (dual-use)	2–3	3–4	4
Legislation (arms)	1–2	2	2–3
Lists of controlled goods (dual-use)	2–3	3–4	4
Lists of controlled goods (arms)	2	2–3	3–4
Lists of sensitive destinations	1–2	2	2–3
Management of export control policy	1–2	2–3	3
Export control criteria	1–2	3	3–4
Regulatory oversight	1–2	2–3	3
2. The administrative structure			
Publication of export guidelines	1–2	2–3	3
Deciding licence applications	1–2	2	2–3
Compliance and enforcement procedures	2	2–3	3

Notes:

[a] This column refers to Germany and the UK only as Sweden did not join the EU until 1995.

[b] In assessing the degree of convergence in some of the elements that make up the policy environment, the situation in the EU as a whole is also considered: see the discussion in the text.

1. = National autonomy; 2. = Mutual recognition; 3. = Coordination; 4. = Explicit harmonization; 5. = Federalist mutual governance. Where two indicators are shown (e.g., 1–2) the assessment is that a mid-point between the two policy responses has been reached.

These policy responses are used in the following analysis as benchmarks to measure progress towards policy convergence in this area. In other words, by locating each of the main elements within the three national policy systems (as described in general in chapter 1, and in detail for each of the three focus countries in chapters 5, 6 and 7) on the appropriate point along the continuum, and by doing this historically, currently and prospectively, it is possible to measure the progress of policy convergence between the UK, Germany and Sweden. An indication of such progress is provided in table 8.5.

The remainder of this section discusses the evidence for such an assessment.

The policy environment and stakeholders

Foreign policy

While the UK, Germany and Sweden continue to adopt different foreign policies in relation to specific countries, the broader systemic and normative differences that help shape those policies have become less and less important in recent years. This is mainly a result of the process of European integration. Even if this process has not brought about a fully functioning CFSP, all three countries are now firmly rooted in the EU where there has been a slow but growing convergence of aspects of foreign policy (including arms export controls) among the member states. This is also true of the three countries examined here.[57]

In the case of Germany, now that full sovereignty has been regained, most of the restrictions on its foreign policy have loosened, including restrictions on the use of German troops abroad. Thus, the normative basis for restrictive arms export restraints is also eroding. Although still only a partial erosion at this stage, eventually it may develop into a new and less restrictive normative base for export controls which is more in keeping with the practice in other prominent European arms-exporting countries (such as France and the UK). This seems unlikely, however, for two reasons. First, the degree of erosion can be overstated. For example, while German armed forces have taken part in military missions outside the traditional NATO area, this has only been done in a multilateral context, which suggests that Germany's commitment to multilateralism is stronger than its aversion to the use of military force.[58] Similarly, any erosion of German export controls is only likely to occur within a multilateral context, either within Wassenaar or as a result of further harmonization within the EU. Second, although Germany may become less restrictive, some other member states are becoming more restrictive. Most clearly this applies to the UK, where recent changes include more emphasis on human rights and closer scrutiny of arms sales to repressive regimes. These changes are mainly the result of changes in the domestic political environment, which in turn have been translated into support for relatively high levels of common standards within the EU (through the adoption of an EU Code of Conduct).[59]

Thus, just as those member states with the most restrictive controls, such as Germany and Sweden, were concerned that their controls could be watered

---

[57] The exact nature of the transformation in foreign policy in each case has yet to be fully realized, and whatever the outcome geography and history will remain important and some differences in emphasis are inevitable. E.g., Germany, Sweden and the UK all have a strong interest in stabilizing the new democracies and market economies in Central and Eastern Europe, but given its status as a front-line state (and for reasons of migration and foreign direct investment) it is an even more important foreign policy goal for Germany and, to a lesser extent, for Sweden in relation to the Baltic states.

[58] The recent German involvement in NATO military action in Kosovo was the first use of German armed forces in external military combat since the end of World War II.

[59] In addition, the decline of the East–West conflict and the final retreat from empire have sharpened the decline in the use of arms transfers by the British state to acquire strategic access or to manipulate the political alignment or behaviour of recipient states.

down if 'lowest common denominator' controls were introduced at the EU level, other member states with less restrictive controls face the prospect of having to strengthen their national controls if tough common standards develop from the EU Code. As discussed in chapters 3 and 4, the current attempts at harmonization arguably fall somewhere in the middle: they are not as restrictive as many proponents of arms trade restraint would like, but certainly not as weak as might have been expected under the lowest common denominator principle.

In the post-cold war environment, the military concerns of the three countries are also converging. While neither Germany nor Sweden is remotely likely to engage in independent 'out of area' military actions in the foreseeable future, neither is as constrained by its past as it was. In the case of Sweden, this has meant a growing debate about membership of a military alliance, and in the case of Germany, consideration of collaborative out-of-area missions. If both Germany and Sweden are less constrained by their pasts, in contrast, the UK is becoming more realistic about its present. Thus, in short, all three countries can expect to make more widespread use of their armed forces in support of multi-national peacekeeping and peacemaking operations, and this argues for more caution in their respective arms export policies.

Strategic industrial policy

It also seems clear that there is growing convergence as a result of changing economic imperatives. With the end of the cold war and increasing competition in the global arms market, all three countries are becoming even more commercially oriented than was previously the case. In addition, the defence industries in Europe are restructuring in the face of shrinking defence budgets both at home and abroad.[60] Companies in each of the three countries are therefore under increasing pressure to find new international markets. While this would seem most pressing in Germany's case, given the huge cuts in German procurement since the end of the cold war,[61] other factors at work in Sweden and the UK have added to the problems facing their domestic defence manufacturers.

In the UK, for example, the application of the 'value for money' principle in British defence procurement has had two main implications. First, UK firms have adopted an international orientation, partly through the demands of collaboration and partly through the need to find less expensive technology and subsystems. Second, the British Government's commitment to maintaining a national defence industrial base for its own sake has been seriously weakened.

---

[60] In each of the 3 states, however, it is broadly accepted that government policy should focus on improving the political framework within which industry has to operate, encouraging and promoting restructuring, and ensuring a 'level playing field' for companies to compete in the international market.

[61] More than the other 2 countries, Germany has been affected by defence budget constraints. However, the reduction in Germany's procurement budget is even more severe—56% in real terms between 1988 and 1997 (compared with a 20% decline in the UK over the same period). Sköns, E. *et al.*, 'Military expenditure', *SIPRI Yearbook 1998: Armaments, Disarmament and International Security* (Oxford University Press: Oxford, 1998), table 6B, p. 236.

With the exception of a few areas,[62] the former policy of maintaining a wide range of national defence capabilities has been supplemented by a willingness to buy off the shelf in the international market place. As a consequence, British-based arms companies are looking to new export markets to offset declining domestic sales. Similarly, Sweden's ongoing restructuring following EU membership is likely to lead to greater commercial pressure for exports. Finally, the involvement of all three countries in the July 2000 Framework Agreement is likely to lead to even closer strategic–industrial alignment.

Policy stakeholders

There has also been growing convergence among a large number of the key policy stakeholders. At the political level, for example, there has been significant convergence around the political programmes of centre–left governments, which enabled agreement on the EU Code of Conduct. Indeed, while there are still many variations in voting patterns as between the national electorates, generally speaking recent swings in electoral support to either the left or the right have tended to be an EU-wide phenomenon (as witnessed by the growing support for most national right-wing parties in the recent European elections). At the industrial level, significant convergence has occurred through the growing number and increasing depth of European collaborative ventures and stronger European networks of trade associations.

Promotion of arms exports

In the UK, defence companies have (since the late 1960s) received high-level political and organizational support from government in their attempts to secure major defence sales. The Al Yamamah contract with Saudi Arabia is the most prominent example. This support occurs in three ways: advocacy on behalf of defence companies; organizational support; and financial support. The British Government has historically sent high-level officials, including ministers of defence, ambassadors or prime ministers, to persuade foreign governments to buy their products. In comparison, because defence exports are a politically sensitive issue in Germany and Sweden, the respective governments have traditionally avoided doing so.

Organizational support in the UK is provided by the DESO, which identifies defence export opportunities, promotes and facilitates such exports, provides assistance with defence equipment demonstrations and trade shows, and provides advice to industry regarding offsets. Although Germany and Sweden have no comparable organization, their companies involved in cross-border collaborative efforts are able to benefit indirectly from the export promotion activities of the DESO (and the French equivalent). Moreover, in the more competitive

---

[62] A classified MOD survey in the 1980s listed 4 areas and their number is not thought to have increased since then. Taylor, T., 'The British restructuring programme', eds M. Brzoska and P. Lock, SIPRI, *Restructuring of Arms Production in Western Europe* (Oxford University Press: Oxford, 1992), p. 90.

climate at the end of the 1990s, Sweden decided to set up its own arms export promotion machinery (which remains very modest in comparison to the DESO), and Germany has also begun to review its options in this area.

Export financing has also been central to the UK's efforts to win and retain its market share and, in the past at least, the ECGD was willing to provide export credit for a wide range of defence products to a large number of destinations, including some 'friendly' countries in the developing world. In contrast, in Germany, with a few exceptions, export credits for military exports have only been provided for sales to developed countries, while Sweden was extremely reluctant to offer any assistance of this kind until 1990. However, since the early 1990s Sweden has been willing to offer credit terms for arms exports and has joined forces with the UK's ECGD to facilitate joint financing of exports of the Gripen.

Thus, while Germany and Sweden have indulged in considerably less overt government promotion of arms exports than the UK, there are clear signs that the gap between their respective policies is slowly closing. This is due partly to the recent initiatives by the German and Swedish governments to extend their export promotion machinery (and this particularly applies to Sweden), and partly to the current British Government's reducing its own activities in this area as a consequence of its declared ethical foreign policy (although so far this has been limited to discussion in the ECGD and reduced levels of export credits for defence exports). It also reflects a new strategy adopted by companies in the defence sector in all three countries during the 1990s. While consolidation and diversification were two key strategies, of equal importance was the strategy of enlisting government support in securing export orders.

The policy-making structure

Legislation

All three countries apply export controls that are based in national law. The basic structure of this legislation has always been broadly consistent in that it requires lists of weapons and dual-use goods to define what is to be regulated and criteria according to which export licences are granted or denied. In the 1990s, the legislative base of all three regimes was influenced in two main ways. First, the end of the cold war and the pressures of trade liberalization and globalization resulted in a reduction in the scope of dual-use goods covered by the legislation. Second, post-cold war proliferation concerns (mainly in connection with WMD) and a number of arms export scandals resulted in some strengthening of export control legislation. These two seemingly contradictory trends resulted in the general principle that now underpins the export legislation of all Western countries—higher fences around fewer goods. However, throughout the Western world (including the three countries discussed here) differences continue to exist in the height and completeness of the fence, and in the type and quantity of goods and technologies kept behind it.

The main area of convergence has been in respect of dual-use legislation. As a result of the EU Dual-Use Regulation, the scope and content of the legislation on the export of dual-use goods in the three countries have converged quite considerably. An export licence granted by any member state is now normally valid throughout the Community and export authorizations to non-EU destinations are now based on common lists of goods and criteria. However, important differences remain in the scope of the legislation, particularly in areas left unregulated by the latest version of the EU Dual-Use Regulation. For example, transit trade transactions and third-party brokering of arms transfers are subject to control in Germany but not in the UK (although the British Government is exploring options for the latter). Sweden, on the other hand, has controls on brokering but not on transit trade. Similarly the legal consequences for breaches of the regulations differ greatly between the three countries (as discussed below). Another area of continuing difference between the three countries in relation to dual-use legislation is the scope of the catch-all clause—only Germany, for example, applies the clause to all goods destined for military uses. This mix of convergence and divergence is in keeping with the overall trend of convergence in some respects, and no convergence in others. However, given the progress made so far, the mid-point between 'coordination' and 'explicit harmonization' seems to be an apt description of the current situation (table 8.5).

Lists of controlled goods

As a result of developments in both the EU (under the Dual-Use Regulation and the EU Code of Conduct) and the Wassenaar Arrangement, lists of controlled items have converged quite closely among all member states. The British, German and Swedish lists of controlled dual-use goods have been almost entirely harmonized under the EU Dual-Use Regulation, with only a few minor differences in the exemption lists. The three countries' respective military lists also show a high degree of convergence, largely because they are based on the current Military List in the Wassenaar Arrangement. However, there are more discrepancies between the three military lists than between their dual-use lists because there are several important omissions in the Wassenaar list, including many types of internal security equipment. The agreement of a common list of military equipment covered by the EU Code of Conduct in June 2000 failed to iron out these discrepancies, and work is continuing to agree a separate EU list for paramilitary and police equipment. Even when such a list is agreed, it seems likely that a few minor differences will remain, both between the various regime control lists and in terms of exemptions and additional controlled items applied by individual countries.

Lists of sensitive destinations

Harmonization within the EU has only led to a partial convergence of the lists of sensitive destinations, and the utility (and even existence) of such listings continues to be controversial.[63] In the UK, for example, the sensitive destination list was withdrawn in 1998 on the grounds that it might cause diplomatic difficulties with some of the countries listed. Similarly, Sweden does not officially have such a list (although clearly both Swedish and British officials have to make a judgement about the country of destination when considering an export licence application, and thus de facto sensitive destination lists do exist in both regimes). Germany, on the other hand, has two sensitive destination lists (recently reduced from four) which continue to be in the public domain.

Moreover, the reasons why a country is designated sensitive are rarely stated explicitly. A 1995 analysis of the sensitive country lists of four major exporters of arms (Germany, Japan, the UK and the USA) sought to identify and explain the concerns which led to the inclusion of countries on those lists.[64] The findings in relation to Germany and the UK were that a total of 57 countries were listed (48 by Germany and 50 by the UK) with 41 common to both lists. The nine countries on the British list but not on the German lists were Angola, Argentina, Brazil, Croatia, Egypt, South Korea, Slovenia, South Africa and Taiwan. The seven countries on the German lists but not the British list were Chile, the Comoros, Djibouti, Jordan, Oman, the UAE and Vanuatu. These differences are largely a reflection of the different foreign policy concerns of Germany and the UK, and confirm the difficulty of reaching a common European perspective in such matters.

In any case, lists of sensitive destinations are not a particularly good guide to the way export controls work in practice. All three countries have exported arms and sensitive technologies to countries they have designated sensitive, and the exact role of lists of sensitive destinations within the export regulations is often unclear:

While they do detail those countries to which 'special procedures apply' the lists do not specify what these 'special procedures' are; nor do they give any indication as to those categories of technologies or arms which will actually be subject to restrictions. The end result is that these lists of countries of concern are not particularly helpful to

---

[63] Several analysts have speculated on the possible groupings of states within a common EU sensitive destinations list. See, e.g., Greene, O., 'Developing and implementing export control guidelines', ed. P. Eavis, *Arms and Dual-Use Exports from the EC: A Common Policy for Regulation and Control* (Saferworld: London, Dec. 1992), pp. 80–83. See also the discussion on typologies of states by Cupitt, R., 'Synthesis and implications: export controls for the 1990s and beyond', eds G. Bertsch, R. Cupitt and S. Elliott-Gower, *International Cooperation on Nonproliferation Export Controls: Prospects for the 1990s and Beyond* (University of Michigan Press: Ann Arbor, Mich., 1994), pp. 297–317.

[64] Overall the study found a wide variety of discrepancies between the 4 lists, indicating that the criteria for deciding which countries should be subject to special procedures are not uniformly applied by these 4 exporting countries. Deltac Ltd and Saferworld, *Proliferation and Export Controls: An Analysis of Sensitive Technologies and Countries of Concern* (Deltac Ltd and Saferworld: Chertsey, 1995), pp. xiii–xiv.

prospective exporters of arms and dual-use technologies, while at the same time they do little to foster greater transparency and international restraint.[65]

Management of export control policy

Authority for the direction of export control policy in each of the three countries is in theory very similar—political direction is said to come from the prime minister, ministers or cabinet committees—but there are clear differences which reflect national constitutional, political and normative differences. In the UK, for example, despite significant differences between departments and sometimes within parliament over the proper direction of policy, throughout the post-war period governments of whichever political hue have had almost total authority to use export controls to serve their conception of the country's security needs and to promote foreign policy and commercial interests. Given the UK's constitutional situation, it can be said that the executive branch of government, and particularly the cabinet and prime minister, have dominated export control policy making. This was particularly true in the 1980s when Prime Minister Margaret Thatcher's interest and involvement in arms exports led to a less restrictive policy. Similarly, German policy is very much centralized at the federal government level, but differs from the British experience in that political direction has tended to come from a special cabinet committee (the Federal Security Council) rather than the head of government, itself a reflection of the lower political priority given to arms exports in Germany.

Political direction in Sweden is centred on the Minister for Foreign Trade within the Ministry for Foreign Affairs and two parliamentary oversight committees, the Advisory Council on Foreign Affairs and the Export Control Council. Prior to 1996 and the formation of an independent licensing agency, the Minister for Foreign Trade was also responsible for deciding on most licence applications. However, the formation of an independent licensing agency is in keeping with the Swedish administrative and political tradition, whereby all the core ministries or political departments are small (usually fewer than 100 people, including clerical staff) and there is a high degree of decentralization to relatively independent governmental agencies. Similarly, in Germany the ministries effectively make policy and leave the day-to-day administrative tasks to an independent agency. This approach is also characteristic of German public administration generally, and is a tradition that predates the creation of the Federal Republic. In the UK, on the other hand, administrative business and policy are handled within specialized departments within the ministries.

Differences can also be found in the degree of diffusion of authority across government ministries and agencies, and in the influence of policy stakeholders, as discussed above. Ministries and agencies have specific and often opposing policy positions that mirror their traditional goals and their standing in the wider policy agenda of the government of the day. In the UK, for example,

---

[65] Deltac Ltd and Saferworld (note 64), p. xiv.

export licences are administered by the DTI and policed by Customs, but the policy guidelines within which the DTI and Customs work are largely driven by the goals of the advisory departments (the MOD, the FCO and since mid-1997, the DFID). These goals have often been poorly defined and each department has sought to bring a unique commercial, military or foreign policy understanding to the problem.[66] These multiple perspectives clearly make coordination of a consistent national position problematic (and often make coordination at the EU level difficult, as discussed in chapters 3 and 4), and have resulted in policy guidelines that are full of contrasts and inconsistencies.

In Germany, the two main advisory ministries—the foreign and defence ministries—have generally displayed more of a shared understanding of policy objectives than their British equivalents, although this cohesiveness broke down in the 1980s when the Foreign Ministry began to favour a more restrictive approach. However, it was not until 1989 (and a change in public opinion following a number of exports scandals) that the Foreign Ministry was able to mount a serious challenge and later end the dominant role of the Economics Ministry. With a similar transformation taking place in the UK in the late 1990s under the New Labour government, and bearing in mind the Ministry for Foreign Affairs' long-standing dominance of Swedish export control policy, there is a clear and growing convergence around the primacy of the foreign office in all three countries.

One of the main remaining differences in the roles of the advisory ministries in the UK as compared with the other two countries (apart from the fact that both Germany and Sweden have delegated responsibility for licensing decisions from their ministries to independent agencies) is the continuing influence of the Ministry of Defence. In Germany and Sweden the defence ministries only have a minor role in export control policy, while in the UK the MOD (and especially the DESO, as described above) continues to have a high-profile role in the direction of both policy and individual licensing decisions.[67]

Export criteria

The criteria for deciding individual export applications are a key policy component for any export control regime. Such criteria have been a long-established tradition within all three export control regimes, but levels of transparency, the

---

[66] E.g., interdepartmental differences over the categorization of machine tools as either dual-use or 'specially designed' for military use were central to the Matrix Churchill case. Scott Report (note 37), paras 151–52, pp. 1125–39.

[67] An illustration of the continuing conflict of interest within and between British government departments and within the government was indicated by leaked Cabinet papers from Sep. 1997. These include a letter from Defence Secretary George Robertson to Foreign Secretary Robin Cook urging him to reconsider the refusal to export 6 armoured Land Rovers to Indonesia because of the cost to British jobs and because they were destined to the 'enlightened' General Prabowo of the Indonesian Special Forces. A month later the general was dismissed from the Indonesian armed forces for human rights abuses. The licence application was eventually refused. *Independent on Sunday*, 26 July 1998; *Jane's Defence Weekly*, 9 Sep. 1998, p. 30; and evidence of Amnesty International UK to the British House of Commons Select Committee on Trade and Industry, *Strategic Export Controls*, HC 1998/99 65 (Her Majesty's Stationery Office: London, 2 Dec. 1998), p. 13.

scope of the guidelines and adherence to them have differed widely between and within the three countries over time. In the UK until 1997, for example, each individual government department was largely responsible for framing its own internal guidelines, and these rarely entered the public domain. The new criteria introduced by the Labour government in 1997 are much more comprehensive and represent the first clear statement of public policy on this issue. Nonetheless, they remain voluntary guidelines as they have not been codified in law. This is also the case in Germany, where a set of export principles was first agreed by the government in 1971. These principles were amended in 1982 and eventually replaced by a new set of policy guidelines in January 2000. In contrast, Sweden's guidelines (first introduced in 1971) are enshrined in national legislation.

The differences between the three sets of criteria as they stood for much of the cold war period (the most recent versions of all three are reproduced in appendix A) were often considerable. For example, Germany had criteria which denied exports to countries at war and selected items to 'areas of tension', while the UK, until the adoption of new criteria in 1997, did not automatically prohibit sales to countries at war. Similarly, the UK specifically mentioned terrorism, while Germany did not.

The ability to formulate national export criteria was traditionally equated with notions of national sovereignty, but by the end of the 1980s many member states saw such thinking as anachronistic. The ensuing discussions within the EU in the 1990s led to the development of common criteria and a growing measure of convergence in this area. This convergence began with the agreement on the eight Common Criteria in 1991–92 and deepened with the adoption of the 1998 EU Code of Conduct—to the extent that all member states now operate from a common policy baseline (although some more restrictive national guidelines continue to be applied by certain countries in certain circumstances[68]). Of course, the adoption of common criteria does not necessarily result in a common interpretation—and there was certainly a failure to adopt a common interpretation or implementation of the eight Common Criteria (the UK, for example, adopted a much looser interpretation than Germany)—but the code is a clear improvement on the Common Criteria. Under it, member states are required to take into account the effect of arms sales on *inter alia* human rights, regional stability and economic and social development. One of the strongest commitments, for example, is that EU governments will not issue export licences if there is a clear risk that the arms will be used for internal repression. Moreover, as discussed in chapter 4, the code's operative provisions offer a new dimension that is designed to secure common interpretation.

The key question now will be how the EU member states apply the operative provisions and implement the guidelines in practice. If they are applied and implemented in full they should lead to increased restraint and a closer align-

---

[68] Sweden, e.g., has since 1993 made the distinction between 'military equipment for combat purposes' and 'other military equipment', with much more restrictive criteria being applied to the former. See chapter 7.

ment of EU states' arms export policies. As the code has only been operating for a short time it is too early to say what effect it is having on the arms export policies of member states or whether some of the potential weaknesses in both the guidelines and the operative provisions, as discussed in chapter 4, are being exploited. Nonetheless, it is an important step towards establishing common responsibility and restraint in conventional arms exports across the EU as a whole.

Regulatory oversight

Regulatory oversight can come in many guises, from prior or subsequent parliamentary scrutiny of export control legislation and/or licensing decisions to transparency mechanisms that allow non-governmental and public oversight. While each state has traditionally chosen a different path in this area, some convergence is beginning to occur as a result of the transparency mechanisms in the EU Code. In Germany the legal framework for export controls requires the assent of Parliament, and this will soon be the case in the UK as well. However, neither Germany nor the UK has traditionally involved its parliament to any significant extent either in the formulation of the export guidelines or in scrutinizing individual licence decisions. These tasks have always been undertaken within the export control bureaucracies of the two countries and without consulting their respective parliaments. Of the three countries, only Sweden subjects its export control policy to sustained and systematic parliamentary attention. This is achieved through a parliamentary advisory council made up of representatives of all political parties, which meets once a month to scrutinize potentially sensitive export licence applications.

In both Germany and the UK there have been sporadic suggestions both within and from outside their parliaments for a similar level of oversight, but for the present this is limited to retrospective and ad hoc consideration by parliamentary committees. There are also differences between the three countries in the amount of information they release on this issue—about the decision making on individual licences and the general reporting of the overall picture of the regulatory environment—and in their reasons for withholding information (as discussed above). These differences have begun to diminish, however, as all three have legislative and administrative actions either planned or already in place which will significantly improve transparency and considerably increase the range of information supplied by each government. The UK, for example, introduced an annual reporting system in March 1999 and Germany did likewise, under the terms of the Code of Conduct, in September 2000. Sweden has been publishing an annual report on arms exports since 1985. However, the new British reporting system appears to be the most detailed by any European state so far and sets a new benchmark for transparency within the EU.

The administrative structure

Publication of export guidelines

The licensing authorities in all three countries produce a wide range of material in different formats—booklets, software training packages, education seminars and so on—to increase awareness of export control policies and procedures. All three countries also make use of the Internet to publish summaries of their arms export policies (in the cases of Germany and Sweden, in a number of different languages) in order to improve awareness of those policies elsewhere in Europe and the wider world.

The decision-making process for licence applications

The three licensing processes have much in common. In all three cases, decision making is the responsibility of a single agency or an agency attached to or under the authority of a specific ministry. However, as discussed above, there are clear differences between the three countries in the level of diffusion of authority across government ministries and agencies. More specifically, only the UK continues to house its licensing authority within a government ministry, the DTI. Moreover, that ministry is responsible for both promoting and restricting exports, a dual role which brings into question the extent to which the balance of export controls is weighted in favour of granting licences.[69] In addition, as stated above, there are potential conflicts within and between the two other main advisory departments in the UK, the FCO and the MOD. In contrast, in both Sweden (since 1996) and Germany (since 1992), principal responsibility for licensing is located in one independent authority which does not have a contradictory promotion role.

In Sweden the ability of ministers to influence individual licensing decisions is also constrained by the constitution. As discussed above, all the core ministries or political departments in Sweden (including the Ministry for Foreign Affairs) are small and there is a high degree of decentralization to relatively independent governmental agencies (including the licensing authority, the ISP). The ISP has to observe the general and particular export control laws, ordinances and instructions, while the Minister for Foreign Trade cannot change the outcome of a specific licensing decision. If the minister disagrees with a particular decision, a general change to the legal framework under which the ISP operates has to be sought. In both Germany and the UK ministers have a much freer hand to dictate individual licensing decisions.

Another area of commonality between the three countries is the process of sending certain licence applications for inter-agency review or scrutiny by individuals with special expertise. Whether or not such scrutiny occurs is left to the discretion of the competent licensing authority. However, not only are there differences in the levels of discretion, but the weight and influence of the

[69] This was a concern in the Scott Report (note 37), para. C2.18.

agencies differ from country to country. In Germany and Sweden the foreign ministry plays a pivotal role in arms transfer decisions, whereas in the UK the MOD shares centre stage with the FCO.

Export licensing practices have changed in all three countries since the end of the cold war, both in terms of the number of licence applications handled and in terms of the numbers of staff working on them, but the changes have been most pronounced in Germany and the UK (largely as a result of the introduction of general licences in an effort to reduce numbers of licence applications). In the late 1980s, for example, the UK received approximately 90 000 licence applications each year and Germany approximately 80 000, but following the introduction of general licences in the early 1990s, the number of licence applications per year currently stands at approximately 16 000 in the UK and 25 000 in Germany. In contrast, the number of applications for export licences in Sweden has remained relatively constant at approximately 2000 per year. Even the introduction in 1993 of licences for 'other military equipment' (mainly dual-use goods for which licences were not previously required) has not significantly altered the picture.

In terms of the number and percentage of licence applications refused, Germany and the UK follow similar patterns (i.e., very low refusal rates). In Sweden there are no statistics for negative decisions because these are weeded out at an earlier, pre-licence stage. Indeed, this reflects a major difference in the decision-making process for licence applications between Sweden on the one hand, and Germany and the UK on the other. Sweden's administrative process operates on the basis of close and regular negotiation between industry and government. This cooperative approach has a number of unique features, including a registration system for all traders and brokers involved in the arms trade within the jurisdiction of the national territory; the requirement of a licence for the manufacture of military equipment (in addition to exporting it); an obligation on the company to provide an annual report on its ownership structure and a quarterly report on its marketing activities; rigorous examination of applications to transfer manufacturing rights or join collaborative development programmes; prior scrutiny of sensitive applications by a parliamentary committee (the Export Control Council); and self-financing of the ISP through a levy on strategic and military exports. In addition, the Swedish system allows the government to object to a potential export early on in the process.

In contrast, the British and German decision-making processes attempt to keep the manufacturers at arm's length (at least in theory) and, as discussed previously, involve a greater degree of interdepartmental rivalry. However, in both countries, before formal application for an export licence is made it is common practice in respect of certain weapon transfers for informal consultation to take place—between industry and the foreign ministry in the case of Germany and between industry and the export-oriented DESO in the case of the UK. Both these informal processes are often the primary locus of decision making on the approval of military exports, rather than the subsequent formal licensing process.

Compliance and enforcement procedures

Compliance and enforcement procedures in the three countries are structured around the same types of mechanisms—end-use controls, border controls, company audits, intelligence work and so on. There are key legal, policy and operational differences between them, but it is in the design and stringency of end-use monitoring and certification that variations between them are most significant.

First, as mentioned already, only Germany applies a military catch-all control to certain non-embargoed destinations (whereas the British and Swedish catch-all is limited to exports in relation to WMD and, once the new EU Regulation enters into force, military dual-use exports to embargoed destinations).

Second, there are many variations in the end-use certificates in operation in the three countries and little commonality between them, especially now that the system devised within COCOM of International Import Certificates and Delivery Verification Certificates has largely been phased out. Efforts are continuing within COARM, the Wassenaar Arrangement and other international forums to develop more effective and common certification but with little sign of success so far.[70]

Third, the monitoring and enforcement of end-use assurances has differed between the three countries (and within each country) over time in terms of the number and scope of end-use certificates monitored and the allocation of resources. Only Germany, for example, has introduced (in 1991) legislation requiring exporting companies to appoint a Person Responsible for Exports and obtain a certificate of reliability from the Federal Export Office. The named company official is also responsible for assessing end-use, and can later be held accountable for any foreseeable diversion. In contrast, British governments have traditionally been unwilling to monitor or enforce end-user assurances (and have tended to accept a greater proportion of end-use statements from non-government recipients than either Sweden or Germany). There is now growing convergence: the current British Government is committed to strengthening end-use controls and is currently reviewing the options. However, the UK will be starting from a much weaker technical and resource baseline than Germany and Sweden. Both these countries already have in place computerized export data collection systems with many innovative tracking and monitoring features (as described in detail in chapters 6 and 7). In contrast, in the UK each government department (the MOD, the DTI, Customs and the FCO) has produced its own information technology solution, but with no means of cross-checking databases. As one insider in Whitehall commented: 'We have all got white elephants, that took so long to design that they were almost out of date by the

---

[70] E.g., at a regional conference in Sofia in 1999 under the auspices of the Stability Pact for South Eastern Europe the participants agreed a Statement on the Harmonization of End-Use/End-User Certificates which made a number of proposals in this area. 'Chairman's summary and contribution of the Bulgarian delegation', Regional Conference on Export Controls, Sofia, 14–15 Dec. 1999.

time they were installed. There is no easy cross-Whitehall link. The DTI, FCO and MoD can't yet speak electronically'.[71]

As a result, the Select Committee on Trade and Industry recommended in 1996 that the DTI, FCO and MoD 'allow mutual access to their computerised information relating to export licensing and that the DTI's export licensing database be developed for the benefit of all three departments'.[72]

There are also marked differences between the three countries in terms of available sanctions and conviction rates for illegal activities. While no accurate record of all pending and concluded court cases concerning breaches of the export regulations in each country has been obtained, it seems that Germany has been more successful in achieving convictions than the UK. The situation in Sweden is not known. In Germany, for example, 117 individuals were sentenced to prison terms following convictions under the War Weapons Control Act (KWKG) between 1986 and 1991.[73] In contrast, the UK has had difficulty in gaining only a handful of convictions, and in a number of high-profile cases (including the 'Supergun' and Matrix Churchill affairs) charges were dropped because of inconclusive evidence.

The severity and nature of sanctions vary widely between the three countries. While all three threaten to punish intentional breaches of the law, the situation is less clear in respect of unintentional breaches or secondary offences, such as instigation, support and assistance. Clear provision for the punishment of secondary acts is made in Germany, but in Sweden and the UK the situation is more ambiguous. Vast differences also remain in the severity of punishment. Germany, for example, currently imposes the strictest sentences for fraudulent exports. Maximum prison sentences range from two years in Sweden and seven years in the UK to the maximum of 10 years in Germany. Fines vary as well, but in all three cases it can be said that these are far outweighed by the likely profits to be made from major transfers. In Germany, there is the possibility of seizing the profits, or the sale value, of the goods concerned, but no such provisions within Swedish or UK law.

V. Conclusions

EU policy making and decision making generally display profound gradualism and incrementalism, and arms export policy making is no exception. Alterations, escape clauses and long transitional periods before full implementation routinely impede promising ideas. Moreover, powerful obstacles to radical change are particularly prevalent in the CFSP field, and arise because of differing national and ideological positions and perspectives. This political and ideological heterogeneity has deep historical roots and member states are under-

---

[71] Personal interview, 1997.

[72] British House of Commons, Select Committee on Trade and Industry, *Third Report: Export Licensing and BMARC*, HC 1995/96 87-I (Her Majesty's Stationery Office: London, 12 June 1996), para. 75, p. xxviii.

[73] Müller *et al.* (note 45), pp. 35–36.

standably reluctant to lose control of their foreign policies. Some also have traditional and special relationships (often cemented through arms deals) with particular parts of the world which they are anxious to maintain.

This does not mean that change and reform are not possible. On the contrary, this study has clearly shown that there has been significant progress since the early 1990s. Indeed, we may look back in time and say that the 1990s was a decade when a lot happened. The changes discussed have been driven by a range of internal and external factors, and have been guided and shaped by complex interactions between EU and national level political forces.

Overall, the policy-making structures in the three countries showed the clearest signs of convergence in the 1990s, and this is likely to deepen in the early years of the new century. Much of the export control legislation (particularly for dual-use goods), the lists of controlled weapons and dual-use goods, and the export guidelines adhered to by national bureaucracies are now virtually identical in all three countries. Even in those areas where differences continue to exist, as with regard to brokering, common approaches are likely to be negotiated in the near future. Other areas traditionally associated with a distinctly national approach, such as regulatory oversight and transparency, also appear to be subject to the functionalist draw of convergence. In the past there has been a considerable lack of transparency and democratic participation in both the German and the British regimes as compared with the Swedish regime. However, there is now a growing convergence among the three towards greater transparency, even though parliamentary control of arms exports continues to be absent in Germany and the UK, and only in Sweden is there a mechanism in place to inform its parliament and allow debate prior to a transfer. Finally, the greatest area of difference within the policy-making framework of the three regimes lies in the identity and make-up of the national policy-making communities themselves. In the absence of a supranational agency, such national differences will continue—a reflection of different political and normative traditions within each of the respective bureaucracies.

A summary of the study and the main conclusions are now discussed in chapter 9. The discussion centres on the questions first raised in the opening chapter.

9. Conclusions

I. Convergence

The main objective of this study was to examine whether the process of European integration (in particular, the harmonization of regulatory policies within the EU) is leading to a convergence of national arms and dual-use export control regimes in EU member states. As a subsidiary objective, it also sought to evaluate the likely consequences arising from such convergence for international efforts to control the proliferation of conventional weapons and dual-use technologies.

As far as the three focus states—the UK, Germany and Sweden—are concerned, the main conclusions that can be drawn with respect to the convergence question are as follows:

1. *The process of European integration in the 1990s led to a significant but incomplete convergence of their arms and dual-use export control regimes.* As shown by table 8.5, the use of more advanced instruments of convergence clearly increased between the mid-1980s and the mid-1990s, and overall this suggests a shift from a position of weak mutual recognition to limited but increasing coordination within the EU during this period.

2. *At the end of the 1990s, convergence was more advanced for dual-use technologies than for military goods.* Dual-use export controls moved from advanced levels of mutual recognition in the mid-1980s to advanced levels of coordination in the mid- to late 1990s, including some aspects of explicit harmonization. In contrast, arms export controls were still being strongly influenced by notions of national autonomy in the mid-1980s and only limited mutual recognition was possible. From this lower base-line convergence of arms export controls progressed to advanced levels of mutual recognition and some limited coordination by the mid-1990s.

3. *Convergence accelerated during the late 1990s.* This acceleration (vis-à-vis the introduction of the EU Code of Conduct and measures to combat illicit trafficking in small arms) was most pronounced with regard to arms export controls which, by the end of 1999, were being subjected to much higher and more rigorous standards of coordination than was the case only two years previously. The introduction of the EU Code also increased the convergence of dual-use export controls, as licensing decisions for these exports also became subject to the common criteria contained in the Code.

4. *Although both policy-making and policy-execution structures in the three countries showed clear signs of convergence in the 1990s, by the end of the decade convergence was more advanced for the former rather than the latter.* In the mid-1980s, policy-making structures tended to display high levels of

mutual recognition and some limited coordination for dual-use exports. By the mid- to late 1990s, however, much more consistent and advanced levels of coordination in policy making were in place, including some explicit harmonization (for dual-use exports). National administrative (policy-execution) structures, on the other hand, were much more autonomous and displayed only limited mutual recognition in the mid-1980s. Again, however, by the mid- to late 1990s convergence had advanced to stronger and more consistent levels of mutual recognition and some limited coordination (particularly in enforcement and compliance procedures).

5. *Further convergence can be expected in the period to 2010 and beyond.* While this is difficult to prove, table 8.5 suggests that the arms and dual-use export controls of the three countries are likely to continue to converge in the coming years around even higher levels of intergovernmental coordination and with further examples of explicit harmonization. While the scope and pace of this convergence will be contingent on future changes in the policy environment (especially the potential for deeper political integration and the development of a Single European Defence Market) and the future actions of policy stakeholders, there are strong grounds for believing that many of the factors which led to significant convergence in the 1990s will continue to shape the policy agenda in the new decade.

There are a number of reasons for reaching these conclusions. This chapter summarizes those reasons and in so doing addresses the other questions outlined in chapter 1. The chapter ends with a brief exploration of the implications that flow from these conclusions for future multilateral arms export controls.

II. The key questions revisited

Why do countries differ in the ways in which they engage in regulation of arms and dual-use transfers?

The differences in the regulatory approaches of the UK, Germany and Sweden (including variations in the export control criteria, the goods and technologies under control, the specific bodies with responsibility for decision making, the execution of those decisions, and the compliance and enforcement procedures) are rooted in the different policy environments that shape policy formulation and execution. Chapter 1 suggested that the policy environment for strategic export controls contains a number of overlapping 'policy shaping' elements, namely the different state strategies adopted towards arms production and exports, systemic and international normative constraints, and the influence of domestic policy stakeholders. Each of these elements was discussed in the individual case studies in chapters 5, 6 and 7. Chapter 8 then evaluated the relative importance of these and another explanation—the different administrative norms associated with policy implementation—for the continuing divergence in the national regulatory approaches.

The main conclusion was that policy differences, including changes in the scope and speed of change of those policies over time, mainly arise as a result of different foreign policy and economic strategies, but that variations in domestic political support for strict export controls between the three countries over time and the national administrative structures can also be significant determining factors. In turn, these differences are rooted in each state's unique historical normative framework.

Germany chose a trading state strategy, emphasized multilateral institutions in its foreign policy and restricted the use of its armed forces largely as a moral response to past German militarism. As a result of this normative framework, German export controls draw a fundamental distinction between military weapons (under the KWKG legislation) and dual-use goods (under the AWG legislation), with a restrictive policy on the former and a much more liberal approach to the latter. In contrast, regulation of both arms and dual-use exports by the UK was dominated by contradictory economic, security and political motives which were largely framed by the retreat from empire, a strong commitment to the fight against communism and a declining manufacturing base. Finally, for Sweden, the concept of armed neutrality was reflected in the high priority that Swedes placed on confidence-building measures, peaceful settlement of conflicts and human rights. These concerns were also central to the criteria that governed their arms and dual-use export control regime.

The relationship between structure and agency in shaping arms and dual-use export controls in the three countries is complex. In summary, the historical normative framework has tended to structure the policy agenda in each case, while political choices have determined how the policy agenda is to be understood and implemented.

Do these differences have consequences for the diffusion of arms and military-related technology?

Even relatively successful multilateral export control regimes (such as the former COCOM regime) can only be expected at best to slow down the diffusion of controlled technology. Thus, the impact of the differences between the three national export control regimes discussed here on global diffusion trends is only likely to be marginal. The evidence suggests that the divergences and variations in regulatory processes and approaches between the three countries have had the most impact on a limited number of specific arms and technologies to specific destinations at specific points in time.

For dual-use goods and technologies, the process of regulation in the three countries tended to be far more divergent (up until the introduction of the EU Dual-Use Regulation in 1995) than the actual levels of control achieved. In other words, the three countries tended to get quite similar results in different ways. Germany was arguably more lax than the UK in licensing dual-use exports throughout the 1980s, and Sweden only applied limited COCOM-related restrictions on dual-use goods until 1993. However, with the exception of a few very sensitive destinations and technologies (e.g., the re-exports of US technologies from Sweden to the Soviet Union in the late 1970s and early 1980s), dual-use export controls in each of the three countries were reasonably effective to COCOM-proscribed destinations but less so to a number of other destinations (most notably Iraq in the late 1980s).

Differences in policy outcomes for arms exports were often (but not always) far more pronounced. While the British Government generally encouraged the sale of defence equipment unless there were compelling reasons not to do so, exports of German arms (with the exception of naval equipment) to non-NATO countries usually faced tighter restrictions, particularly to regions of tension and developing nations. Swedish arms export controls were also generally more prohibitive than the UK's but with a number of exemptions which allowed some exports to the developing world. East and South Asia, the Middle East and Europe are the regions where these policy differences have had the most impact (as discussed in chapter 8).

What are the main obstacles to agreement on EU export control regimes?

Although Article 223 has been the main legal obstacle to EU involvement in defence trade matters, it is the differing national foreign, security and trade policy interests underpinning the legislation that are the main obstacles. This political and ideological heterogeneity has deep historical roots and member states are understandably reluctant to yield sovereignty in this area.

Is the current framework for harmonizing European arms and dual-use export controls based on intergovernmentalism, supranationalism or a 'middle way'?

European integration is a multifaceted and complex phenomenon, capable of being approached in a number of ways. Two opposing theoretical perspectives from the discipline of international relations—functionalism and intergovernmentalism—tended to dominate the early debates on the nature of European integration. The former was developed from functional theories of macro-regional integration and the latter from neo-realist theories of international relations. A third perspective—policy network theory—has tended to dominate research in this area in recent years. However, functionalism, intergovernmentalism and the study of policy networks offer complementary rather than competitive approaches to understanding the process of European integration. The integration of member states' arms and dual-use export controls is also best explained by a synthesis of these approaches.

Overall, the concept of 'reactive spillover'[1] seems to have the strongest resonance, in that it captures elements of both intergovernmentalism and func-

---

[1] Guay, T., 'The limits of regional integration: the European Union and Europe's defense industry', Paper presented at the International Studies Association Annual Conference, San Diego, Calif., 18 Apr. 1996, p. 8 (unpublished), uses the term to describe the process of integration within the European defence

tionalism, as well as being sensitive to external factors (such as international trade liberalization and the ending of the cold war). Here the concept is taken to mean a combination of the reaction within the national policy-making bodies to external forces—one possible reaction is an increase or decrease in the level of intergovernmental bargaining within multilateral control regimes—with the spillover effect from EU economic and political integration.

Reactive spillover offers a particularly strong explanation for the creation of the EU Dual-Use Regulation. Although the regulation started out as a European Commission initiative (demonstrating 'cultivated spillover') as a result of the Single European Market imperative (demonstrating 'functional spillover'), it was later commandeered by national governments and turned into a partial foreign policy and defence issue (demonstrating intergovernmental bargaining). Prior to the introduction of a new Regulation in June 2000, the result was a compromise between a Community Regulation and an intergovernmental Decision (under the Joint Action procedure). However, the new Regulation returns competence to the European Community.

While the 'spillover effect' is strong in respect of dual-use goods, it is much weaker in respect of major conventional weapon systems. The lack of supra-national regulatory legitimacy in the security field has led to the construction of separate EU control regimes for weaponry and sensitive dual-use items, with convergence more advanced for the latter than the former. Moreover, the har-monization of EU dual-use controls was facilitated by a simultaneous liberaliza-tion of international dual-use controls (as witnessed by the replacement of COCOM with the much weaker Wassenaar Arrangement). For arms export controls, however, despite the Commission and European Parliament making a strong contribution to agenda setting, the most influential EU bodies in this area (namely the Council of the European Union and COARM) remain pre-dominantly intergovernmental, and overall authority on licensing decisions continues to rest with national governments (as it also does for dual-use exports).

Reactive spillover is also useful for explaining the acceleration in the pace of integration in arms export controls in the latter part of the 1990s. From 1957 until entry into force of the Maastricht Treaty in 1993, there was little effort by member states to collectively coordinate, control or restrain arms and dual-use exports. The only concrete exception was the limited coordination of arms embargoes against specific countries in the 1980s through the EPC framework. With the replacement of the EPC process by the CFSP in 1993, intergovern-mental cooperation became a more formal affair and enabled greater and more effective cooperation on defence-related trade matters through information exchange, common positions and joint actions (chapter 4). The acceleration in

sector, which is said to involve a combination of the defence sector's reaction to external forces and the spillover effect from EU economic integration. Guay also describes 3 other forms of spillover: 'functional' (the technical pressures that build up to integrate other areas of policy once one set of policies has been developed at the EU level); political (the shift in focus of interest groups, political parties and other national political elites from the national level to EU institutions); and 'cultivated' (the setting of agendas and pushing for policies that favour further integration by European institutions).

the process of integration in this policy area during 1997 and 1998 produced agreement on the EU Code of Conduct on Arms Exports, and the introduction of the EU Programme for Preventing and Combating Illicit Arms Trafficking and the EU Joint Action on Small Arms.

Although all three measures started out as initiatives of one or more individual member states and were developed within the framework of COARM (thus demonstrating strong intergovernmentalism), all had a strong external stimulus. Growing international and domestic concern over small arms proliferation in the late 1990s, for example, provided pressure for the development of the EU Programme and EU Joint Action. Similarly, the introduction of the EU Code was facilitated by the efforts of an EU-wide campaign by NGOs for tighter restrictions on arms exports and by the advent of left-of-centre governments in many of the EU member states (and especially in France and the UK).

Moreover, as all three measures have begun to be implemented there are increasing signs of functional and cultivated spillover, and the emergence of an EU-level policy network. The issue of arms trafficking, in particular, cuts across important institutional and organizational divisions, both nationally and within the EU. Effective administrative cooperation between the member states and consultations on policy issues have therefore necessitated the development of a network of national officials responsible for export controls. Thus, having started out as intergovernmental initiatives, they are now being commandeered by EU institutions and EU-wide policy networks. In addition, the EU Code of Conduct, if it works well, is likely to lead to further functional spillover and a strengthening of the EU-level policy network (which is currently centred on COARM).

What are the norms and control standards around which convergence is taking place?

In her critique of regime analysis, Susan Strange argues that 'the tendency toward symbolism, expressed in a proliferation of Declarations, Charters, Codes of Conduct, and other rather empty texts, has strengthened as the ability to reach agreement on positive action to solve real global problems has weakened'.[2] It is the contention of this study, however, that the symbolism and rather empty texts of the early 1990s (including the eight Common Criteria agreed within the EU and the P5, UNDC and OSCE principles) have been replaced in the EU by much stronger normative control standards in the late 1990s. In short, the recent changes discussed in chapters 3 and 4 represent a clear turning point. From a previous position of simply coordinating shared national interests, the EU Code of Conduct and the Dual-Use Regulation now allow member states to negotiate to reconcile divergent national interests. The importance of the earlier 'empty declarations' should not be underestimated, however, as they

---

[2] Strange, S., 'Cave! Hic dragones: a critique of regime analysis', ed. S. Krasner, *International Regimes* (Cornell University Press: Ithaca, N.Y., 1983), p. 342.

helped to create the conditions for the Code of Conduct to be agreed by establishing the principle of common action in this policy area.

While the UK, Germany and Sweden continue to adopt different foreign policies in relation to specific countries, the broader systemic and normative differences that help shape those policies have increasingly become less important in recent years. The reality is that there are now more areas of agreement between the three countries than there are areas of disagreement and controversy. The core security interests and humanitarian concerns around which their arms and dual-use export control policies are converging were discussed in chapter 2 and are reflected in the EU Code of Conduct (chapter 4 and appendix A). In summary, these shared beliefs are that :

1. The acquisition of military or sensitive dual-use technologies by certain proscribed states and sensitive end-users poses a security threat to both national security and their 'extended' common interests.

2. Extended common interests include preventing the export of military equipment which might (*a*) be used for internal repression or international aggression, (*b*) contribute to regional instability or (*c*) undermine the sustainable development of the recipient country.

3. A code of conduct can be an effective and efficient means of addressing these security threats, but only if the export guidelines are supported by confidence-building provisions that enhance transparency and information exchange, and prevent 'undercutting'.

4. The decision to transfer or deny the transfer of any item of military or dual-use equipment ultimately remains a national prerogative.

What policy measures are needed for achieving a credible and effective EU control regime?

In particular, what changes would be necessary in the oversight and regulatory functions of the various national government departments and agencies of member states, whose responsibilities touch on arms and dual-use export controls?

It was predicted in chapter 8 that the convergence of member states' arms and dual-use export controls will be a long and evolutionary process. The subjection to Community competence (if it happens at all) will be the final stage and is likely to be preceded by various transitional stages. The EU Dual-Use Regulation, the Code of Conduct and measures to combat illicit trafficking of small arms are all transitional measures, which are made less effective by the continuing disparities in national practice and attitudes alluded to in chapter 8.

Given that these controls now focus more on end-users and end-use (where previous regimes like COCOM focused on countries), a key priority is to improve current procedures for monitoring and enforcing end-use. End-use provisions are clearly inadequate in the EU (as shown by the case studies in part III of this volume) and elsewhere. A variety of end-use documents and procedures are currently in operation across the 15 member states, and as first step these need to be harmonized around 'best practice'. More far-reaching and more difficult to achieve would be an international agreement which gives end-use certificates the status of legally binding contracts, with clauses that allow follow-up checks and which debar future deliveries if the goods are found to have been used for proscribed purposes.

Given also that end-use controls require cooperation on intelligence gathering and analysis, the absence of a Community database of information on licences and sensitive end-users is another cause for concern. Although some intelligence dissemination does occur within the other non-proliferation regimes, and between individual member states on an ad hoc basis, a more coordinated and systematic approach by member states will probably be necessary to ensure an effective external 'fence'. There may also be scope to adapt and develop existing cooperative structures between police forces, intelligence services and justice ministries to the control of dual-use and arms exports (see below).

Will the EU need to cooperate with other major suppliers outside the EU (particularly the USA) and, if so, what form should that cooperation take?

Because the EU still only accounts for less than one-third of the global market in arms exports, member states will still need to cooperate closely with other major suppliers (especially the USA) in building effective multilateral arms and dual-use export control regimes. Nonetheless, the EU is a vital link in the argument that a mixture of specific international agencies and common policies of the major countries can regulate the international arms and dual-use trade.

Now that the EU member states have developed the first stages of a viable institutional architecture and common policies towards the regulation of arms and dual-use goods within their own sphere of influence, the scope for wider international regulation has been significantly increased.

Indeed, one of the key commitments within the EU Code—the requirement that member states work for wider subscription to the principles of the code among other arms-exporting countries—began to be realized almost immediately with declarations of support for the principles by the 13 non-EU associate countries and others (as discussed in chapter 4). However, it still remains to be seen where the EU Code will fit in the division of labour between the different multilateral security structures. In other words, if the EU Code is to be extended across Central and Eastern Europe, and to the United States and Russia, what is the best way to do this? Should it be through the Wassenaar Arrangement, through the OSCE, through other regional and international forums, or through a combination of all of these approaches? How the member states go about widening adherence to the EU Code will be as important a challenge as deepening the existing ties within the EU.

One way forward, for example, would be for other regimes and organizations, especially the OSCE and the Wassenaar Arrangement, to establish a group of experts to consider some of the options in more detail. In the case of the OSCE, for example, these include building on the 1993 OSCE Principles (discussed in chapter 2 and reproduced in appendix A) and the 2000 OSCE Document on Small Arms and Light Weapons[3] so that they eventually match the EU Code's guidelines, and developing a programme and timetable for the implementation of the code's operative provisions within the OSCE. EU member states could assist in this process by sharing information on the implementation of the code within the OSCE and other international forums. In the beginning, such an information exchange might only involve fairly basic material, such as the annual consolidated report and information on current export control legislation. Later it could be extended to the circulation of licence denials either as they are issued or on an aggregate basis every six months.

Eventually it is possible to see the international community moving beyond the partial governance of specific weapon systems and the periodic crisis management of excessive arms transfers to a cooperative regulatory regime consisting of a number of core elements. This study ends with a brief discussion of these core elements and some suggestions for further research.

III. The next steps in multilateral arms and dual-use export controls

The overview of multilateral arms export control measures in chapter 2 illustrated the ad hoc nature of existing regimes. The wide range of mechanisms that are in place have many inadequacies which appear difficult to address within the traditional security and arms control framework. This concluding section considers the case for new conceptual thinking based on the lessons from developments within the EU.

Whither arms and dual-use export controls?

What is the role of arms and dual-use export controls a decade or so after the end of the cold war? There are broadly three post-cold war models of strategic thought—hard realism, soft neo-realism and common security[4]—and each carries a range of possibilities concerning the future shape of European security and defence integration. The first adheres to a cold war containment paradigm in which defence remains a matter for states and alliances, with the core problem of how to organize the security of the European continent being met by the 'collective security' arrangement in NATO. The re-nationalization of security policy also remains an option within this perspective.

---

[3] Organization for Security and Co-operation in Europe, 'Document on small arms and light weapons', approved by the OSCE Ministerial Council at Vienna on 27–28 Nov. 2000. The document in reproduced in *SIPRI Yearbook 2001: Armaments, Disarmament and International Security* (Oxford University Press: Oxford, 2001), pp. 590–98.

[4] Adapted from Chilton, P., 'Common, collective, or combined? Theories of defense integration in the European Union', eds C. Rhodes and S. Mazey, *The State of the European Union, Vol. 3: Building a European Polity?* (Longman: Harlow, 1995), p. 82.

The second and dominant model, subscribed to by both neo-realist and liberal traditions, recognizes that member states of the EU are no longer part of a tight bipolar political and ideological international system but urges caution and a step-wise approach to change. Thus, although there may be a growing awareness of an extended concept of security, preference continues to be given to the military 'collective security' option, either through NATO or through the WEU, rather than reliance on predominantly non-military multilateral institutions.

The third model, critical of realist and neo-realist world views, urges proactive change based on wider conceptions of security, with efforts to strengthen other multilateral institutions (such as the UN and the OSCE) given preference over defence. Advocates of this common or cooperative security approach stress the importance of negotiated common goals, norms, institutions and procedures.[5]

The process of shaping a cooperative security system is still in its infancy, however. The process is not automatic and the outcome is by no means certain. The continued emphasis on military security and power projection within NATO and the proliferation of intra-state conflicts suggest that the second perspective continues to dominate European and transatlantic security thinking.[6] Thus, European defence integration continues to take place primarily within the context of developments within NATO and the transatlantic partnership (the NATO–WEU nexus) rather than in the context of the EU and Maastricht (the EU–WEU nexus).

It is also clear that these three frameworks provide for a range of possibilities within the field of arms and dual-use export controls. In both the first and the second models, control strategies for exports will continue to be based largely on technology denial, combined on occasions with more coercive forms of arms control.[7] Another alternative (within the first model) is a resurrection of the types of barrier to international trade and finance that allow for more traditional controls. However, this forced disintegration of the international economy would be very difficult to realize.

In the cooperative security model an expanding network of generally applicable limitations on weapons systems, technologies and force structures is suggested, combined with a more open system of arms and technology transfer

---

[5] Rotfield, A., 'Introduction: the search for a new security system', *SIPRI Yearbook 1994* (Oxford University Press: Oxford, 1994), p. 4; and Halliday, F., 'International relations: is there a new agenda?', *Millennium: Journal of International Studies,* vol. 20, no. 1 (1991), pp. 57–72.

[6] NATO's reworking of its 1991 Strategic Concept reflects this agenda. Cornish, P., 'NATO at the millennium: new missions, new members . . . new strategy?', *NATO Review,* Sep./Oct. 1997, pp. 21–24; and all of *NATO Review,* summer 1998.

[7] On a spectrum of options, coercive arms control measures range from UN-sanctioned disarmament operations against 'rogue states', such as the United Nations Special Commission on Iraq (UNSCOM) and International Atomic Energy Authority (IAEA) activity in Iraq after the 1991 Persian Gulf War, to counter-military responses, such as Israel's 1981 attack on Iraq's nuclear reactor at Osirak. In a cooperative security system the former would be acceptable but the latter problematic and not in keeping with the message of global restraint. Such 'technological fixes' and counter-military responses also detract from diplomatic efforts at non-proliferation. Nolan, J. (ed.), *Global Engagement: Cooperation and Security in the 21st Century* (Brookings Institution: Washington, DC, 1994), p. 534.

based on the principle of disclosure.[8] Greater transparency will be needed at all stages of the export control decision-making process if this model is to be realized. Transparency engenders compliance with national and international regulatory regimes in a number of ways: by permitting coordination between officials making independent decisions; by providing reassurance to officials and governments which cooperate or comply with the norms of the regime that they are not being taken advantage of; and by deterring officials and governments which contemplate non-compliance or defection.[9] The EU Code's information exchanges and no-undercutting rule are crucial transparency mechanisms in this regard. Of course, transparency cannot be total, and in terms of both scope and level of specificity the optimal balance between disclosure and secrecy will require careful analysis. This is a particular area where much more research is needed.[10]

During the cold war transparency was mainly a confidence-building measure, but within a cooperative control regime it is also a gateway to advanced dual-use technologies and arms. In a cooperative system that encouraged transparency the emphasis would gradually shift from supply controls and protectionism to a control strategy 'stressing much freer availability of technology to all states if such states agreed to free disclosure of technology's disposition and application'.[11] In effect, importing countries would be expected to agree to self-imposed restrictions on the end-use (i.e., military application) of such technologies in exchange for greater market access. This study has shown that there is already a strong shift within the EU and by other major suppliers to controlling end-use. However, more research is needed on: (*a*) how to improve the effectiveness of end-use provisions; (*b*) how to develop a strong legal or normative basis for their application which reconciles issues of extra-territoriality and national sovereignty; and (*c*) how to harmonize such provisions within the EU and among other major supplier countries.

As part of the greater application of end-use controls, governments could also seek to impose control and information-gathering efforts at different stages in the life cycle of a product. 'To allow, therefore, for continued integration and liberalization of the world economy as well as effective control, new regulations will have to be applied further "upstream" in the chain of proliferation,

---

[8] The authors of a major US study on cooperative security identify a number of fundamental design elements and principles that are needed to achieve a functioning cooperative strategic export control regime. Nolan (note 7): see in particular Reinicke, W., 'Cooperative security and the political economy of non-proliferation', pp. 175–234; Chayes, A. H. and Chayes, A., 'Regime architecture: elements and principles', pp. 65–130; Nolan, pp. 1–14, 530–35; and Nolan, J. and Steinbruner, J., 'A transition strategy for the 1990s', pp. 582–84.

[9] Chayes and Chayes (note 8), p. 81.

[10] For a rare and detailed discussion on the challenge of protecting confidential business information see Kellman, B., Gualtieri, D. and Tanzman, E., 'Disarmament and disclosure: how arms control verification can proceed without threatening confidential business information', *Harvard International Law Journal*, vol. 36, no. 1 (winter 1995), pp. 71–126. See also Mariani, B. and Urquhart, A., *Transparency and Accountability in European Arms Export Controls: Towards Common Standards and Best Practice* (Saferworld: London, Dec. 2000).

[11] Nolan (note 7), p. 14.

closer to or at the level of production and relying on the principle of disclosure, which allows regulators to gather the necessary information.'[12]

Such an approach would necessitate a data collection system that provides effective monitoring of the source, quantity, foreign destination, user and purpose of arms and dual-use items. A potential model is the existing KOBRA system used in Germany (chapter 6) or the Schengen Information System (SIS).[13] The latter could be developed to track illicit arms trafficking and brokering networks, for example.

Another option is develop further the mixed model of regulation, and in particular to increase the proportion of self-regulation in the larger control effort by governments. Currently, self-regulation is rather limited and mainly focuses on the 'preventive' aspects of controls, while government regulations focus on the 'protective' aspects as well as on enforcement of preventive regulations. Within the EU, however, there is already an increased onus on industry to engage in self-regulation, particularly with the advent of the catch-all clause (chapter 3), which requires industry to ensure that exports of dual-use goods are intended for legitimate purposes. In addition, German companies are required to appoint a director with responsibility for exports who can be held accountable for any diversion (chapter 6). Further shifts of the regulatory burden onto industry can be expected in the future and, as in the past, these are likely to be facilitated by compensatory liberalization of export controls. In the EU, for example, the introduction of the catch-all clause was balanced by Article 6 in the EU Dual-Use Regulation which allows simplified licensing to friendly destinations and greater use of open and general licences.

The mixed regulation in the British and US financial markets provides a potential signpost to the future, and particularly the institutional frameworks provided by the National Association of Securities Dealers Automated Quotation (NASDAQ)[14] and the Integrated Monitoring and Surveillance (IMAS)[15] systems. Reinicke argues that all major states that supply advanced technologies could establish an Automated Technology Transfer Registry (ATTR) to register and track the flow of arms and technology.[16] This could be based on existing technology utilized in the NASDAQ, IMAS, SIS and KOBRA systems. An EU-

[12] Reinicke (note 8), pp. 179–80.

[13] SIS is a trans-European database with descriptions of people and objects wanted or missing in each Schengen country which police, customs officers, etc. can access at any time. According to Martin Walker, the database contains about 8 million names of criminals, suspected terrorists, drug smugglers and illegal immigrants. Walker, M., *The Guardian*, 10 Jan. 1998.

[14] NASDAQ is a computerized market surveillance system that continually monitors securities trading activities, tracking about 150 000 trades and 40 000 price quotes generated daily across the USA. Any unusual price and volume movements trigger an alert and possible subsequent investigation. In 1992, the system triggered 5839 alerts, leading to 96 formal investigations and the referral of 28 cases for further examination or prosecution. In addition, compliance and arbitration committees, composed of industry members, expelled 62 companies, suspended 11 others and barred 491 individuals from membership in the same year. Reinicke (note 8), p. 187.

[15] IMAS is used by the Market Surveillance Department in the London Stock Exchange to identify wrongdoing in the market (such as insider dealing). It covers all price movements, plots each deal in each share and can trace each deal back to the end-buyer. 'Man vs the Brain is no contest', *The Guardian*, 21 Mar. 1997.

[16] Reinicke (note 8), pp. 187–89.

wide registry, for example, could also be responsible for updating and explaining new export control guidelines to companies; alerting suppliers to new techniques used by front companies and countries to circumvent regulations; and sharing intelligence information via a computer network.

The development of a system that records and monitors trade flows internationally poses several challenges, both technological and political.[17] Probably the most difficult political issue is the potential regulatory burden on business. A requirement for reporting, product labelling and monitoring the make-up of technology would at first sight appear to impose enormous regulatory burdens for industry and recipients. Indeed, the feasibility and cost of monitoring large numbers of dual-use items have yet to be fully examined. KOBRA, for example, has been criticized by German industrial associations for being too cumbersome and bureaucratic. In terms of the company compliance requirement, companies also argue that they cannot know the exact nature of a particular contract and its intended uses, nor do they have adequate intelligence information about possible arms-related activities by foreign companies.

Political difficulties also exist on the demand side, particularly with regard to encouraging recipient countries to comply with such an arrangement, but there are strong and as yet largely underdeveloped inducements that could be offered to countries to encourage compliance. Access to trade credits and other sources of international capital could be made contingent on participation in and compliance with an international ATTR system. A number of countries (including Germany, Japan and the UK—see chapter 2) already include aid conditionality in some of their bilateral programmes, including measures to encourage transparency, restraint and reform in the recipient's security programmes. In the future technical and financial assistance of the kind being granted to the Commonwealth of Independent States (CIS) countries for weapon destruction and dismantling could become a more significant instrument for cooperative technology and arms transfer. In turn, development goals in less-developed countries (LDCs) could be based on the transfer of the computer and communications infrastructure necessary to create the monitoring mechanisms required for a cooperative security approach.[18]

Verification can never be perfect and membership is unlikely to be total. Indeed, even the most successful control regime is likely to drive potential proliferators underground into covert actions.[19] Thus, any arms and dual-use export control regime must also be able to impose mandatory curbs, with well-defined enforcement mechanisms and clear penalties for violations. Within the

---

[17] The technological problems may be eased considerably by the eventual introduction of a standardized coding system, which is currently under development, known as the Unique Identification Code (UNIC) methodology. Technology is also becoming available to tag or label items of particular concern in a way that reveals their location. Even so, other arms control treaties have shown how technically complex the setting up and maintaining of adequate and reliable databases can be.

[18] This argument is advanced by Nolan and Steinbruner (note 8), p. 581.

[19] See the discussion on the 'evasive' and 'illegal' procurement strategies of would-be proliferators in Müller, H. *et al.*, *From Black Sheep to White Angel? The New German Export Control Policy*, PRIF Reports no. 32 (Peace Research Institute Frankfurt: Frankfurt, Jan. 1994).

EU such protective regulatory mechanisms include monetary fines, the revocation of manufacturing and trading licences, criminal penalties on violators at the domestic level and sanctions or other forms of economic and political isolation at the international level.

Finally, if the past emphasis on supplier controls and technology denial is to give way to some new form of cooperative arrangement between suppliers and recipients, this study has suggested that the EU is likely to be at the forefront of such a change. The EU itself has already been reworked into a virtual free-trade zone for conventional arms and technology transfer, and control regimes are now in place for exports of arms and dual-use technologies to third countries. Further evolution is now required to shift the emphasis from technology denial to end-use. In exchange for access to sensitive technologies, third countries could be obligated to supply proof of established end-use. End-use certification of this kind, along with ongoing surveillance of transfer arrangements (in time, possibly through electronic registries) could do much to allay fears of the proliferation of advanced weapons and military equipment.

The response of recipient countries to such a new supplier–recipient bargain will be key. Some countries may be willing to accept more effective end-use controls, while others are likely to object that it is a further infringement on their sovereignty. It seems likely, therefore, that this cooperative model, if it progresses at all, will do so within three tiers. The first tier, consisting of the EU 'non-discriminatory core', will gradually be extended to other countries (such as the USA, other members of the OECD, and associate countries in Central and Eastern Europe) as they begin to accept and work within the normative framework outlined above. The second tier will consist of recipient (and supplier) countries that have accepted the 'end-use bargain' with the EU and other OECD suppliers. The bargain may well be developed through regional accords between the EU and other regional groupings such as the Organization of American States (OAS), ASEAN, ECOWAS and the Southern African Development Community (SADC). The third tier would consist of those countries that are the targets of extensive denial of arms and dual-use technologies. The aim would be for the third tier to steadily reduce as the first and second tiers grow.

Building a political consensus for such an approach will be difficult. This study has shown that reaching consensus among the 15 EU member states was difficult enough. It has also shown that the nature and purpose of arms and dual-use export controls changed profoundly in the past decade. However, the EU member states are now well placed to help further shape those controls towards a new cooperative model.

Part IV
Appendices

Appendix A. National and multilateral statements on controlling arms exports

1. THE GUIDELINES FOR CONVENTIONAL ARMS TRANSFERS AGREED BY THE FIVE PERMANENT MEMBERS OF THE UN SECURITY COUNCIL

London, 18 October 1991

The People's Republic of China, the French Republic, the Union of Soviet Socialist Republics, the United Kingdom of Great Britain and Northern Ireland, and the United States of America,

recalling and reaffirming the principles which they stated as a result of their meeting in Paris on 8 and 9 July 1991,

mindful of the dangers to peace and stability posed by the transfer of conventional weapons beyond levels needed for defensive purposes,

reaffirming the inherent right to individual or collective self-defence recognized in Article 51 of the Charter of the United Nations, which implies that States have the right to acquire means of legitimate self-defense,

recalling that in accordance with the Charter of the United Nations, United Nations Member States have undertaken to promote the establishment and maintenance of international peace and security with the least diversion for armaments of the world's human and economic resources,

seeking to ensure that arms transferred are not used in violation of the purposes and principles of the United Nations Charter,

mindful of their special responsibilities for the maintenance of international peace and security,

reaffirming their commitment to seek effective measures to promote peace, security, stability and arms control on a global and regional basis in a fair, reasonable, comprehensive and balanced manner,

noting the importance of encouraging international commerce for peaceful purposes,

determined to adopt a serious, responsible and prudent attitude of restraint regarding arms transfers,

declare that, when considering under their national control procedures conventional arms transfers, they intend to observe rules of restraint, and to act in accordance with the following guidelines:

1. They will consider carefully whether proposed transfers will:

(*a*) promote the capabilities of the recipient to meet needs for legitimate self-defence;

(*b*) serve as an appropriate and proportionate response to the security and military threats confronting the recipient country;

(*c*) enhance the capability of the recipient to participate in regional or other collective arrangements or other measures consistent with the Charter of the United Nations or requested by the United Nations;

2. They will avoid transfers which would be likely to

(*a*) prolong or aggravate an existing armed conflict;

(*b*) increase tension in a region or contribute to regional instability;

(*c*) introduce destabilizing military capabilities in a region;

(*d*) contravene embargoes or other relevant internationally agreed restraints to which they are parties;

(*e*) be used other than for the legitimate defense and security needs of the recipient State;

(*f*) support or encourage international terrorism;

(*g*) be used to interfere with the internal affairs of sovereign States;

(*h*) seriously undermine the recipient State's economy.

———

Source: Meeting of the Five on Arms Transfers and Non-Proliferation, London, 17–18 Oct. 1991, Conference on Disarmament document CD/113.

2. THE CSCE PRINCIPLES GOVERNING CONVENTIONAL ARMS TRANSFERS

Agreed by the CSCE in Vienna, 25 November 1993

1. The participating States reaffirm their commitment to act, in the security field, in accordance with the Charter of the United Nations and the Helsinki Final Act, the Charter of Paris and other relevant CSCE documents.

2. They recall that in Prague on 30 January 1992 they agreed that effective national control of weapons and equipment transfer is acquiring the greatest importance and decided to include the question of the establishment of a responsible approach to arms transfers as a matter of priority in the work programme of the post-Helsinki arms control process. They also recall their declaration in the Helsinki Document of 10 July 1992 that they would intensify their co-operation in the field of effective export controls applicable, inter alia, to conventional weapons.

I.

3. The participating States reaffirm:

(*a*) their undertaking, in accordance with the Charter of the United Nations, to promote the establishment of international peace and security with the least diversion for armaments of human and economic resources and their view that the reduction of world military expenditures could have a significant positive impact for the social and economic development of all peoples;

(*b*) the need to ensure that arms transferred are not used in violation of the purposes and principles of the Charter of the United Nations;

(*c*) their adherence to the principles of transparency and restraint in the transfer of conventional weapons and related technology, and their willingness to promote them in the security dialogue of the Forum for Security Co-operation;

(*d*) their strong belief that excessive and destabilising arms build-ups pose a threat to national, regional and international peace and security;

(*e*) the need for effective national mechanisms for controlling the transfer of conventional arms and related technology and for transfers to take place within those mechanisms;

(*f*) their support for and commitment to provide data and information as required by the United Nations resolution establishing the Register of Conventional Arms in order to ensure its effective implementation.

II.

4. In order to further their aim of a new co-operative and common approach to security, each participating State will promote and, by means of an effective national control mechanism, exercise due restraint in the transfer of conventional arms and related technology. To give this effect:

(*a*) each participating State will, in considering proposed transfers, take into account:

i. the respect for human rights and fundamental freedoms in the recipient country;

ii. the internal and regional situation in and around the recipient country, in the light of existing tensions or armed conflicts;

iii. the record of compliance of the recipient country with regard to international commitments, in particular on the non-use of force, and in the field of non-proliferation, or in other areas of arms control and disarmament;

iv. the nature and cost of the arms to be transferred in relation to the circumstances of the recipient country, including its legitimate security and defence needs and the objective of the least diversion for armaments of human and economic resources;

v. the requirements of the recipient country to enable it to exercise its right to individual or collective self-defence in accordance with Article 51 of the Charter of the United Nations;

vi. whether the transfers would contribute to an appropriate and proportionate response by the recipient country to the military and security threats confronting it;

vii. the legitimate domestic security needs of the recipient country;

viii. the requirements of the recipient country to enable it to participate in peacekeeping or other measures in accordance with decisions of the United Nations or the Conference on Security and Co-operation in Europe.

(*b*) Each participating State will avoid transfers which would be likely to:

i. be used for the violation or suppression of human rights and fundamental freedoms;

ii. threaten the national security of other States and of territories whose external relations are the internationally acknowledged responsibility of another State;

iii. contravene its international commitments, in particular in relation to sanctions adopted by the Security Council of the United Nations, or to decisions taken by the CSCE Council, or agreements on non-proliferation, or other arms control and disarmament agreements;

iv. prolong or aggravate an existing armed conflict, taking into account the legitimate requirement for self-defence;

v. endanger peace, introduce destabilizing military capabilities into a region, or otherwise contribute to regional instability;

vi. be diverted within the recipient country or re-exported for purposes contrary to the aims of this document;

vii. be used for the purpose of repression;

viii. support or encourage terrorism;

ix. be used other than for the legitimate defence and security needs of the recipient country.

III.

5. Further, each participating State will:

(*a*) reflect, as necessary, the principles in Section II in its national policy documents governing the transfer of conventional arms and related technology;

(*b*) consider mutual assistance in the establishment of effective national mechanisms for controlling the transfer of conventional arms and related technology;

(*c*) exchange information, in the context of security co-operation within the Forum for Security Co-operation, about national legislation and practices in the field of transfers of conventional arms and related technology and on mechanisms to control these transfers.

———

Source: Organization for Security and Co-operation in Europe, 'Principles governing conventional arms transfers', Nov. 1993, Programme for Immediate Action series no. 3, DOC.FSC3//96 [1996].

3. GUIDELINES FOR INTERNATIONAL ARMS TRANSFERS IN THE CONTEXT OF GENERAL ASSEMBLY RESOLUTION 46/36 H OF 6 DECEMBER 1991

Agreed by the UN Disarmament Commission, 1996

Excerpts

I. Introduction

1. Arms transfers are a deeply entrenched phenomenon of contemporary international relations. All States have the inherent right to self-defence, as enshrined in the Charter of the United Nations, and consequently the right to acquire arms for their security, including arms from outside sources. However, international transfers of conventional arms have, in recent decades, acquired a dimension and qualitative characteristics which, together with the increase in illicit arms trafficking, give rise to serious and urgent concerns.

2. Arms transfers should be addressed in conjunction with the question of maintaining international peace and security, reducing regional and international tensions, preventing and resolving conflicts and disputes, building and enhancing confidence, and promoting disarmament as well as social and economic

development. Restraint and greater openness, including various transparency measures, can help in this respect and contribute to the promotion of international peace and security.

3. The problem of the illicit traffic in arms has a social and humanitarian component in addition to its technical, economic and political dimensions. The human suffering that is caused, inter alia, by the devastating consequences of war, destabilizing violence and conflicts, terrorism, mercenary activities, subversion, drug trafficking, common and organized crime and other criminal actions cannot be ignored. The negative effects of illicit arms trafficking can often be disproportionately large, particularly for the internal security and socio-economic development of affected States. Illicit arms trafficking, which affects many countries and several regions of the world, puts to the test the capacity of States to find a solution to it.

4. Legal, political and technical differences in internal control of armaments and their transfer and, in some cases, inadequacy or absence of such controls can contribute to the growing illicit traffic in arms.

5. International cooperation in curbing illicit arms trafficking and in condemning it will assist in focusing the attention of the international community on this phenomenon and will be an important factor in combating it.

6. The United Nations, in keeping with its overall purposes and principles, has a legitimate interest in the field of arms transfers, recognized by the Charter, which refers specifically to the importance of the regulation of armaments for the maintenance of international peace and security.

7. Illicit arms trafficking is understood to cover that international trade in conventional arms, which is contrary to the laws of States and/or international law.

8. Limitations on arms transfers can be found in international treaties, binding decisions adopted by the Security Council under Chapter VII of the Charter of the United Nations and the principles and purposes of the Charter.

II. Scope

9. According to paragraph 1 of General Assembly resolution 43/75 I of 7 December 1988, entitled 'International arms transfers', arms transfers in all their aspects deserve serious consideration by the international community. The General Assembly, in paragraph 4 of its resolution 48/75 F of 16 December 1993, of the same title, noted that the Disarmament Commission had included the question of international arms transfers, with particular reference to resolution 46/36 H of 6 December 1991, also of the same title, in the agenda of its substantive session in 1994.

10. In its resolution 46/36 H, the General Assembly called upon all States to give high priority to eradicating illicit arms trafficking in all kinds of weapons and military equipment; urged Member States to exercise effective control over their weapons and military equipment and their arms imports and exports to prevent them from getting into the hands of parties engaged in illicit arms trafficking; and also urged Member States to ensure that they had in place an adequate system of laws and administrative machinery for regulating and monitoring effectively their transfer of arms, to strengthen or adopt strict measures for their enforcement, and to cooperate at the international, regional and subregional levels to harmonize, where appropriate, relevant laws, regulations and administrative procedures as well as their enforcement measures, with the goal of eradicating illicit arms trafficking.

11. Licit transfers of conventional arms can be addressed, inter alia, through national legislative and administrative actions and increased transparency. The objective in the case of illicit arms trafficking must be the eradication of this phenomenon.

12. All stages of illicit arms trafficking should be the focus of scrutiny. An essential factor in eradicating illicit arms trafficking is the effective control of arms to prevent them from being acquired by unauthorized persons.

III. Principles

13. In their efforts to control their international arms transfers and to prevent, combat and eradicate illicit arms trafficking, States should bear in mind the principles listed below.

14. States should respect the principles and purposes of the Charter of the United Nations,

including the right to self-defence; the sovereign equality of all its Members; non-interference in the internal affairs of States; the obligation of Members to refrain in their international relations from the threat or use of force against the territorial integrity or political independence of any State; the settlement of disputes by peaceful means; and respect for human rights; and continue to reaffirm the right of self-determination of all peoples, taking into account the particular situation of peoples under colonial or other forms of alien domination or foreign occupation, and recognize the right of peoples to take legitimate action in accordance with the Charter of the United Nations to realize their inalienable right of self-determination. This shall not be construed as authorizing or encouraging any action that would dismember or impair, totally or in part, the territorial integrity or political unity of sovereign and independent States conducting themselves in compliance with the principle of equal rights and self-determination of peoples and thus possessed of a Government representing the whole people belonging to the territory without distinction of any kind.

15. States should recognize the need for transparency in arms transfers.

16. States should recognize the responsibility to prohibit and eradicate illicit arms trafficking and the need for measures to achieve this end, taking into account the inherently clandestine nature of this traffic.

17. States, whether producers or importers, have the responsibility to seek to ensure that their level of armaments is commensurate with their legitimate self-defence and security requirements, including their ability to participate in United Nations peace-keeping operations.

18. States have responsibilities in exercising restraint over the production and procurement of arms as well as transfers.

19. Economic or commercial considerations should not be the only factors in international arms transfers. Other factors include, inter alia, the maintenance of international peace and security and efforts aimed at easing international tensions, promoting social and economic development, peacefully resolving regional conflicts, preventing arms races and achieving disarmament under effective international control.

20. Arms-producing or supplier States have a responsibility to seek to ensure that the quantity and level of sophistication of their arms exports do not contribute to instability and conflict in their regions or in other countries and regions or to illicit trafficking in arms.

21. States receiving arms have an equivalent responsibility to seek to ensure that the quantity and the level of sophistication of their arms imports are commensurate with their legitimate self-defence and security requirements and that they do not contribute to instability and conflict in their regions or in other countries and regions or to illicit trafficking in arms.

22. International arms transfers should not be used as a means to interfere in the internal affairs of other States.

. . . .

[The Guidelines go on to discuss the 'ways and means' in which these principles can be implemented.]

Source: United Nations, General Assembly, Review of the implementation of the recommendations and decisions adopted by the General Assembly at its 10th Special Session: Report of the Disarmament Commission, UN document A/51/182, 1 July 1996.

---

4. THE NOBEL PEACE LAUREATES' INTERNATIONAL CODE OF CONDUCT ON ARMS TRANSFERS

Prepared by a commission of recipients of the Nobel Peace Prize, January 1997

Introductory memorandum

We come from different nations with varied histories, and in the past, the world has honored each of our struggles for peace and justice with the Nobel Prize for Peace. Today, we speak as one to voice our common concern regarding the destructive effects of the unregulated arms trade. Together, we have written an International Code of Conduct on Arms Transfers, which, once adopted by all arms-selling nations, will benefit all of humanity, nationalities, ethnicites and religions.

This International Code of Conduct would govern all arms transfers, including conventional weapons and munitions, military and security training, and sensitive military and dual-use technologies. The Code stipulates that any country wishing to purchase arms must meet certain criteria, including the promotion of democracy, the protection of human rights, and transparency in military spending. It would also prohibit arms sales to nations that support terrorism and to states that are engaged in aggression against other nations or peoples.

The international community can no longer ignore the repercussions of irresponsible arms transfers. Indiscriminate weapons sales foster political instability and human rights violations, prolong violent conflicts, and weaken diplomatic efforts to resolve differences peacefully. Arms transfers often take place under a cloud of secrecy, and generally respond to the desires of a few while ignoring the needs and rights of the many. Sadly, many governments continue to divert scarce resources toward arms purchases while their people live in abject poverty.

Millions of civilians have been killed in conflict this century, and many more have lost their loved ones, their homes, their spirit. In a world where 1.3 billion people earn less than 1 dollar a day, the sale of weapons simply perpetuates poverty. Our children urgently need schools and health centers, not machine guns and fighter planes. Our children also need to be protected from violence. The dictators of this world, not the poor, clamor for arms.

Once in effect, this International Code of Conduct on Arms Transfers would prevent undemocratic governments from building sophisticated arsenals. Governments which systematically abuse internationally recognized human rights through practices such as torture or arbitrary executions would not receive military training. Countries who commit genocide would not be able to buy munitions. Governments engaged in armed aggression against other countries or peoples could not buy missiles. States that support terrorism would be prevented from acquiring weapons. In addition, all nations would be required to report their arms purchases to the United Nations. This Code of Conduct would undeniably promote global peace and security, and protect human rights.

We call on all nations to endorse this International Code of Conduct on Arms Transfers. The citizens of the world must demand that leaders support this Code as well as similar efforts on the national and regional level. Only through solidarity, compassion, and courageous leadership can we make violence and its vestiges a distant memory of the past.

INTERNATIONAL CODE OF CONDUCT ON ARMS TRANSFERS

Preamble

Gravely concerned that international transfers of major conventional weapons, small arms and light weapons, and ammunition result every year in human misery and countless deaths, the majority of which are suffered by civilian populations;

Recognising that, according to the UN Charter, every state has a right to individual and collective self-defence against acts of aggression, and that every human being has the inalienable right to life, liberty, and security of person, as stated in the Universal Declaration of Human Rights;

Convinced that conflicts should be settled by peaceful means rather than by the use or threat of force;

Alarmed by the excessive stockpiling of conventional weapons and by their increasingly sophisticated and lethal levels of technology, both of which tend to increase instability through regional arms races;

Recognising that internationally transferred arms and ammunition are frequently used to facilitate and commit human rights abuses and to prevent democratic governance, in contravention of international human rights law;

Recognising, moreover, that these weapons transferred internationally are frequently used to commit acts of aggression between and within states;

Mindful that weapons transfers often result in situations whereby vendor states confront enemies that they themselves have helped to arm;

Concerned that international arms transfers can undermine social and economic development in both exporting and importing countries by diverting scarce resources;

Noting that reduction of global military spending in many countries could release substantial resources for the social and economic development of all peoples and would permit dramatic increases in funding for demobilisation and conversion of resources to peaceful, productive uses;

Reaffirming that the United Nations has an important role to play in maintaining international peace and security through the regulation of armaments, as set forth in the Charter;

Welcoming, in this context, steps taken by Member States to provide for transparency and restraint of arms transfers, such as: the United Nations Register of Conventional Arms, the Panel of Governmental Experts on Small Arms, General Assembly resolutions on curbing the illicit transfer of conventional arms, the standardised reporting form of military expenditures, and the UN Disarmament Commission's Guidelines for International Arms Transfers;

Welcoming also that, in addition to measures of transparency and restraint, regulations on arms transfers have been achieved in specific cases, such as anti-personnel land mine export moratoria and arms embargoes;

Noting, however, that existing regulations are inadequate and that, in order to further the cause of global peace, security, and human rights, a more comprehensive international mechanism to regulate and monitor the transfer of arms must be established.

We hereby call on all governments to abide by the following rules and principles to govern international arms transfers:

Section 1: Definitions

Article 1. Arms

For the purposes of this Code, arms include:

A. All weapons, munitions, sub-components and delivery systems, including, for example:

battle tanks, armoured combat vehicles, military aircraft, artillery systems, military helicopters, missiles, paramilitary police equipment, mortars, machine guns and sub-machine guns, rifles, pistols, anti-tank weapons, mines, grenades, cluster bombs, and all types of ammunition.

B. Sensitive military and dual-use technologies, including, for example: encryption devices, certain machine tools, supercomputers, gas-turbine and rocket-propulsion technology, avionics, thermal-imaging equipment and chemical irritants.

C. Military and security training including the provision of expertise, knowledge or skill in the use of such weapons, munitions, subcomponents and sensitive technologies.

Article 2. Transfers

For the purposes of this Code, transfers are defined as:

A. Any transaction resulting in a change of title to, and/or control over, any arms defined in Article 1, and any physical movement of any arms defined in Article 1 from one jurisdiction to another. Such transfers include those conducted in return for direct payment, credit, foreign aid, grants, and goods received as a result of off-set or barter arrangements. They also include transfers of expertise, information, designs, technology or goods under licensing and coproduction agreements, leasing arrangements, and arms deliveries in return for which the supplier receives no financial compensation, goods or services. Logistical and financial support for any of the above arrangements are also included.

B. Any provision by one or more persons to another in a different jurisdiction of expertise, knowledge or skill in the use of arms as defined in Article 1 above.

Section II: Principles

Arms transfers may be conducted only if the proposed recipient state, or recipient party in the country of final destination, is in compliance with all of the following principles:

Article 3. Compliance with international human rights standards

A. Arms transfers may be conducted only if it can be reasonably demonstrated that the proposed transfer will not be used by the recipient state, or recipient party in the country of final destination, to contribute to grave violations of human rights, such as:

– genocide and other crimes against humanity, for example 'ethnic cleansing'[1].

– extra-legal, summary or arbitrary executions;

– enforced disappearances;

– torture or other forms of cruel, inhuman or degrading treatment or punishment;

– detentions in violation of international human rights standards.

B. Arms transfers may be conducted only if the proposed recipient state, or recipient party in the country of final destination:

– Vigorously investigates, prosecutes and brings to justice those responsible for the above-mentioned violations and abuses of human rights and violations of the laws and customs of war;

– Makes it part of the training of the armed forces and law enforcement agencies that any-one ordered to commit the above-mentioned grave violations has a duty to refuse;

– Works towards the establishment of impartial and independent bodies that oversee the protection of human rights and does not impede the free functioning of domestic and international human rights organisations.

Article 4. Compliance with international humanitarian law

Arms transfers may be conducted only if the proposed recipient state, or recipient party in the country of final destination:

A. Does not engage in, or sponsor, grave breaches of the laws and customs of war as set forth in the Geneva Conventions of 1949, and additional Protocols of 1977, and other rules and principles of international humanitarian law applicable during inter-state or intra-state armed conflict which, for example, prohibit arbitrary and summary execution, indiscrim-inate killing, mutilation, torture and cruel treatment, and hostage taking;

B. Provides access on a regular basis to humanitarian non-governmental organisations in time of conflict or humanitarian emergency, including access of the International Com-mittee of the Red Cross to detainees.

C. Co-operates with international tribunals, either ad-hoc or general, with the power to adjudicate violations of the rules listed under (A).

Article 5. Respect for democratic rights

Arms transfers may be conducted only if the proposed recipient state:

A. Allows its citizens to choose their representatives through free and fairly-contested periodic elections that feature secret balloting;

B. Permits its citizens to express their political views through the freedom to speak, disseminate ideas and information, assemble, associate, and organise, including the organisation of political parties.

C. Has civilian institutions that determine national security policy and control the opera-tions and spending of the armed forces and law enforcement agencies;

Article 6. Respect for international arms embargoes and military sanctions

Arms transfers may be conducted only if the proposed recipient state, or recipient party in the country of final destination:

A. Is in compliance with international agreements relating to arms embargoes and other military sanctions decreed by the United Nations Security Council, whether or not they have been adopted specifically under Chapter VII of the UN Charter;

B. Is in compliance with arms embargoes and other military sanctions decreed by regional organisations or regional arrange-ments to which it is a party.

Article 7. Participation in the United Nations Register of Conventional Arms

Transfers may be conducted only if the recipient state fully participates in reporting arms transfers to the United Nations Register of Conventional Arms, as defined in United Nations General Assembly Resolution 46/36 L of December 9, 1991.

---

[1] Ethnic cleansing is here defined as mass killings and/or forced displacement on the grounds of ethnicity.

Article 8. Commitment to promote regional peace, security and stability

Arms transfers may be conducted only if the proposed recipient state or recipient party in the country of final destination:

A. Is not involved in an armed conflict in the region, unless it is recognised by the UN as being engaged in an act of self-defence in accordance with Article 51 of the UN Charter; or is playing a role in a UN-mandated operation;

B. Is not, as a result of this transfer, introducing weapons beyond those considered appropriate for its legitimate self-defence; or introducing a significantly more advanced military technology into the region;

C. Recognises the right of other UN-recognised states in the region to exist within agreed boundaries, and agrees to submit disputes relating to territorial claims to third party settlement;

D. Carries out and/or respects an agreed cease-fire as party to a former conflict;

E. Does not advocate national, racial or religious hatred that constitutes incitement to discrimination, hostility or violence, in particular propaganda inciting individuals to overthrow their own or a foreign government, or inflammatory propaganda in pursuit of the vindication of territorial claims;

F. Is not engaged in armed actions or practices which are likely to lead to a significant number of displaced persons or refugees.

Article 9. Opposition to terrorism

Arms transfers may be conducted only if the proposed recipient state, or recipient party in the country of final destination:

A. Has ratified, and is not in violation of, the international conventions and instruments concerning terrorism or acts associated with terrorism, including, for example: the Tokyo Convention on Offences and Certain Acts Committed Onboard Aircraft; the Hague Convention for the Suppression of Unlawful Seizure of Aircraft; the Montreal Convention for the Suppression of Unlawful Acts Against the Safety of Civilian Aircraft; the Convention on Offences Against Internationally Protected Persons (New York Convention); the International Convention Against the Taking of Hostages (Hostages Convention); and the Convention on the Physical Protection of Nuclear Material;

B. Is in compliance with the international obligations relating to the apprehension and prosecution or extradition of terrorist suspects found within the territory of the recipient state; or of persons indicted by an international ad-hoc War Crimes Tribunal or by an international criminal tribunal;

C. Does not allow its territory to be used as a base for terrorists, or as a base to supply or direct terrorists.

Article 10. Promotion of human development

Arms transfers may be conducted only if the recipient state's expenditures on health and education combined exceed its military expenditures, unless the recipient state can reasonably demonstrate that such transfers are justified by exceptional needs to counter acts of aggression.

Section III: Implementation

Article 11. Enacting the Code

All States shall introduce national legislation and regulations which ensure effective implementation and enforcement of this Code. Such laws and regulations shall:

A. Incorporate this Code;

B. Provide mechanisms for public scrutiny of all transfers in advance of any decision to authorise a transfer;

C. Require end-use certification which incorporates the principles of the Code into legally binding conditions for the receipt of arms. End-user certification must identify both the recipient, and the actual use to which the equipment will be put;

D. Establish effective channels for receiving information on implementation of the Code from non-governmental organisations.

E. Require States to make a criminal offence any transfers made in violation of the Code, or any attempt to effect, to conspire to effect, or to incite any such transfer.

Article 12. Monitoring the Code internationally

All States shall:

A. Provide an annual report on the implementation of the Code to the Secretary-General of the United Nations who will report to the General Assembly;

B. Consult each other and cooperate with each other bilaterally, through the Secretary General of the UN, or through other appropriate international procedures to resolve any problems that may arise with regard to the interpretation and application of the provisions of this Code; and shall consider measures designed to encourage compliance, including collective measures in conformity with international law.

Article 13. Verification

C. Parties to the Code shall convene a review two years after this Code comes into operation with the specific purpose of developing an effective verification commission.

———

Source: 'Nobel Peace Laureates' international code of conduct on arms transfers', British American Security Information Council, URL <http://www.basicint.org/code_itl.htm>.

5. THE EU COMMON CRITERIA FOR ARMS EXPORTS

Adopted by the Council of Ministers, 30 June 1991 in Luxembourg and 27 June 1992 in Lisbon

The European Council is deeply concerned at the danger arising from the proliferation of weapons of mass destruction . . .

The European Council is also alarmed by the stockpiling of conventional weapons in certain regions of the world. To prevent situations of instability recurring in entire regions as a result of such over-armament, the European Council believes that far-reaching international action is needed immediately to promote restraint and transparency in the transfers of conventional weapons and of technologies for military use, in particular towards areas of tension.

The European Council notes with satisfaction that work in progress in the organs of European political cooperation has already, by comparing national policies on arms exports, identified a number of common criteria on which these policies are based, such as:

– respect for the international commitments of the member States of the Community, in particular the sanctions decreed by the Security Council of the United Nations and those decreed by the Community, agreements on non-proliferation and other subjects, as well as other international obligations;

– respect of human rights in the country of final destination;

– the internal situation in the country of final destination, as a function of the existence of tensions or internal armed conflicts;

– the preservation of regional peace, security and stability;

– the national security of the member States and of territories whose external relations are the responsibility of a member State, as well as that of friendly and allied countries;

– the behaviour of the buyer country with regard to the international community, as regards in particular its attitude to terrorism, the nature of its alliances, and respect for international law;

– the existence of a risk that the equipment will be diverted within the buyer country or re-exported under undesirable conditions.

– The compatibility of the arms exports with the technical and economic capacity of the recipient country, taking into account the desirability that states should achieve their legitimate needs of security and defence with the least diversion for armaments of human and economic resources.

———

Source: 'Declaration on non-proliferation and the export of weapons', appendix VII to the Communiqué of the Meeting of EC Heads of State, Luxembourg, 28–29 June 1991, EPC Press Release, 29 June 1991; and 'Conclusions of the Presidency of the European Council held in Lisbon on 26 and 27 June 1992', EPC Press Release, 27 June 1992.

6. THE EU CODE OF CONDUCT ON ARMS EXPORTS

Adopted by the General Affairs Council, 8 June 1998

The Council of the European Union,

BUILDING on the Common Criteria agreed at the Luxembourg and Lisbon European Councils in 1991 and 1992,

RECOGNISING the special responsibility of arms exporting states,

DETERMINED to set high common standards which should be regarded as the minimum for the management of, and restraint in, conventional arms transfers by all EU Member States, and to strengthen the exchange of relevant information with a view to achieving greater transparency,

DETERMINED to prevent the export of equipment which might be used for internal repression or international aggression, or contribute to regional instability,

WISHING within the framework of the CFSP to reinforce their cooperation and to promote their convergence in the field of conventional arms exports,

NOTING complementary measures taken by the EU against illicit transfers, in the form of the EU Programme for Preventing and Combating Illicit Trafficking in Conventional Arms,

ACKNOWLEDGING the wish of EU Member States to maintain a defence industry as part of their industrial base as well as their defence effort,

RECOGNISING that states have a right to transfer the means of self-defence, consistent with the right of self-defence recognised by the UN Charter,

have adopted the following Code of Conduct and operative provisions:

CRITERION ONE
Respect for the international commitments of EU member states, in particular the sanctions decreed by the UN Security Council and those decreed by the Community, agreements on non-proliferation and other subjects, as well as other international obligations

An export licence should be refused if approval would be inconsistent with, inter alia:

(*a*) the international obligations of member states and their commitments to enforce UN, OSCE and EU arms embargoes;

(*b*) the international obligations of member states under the Nuclear Non-Proliferation Treaty, the Biological and Toxin Weapons Convention and the Chemical Weapons Convention;

(*c*) their commitments in the frameworks of the Australia Group, the Missile Technology Control Regime, the Nuclear Suppliers Group and the Wassenaar Arrangement;

(*d*) their commitment not to export any form of anti-personnel landmine.

CRITERION TWO
The respect of human rights in the country of final destination

Having assessed the recipient country's attitude towards relevant principles established by international human rights instruments, Member States will:

(*a*) not issue an export licence if there is a clear risk that the proposed export might be used for internal repression;

(*b*) exercise special caution and vigilance in issuing licences, on a case-by-case basis and taking account of the nature of the equipment, to countries where serious violations of human rights have been established by the competent bodies of the UN, the Council of Europe or by the EU;

For these purposes, equipment which might be used for internal repression will include, inter alia, equipment where there is evidence of the use of this or similar equipment for internal repression by the proposed end-user, or where there is reason to believe that the equipment will be diverted from its stated end-use or end-user and used for internal repression. In line with operative paragraph 1 of this Code, the nature of the equipment will be considered carefully, particularly if it is intended for internal security purposes. Internal repression includes, inter alia, torture and other cruel, inhuman and degrading treatment or punishment, summary or arbitrary executions, disappearances, arbitrary detentions and other major violations of human rights and fundamental freedoms as set out in relevant international human rights instruments, including the Universal Declaration on Human Rights and the International Covenant on Civil and Political Rights.

CRITERION THREE
The internal situation in the country of final destination, as a function of the existence of tensions or armed conflicts

Member States will not allow exports which would provoke or prolong armed conflicts or aggravate existing tensions or conflicts in the country of final destination.

CRITERION FOUR
Preservation of regional peace, security and stability

Member States will not issue an export licence if there is a clear risk that the intended recipient would use the proposed export aggressively against another country or to assert by force a territorial claim.

When considering these risks, EU Member States will take into account inter alia:

(*a*) the existence or likelihood of armed conflict between the recipient and another country;

(*b*) a claim against the territory of a neighbouring country which the recipient has in the past tried or threatened to pursue by means of force;

(*c*) whether the equipment would be likely to be used other than for the legitimate national security and defence of the recipient;

(*d*) the need not to affect adversely regional stability in any significant way.

CRITERION FIVE
The national security of the member states and of territories whose external relations are the responsibility of a Member State, as well as that of friendly and allied countries

Member States will take into account:

(*a*) the potential effect of the proposed export on their defence and security interests and those of friends, allies and other member states, while recognising that this factor cannot affect consideration of the criteria on respect of human rights and on regional peace, security and stability;

(*b*) the risk of use of the goods concerned against their forces or those of friends, allies or other member states;

(*c*) the risk of reverse engineering or unintended technology transfer.

CRITERION SIX
The behaviour of the buyer country with regard to the international community, as regards in particular to its attitude to terrorism, the nature of its alliances and respect for international law

Member States will take into account inter alia the record of the buyer country with regard to:

(*a*) its support or encouragement of terrorism and international organised crime;

(*b*) its compliance with its international commitments, in particular on the non-use of force, including under international humanitarian law applicable to international and non-international conflicts;

(*c*) its commitment to non-proliferation and other areas of arms control and disarmament, in particular the signature, ratification and implementation of relevant arms control and disarmament conventions referred to in sub-para (*b*) of Criterion One.

CRITERION SEVEN
The existence of a risk that the equipment will be diverted within the buyer country or re-exported under undesirable conditions

In assessing the impact of the proposed export on the importing country and the risk that exported goods might be diverted to an undesirable end-user, the following will be considered:

(*a*) the legitimate defence and domestic security interests of the recipient country, including any involvement in UN or other peace-keeping activity;

(*b*) the technical capability of the recipient country to use the equipment;

(*c*) the capability of the recipient country to exert effective export controls;

(*d*) the risk of the arms being re-exported or diverted to terrorist organisations (anti-terrorist equipment would need particularly careful consideration in this context).

CRITERION EIGHT
The compatibility of the arms exports with the technical and economic capacity of the recipient country, taking into account the desirability that states should achieve their legitimate needs of security and defence with the least diversion for armaments of human and economic resources

Member States will take into account, in the light of information from relevant sources such as UNDP, World Bank, IMF and OECD reports, whether the proposed export would seriously hamper the sustainable development of the recipient country. They will consider in this context the recipient country's relative levels of military and social expenditure, taking into account also any EU or bilateral aid.

OPERATIVE PROVISIONS

1. Each EU Member State will assess export licence applications for military equipment made to it on a case-by-case basis against the provisions of the Code of Conduct.

2. This Code will not infringe on the right of Member States to operate more restrictive national policies.

3. EU Member States will circulate through diplomatic channels details of licences refused in accordance with the Code of Conduct for military equipment together with an explanation of why the licence has been refused. The details to be notified are set out in the form of a draft pro-forma at Annex A. Before any Member State grants a licence which has been denied by another Member State or States for an essentially identical transaction within the last three years, it will first consult the Member State or States which issued the denial(s). If following consultations, the Member State nevertheless decides to grant a licence, it will notify the Member State or States issuing the denial(s), giving a detailed explanation of its reasoning.

The decision to transfer or deny the transfer of any item of military equipment will remain at the national discretion of each Member State. A denial of a licence is understood to take place when the member state has refused to authorise the actual sale or physical export of the item of military equipment concerned, where a sale would otherwise have come about, or the conclusion of the relevant contract. For these purposes, a notifiable denial may, in accordance with national procedures, include denial of permission to start negotiations or a negative response to a formal initial enquiry about a specific order.

4. EU Member States will keep such denials and consultations confidential and not use then for commercial advantage.

5. EU Member States will work for the early adoption of a common list of military equipment covered by the Code, based on similar national and international lists. Until then, the Code will operate on the basis of national control lists incorporating where appropriate elements from relevant international lists.

6. The criteria in this Code and the consultation procedure provided for by paragraph 3 of the operative provisions will also apply to dual-use goods as specified in Annex I of Council Decision 94/942/CFSP as amended, where there are grounds for believing that the end-user of such goods will be the armed forces or internal security forces or similar entities in the recipient country.

7. In order to maximise the efficiency of this Code, EU Member States will work within the framework of the CFSP to reinforce their cooperation and to promote their convergence in the field of conventional arms exports.

8. Each EU Member State will circulate to other EU Partners in confidence an annual report on its defence exports and on its implementation of the Code. These reports will be discussed at an annual meeting held within the framework of the CFSP. The meeting will also review the operation of the Code, identify any improvements which need to be made and submit to the Council a consolidated report, based on contributions from Member States.

9. EU Member States will, as appropriate, assess jointly through the CFSP framework the situation of potential or actual recipients of arms exports from EU Member States, in the light of the principles and criteria of the Code of Conduct.

10. It is recognised that Member States, where appropriate, may also take into account the effect of proposed exports on their economic, social, commercial and industrial interests, but that these factors will not affect the application of the above criteria.

11. EU Member States will use their best endeavours to encourage other arms exporting states to subscribe to the principles of this Code of Conduct.

12. This Code of Conduct and the operative provisions will replace any previous elaboration of the 1991 and 1992 Common Criteria.

[Annex A not reproduced here]

———

Source: European Commission Internet site, URL <http://europa.eu.int/comm/development/prevention/codecondarmsexp.htm>.

---

7. FRAMEWORK AGREEMENT BETWEEN FRANCE, GERMANY, ITALY, SPAIN, SWEDEN, AND THE UNITED KINGDOM CONCERNING MEASURES TO FACILITATE THE RESTRUCTURING AND OPERATION OF THE EUROPEAN DEFENCE INDUSTRY

Farnborough, 27 July 2000

Excerpts

PREAMBLE

The French Republic, The Federal Republic of Germany, The Italian Republic, The Kingdom of Spain, The Kingdom of Sweden, and The United Kingdom of Great Britain and Northern Ireland, (hereinafter referred to as the 'Parties'):

Recalling the Statement signed by the Heads of State and Government of the French Republic and the Heads of Government of the Federal Republic of Germany and the United Kingdom of Great Britain and Northern Ireland on 9 December 1997, and supported by the Heads of Government of the Italian Republic, the Kingdom of Spain, and the Kingdom of Sweden, designed to facilitate the restructuring of the European aerospace and defence electronics industries;

Recalling the Joint Statement of 20 April 1998 by the Minister of Defence of the French Republic, the Federal Minister of Defence of the Federal Republic of Germany, the Minister of Defence of the Italian Republic, the Minister of Defence of the Kingdom of Spain and the Secretary of State for Defence of the United Kingdom of Great Britain and Northern Ireland, and also supported by the Minister for Defence of the Kingdom of Sweden;

Recalling the Letter of Intent concerning Measures to Facilitate the Restructuring of European Defence Industry of 6 July 1998 signed by the Ministers of Defence of the Parties and wishing to define a framework of co-operation to facilitate the restructuring of the European defence industry;

Recognising that creation of Transnational Defence Companies is a matter for industry to determine, in accordance with competition regulations. Noting in this connection that a degree of interdependency already exists in Europe as a result of current co-operation on major defence equipment;

Wishing to create the political and legal framework necessary to facilitate industrial restructuring in order to promote a more competitive and robust European defence technological and industrial base in the global defence market and thus to contribute to the construction of a common European security and defence policy;

Recognising that industrial restructuring may lead to the creation of Transnational Defence Companies and the acceptance of mutual dependence. Emphasising, in this connection, that industrial restructuring in the field of defence must take account of the imperative of ensuring the Parties' security of supply, and a fair and efficient distribution and maintenance of strategically important assets, activities and skills;

Desiring to simplify Transfers of Defence Articles and Defence Services between them and to increase co-operation in Exports, and acknowledging that this will help foster industrial restructuring and maintain industry's capacity to export; wishing to ensure that the Export of equipment produced in co-operation between them will be managed responsibly in accordance with each participating State's international obligations and commitments in the export control area, especially the criteria of the European Union Code of Conduct;

Wishing to adapt procedures relating to security clearances, transmission of Classified Information and visits, with a view to facilitating industrial co-operation without undermining the security of Classified Information;

Acknowledging the need to improve the use of the limited resources devoted to defence research and technology by each Party and wishing to increase their co-operation in this field;

Acknowledging the need, in order to make possible the efficient functioning and the restructuring of the European defence industry, to simplify the transfer of Technical Information, to harmonise national con-ditions relating to treatment of Technical Information, and to reduce restrictions put upon the disclosure and use of Technical Information;

Recognising that European armed forces must be of a sufficient quality, quantity and level of readiness to meet future requirements for flexibility, mobility, deployability, sustainability and interoperability, reflecting also the additional challenges and possibilities provided for by future developments in research and technology. Also recognising that these forces must be capable of operating jointly or as a part of a coalition in a wide range of roles with, in particular, assured augmentation and effective command, control, communications and support;

Desiring, in this field, to organise consultations between the Parties in order to harmonise the military requirements of their armed forces and acquisition procedures, by co-operating at the earliest possible stage and in the definition of the specifications for the weapon systems to be developed or acquired;

Recognising that this Agreement does not require any modification of their Constitutions;

Acknowledging that any activity undertaken under this Agreement shall be compatible with the Parties' membership of the European Union and their obligations and commitments resulting from such membership;

Have agreed as follows:

PART 1
Objectives, use of terms and general organisation

. . .

PART 2
Security of supply

. . .

PART 3
Transfer and export procedures
Article 12

1. This article deals with Transfers between Parties of Defence Articles and related Defence Services in the context of a Co-operative Armament Programme.

2. Global Project Licences shall be used as the necessary authorisation, if required by the national regulations of each of the Parties, when the Transfer is needed to achieve the programme or when it is intended for national military use by one of the Parties.

3. The granting of a Global Project Licence has the effect of removing the need for specific authorisations, for the Transfer of the concerned Defence Articles and related Defence Services to the destinations permitted by the said licence, for the duration of that licence.

4. The conditions for granting, withdrawing and cancelling the Global Project Licence shall be determined by each Party, taking into consideration their obligations under this Agreement.

Article 13

1. This article deals with Exports to a non-Party of Defence Articles and the related Defence Services developed or produced in the context of a Co-operative Armament Programme carried out according to Article 12.

2. Parties undertaking a Co-operative Armament Programme shall agree basic principles governing Exports to non-Parties from that programme and procedures for such Export decisions. In this context, for each programme, the participating Parties shall set out, on the basis of consensus:

(*a*) The characteristics of the equipment concerned. These can cover final specifications or contain restrictive clauses for certain functional purposes. They shall detail, when necessary, the agreed limits to be imposed in terms of function, maintenance or repairs for Exports to different destinations. They shall be updated to take into account technical improvements to the Defence Article produced within the context of the programme.

(*b*) Permitted Export destinations established and revised according to the procedure detailed in paragraph 3 of the present article.

(*c*) References to embargoes. These references shall be automatically updated in the light of any additions or changes to relevant United Nations resolutions and/or European Union decisions. Other international embargoes could be included on a consensus basis.

3. The establishment and revision of permitted Export destinations shall follow the procedures and principles below:

(*a*) Establishment of permitted Export destinations and later additions is the responsibility of the participating Parties in the Co-operative Armament Programme. Those decisions shall be made by consensus following consultations. These consultations will take into account, inter alia, the Parties' national export control policies, the fulfilment of their international commitments, including the EU code of conduct criteria, and the protection of the Parties defence interests, including the preservation of a strong and competitive European defence industrial base. If, later, the addition of a permitted destination is desired by industry, it should, as early as possible, raise this issue with relevant Parties with a view to taking advantage of the procedures set out in this article.

(*b*) A permitted Export destination may only be removed in the event of significant changes in its internal situation, for example full scale civil war or a serious deterioration of the human rights situation, or if its behaviour becomes a threat to regional or international peace, security and stability, for example as a result of aggression or the threat of aggression against other nations. If the participating Parties in the programme are unable to reach consensus on the removal of a permitted Export destination at the working level, the issue will be referred to Ministers for resolution. This process should not exceed three months from the time removal of the permitted Export destination was first proposed. Any Party involved in the programme may require a moratorium on Exports of the product to the permitted destination in question for the duration of that process. At the end of that period, that destination shall be removed from the permitted destinations unless consensus has been reached on its retention.

4. Once agreement has been reached on the Export principles mentioned in paragraph 2, the responsibility for issuing an Export licence for the permitted Export destinations lies with the Party within whose jurisdiction the Export contract falls.

5. Parties who are not participants in the Co-operative Armament Programme shall obtain approval from the Parties participating in the said programme before authorising any re-Export to non-Parties of Defence Articles produced under that programme.

6. Parties shall undertake to obtain end-user assurances for Exports of Defence Articles to permitted destinations, and to exchange views with the relevant Parties if a re-export request is received. If the envisaged re-export destination is not among permitted export destinations, the procedures defined in paragraph 13.3(a) shall apply to such consultations.

7. The Parties shall also undertake to review on a case by case basis existing Co-operative Armament Programme agreements or arrangements and the commitments relating to current Co-operative Armament Programmes, with a view to agreeing, where possible, to apply to these programmes the principles and procedures outlined in Article 12 and the present article.

Article 14

1. This article deals with Transfers and Exports relating to a programme which has been carried out in co-operation between manufacturers within the jurisdiction of two or more Parties.

2. When TDCs or other defence companies carry out a programme of development or production of Defence Articles on the territory of two or more Parties, which is not conducted pursuant to an inter-governmental programme,

they can ask their relevant national authorities to issue an approval that this programme qualifies for the procedures outlined in Articles 12 and 13.

3. If approval is obtained from all Parties concerned, the procedures outlined in Article 12 and Article 13 paragraphs 2, 3, 4 and 6 shall be fully applied to the programme in question. The Parties concerned shall inform the other Parties of the status of the programme resulting from this approval. These other Parties shall then be committed to apply the provisions of Article 13, paragraph 5.

Article 15

At early stage of development of an industrial co-operation, Transfers between Parties for the exclusive use of the industries involved can be authorised on the basis of Global Project Licences granted by the respective Parties.

Article 16

1. The Parties commit themselves to apply simplified licensing procedures for Transfers, outside the framework of an intergovernmental or an approved industrial co-operation programme, of components or sub-systems produced under sub-contractual relations between industries located in the territories of the Parties.

2. Parties shall minimise the use of governmentally issued End-User Certificate and international import certificate requirements on Transfers of components in favour of, where possible, company certificates of use.

Article 17

1. This article deals with Transfers between Parties of Defence Articles and related Defence Service that are nationally produced and do not fall within the scope of Articles 12 or Articles 13 to 16.

2. As a contribution to security of supply, Parties shall make their best efforts to streamline national licensing procedures for such Transfers of Defence Articles and related Defence Services to another Party.

Article 18

The granting of a Global Project Licence shall not exempt related Transfers of Defence Articles between Parties from other relevant regulations, for example transit requirements or customs documentation requirements. Parties agree to examine the possibility of simplifying or reducing administrative requirements for Transfers covered by this Agreement.

PART 4
Security of classified information
Articles 19–27

. . .

PART 5
Defence related research and technology
Articles 28–36

. . .

PART 6
Treatment of technical information
Articles 37–44

. . .

PART 7
Harmonisation of military requirements
Articles 45–49

. . .

PART 8
Protection of commercially sensitive information
Articles 50–54

. . .

PART 9
Final provisions
Articles 55–60

. . .

———

Source: Framework Agreement between the French Republic, the Federal Republic of Germany, the Italian Republic, the Kingdom of Spain, the Kingdom of Sweden, and the United Kingdom of Great Britain and Northern Ireland concerning Measures to Facilitate the Restructuring and Operation of the European Defence Industry, Farnborough, 27 July 2000 (SIPRI archive).

8. CRITERIA TO BE USED IN CONSIDERING LICENCE APPLICATIONS FOR THE EXPORT OF CONVENTIONAL ARMS FROM THE UK

Statement by the Secretary of State for Foreign and Commonwealth Affairs, 28 July 1997

Parliamentary Question

Mr Stephen Timms (East Ham) (L)

To ask the Secretary of State for Foreign and Commonwealth Affairs what criteria will be used in considering licence applications for the export of conventional arms; and if he will make a statement.

Answer [The Secretary of State for Foreign and Commonwealth Affairs]

The Government are committed to the maintenance of a strong defence industry which is a strategic part of our industrial base as well as of our defence effort. Defence exports can also contribute to international stability by strengthening bilateral and collective defence relationships in accordance with the right of self-defence recognised by the UN charter, but arms transfers must be managed responsibly, in particular so as to avoid their use for internal repression and international aggression.

It will be important to avoid a situation in which our policy of seeking to prevent certain regimes from acquiring certain equipment is undermined by foreign competitors supplying them. We will therefore work for the introduction of a European code of conduct, setting high common standards to govern arms exports from all EU member states.

Licences to export strategic goods are issued by the President of the Board of Trade and the export control organisation of the Department of Trade and Industry is the licensing authority. All relevant individual licence applications are circulated by DTI to other Government Departments with an interest, as determined by them in line with their policy responsibilities. These include the Foreign and Commonwealth Office, the Ministry of Defence and the Department for International Development.

The present Government were not responsible for the decisions on export licences made by the previous Administration. We do not, however, consider that it would be realistic or practical to revoke licences that were valid and in force at the time of our election.

The criteria set out below will be used when considering all future individual applications for licences to export goods entered in part III of schedule 1 to the Export of Goods (Control) Order 1994 and existing licence applications on which a decision has not yet been made. The criteria will also be applied when considering advance approvals for promotion prior to formal application for an export licence and licence applications for the export of dual-use goods when there are grounds for believing that the end user of such goods will be the armed forces or the internal security forces of the recipient country.

The criteria will constitute broad guidance. They will not be applied mechanistically and judgment will always be required. Individual applications will be considered case by case.

CRITERIA USED IN CONSIDERING CONVENTIONAL ARMS EXPORT LICENCE APPLICATIONS

1. An export licence will not be issued if the arguments for doing so are outweighed by the need to comply with the UK's international obligations and commitments, or by concern that the goods might be used for internal repression or international aggression, or by the risks to regional stability, or other considerations as described in these criteria.

The United Kingdom's international obligations

2. An export licence should be refused if approval would be inconsistent with:

(*a*) the UK's international obligations and commitments to enforce United Nations, Organisation for Security and Co-operation in Europe and European Union arms embargoes, together with any national embargoes or other commitments regarding the application of strategic export controls;

(*b*) the UK's international obligations under the nuclear non-proliferation treaty, the biological weapons convention and the chemical weapons convention;

(*c*) the UK's commitments to the international export control regimes—the Australia group, the missile technology control regime, the nuclear suppliers group and the Wassenaar arrangement;

(*d*) the EU common criteria for arms exports, the guidelines for conventional arms transfers agreed by the permanent five members of the UN Security Council, and the OSCE principles governing conventional arms transfers;

(*e*) the UK's commitment not to export all forms of anti-personnel land mines and their components.

The United Kingdom's national interests

3. Full weight should be given to the UK's national interests when considering applications for licences, including:

(*a*) the potential effect on the UK's defence and security interests and those of allies and EU partners;

(*b*) the potential effect on the UK's economic, financial and commercial interests, including our long-term interests in having stable, democratic trading partners;

(*c*) the potential effect on the UK's relations with the recipient country;

(*d*) the potential effect on any collaborative defence production or procurement project with allies or EU partners;

(*e*) the protection of the UK's essential strategic industrial base.

Human rights and internal repression

4. The Government:

(*a*) will take into account respect for human rights and fundamental freedoms in the recipient country;

(*b*) will not issue an export licence if there is a clearly identifiable risk that the proposed export might be used for internal repression.

5. For these purposes equipment which might be used for internal repression will include:

(*a*) Equipment where there is clear evidence of the recent use of similar equipment for internal repression by the proposed end user, or where there is reason to believe that the equipment will be diverted from its stated end use or end user and used for internal repression;

(*b*) Equipment which has obvious application for internal repression, in cases where the recipient country has a significant and continuing record of such repression, unless the end use of the equipment is judged to be legitimate, such as protection of members of security forces from violence.

6. The nature of the equipment proposed for export will also be carefully considered. Certain goods have more obvious potential for use in internal repression than others, such as armoured personnel carriers specially designed for internal security. In other cases, there may be *prima facie* reasons for believing that a particular equipment might be used in such roles in certain circumstances. Any proposed export which is to be used by the recipient country for internal security purposes should be considered particularly carefully.

7. Internal repression includes extra-judicial killings, arbitrary arrest, torture, suppression or major violation of human rights and fundamental freedoms. In some cases, the use of force by a Government within its own borders does not constitute internal repression. The use of such force by Governments is legitimate in some cases, for example to preserve law and order against terrorists or other criminals. However, force may be used only in accordance with international human rights standards.

International aggression

8. The Government will not issue an export licence if there is a clearly identifiable risk that the intended recipient would use the proposed export aggressively against another country, or to assert by force a territorial claim. However, a purely theoretical possibility that the items concerned might be used in the future against another state will not of itself lead to a licence being refused.

9. When considering the risk that the country for which arms are destined might use them for international aggression, the Government will take into account:

(*a*) the existence or likelihood of armed conflict between the recipient and another country;

(*b*) a claim against the territory of a neighbouring country which the recipient has in the past tried or threatened to pursue by means of force;

(*c*) whether the equipment [would] be likely to be used other than for the legitimate national security and defence of the recipient.

Regional stability

10. The need not to affect adversely regional stability in any significant way will also be considered. The balance of forces between neighbouring states, their relative expenditure on defence, and the need not to introduce into the region new capabilities which would be likely to lead to increased tension, will all be taken into account.

Other criteria

11. In assessing the impact of the proposed export on the importing country and the risk that exported goods might be diverted to an undesirable end user, the following will be considered:

(*a*) the legitimate defence and domestic security interests of the recipient country, including any involvement in UN or other peacekeeping activity;

(*b*) the technical capability of the recipient country to use the equipment;

(*c*) whether the purchase would seriously undermine the economy of the recipient country, taking into account its public finances, balance of payments, external debt, economic and social development and any International Monetary Fund/World bank-sponsored economic reform programme;

(*d*) the risk of the arms being re-exported or diverted to an undesirable end user, including terrorist organisations—anti-terrorist equipment would need particularly careful consideration in this context.

12. The following factors will also be taken into account:

(*a*) the risk of use of the goods concerned against UK forces;

(*b*) the need to protect UK military classified information and capabilities;

(*c*) the potential for the equipment to be a force multiplier in the region;

(*d*) the risk of reverse engineering or technology transfer.

13. In the application of all the above criteria, account should also be taken of, for example, reporting from diplomatic posts, relevant reports by international bodies, intelligence, and information from open sources and non-governmental organisations.

Reporting to Parliament

To ensure full transparency and accountability to Parliament the Government will report annually on the state of strategic export controls and their application, thereby providing for parliamentary consideration of the application of the criteria. The Government will also inform Parliament of any changes to the criteria.

———

Source: British House of Commons, *Parliamentary Debates: Official Report* (Hansard), written answers, 28 July 1997, cols 27–29, URL <http://www.parliament.the-stationery-office.co.uk/pa/cm199798/cmhansrd/vo97072 8text>.

9. POLITICAL PRINCIPLES OF THE GOVERNMENT OF THE FEDERAL REPUBLIC OF GERMANY FOR THE EXPORT OF WAR WEAPONS AND OTHER MILITARY EQUIPMENT

Berlin, 19 January 2000

The Government of the Federal Republic of Germany, desiring

– to pursue a restrictive policy on arms exports,

– with regard to the international and statutory obligations of the Federal Republic of Germany, to gear arms exports to Germany's security needs and foreign policy interests,

– through the restriction and control of such exports to contribute to safeguarding peace, preventing the threat or use of force, securing respect for human rights and promoting sustainable development in all parts of the world,

– hence to take account also of decisions adopted by international institutions with a view to disarmament and designed to restrict the international arms trade,

– to press for such decisions to be made legally binding at the international as well as the European level,

has modified its principles for the export of war weapons and other military equipment as follows:

I. General principles

1. The Federal Government's decisions regarding the export of war weapons[1] and other military equipment[2] are made in accordance with the provisions of the War Weapons Control Act and the Foreign Trade and Payments Act as well as the EU Code of Conduct for Arms Exports adopted by the European Council on 8 June 1998[3] and such arrangements as may be agreed subsequently as well as the Principles Governing Conventional Arms Transfers adopted by the Organization for Security and Co-operation in Europe (OSCE) on 25 November 1993. The criteria laid down in the EU Code of Conduct are an integral part of these Policy Principles. The standards stipulated in the Code of Conduct will be superseded by any more stringent standards that may be derived from the following principles:

2. The issue of respect for human rights in the countries of destination and end-use is a key factor in deciding whether or not to grant licences for the export of war weapons and other military equipment.

3. On principle export licences for war weapons and other military equipment will not be granted where there are reasonable grounds to suspect they may be used for internal repression as defined in the EU Code of Conduct for Arms Exports or the sustained and systematic abuse of human rights. In this context the assessment of the human rights situation in the recipient country is an important factor to be considered.

---

[1] Weapons (complete weapons as well as components classed separately as weapons) listed in the Schedule of War Weapons (Annex to the War Weapons Control Act).

[2] Goods specified in Part I, Section A of the Schedule of Exports (Annex to the Foreign Trade and Payment Act) with the exception of war weapons.

[3] Enclosed as annex [not reproduced here].

4. Such assessments will take into account the views of the European Union, the Council of Europe, the United Nations (UN), the OSCE and other international bodies. Reports issued by international human rights organizations will also be taken into consideration.

5. The end-use of war weapons and other military equipment must be definitively determined.

II. NATO countries[4], EU member states, countries with NATO-equivalent status[5]

1. The export of war weapons and other military equipment to these countries will be geared to the security interests of the Federal Republic of Germany with regard to the Alliance and the European Union.

In principle, such exports will not be restricted unless in specific cases this is warranted on particular political grounds.

2. Cooperative ventures in this area should be in the interest of the Alliance and/or European policy. In the case of coproduction projects covered by intergovernmental agreements with countries referred to in this Section, these arms export principles will be given practical effect as far as possible. While mindful of its special interest in its cooperation standing, the Federal Government will not forgo any opportunities it may have to influence export projects envisaged by its cooperation partners (Section II (3)).

3. Before concluding any cooperation agreement, a timely joint assessment of its export policy implications is to be made.

To give effect to its arms exports policy principles, the Federal Government reserves the right by way of consultations to object to particular export projects envisaged by its cooperation partners. All new cooperation agreements should therefore aim in principle to incorporate a consultations procedure enabling the Federal Government to raise effectively any objections it might have to exports envisaged by its partner country. In so doing the Federal Government will seek, in the light of the human rights criterion, to strike a balance between its interest in cooperation and its fundamentally restrictive arms exports policy.

---

[4] Area of application of NATO Treaty, Article 6.

[5] Australia, Japan, New Zealand, Switzerland.

4. Before any exports of war weapons or other military equipment involving German components take place, the Federal Foreign Office, the Federal Ministry of Economics and the Federal Ministry of Defence, in conjunction with the Federal Chancellery, will evaluate whether in any specific case the relevant conditions for initiating such consultations exist.

The Federal Government will raise objections—generally following consideration of the matter by the Federal Security Council—against such exports involving the use of German components in the following cases:

– exports to countries involved in armed conflict, unless such conflict is covered by Article 51 of the UN Charter,

– exports to countries where an outbreak of armed conflict is imminent or where exports may stir up, perpetuate or exacerbate latent tensions and conflicts,

– exports where there are reasonable grounds to suspect they may be used for internal repression as defined by the EU Code of Conduct for Arms Exports or the sustained and systematic abuse of human rights,

– exports that would impair vital security interests of the Federal Republic of Germany,

– exports that would impose such a strain on relations with third countries that even Germany's own interest in the cooperative venture and in maintaining good relations with its cooperation partner must rank second.

Objections will not be raised if in the light of the considerations outlined in Section III (4) to (7) below licences for the export of direct deliveries of war weapons and other military equipment are likely to be granted.

5. In the case of cooperative ventures between German companies and companies in countries referred to in Section II above not covered by intergovernmental agreements, supplies of components will, as with direct deliveries of war weapons and other military equipment to those countries, in principle not be restricted. The Federal Government will, however, as in the case of cooperative ventures covered by inter-governmental agreements, bring its influence to bear in the matter of exports resulting from cooperative ventures between commercial companies.

To that end it will require German cooperative venture partners to enter a contractual obligation that, should they supply components of a quantity or type that could be relevant to the manufacture of war weapons, they will inform the Federal Government in good time as to their partners' export intentions and seek legally binding arrangements on end-use.

6. In the case of German supplies of components (separate components or sub-systems) that constitute war weapons or other military equipment, the partner country is in terms of exports law both purchaser and user. Where such components are built into a weapons system as fixed features, that process in terms of exports law makes the partner country the country of origin of the goods in question.

III. Other countries

1. A restrictive policy will be pursued regarding exports of war weapons and other military equipment to countries other than those covered by Section II. Notably the development of additional, specifically export-oriented capacities must be avoided. The Federal Government will not take the initiative to privilege any specific country or region.

2. Export licences for war weapons (subject to licensing under the War Weapons Control Act and the Foreign Trade and Payments Act) will not be granted unless in a specific case this is exceptionally warranted on particular foreign and security policy grounds, having due regard to Alliance interests. Labour policy considerations must not be a decisive factor.

3. Export licences for other military equipment (subject to licensing under the Foreign Trade and Payments Act) will be granted only where such exports will not prejudice interests that German law on foreign trade and payments serves to protect, namely, security, peace among the nations and Germany's foreign relations.

The protection of these interests takes priority over economic interests as defined in Section 3(1) of the Foreign Trade and Payments Act.

4. Export licences pursuant to the War Weapons Control Act and/or the Foreign Trade and Payments Act will not be granted where the internal situation in the country

concerned precludes such action, e.g. in the case of armed conflict or where there are reasonable grounds for suspecting such exports may be used for internal repression or the sustained and systematic abuse of human rights. In this context the human rights situation in the recipient country is a major factor to be considered.

5. No licences will be granted for the export of war weapons and other military equipment related to war weapons[6] to countries

– involved in armed conflict or where armed conflict is imminent,

– where the outbreak of armed conflict is imminent or where such exports would stir up, perpetuate or exacerbate latent tensions and conflicts.

Exports to countries involved in external armed conflicts or where there is a danger such conflicts may erupt are therefore ruled out on principle except in cases covered by Article 51 of the UN Charter.

6. Decisions on whether to grant export licences for war weapons and other military equipment will take into account whether sustainable development in the recipient country is being seriously impeded by excessive arms spending.

7. Also to be taken into account is the recipient country's conduct in terms of whether it

– supports and promotes terrorism and international organized crime,

– complies with international obligations, especially renunciation of the threat or use of force, including obligations under humanitarian law on international or non-international conflicts,

– has assumed obligations in the area of non-proliferation and other aspects of arms control and disarmament, notably by signing, ratifying and implementing the arms control and disarmament arrangements specified in the EU Code of Conduct for arms exports,

– supports the UN Arms Register.

IV. Definitive determination of end-use

1. Export licences for war weapons and other military equipment will be granted only on the basis of prior knowledge of definitive end-use in the country of final destination.

This will generally require a written assurance by the end-user as well as other appropriate documentation.

2. Export licences for war weapons or other military equipment of a quantity and type relevant to war weapons may be granted only on presentation of governmental end-use certificates that preclude re-exports without prior authorization. This applies mutatis mutandis to any other military equipment related to war weapons exported in connection with a manufacturing licence. For the export of such equipment used for the manufacture of war weapons definitive end-use certificates must be furnished.

Stringent standards are to be applied in assessing whether the recipient country is capable of carrying out effective export controls.

3. War weapons and other military equipment relevant to war weapons may only be re-exported to third countries or transferred inside the EU Internal Market with the written approval of the Federal Government.

4. A recipient country that, in breach of an end-use certificate, authorizes or does not seek to prevent or sanction the unauthorized re-export of war weapons or other military equipment relevant to war weapons will on principle, as long as such conditions persist, be excluded from receiving any further deliveries of war weapons or other military equipment related to war weapons.

V. Arms exports report

The Federal Government will submit to the German Bundestag an annual report on the principle and practice of its arms exports policy listing, with details of the relevant legislation, the export licences for war weapons and other military equipment it has granted over the past year.

___

Source: SIPRI archive, URL <http://projects. sipri.se/expcon/natexpcon/Germany/frg_guide. htm>.

___

[6] Plant and documentation for the manufacturer of war weapons.

10. SWEDISH GUIDELINES FOR THE EXPORTATION OF MILITARY EQUIPMENT AND OTHER FORMS OF COLLABORATION ABROAD

Excerpts from the Military Equipment Act, 1992

A permit for the exportation of military equipment, or for other forms of collaboration abroad involving military equipment, may only be granted if such exportation or cooperation:

1. is considered necessary to fulfil the Swedish defence forces' requirements for materiél or know-how, or otherwise desirable for reasons of national security, and

2. is not in conflict with the principles and aims of Swedish foreign policy.

When considering a request for a permit, the Government is responsible for making an overall assessment, taking into account all the relevant circumstances and applying the basic principles stated above.

There are no obstacles of a foreign policy nature to collaboration with, or exportation to, the Nordic countries and the traditionally neutral countries of Europe. In principle, collaboration with these countries is consistent with the requirements of Sweden's national security. To the extent that collaboration with other members of the European Community is extended, the same principles should be applied to collaboration with, and exports to, these countries.

A permit may only be granted with regard to a Government, a Government Authority or a Government-authorized recipient; furthermore, an End User Declaration (EUC) or an Own Production Declaration (OPD) should be presented when equipment is to be transferred abroad. A Government which, despite assurances to the Swedish Government, has allowed or neglected to prevent the unauthorized re-exportation of Swedish military equipment, shall not in principle be eligible to receive further equipment from Sweden as long as these circumstances remain.

A permit for exportation or for other forms of collaboration abroad under the Military Equipment Act may not be granted if this would contravene an international agreement which Sweden has signed, a Resolution adopted by the United Nations Security Council, or a rule of international law concerning exports from neutral states in times of armed conflict (unconditional obstacles).

A permit for the exportation of military equipment, or for other forms of collaboration abroad comprising military equipment, may not be granted when it involves a country in which widespread and serious violations of human rights occur. Respect for human rights is an essential condition for the issuance of permits.

A permit for the exportation of Military Equipment for Combat Purposes (MEC), or for other collaboration involving MEC or Other Military Equipment (OME), should not be granted for a country involved in armed conflict with another country—whether or not war has been declared—or for a country involved in an international conflict which may lead to an armed conflict, or for a country in which internal armed disturbances are taking place.

A permit should be granted for the exportation of equipment designated as Other Military Equipment (OME), on condition that the recipient country is not involved in an armed conflict with another country, that it is not the scene of internal armed disturbances or widespread and serious violations of human rights, and that no unconditional obstacle exists.

A permit which has been granted should be revoked if an unconditional obstacle arises, or if the recipient country becomes involved in an armed conflict with another country or the scene of internal armed disturbances. When one of the latter two situations has arisen, the Government may refrain from revoking the permit in exceptional cases, if this is consistent with the rules of international law and with the principles and aims of Swedish foreign policy.

Permits should be granted for the exportation of spare parts pertaining to equipment exported previously with the requisite permission, unless an unconditional obstacle exists. The same applies to other deliveries, of, for example, ammunition, linked with previous exports of equipment, or otherwise in cases where denial of permission would be unreasonable.

With reference in particular to agreements with a foreign Party on the joint development or production of military equipment, the examination of each case shall be based on the basic principles given above. Exports to the cooperating country under the agreement should be permitted unless an unconditional obstacle arises.

If an agreement with a foreign Party is based on an assumption of exportation from the cooperating country to third countries, and the equipment concerned has a predominantly Swedish identity, the question of such exports should be assessed in accordance with Swedish guidelines. Regarding equipment with a predominantly foreign identity, exports from the cooperating country to third countries should be assessed in accordance with the export regulations of the cooperating country.

If there is a strong Swedish defence policy interest in a certain agreement, and the cooperating country requires that certain exports take place from that country, exports to third countries under the export regulations of the cooperating country may be allowed in other circumstances too.

In cases where collaboration with another country in the area of military equipment is of considerable magnitude and importance to Sweden, a government-to-government agreement should be reached between Sweden and the cooperating country. Before agreements of this kind are signed, the Advisory Council on Foreign Affairs should be consulted.

______

Source: Government Bill 1991/92:174 'The Military Equipment Act'; Parliamentary Report 1992/93: UUl, Parliamentary Authorization 1992/93:61 (unofficial translation).

Appendix B. Other EU documents relating to non-proliferation of conventional arms

1. ARTICLES 223–225 OF THE TREATY OF ROME

1957

Article 223

1. The provisions of this Treaty shall not preclude the application of the following rules:

(*a*) no Member State shall be obliged to supply information the disclosure of which it considers contrary to the essential interests of its security;

(*b*) any Member State may take such measures as it considers necessary for the protection of the essential interests of its security which are connected with the production of or trade in arms, munitions and war material; such measures shall not adversely affect the conditions of competition in the common market regarding products which are not intended for specifically military purposes.

2. During the first years after the entry into force of this Treaty, the Council shall, acting unanimously, draw up a list of products to which the provisions of paragraph 1(b) shall apply.

3. The Council may, acting unanimously on a proposal from the Commission, make changes in this list.

Article 224

Member States shall consult each other with a view to taking together the steps needed to prevent the functioning of the common market being affected by measures which a Member State may be called upon to take in the event of serious internal disturbances affecting the maintenance of law and order, in the event of war, serious international tension constituting a threat of war, or in order to carry out obligations it has accepted for the purpose of maintaining peace and international security.

Article 225

If measures taken in the circumstances referred to in Articles 223 and 224 have the effect of distorting the conditions of competition in the common market, the Commission shall, together with the State concerned, examine how these measures can be adjusted to the rules laid down in the Treaty.

By way of derogation from the procedure laid down in Articles 169 and 170, the Commission or any Member State may bring the matter directly before the Court of Justice if it considers that another Member State is making improper use of the powers provided for in Articles 223 and 224. The Court of Justice shall give its rulings in camera.

———

Source: URL <http://europa.eu.int/abc/treaties/en/entr6g.htm#Article–223>.

2. THE EU COMMON EMBARGO LIST

Agreed by the Council of Ministers 1991

When an arms embargo is applied to a particular country, EC States will agree to it being interpreted either as a 'full scope' embargo, or as less than full scope.

If the agreement is that it is to be full scope, then the embargo is defined as being on 'arms, munitions and military equipment'. In that case, it will apply to all the goods on the common embargo list below.

In the case of an embargo which is less than full scope, it will be defined as 'an embargo on arms and munitions'. The Member States will then agree to specify the categories within the common list which the embargo will cover.

The Common Embargo List

a. Weapons designed to kill and their ammunition

1. Small arms and machine guns, and specially designed components thereof.

2. Large calibre armament or weapons and projectors, and specially designed components and 'specially designed software' thereof.

3. Ammunition and specially designed components and 'specially designed software' thereof, for weapons embargoed.

4. Bombs, torpedoes, rockets and missiles, and specially designed components and 'specially designed software' therefor.

5. Fire control systems and sub-systems, specially designed for military use, specially designed components and accessories and 'specially designed software' therefor.

6. Tanks and self-propelled guns.

7. Toxological agents, related equipment components, materials and technology, and 'specially designed software' therefor.

8. Military explosives.

9. Forgings, castings and semi-finished products specially designed for the products embargoed by items (a) 1, 2, 3, 4 and 6 on this list.

10. Fire-arms silencers (mufflers), specially designed components and 'specially designed software' therefor.

11. Directed energy weapons systems and specially designed components, and 'specially designed software' therefor.

12. Kinetic energy weapons systems and associated equipment, specially designed components and 'specially designed software' therefor.

b. Weapon Platforms

1. Armed, armoured vehicles or vehicles fitted with mounting for arms.

2. Vessels of war and special naval equipment, and specifically designed components and 'specially designed software' therefor.

3. Aircraft and helicopters, aero-engines and aircraft or helicopter equipment, associated equipment and components; specially designed for military purposes, and 'specially designed software' therefor.

4. Forgings, casting and semi-finished products specially designed for the products embargoed by Item (b) on this list.

c. Non-weapon Platforms

1. Vehicles, as follows, specially designed or modified for military use, specially designed components and 'specially designed software' therefor:

– armoured railway trains

– half-tracks

– gun-carriers and tractors specially designed for towing artillery

– recovery vehicles

– amphibious and deep water fording vehicles

– mobile repair shops specially designed to service military equipment

– all other vehicles specially designed or modified for military use.

2. Specially armoured equipment.

3. Forgings, castings and semi-finished products specially designed for products embargoed by Item (c) 1 on this list.

d. Ancillary Equipment

1. Military infrared, thermal imaging and image intensifier equipment, specially designed components and 'specially designed software' therefor.

2. Power-controlled searchlights and control units, specially designed components and 'specially designed software' therefor, designed for military use.

3. Unmanned airborne vehicles, associated equipment and components, specially designed for military purposes, and 'specially designed software' therefor.

4. Electronic equipment specially designed for military use and specially designed components and 'specially designed software' therefor.

5. Photographic and electro-optical imaging equipment, and specially designed components and 'specially designed software' therefor.

6. Specialised equipment for military training or for simulating military scenarios, specially designed components and accessories and 'specially designed software' therefor.

7. Miscellaneous equipment and materials, as follows, specially designed components, and 'specially designed software' therefor.

– self-contained diving and underwater swimming apparatus.

– construction *equipment built to military* specifications, specially designed for airborne transport.

– external fittings, coatings and treatments for the suppression of acoustic, radar, infrared and other emissions, specially designed for military use.

– field engineer equipment specially designed for use in a combat zone.

8. Cryogenic and superconductive equipment, specially designed components and accessories, and 'specially designed software' therefor.

9. 'Software', as follows:

(*a*) 'Software' specially designed for:

– modelling, simulation or evaluation of military weapons systems

– developmental, monitoring, maintenance or up-dating of 'software' embedded in military weapon systems

– modelling or simulating military operation scenarios, not embargoed by item (d) 6.

– command communications, control and intelligence (C^3I) applications.

(*b*) 'Software' for determining the effects of conventional, nuclear, chemical or biological warfare weapons.

Source: SIPRI archive, URL <http://projects.sipri.se/expcon/euframe/eu_commonlist.htm>.

3. THE EU PROGRAMME FOR PREVENTING AND COMBATING ILLICIT TRAFFICKING IN CONVENTIONAL ARMS

Adopted by the Council of the European Union, 26 June 1997

The Council of the European Union,

Convinced that peace and security are inextricably interlinked with economic development and reconstruction,

Recognizing that the availability and accumulation of massive quantities of conventional arms and especially their illicit trafficking, often associated with destabilizing activities, are disturbing and dangerous phenomena, particularly for the internal situation of affected states and for the respect of human rights,

Stressing the need for effective national control measures on the transfer of conventional arms,

Recognizing also the curbing of illicit trafficking of conventional arms as an important contribution to the relaxation of tension and to reconciliation processes,

Desirous to take concrete measures to curb the illicit traffic and use of conventional arms, as called for in UNGA resolution 51/45 F, to take practical disarmament measures, as called for in UNGA resolution 51/45 N, and to provide assistance to states for curbing the illicit traffic in small arms and collecting them, as called for in UNGA resolution 51/45 L, all of 10 December 1996,

Recalling the EU Member States' common reply to UNGA resolution 50/70 B of 12 December 1995,

has adopted the following:

1. EU Member States will strengthen their collective efforts to prevent and combat illicit trafficking of arms[1], particularly of small arms, on and through their territories. In particular, they will vigilantly discharge their national responsibility to ensure the effective implementation of obligations resulting from Conventions and Joint Actions adopted in this field. Furthermore, consideration could be given to, inter alia:

– Fostering enhanced co-operation and co-ordination, whilst respecting national legislation and policies, amongst intelligence, customs and other law enforcement agencies, both at the national and international level, in order to ensure adequate (customs) checks, as

------

[1] For the purpose of this Programme and in conformity with the definition in paragraph 7 of the Guidelines for International Arms Transfers (UN Disarmament Commission, 7 May 1996), 'illicit trafficking in arms' is understood to cover that international trade in conventional arms which is contrary to the laws of states and/or international law.

well as prompt investigation and effective prosecution in cases of illicit trafficking of arms;

– Improving the exchange of information and data on illicit trafficking of arms, e.g. through the use of international data bases and risk analyses.

2. The EC and its Member States, each within the limits of its respective competence, will take concerted action to assist other countries in preventing and combating illicit trafficking of arms, particularly of small arms. Specifically, this assistance could aim to:

– Set up or strengthen, as appropriate, an adequate body of laws and administrative measures for regulating and monitoring effectively transfers of arms;

– Adopt strict measures, and provide an adequate number of appropriately trained police and customs officials, for the enforcement of national arms export control legislation;

– Set up (sub) regional points of contact to report illicit trafficking of arms;

– Set up national commissions against illicit trafficking of arms;

– Prevent corruption and bribery in connection with illicit trafficking of arms;

– Promote (sub) regional and national co-operation amongst police, customs authorities and intelligence services in this field;

– Promote the use of relevant existing international data bases.

3. The EC and its Members States, each within the limits of its respective competence, will take concerted action to assist affected countries, especially in post-conflict situations, and situations where a minimal degree of security and stability exists, in suppressing the illicit circulation and trafficking of arms, particularly of small arms, Specifically, they could aim to:

– Ensure the incorporation of appropriate measures for suppressing the illicit circulation and trafficking of arms in peace-keeping operations and cease fire or peace agreements preceding such operations. To this end, they will co-operate closely, where appropriate, with the United Nations;

– Set up weapons collection, buy back, and destruction programmes;

– Promote the integration of former combatants in civilian life.

4. EU Member States will ensure adequate co-operation amongst the competent branches of their national authorities in giving concrete form to the objectives of this Programme. The Presidency of the Council will ensure the necessary co-ordination in this field.

5. The EC, according to its own procedures, and its Member States are prepared, where appropriate, to make funds available in pursuit of the objectives of this Programme.

6. The Council will annually review the actions taken in the framework of this programme.

Source: URL <http://europa.eu.int/comm/development/prevention/programconventarms.htm>.

Select bibliography

Interviews*

1. United Kingdom

4 July 1997	Dr Susan Willett, Senior Research Fellow, Centre for Defence Studies, King's College, London
8 July 1997	Will McMahon, Joint Coordinator, Campaign Against the Arms Trade, London
9 July 1997	Elisabeth Clegg, Arms Trade Researcher, Saferworld, London
10 July 1997	Dr Joanna Spears, Department of War Studies, King's College, London
14 July 1997	John Thurlow, Managing Director, Deltac Ltd, Export Control Consultants, Chertsey, Surrey
15 July 1997	Dr Paul Cornish, Visiting Fellow, Centre for International Studies, University of Cambridge
26 Aug. 1997	Brinley Salzmann, Manager, Market Information, DMA, Grayshott, Surrey
28 Aug. 1997	Martin Day, Head of Export Control Policy Section, Foreign and Commonwealth Office, London
1 Sep. 1997	Chris Savage, Senior Policy Officer, Economic and Social Affairs Department, Trades Union Congress, London
	Graham Jenkins and Elspeth Paton, Export Licensing and Sanctions, Criminal and Enforcement Policy Group (CEP), Customs Policy Directorate, HM Customs and Excise, London
3 Sep. 1997	Ashley Adams, Head of Defence Export Services Secretariat, Ministry of Defence, London
24 Nov. 1997	Tony Medawar, Head of Policy Unit, Export Control Organisation, Department of Trade and Industry, London

2. Federal Republic of Germany

23 Sep. 1997	Volker Hahn, Ministry of Economics, Bonn
	Dr Günther Sprögel and Mr Warnken, Ministry of Economics, Bonn
24 Sep. 1997	Michael Brzoska, Head of Research, Bonn International Centre for Conversion (BICC), Bonn
26 Sep. 1997	Mr Wienicke and Mr Ricke (Departmental Head), Customs Criminal Investigation Service (ZKA), Cologne
	Mr Maer, Federation of German Industries (BDI), Cologne

* The author is indebted to the interviewees for their kind cooperation with this research work. The views expressed in this book are the responsibility of the author and of no one else. The titles of the interviewees reflect their professional positions at the time of the interviews.

Michael Masberg, Director of Section, Department of International Affairs, Economic Policy, Federation of German Industries (BDI)

Jorg Wessels, freelance researcher/assistant to Klaus Bachmeier, MP (SPD), Cologne

30 Sep. 1997   Peter Darmstadt, Assistant to Dr Andreas Schockenhoff, MP (CDU), Bonn

2 Oct. 1997   Susanne Bös, Federal Export Office, Eschborn

Gerhard Rein, Federal Export Office, Eschborn

6 Oct. 1997   Annette Schaper, Senior Research Associate, Peace Research Institute Frankfurt

15 Oct. 1997   Michaela Elany, part-time NGO researcher, BUKO, Bremen

17 Oct. 1997   Andrea Kolling, founder member and trustee of BUKO, Bremen

Michael Ahlmann, Senior Works Councillor, STN Atlas Electronik GmbH, Bremen

24 Nov. 1997   Bernhard Sauer, Head of Legal Affairs, BAFA, Eschborn (interview took place in London)

3. Sweden

8 Oct. 1997   Dr Ian Anthony, Project Leader, SIPRI, Stockholm

9 Oct. 1997   Pär Ahlberger, Ministry for Trade and Industry, Stockholm

Ambassador Staffan Sohlman, Inspector-General, National Inspectorate of Strategic Products (ISP), Stockholm

Paul Beijer, Principal Administration Officer, National Inspectorate of Strategic Products (ISP), Stockholm

10 Oct. 1997   Birgitta Alani, Senior Administrative Officer, Ministry for Foreign Affairs, Stockholm

Peter Kröjs, Board of Customs, Control Division, Stockholm

4. EU

24 Oct. 1997   Martin Butcher, Director of the Centre for European Security and Disarmament, Brussels

27 Oct. 1997   Muriel Guin, European Commission, DGIA

Antonis Antanasiotis, European Commission, DGIA

Fredrik Linton, European Commission, DGIII

28 Oct. 1997   Graham Woodcock, Secretary General, European Defence Industry Group, Brussels

29 Oct. 1997   Peter Lennon, European Commission, DGIIIA

Giancarlo Chevallard, European Commission, DGIA

30 Oct. 1997   Oliver Nette, European Commission, DGI

Ernst Gulcher, MEP, Green Group in the European Parliament and European Network Against the Arms Trade, Brussels

12 Dec. 1997   Gary Titley, MEP, Labour Party, Manchester

B. Publications

1. Primary sources

Data reference material

International Institute for Strategic Studies (IISS), *The Military Balance* (Oxford University Press, annual)

Stockholm International Peace Research Institute, *SIPRI Yearbook: World Armaments and Disarmament* (Oxford University Press, annual)

US Department of State, Bureau of Arms Control (previously US Arms Control and Disarmament Agency, ACDA), *World Military Expenditures and Arms Transfers* (annual)

Worldwide Guide to Export Controls (Export Control Publications: Chertsey, updated three or four times each year)

Germany

German Federal Export Office, 'BAFA export controls: summary', Eschborn, 15 Apr. 1998

German Federal Ministry of Economics, 'Report by the Government of the Federal Republic of Germany on the tightening of export controls for goods with civilian and military applications (dual-use)', BMWi, Bonn, 11 Mar. 1992

German Customs Criminal Investigation Service, 'Zollkriminalamt: development and tasks', Cologne, Mar. 1996

Sweden

Swedish Ministry for Foreign Affairs, 'Sweden's policy on arms exports' (unofficial translation), Stockholm, 1989

—, Strategic Export Control Division, *Swedish Arms Exports in 1996: A Government Report*, Swedish Government Report to Parliament 1996/97:138 (Ministry for Foreign Affairs: Stockholm, June 1997)

—, Strategic Export Control Division, *Swedish Arms Exports in 1997: A Government Report*, Swedish Government Report to Parliament 1997/98:147 (Ministry for Foreign Affairs: Stockholm, May 1998)

—, Strategic Export Control Division, *Swedish Arms Exports in 1998: A Government Report*, Swedish Government Report to Parliament 1998/99:128 (Ministry for Foreign Affairs: Stockholm, May 1999)

—, Strategic Export Control Department, *Swedish Arms Exports and Strategic Export Controls in 1999: A Government Report*, Swedish Government Report to Parliament 1999/2000:110 (Ministry for Foreign Affairs: Stockholm, Mar. 2000)

—, *Report on Sweden's Export Control Policy and Exports of Military Equipment in 2000*, Swedish Government Report to Parliament 2000/01:114 (Stockholm, Apr. 2001)

Swedish National Inspectorate of Strategic Products, 'National Inspectorate of Strategic Products: presentation in brief', Stockholm, 1996

United Kingdom

British Department of Trade and Industry, 'The end-use control: a guide for exporters', DTI/Pub 1280/5K/4/94/NP, London, 1994

—, 'Non-proliferation controls (revised July 1995): a guide for exporters', London, July 1995

—, 'Responses to the Department of Trade and Industry's consultative document on strategic export controls', Ref: URN 97/752, London, 5 June 1997

—, *Strategic Export Controls: A Consultative Document*, Cm 3349 (Her Majesty's Stationery Office: London, July 1996)

—, *Strategic Export Controls*, Cm 3989 (Her Majesty's Stationery Office: London, July 1998)

British Department of Trade and Industry, Export Control Organisation, 'Code of practice for enforcement', DTI/Pub 1220/5K/2.94/AR, London, Dec. 1993

—, Export Control Organisation, *Export Control Organisation Annual Report 1995* (Department of Trade and Industry: London, Oct. 1996)

—, Non-Proliferation Department, 'Export Licence and Arms Working Party (MoD Form 680) applications: guidance for desk officers', Mar. 1997

British Foreign and Commonwealth Office, *Report of the Sierra Leone Arms Investigation*, HC 1997/98 1016 (Her Majesty's Stationery Office: London, 27 July 1998)

British House of Commons, *The Right Honourable Sir Richard Scott, Report of the Inquiry into the Export of Defence Equipment and Dual-Use Goods to Iraq and Related Prosecutions: Return to an Address of the Honourable the House of Commons dated 15th February*, HC 1995/96 115 (Her Majesty's Stationery Office: London, 1996), 5 vols and index (the Scott Report)

British House of Commons, Public Accounts Committee, *Pergau Hydro-Electric Project*, HC 1993/94 7 (Her Majesty's Stationery Office: London, 21 Mar. 1994)

British House of Commons, Select Committee on Defence and Select Committee on Trade and Industry, *Aspects of Defence Procurement and Industrial Policy*, HC 1995/96 333 (Her Majesty's Stationery Office: London, 1995)

British House of Commons, Select Committee on Foreign Affairs, *Foreign Policy and Human Rights*, HC 1998/99 100-I (Her Majesty's Stationery Office: London, 10 Dec. 1998)

—, *Overseas Arms Sales: Foreign Policy Aspects*, HC 1981/82 41 (Her Majesty's Stationery Office: London, 4 Mar. 1982)

—, *Public Expenditure: The Pergau Hydro-Electric Project, Malaysia: The Aid and Trade Provisions and Related Matters, Third Report*, HC 1993/94 271-I (Her Majesty's Stationery Office: London, 1994), vol. 1

—, *UK Policy on Weapons Proliferation and Arms Control in the Post Cold War Era*, HC 1994/95 34-I and 34-II (Her Majesty's Stationery Office: London, 30 Mar. 1995), vols I and II

British House of Commons, Select Committee on Trade and Industry, *Exports to Iraq: Project Babylon and Long Range Guns*, HC 1991/92 86 (Her Majesty's Stationery Office: London, Mar. 1992)

—, *Strategic Export Controls*, HC 1998/99 65 (Her Majesty's Stationery Office: London, 2 Dec. 1998)

—, *Third Report: Export Licensing and BMARC*, HC 1995/96 87-I (Her Majesty's Stationery Office: London, 12 June 1996)

British Interdepartmental Committee, 'Trafficking in arms: controls and procedures', Cabinet Office, 17 Dec. 1996

British Ministry of Defence, 'The release of information on defence related exports', Ministry of Defence, London, July 1996

—, Foreign and Commonwealth Office and Department of Trade and Industry, *Annual Report on Strategic Export Controls* (Foreign and Commonwealth Office: London, Mar. 1999)

—, Foreign and Commonwealth Office and Department of Trade and Industry, *Annual Report on Strategic Export Controls* (Foreign and Commonwealth Office: London, Nov. 1999)

—, Foreign and Commonwealth Office and Department of Trade and Industry, *Annual Report on Strategic Export Controls* (Foreign and Commonwealth Office: London, July 2000)

—, Foreign and Commonwealth Office and Department of Trade and Industry, *Strategic Export Controls: Annual Report* (Stationery Office: London, July 2001)

British National Audit Office, *Overseas Development: Aid to Indonesia*, HC 1996/97 101 (Her Majesty's Stationery Office: London, Nov. 1996)

—, *Ministry of Defence: Support for Defence Exports*, HC 1988/89 303 (Her Majesty's Stationery Office: London, 10 Apr. 1989)

European Union

Council of the European Union, 'Code of Conduct on Arms Exports', 8 June 1998, URL ‹http://europa.eu.int/comm/development/prevention/codecondarmsexp.htm›

—, Council Decision no. 94/942/CFSP of 19 Dec. 1994 on the joint action adopted by the Council on the basis of Article J.3 of the Treaty on European Union concerning the control of exports of dual-use goods

—, Council Regulation (EC) no. 3381/94 of 19 Dec. 1994 setting up a Community regime for the control of exports of dual-use goods

—, 'Draft regulation, control of exports of dual-use goods and technologies', document no. 7672/94, Brussels, 9 June 1994

—, 'EU programme for preventing and combating illicit trafficking in conventional arms', June 1997

—, 'Joint Action adopted by the Council on the basis of Article J.3 of the Treaty on European Union on the European Union's contribution to combating the destabilising accumulation and spread of small arms and light weapons', Brussels, 17 Dec. 1998

European Commission, 'Action plan for the Single Market', Communication of the Commission to the European Council, CSE(97)1 final, 4 June 1997

—, 'Agenda 2000', Communication of the Commission, DOC97/6, Strasbourg, 15 July 1997

—, 'The challenges facing the European defence-related industry: a contribution for action at European level', Communication from the Commission to the Council, the European Parliament, the Economic and Social Committee and the Committee of the Regions, Brussels, Jan. 1996

—, 'Commission opinion of the 21 October 1990 on the proposal for amendment of the Treaty Establishing the European Economic Community with a view to political union', COM(90)600 (final), Brussels, 23 Oct. 1990

—, 'Export controls on dual-use goods and technologies and the completion of the internal market', Communication from the Commission to the Council and the Parliament, SEC(92)85 final, Brussels, 31 Jan. 1992

—, 'Implementing European Union strategy on defence-related industries', COM(97)583 (final), Communication from the Commission to the Council, the European Parliament, the Economic and Social Committee and the Committee of the Regions, Brussels, 4 Dec. 1997

—, 'Proposal for a Council Regulation (EEC) on the control of exports of certain dual-use goods and technologies of certain nuclear products and technologies', COM(92)317, Brussels, 31 Aug. 1992

—, 'Proposal for a Council Regulation (EC) setting up a Community regime for the control of exports of dual-use goods and technology', COM(1998)257 (final), Brussels, Apr. 1998

—, 'Report to the European Parliament and the Council on the application of Regulation (EC) 3381/94 setting up a Community system of export controls regarding dual-use', COM(98)258 (final), Brussels, Apr. 1998

European Communities, *Treaty on European Union* (Office for Official Publications of the European Communities: document no. 1759/60, Luxembourg, 7 Feb. 1992

European Parliament, 'Report drawn up on the behalf of the Political Affairs Committee on arms procurement within a common industrial policy and arms sales, Rapporteur Adam Fergusson', PE 78.344/fin., Strasbourg, 27 June 1983

—, 'Report drawn up on behalf of the Political Affairs Committee on European Arms Exports, Rapporteur Glyn Ford', document A2-0398/88, PE 118.374/fin., Strasbourg, 22 Feb. 1989

—, 'Report drawn on up on behalf of the Political Affairs Committee on the outlook for a European security policy: the significance of a European security policy and its implications for European Political Union, Rapporteur Hans-Gert Poettering', PE 146.269/fin., Strasbourg, 29 Apr. 1991

—, Committee on Economic and Monetary Affairs and Industrial Policy, 'Report on the Commission proposal for a Council Regulation on the control of exports of certain dual-use goods and technologies and of certain nuclear products and technologies, Rapporteur Gerard Fuchs', document A3-0398/92Part A and Part B, PE 201.553/fin., Strasbourg, 3 Dec. 1992

—, Committee on Foreign Affairs, Security and Defence Policy, within the European Parliament, 'Working document on the challenges facing the European defence-related industry', COM(96)0010, Rapporteur Mr Gary Titley, 5 Sep. 1996

—, Directorate-General for Research, 'International transfers of dual-use technologies: CoCom and the European Community', Working Papers, External Economic Relations Series, DOC_EN\DV\239\239598, W-5 10/1993

Others

Council of Europe, Political Affairs Committee, 'Drawing up a European code of conduct on arms sales', Rapporteur Mr Borut Pahor, Slovenia, Socialist Group, doc. 8188, 10 Sep. 1998

Independent European Programme Group (IEPG), 'Towards a stronger Europe', Report by an independent study team established by the defence ministers of nations of the IEPG, Brussels, 1986

OECD, Development Assistance Committee, *Military Expenditure in Developing Countries: Security and Development* (OECD: Paris, 1998)

—, *Participatory Development and Good Governance*, Development Co-operation Guidelines Series (OECD: Paris, 1995)

United Nations, Panel of Governmental Experts on Small Arms, Report of the UN Secretary-General on small arms, UN document A/52/298, 1997

United Nations Disarmament Commission, Guidelines for international arms transfers in the Context of General Assembly Resolution 46/36H of 6 Dec. 1991, UN document A/CN.10/1996/CRP.3, 3 May 1996

US General Accounting Office (GAO), *Export Controls: License Screening and Compliance Procedures Need Strengthening*, GAO/NSIAD-94-178 (GAO: Washington, DC, June 1994)

—, *Military Exports: A Comparison of Government Support in the United States and Three Major Competitors*, GAO/NSIAD-95-86 (GAO: Washington, DC, May 1995)

The Wassenaar Arrangement on Export Controls for Conventional Arms and Dual-Use Goods and Technologies, Initial Elements, as adopted by the Plenary of 11–12 July 1996

2. Books, special studies and reports

Action from Ireland, *Ireland's Links with the Arms Trade and Military Industry* (AFrI: Dublin, 1996)

Adam, B. (ed.), *European Union and Arms Exports* (Groupe de Recherche et d'Information sur la Paix et la Sécurité (GRIP): Brussels, Dec. 1995)

Alic, J. *et al.*, *Beyond Spinoff: Military and Commercial Technology in a Changing World* (Harvard Business School Press: Boston, Mass., 1992)

Altes, P., *Access to Outer Space Technologies: Implications for International Security*, UNIDIR Research Paper no. 15 (United Nations: Geneva, Dec. 1992

American Academy of Arts and Sciences, 'Arms control: thirty years on', *Daedalus*, vol. 120, no. 1 (winter 1991)

Amnesty International, *Repression Trade (UK) Ltd: How the United Kingdom Makes Torture and Death its Business* (Amnesty International: London, 1992)

Anthony, I. (ed.), SIPRI, *Arms Export Regulations* (Oxford University Press: Oxford, 1991)

—, Eavis, P. and Greene, O., *Regulating Arms Exports: A Programme for the European Community* (Saferworld: London, Sep. 1991)

Bailey, K. and Rudney, R. (eds), *Proliferation and Export Controls* (University Press of America: Lanham, Md., 1993)

Baldwin, D., *Neorealism and Neoliberalism: The Contemporary Debate* (Columbia University Press: New York, 1993)

Barratt Brown, M., *Models in Political Economy*, 2nd edn (Penguin: London, 1995)

Bauer, H., Brzoska, M. and Karl, W., *Co-ordination and Control of Arms Exports from EC Member States and the Development of a Common Arms Export Policy, Study Prepared for the European Parliament, Directorate General for Research, European Parliament Research Project no. 4/90/9*, Arbeitspapiere/Working Papers no. 48 (Berghof Foundation: Berlin, 1992)

Benson, W., *Light Weapons Controls and Security Assistance: A Review of Current Practice* (Saferworld/International Alert: London, Sep. 1998)

Bertsch, G., Cupitt, R. and Elliott-Gower, S. (eds), *International Cooperation on Nonproliferation Export Controls: Prospects for the 1990s and Beyond* (University of Michigan Press: Ann Arbor, Mich., 1994)

— and Elliott-Gower, S. (eds), *Export Controls in Transition: Perspectives, Problems, and Prospects* (Duke University Press: Durham, Ga., 1992)

— and Grillot, S. (eds), *Arms on the Market: Reducing the Risk of Proliferation in the Former Soviet Union* (Routledge: New York, 1998)

—, Vogel, H. and Zielonka, J. (eds), *After the Revolutions: East–West Trade and Technology Transfer in the 1990s* (Westview Press: Boulder, Colo., 1991)

Brandt, W., *Common Responsibilities for the 1990s* (Foundation for Development and Peace: Bonn, 1991)

Brauch, H. G. *et al.* (eds), *Controlling the Development and Spread of Military Technology: Lessons from the Past and Challenges for the 1990s* (VU University Press: Amsterdam, 1992)

British American Security Information Council (BASIC), 'Showing no restraint: missed opportunities for arms trade control', *Basic Report*, no. 93:2 (Apr. 1993)

Brittleson, M., *Co-operation or Competition? Defence Procurement Options for the 1990s*, Adelphi Papers no. 250 (International Institute for Strategic Studies: London, 1990)

Brzoska, M., *Spread of Conventional Weapons Production Technology*, Working Papers 76 (Institut für Politische Wissenschaft: Hamburg, 1994)

— and Lock, P. (eds), SIPRI, *Restructuring of Arms Production in Western Europe* (Oxford University Press: Oxford, 1992)

— and Ohlson, T. (eds), SIPRI, *Arms Transfers to the Third World 1971–85* (Oxford University Press: Oxford, 1987)

— and Pearson, F., *Arms and Warfare: Escalation, De-escalation and Negotiation* (University of South Carolina: Columbia, S.C., 1994)

Bull, H., *The Control of the Arms Race* (Weidenfeld & Nicolson: London, 1961)

Buzan, B., *People, States and Fear* (Wheatsheaf Books: London, 1991)

Carlton, D. *et al.* (eds), *Controlling the International Transfer of Weaponry and Related Technology* (Dartmouth: Aldershot, 1995)

Centre for European Studies, *The Member States of the European Union and the Inter-Governmental Conference,* Briefing Paper (University of Leeds: Leeds, Feb. 1997)

Center for Strategic and International Studies, *Breaking Down the Barricades: Reforming Export Controls to Increase US Competitiveness*, Final Report of the Project on Export Controls in a Changing World, Project Chairman Boyd McKelvain (Center for Strategic and International Studies: Washington, DC, 1994)

Chalmers, M., *British Arms Export Policy and Indonesia* (Saferworld: London, May 1997)

—, Donowaki, M. and Greene, O. (eds), *Developing Arms Transparency: The Future of the UN Register* (University of Bradford: Bradford, 1997)

— and Greene, O., *A Maturing Regime? The UN Register in its Sixth Year*, BARS Working Paper no. 6 (University of Bradford: Bradford, Jan. 1999)

— *et al.*, *Developing the UN Register of Conventional Arms* (University of Bradford: Bradford, 1994)

Chayes, A. and Chayes, A. H., *The New Sovereignty: Compliance with International Regulatory Agreements* (Harvard University Press: Cambridge, Mass., 1996)

Clegg, E. and Thurlow, J., *The EU Regulation on Dual-Use Goods after One Year* (Export Control Publications (Deltac Ltd): Chertsey, 1996)

Collinson, H., *Death on Delivery: The Impact of the Arms Trade on the Third World* (Campaign Against the Arms Trade (CAAT): London, 1989)

Cooper, N., *The Business of Death: Britain's Arms Trade at Home and Abroad* (I. B. Tauris: London, 1997)

Cornish, P., *The Arms Trade and Europe*, Chatham House Papers (Royal Institute of International Affairs and Pinter: London, 1995)

—, van Ham, P. and Krause, J. (eds), *Europe and the Challenge of Proliferation*, Chaillot Paper no. 24 (Western European Union, Institute for Security Studies: Paris, May 1996)

Cottey, A., *The European Union and Conflict Prevention: The Role of the High Representative and the Policy Planning and Early Warning Unit* (Saferworld/International Alert: London, 1998)

Cowen, R., *Defense Procurement in the Federal Republic of Germany: Politics and Organization* (Westview Press: Boulder, Colo., 1986)

van Creveld, M., *On Future War* (Brassey's: London, 1991)

Croft, S., *Strategies of Arms Control: A History and Typology* (Manchester University Press: Manchester, 1996)

Davis, I. (ed.), *An Independent Audit of the First UK Annual Report on Strategic Export Controls* (Saferworld: London, Sep. 1999)

—, *Military R&D in Europe: Collaboration Without Control?*, Current Decisions Report no. 11 (Oxford Research Group: Oxford, Oct. 1992)

—, *The UK Peace Dividend: Whence It Came, Where it Went*, Peace Studies Papers, 3rd series (University of Bradford, Department of Peace Studies: Bradford, Sep. 1996)

— and Schofield, S., *Upgrades and Surplus Weapons: Lessons from the UK Disposal Sales Agency*, BICC Papers no. 11 (Bonn International Center for Conversion: Bonn, Aug. 1997)

Deltac Ltd and Saferworld, *Proliferation and Export Controls: An Analysis of Sensitive Technologies and Countries of Concern* (Deltac Ltd and Saferworld: Chertsey, 1995)

Duff, A. (ed.), *The Treaty of Amsterdam: Text and Commentary* (Federal Trust: London, 1997)

Dunn, W., *Public Policy Analysis: An Introduction*, 2nd edn (Prentice-Hall: Englewood Cliffs, N.J., 1994)

Eavis, P. (ed.), *Arms and Dual-Use Exports from the EC: A Common Policy for Regulation and Control* (Saferworld: London, Dec. 1992)

Edmonds, M., *Defence Manufacturing Trends Within Europe: Sweden's Potential in Partnership and Co-operative Development*, Bailrigg Memorandum 31 (Centre for Defence and International Security Studies, Lancaster University: Lancaster, 1997)

European Round Table of Industrialists (ERT), 'Towards a single European export control system: harmony or chaos?', ERT, Brussels, June 1991

EuroStrategies, *Dual-Use Industries in Europe*, Executive Summary, Study carried out for the Commission of the European Communities, DG III, Apr. 1991

Foray, D. and Freeman, C. (eds), *Technology and the Wealth of Nations: The Dynamics of Constructed Advantage* (OECD and Pinter: London, 1993)

Frankfort-Nachmias, C. and Nachmias, D., *Research Methods in the Social Sciences*, 4th edn (Edward Arnold: Sevenoaks, 1992)

Gilpin, R., *The Political Economy of International Relations* (Princeton University Press: Princeton, N.J., 1987)

Gleditsch, N. P. and Njølstad, O. (eds), *Arms Races: Technological and Political Dynamics* (Sage: London, 1990)

Goodman, S., Wolcott, P. and Burkhart, G., *Building on the Basics: An Examination of High Performance Computing Export Control Policy in the 1990s* (Stanford University Center for International Security and Arms Control: Stanford, Calif., Nov. 1995)

Gordon, P., *France, Germany and the Western Alliance* (Westview Press: Boulder, Colo., 1995)

Greene, O., *Tackling Illicit Trafficking in Conventional Arms: Strengthening Collective Efforts by EU and Associate Countries* (Saferworld: London, Apr. 1999)

—, *Tackling Light Weapons Proliferation: Issues and Priorities for the EU* (Saferworld: London, Apr. 1997)

Gregory, W., *The Price of Peace: The Future of the Defence Industry and High Technology in a Post Cold War World* (Lexington Books: New York, 1993)

Gummett, P. and Stein, J., 'European defence technology in transition: issues for the UK', a CREDIT (Capacity for Research on European Defence and Industrial Technology) Network Study, Science Policy Support Group Review Paper no. 7, London, Sep. 1994

Gutjahr, L., *German Foreign and Defence Policy After Unification* (Pinter: London, 1994)

Hague, R., Harrop, M. and Breslin, S., *Comparative Government and Politics: An Introduction*, 3rd edn (Macmillan: London, 1994)

Ham, C. and Hill, M., *The Policy Process in the Modern Capitalist State*, 2nd edn (Harvester Wheatsheaf: Brighton, 1984)

Hampden-Turner, C. and Trompenaars, F., *The Seven Cultures of Capitalism* (Piatkus: London, 1994)

Harkavy, R., *The Arms Trade and International Systems* (Ballinger: Cambridge, Mass., 1975)

Hartung, W., *And Weapons for All* (HarperCollins: New York, 1994)

Hayward, K., *Towards a European Weapons Procurement Process: The Shaping of Common European Requirements for New Arms Programmes*, Chaillot Paper no. 27 (Western European Union, Institute for Security Studies: Paris, June 1997)

Hewitt, D., *Military Expenditures 1972–1990: the Reasons Behind the Post-1985 Fail in World Military Spending*, IMF Working Paper WP/93/18 (International Monetary Fund: Washington, DC, Mar. 1993)

Hoffman, M. (ed.), *UK Arms Control in the 1990s* (Manchester University Press: Manchester, 1990)

Hofhansel, C., *Commercial Competition and National Security: Comparing US and German Export Control Policies* (Praeger: Westport, Conn., 1996)

Jackson, B., *Gunrunners Gold: How the Public's Money Finances Arms Sales* (World Development Movement: London, May 1995)

Jopp, M., International Institute for Strategic Studies, *The Strategic Implications of European Integration*, Adelphi Paper no. 290 (Brassey's: London, July 1994)

Kahler, M., *International Institutions and the Political Economy of Integration* (Brookings Institution: Washington, DC, 1995)

Kapstein, E. B., *The Political Economy of National Security: A Global Perspective* (McGraw-Hill: New York, 1992)

— (ed.), *Global Arms Production: Policy Dilemmas for the 1990s* (University Press of America: Lanham, Md., 1992)

Keller, W., *Arm in Arm: The Political Economy of the Global Arms Trade* (Basic Books: New York, 1995)

Kołodziej, E. A., *Making and Marketing Arms: The French Experience and its Implications for the International System* (Princeton University Press: Princeton, N.J., 1987)

Krasner, S. (ed.), *International Regimes* (Cornell University Press: Ithaca, N.Y., 1983)

Krause, K., *Arms and the State: Patterns of Military Production and Trade* (Cambridge University Press: New York, 1992)

— *et al.*, 'Constraining conventional proliferation: a role for Canada', Research Report Prepared for the Non-Proliferation, Arms Control and Disarmament Division, Department of Foreign Affairs and International Trade, Ottawa, Mar. 1996

Krell, G., *The Federal Republic of Germany and Arms Control*, PRIF Reports no. 10 (Peace Research Institute Frankfurt: Frankfurt, Feb. 1990)

Laurance, E., *The International Arms Trade* (Lexington Books: New York, 1992)

—, Wezeman, S. and Wulf, H. (eds), *Arms Watch: SIPRI Report on the First Year of the UN Register of Conventional Arms*, SIPRI Research Report no. 6 (Oxford University Press: Oxford, 1993)

Lodgaard, S. and Rønnfeldt, C., *A Moratorium on Light Weapons in West Africa* (Norwegian Institute of International Affairs/ Norwegian Initiative on Small Arms Transfers: Oslo, 1998)

Louise, C., *The Social Impacts of Light Weapons Availability and Proliferation* (United Nations Research Institute for Social Development: Geneva, Mar. 1995)

Mackenzie, D., *Inventing Accuracy: A Historical Sociology of Nuclear Missile Guidance* (MIT Press: Cambridge, Mass., 1990)

Maddock, R. T., *The Political Economy of the Arms Race* (Macmillan: London, 1990)

Majone, G. *et al.*, *Regulating Europe* (Routledge: London, 1996)

Mariani, B. and Urquhart, A., *Transparency and Accountability in European Arms Export Controls: Towards Common Standards and Best Practice* (Saferworld: London, Dec. 2000)

May, T., *Social Research: Issues, Methods and Process* (Open University Press: Buckingham, 1993)

Miles, L., *Sweden and European Integration* (Ashgate: Aldershot, 1997)

Miller, D., *Export or Die: Britain's Defence Trade with Iran and Iraq* (Cassell: London, 1996)

Mollas-Gallart, J. and Perry Robinson, J., 'Assessment of dual technologies in the context of European security and defence', PE 166 819/Final, European Parliament, Directorate General for Research, Luxembourg, Oct. 1997

Molle, W., *The Economics of European Integration: Theory, Practice, Policy*, 2nd edn (Dartmouth: Aldershot, 1994)

Morgenthau, H., *Politics Among Nations* (Alfred Knopf: New York, 1973)

Mueller, J., *Retreat from Doomsday: The Obsolescence of Major War* (Basic Books: New York, 1989)

Müller, H., *European Non-Proliferation Policy 1993–1995* (European InterUniversity Press: Brussels, 1996)

—, *Nuclear Export Controls in Europe* (European InterUniversity Press: Brussels, 1995)

— *et al.*, *From Black Sheep to White Angel? The New German Export Control Policy*, PRIF Reports no. 32 (Peace Research Institute Frankfurt: Frankfurt, Jan. 1994)

— and Prystrom, J. (eds), *Central European Countries and Non-Proliferation Regimes* (Polish Foundation of International Affairs and Peace Research Institute Frankfurt: Warsaw, 1996)

Mussington, D., International Institute for Strategic Studies, *Understanding Contemporary International Arms Transfers: An Analysis of the Post-Cold War Arms Trade and Supplier Strategies for Limiting Conventional Weapons Proliferation*, Adelphi Paper no. 291 (Brassey's: London, Sep. 1994)

Myrdal, A., *The Game of Disarmament: How the United States and Russia Run the Arms Race* (Spokesman: Nottingham, 1980)

Nolan, J. (ed.), *Global Engagement: Cooperation and Security in the 21st Century* (Brookings Institution: Washington, DC, 1994)

Norton-Taylor, R. and Lloyd, M., *Truth Is a Difficult Concept: Inside the Scott Inquiry* (Fourth Estate: London, 1995)

Nugent, N., *The Government and Politics of the European Union*, 3rd edn (Macmillan: London, 1994)

Ohlson, T. (ed.), SIPRI, *Arms Transfer Limitations and Third World Security* (Oxford University Press: Oxford, 1988)

Oxford Research Group, *International Control of the Arms Trade*, Current Decisions Report no. 8 (Oxford Research Group: Oxford, Apr. 1992)

—, *Weapons Decisions: Proposals for An Informed Parliament*, Current Decisions Report no. 17 (Oxford Research Group: Oxford, Oct. 1996)

Parsons, W., *Public Policy: An Introduction to the Theory and Practice of Policy Analysis* (Edward Elgar: Aldershot, 1995)

Pearson, F., *The Global Spread of Arms: Political Economy of International Security* (Westview Press: Boulder, Colo., 1994)

Pierre, A., *The Global Politics of Arms Sales* (Princeton University Press: Princeton, N.J., 1982)

— (ed.), *Cascade of Arms: Managing Conventional Weapons Proliferation* (Brookings Institution/World Peace Foundation: Cambridge, Mass., 1997)

Rana, S., 'Small arms and intra state conflicts', Centre for Disarmament Affairs, United Nations, Washington, DC, 1995 (mimeo)

Ray, J. E., *Managing Official Export Credits: The Quest for a Global Regime* (Institute for International Economics: Washington, DC, July 1995)

Rhodes, C. and Mazey, S. (eds), *The State of the European Union, Vol. 3: Building a European Polity?* (Longman: Harlow, 1995)

Rosecrance, R., *The Rise of the Trading State: Commerce and Conquest in the Modern World* (Basic Books: New York, 1986)

Sampson, A., *The Arms Bazaar* (Coronet Books/Hodder & Stoughton: Sevenoaks, 1992)

Sapsford, R. and Jupp, V. (eds), *Data Collection and Analysis* (Sage: London, 1996)

Sbragia, A. (ed.), *Euro-Politics: Institutions and Policymaking in the 'New' European Community* (Brookings Institution: Washington, DC, 1992)

Scholte, J. A., *International Relations of Social Change* (Oxford University Press: Oxford, 1993)

Singh, J. (ed.), *Light Weapons and International Security* (Indian Pugwash Society and British American Security Information Council: Delhi, 1995)

Stoessinger, J., *Why Nations Go To War*, 4th edn (St Martin's Press: London, 1985)

Stubbs, R. and Underhill, G. (eds), *Political Economy and the Changing Global Order* (Macmillan: London, 1994)

Swedish Fellowship of Reconciliation/Saferworld, *Report on the International Conference on European Arms Export Controls*, 13–14 November 1997 (Swedish Fellowship of Reconciliation and Saferworld: Stockholm, 1998)

Taylor, T. and Imai, R. (eds), *The Defence Trade: Demand, Supply and Control, Security Challenges for Japan and Europe in a Post-Cold War World, Vol. III*

(Royal Institute of International Affairs (RIIA) and Institute for International Policy Studies: London, 1994)

Thayer, G., *The War Business: The International Trade in Armaments* (Simon & Schuster: New York, 1969)

Thorsson, I., Chairwoman, UN Group of Government Experts, *The Relationship between Disarmament and Development* (United Nations: New York, 1982)

Timmerman, K., *The Death Lobby: How the West Armed Iraq* (Fourth Estate: London, 1992)

de Vestel, P., *Defence Markets and Industries in Europe: Time for Political Decisions*, Chaillot Paper no. 21 (Western European Union, Institute for Security Studies: Paris, Nov. 1995)

Wallace, W. (ed.), *The Dynamics of European Integration* (Pinter: London, 1990)

Waltz, K., *Theory of International Politics* (Addison-Wesley: Reading, Mass., 1979)

Wander, W. T., Arnett, E. and Bracken, P. (eds), *The Diffusion of Advanced Weaponry: Technologies, Regional Implications, and Responses* (American Association for the Advancement of Science: Washington, DC, 1994)

Wulf, H. (ed.), SIPRI, *Arms Industry Limited* (Oxford University Press: Oxford, 1993)

3. Articles and papers

Abbott, K., '"Trust but verify": the production of information in arms control treaties and other international agreements', *Cornell International Law Journal*, vol. 26, no. 1 (1993), pp. 1–58

Anderson, D. G., 'The international arms trade: regulating conventional arms transfers in the aftermath of the Gulf War', *American University Journal of International Law and Policy*, vol. 7, no. 4 (summer 1992), pp. 749–806

Anthony, I., 'Current trends and developments in the arms trade', *Annals of the American Academy of Political and Social Science*, 535 (Sep. 1994), pp. 29–42

—, 'The global arms trade', *Arms Control Today*, June 1991, pp. 3–8

—, 'Measuring conventional arms transfers: definitions, data and evaluation', *Strategic Analysis*, Mar. 1995, pp. 1453–79

—, 'The United Kingdom', ed. I. Anthony, SIPRI, *Arms Export Regulations* (Oxford University Press: Oxford, 1991), pp. 175–81

Bailes, A., 'Europe's defense challenge: reinventing the Atlantic Alliance', *Foreign Affairs*, vol. 76, no. 1 (Jan./Feb. 1997), pp. 15–20

Beach, H., 'Peacekeeping and weapons proliferation', Occasional Paper, Council for Arms Control, London, Feb. 1994

Beard, R., 'NATO armaments cooperation in the 1990s', *NATO Review*, Apr. 1993, pp. 23–28

Bersten, F., 'Globalizing free trade', *Foreign Affairs*, vol. 75, no. 3 (May/June 1996), pp. 105–20

Bertsch, G. and Cupitt, R., 'Nonproliferation in the 1990s: enhancing international cooperation on export controls', *Washington Quarterly*, vol. 16, no. 4 (1993), pp. 119–36

Betts, R., 'Systems for peace or causes of war? Collective security, arms control and the new Europe', *International Security*, vol. 17, no. 1 (summer 1992), pp. 5–43

Bitzinger, R., 'The globalisation of the arms industry: the next proliferation challenge', *International Security*, vol. 19, no. 2 (1994), pp. 170–98

—, 'Gorbachev and GRIT, 1985–89: Did arms control succeed because of unilateral actions or in spite of them?', *Contemporary Security Policy*, vol. 15, no. 1 (Apr. 1994), pp. 68–79

Blunden, M., 'Collaboration and competition in European weapons procurement: the issue of democratic accountability', *Defense Analysis*, vol. 5, no. 4 (1989), pp. 291–304

Boyer, Y., 'Conventional and non-conventional weapons: their changing characteristics and challenges for arms control', eds T. Taylor and R. Imai, *The Defence Trade: Demand, Supply and Control* (Royal Institute of International Affairs and Institute for International Policy Studies: London, 1994)

British Labour Party, 'Labour's policy pledges for a responsible arms trade', 13 Feb. 1997

Brzoska, M., 'Arms transfer data sources', *Journal of Conflict Resolution*, vol. 26, no. 1 (Mar. 1982), pp. 77–108

—, 'Assessing proposals for a conventional arms export control regime', eds H. G. Brauch *et al.*, *Controlling the Development and Spread of Military Technology: Lessons from the Past and Challenges for the 1990s* (VU University Press: Amsterdam, 1992), chapter 22

—, 'Behind the German export scandals', *Bulletin of the Atomic Scientists* (July/Aug. 1989), pp. 32–35

—, 'The erosion of restraint in West German arms transfer policy', *Journal of Peace Research*, vol. 26, no. 2 (1989), pp. 165–77

—, 'The financing factor in military trade', *Defence and Peace Economics*, vol. 5 (1994), pp. 67–80

— and Pearson, F., 'Developments in the global supply of arms: opportunity and motivation', *Annals of the American Academy of Political and Social Science*, 535 (Sep. 1994), pp. 58–72

Bullens, H., 'Arms industry and arms trade in crisis? Rhetoric and reality in post-cold-war Germany', eds H. Bullens and S. Tachibana, *Restructuring Security Concepts, Postures and Industrial Base*, IPPRA Security and Disarmament Commission Paper 9, Arbeitsgruppe Friedensforschung und Europäische Sicherheitspolitik (AFES) Press Report no. 63 (AFES Press: Mosbach, 1997), pp. 75–89

Buzan, B., 'From international system to international society: structural realism and regime theory meet the English school', *International Organization*, vol. 47, no. 3 (summer 1993), pp. 227–352

Carus, S., 'Military technology and the arms trade: changes and their impact', *Annals of the American Academy of Political and Social Science*, 535 (Sep. 1994), pp. 163–74

Catrina, C., 'Main directions of research in the arms trade', *Annals of the American Academy of Political and Social Science*, 535 (Sep. 1994), pp. 190–205

Chalmers, M., 'Beyond CFE: cutting conventional procurement', *Arms Control Today*, June 1990, pp. 13–17

—, 'Conceptualising arms control after the cold war', *Brassey's Defence Yearbook 1997* (Brassey's: London, 1997), pp. 273–88

Chilton, P., 'Common, collective, or combined? Theories of defense integration in the European Union', eds C. Rhodes and S. Mazey, *The State of the European Union, Vol. 3: Building A European Polity?* (Longman: Harlow, 1995), pp. 81–109

Clegg, E., 'Controlling legal arms transfers: the EU Code of Conduct', eds P. Cross and G. Rasamoelina, *Conflict Prevention Policy of the European Union: Recent Engagements, Future Instruments, Yearbook 1998/99* (Nomos Verlagsgesellschaft and Conflict Prevention Network: Baden-Baden, 1999), pp. 163–78

—, 'Developing the Wassenaar Arrangement: a new arms export control regime', *CDS Bulletin of Arms Control*, no. 23 (Sep. 1996), pp. 5–9

Cornish, P., 'European security: the end of architecture and the new NATO', *International Affairs*, vol. 72, no. 4 (1996), pp. 751–69

—, 'NATO at the millennium: new missions, new members . . . new strategy?', *NATO Review,* Sep./Oct. 1997, pp. 21–24

Cragg, A., 'The Combined Joint Task Force concept: a key component of the Alliance's adaptation', *NATO Review*, July 1996, pp. 7–10

—, 'Internal adaptation: reshaping NATO for the challenges of tomorrow', *NATO Review*, July/Aug. 1997, pp. 30–35

Davis, Z., 'Devolution of the nonproliferation regime? United States and European export control policies in the post cold war era', Paper presented at the Seminar on the European Arms Trade and the EC, Centre for Defence Studies/Department of War Studies, London, 17–18 Jan. 1994 (unpublished)

Dean, J. and Forsberg, R. W., 'CFE and beyond: the future of conventional arms control', *International Security*, vol. 17, no. 1 (summer 1992), pp. 76–121

Donowaki, M., 'Developing a code of conduct for conventional weapons', *Nonproliferation Review*, fall 1995, pp. 60–65

Dowdy, J. J., 'Winners and losers in the arms industry downturn', *Foreign Policy*, vol. 107 (summer 1997), pp. 88–101

Druckman, D., 'The social psychology of arms control and reciprocation', *Political Psychology*, vol. 11, no. 3 (1990), pp. 553–81

Dunne, P., 'The economic effects of military expenditure in developing countries', Paper presented to the Project LINK conference, Salamanca, Spain, Sep. 1994

Eavis, P. and Greene, O., 'Regulating arms exports: a programme for the European Community', eds H. G. Brauch *et al.*, *Controlling the Development and Spread of Military Technology: Lessons from the Past and Challenges for the 1990s* (VU University Press: Amsterdam, 1992), chapter 21

— and Shannon, A., 'Arms and dual-use export controls: priorities for the European Union', Saferworld Briefing, London, June 1994

Edmonds, M., 'The domestic and international dimensions of British arms sales', ed. C. Cannizzo, *The Gun Merchants: Politics and Policies of the Major Arms Suppliers* (Pergamon Press: New York, 1980)

European Defence Industries Group, 'EDIG policy paper on conventional defence equipment export', Reference EPP/94/07, 13 Jan. 1994

—, 'European defence industry: an agenda item for the 1996 Intergovernmental Conference', Memorandum by the European Defence Industries Group, 30 May 1995

Foot, P. and Laxton, T., 'Not the Scott Report', A *Private Eye* Arms to Iraq Special, Nov. 1994

Ford, G., 'European arms exports', ed. K. Coates, *ENDpapers Nineteen: The Hole in the Sky* (Spokesman: Nottingham, 1989), pp. 59–81

Forland, T. E., '"Economic warfare" and "strategic goods": a conceptual framework for analyzing COCOM', *Journal of Peace Research*, vol. 28, no. 2 (1991), pp. 191–204

—, 'The history of economic warfare: international law, effectiveness, strategies', *Journal of Peace Research*, vol. 30, no. 2 (1993), pp. 151–62

Freeman, R., 'Moving Britain forward: defence exports in the 1990s', *RUSI Journal*, Feb. 1995, pp. 1–5

Gibbs, D., 'Secrecy and international relations', *Journal of Peace Research*, vol. 32, no. 2 (1995), pp. 213–28

Gordon, P., 'Europe's uncommon foreign policy', *International Security*, vol. 22, no. 3 (winter 1997/98), pp. 74–100

Gray, C., 'Arms control does not control arms', *Orbis,* summer 1993, pp. 333–48

Greene, O., 'Launching the Wassenaar Arrangement: challenges for the new arms export control regime', Saferworld Briefing, London, Mar. 1996

—, 'Strengths and weaknesses of the EU programme for preventing and combating illicit arms trafficking, and their relevance for the OSCE', Paper presented at a workshop on Small Arms and Light Weapons: An Issue for the OSCE?, hosted by the Netherlands, Norway and Switzerland in association with BASIC, Vienna, 9–10 Nov. 1998 (unpublished)

— and Gamba, V., 'Responding to small arms and light weapons proliferation in Southern Africa: developing a regional action programme', *African Security Review,* no. 4 (1998)

Grobar, L. M., Stern, R. M. and Deardorff, A. V., 'The economic effects of international trade in armaments in the major Western industrialized and developing countries', *Defence Economics*, vol. 1 (1990), pp. 97–120

Guay, T., 'The limits of regional integration: the European Union and Europe's defense industry', Paper presented at the International Studies Association Annual Conference, San Diego, Calif., 18 Apr. 1996 (unpublished)

Gutjahr, L., 'Continuity or change? Germany's foreign policy after the 1994 general elections', *Coexistence,* no. 32 (1995), pp. 99–118

Hagelin, B., 'Sweden's search for military technology', eds M. Brzoska and P. Lock, SIPRI, *Restructuring of Arms Production in Western Europe* (Oxford University Press: Oxford, 1992)

Halliday, F., 'International relations: is there a new agenda?', *Millennium: Journal of International Studies*, vol. 20, no. 1 (1991), pp. 57–72

Happe, N. and Wakeham-Linn, J., 'Military expenditure and arms trade: alternative data sources, Part I', *Peace Economics, Peace Science and Public Policy,* vol. 1, no. 4 (1994), pp. 3–38

— and Wakeham-Linn, J., 'Military expenditure and arms trade: alternative data sources, Part II', *Peace Economics, Peace Science and Public Policy*, vol. 2, no. 1 (1994), pp. 10–23

Harkavy, R., 'The changing international system and the arms trade', *Annals of the American Academy of Political and Social Science*, 535 (Sep. 1994), pp. 11–28

Hartung, W., 'Curbing the arms trade: from rhetoric to restraint', *World Policy Journal*, vol. 9, no. 3 (spring 1992), pp. 219–47

Harvey, M., 'Arms export control: an analysis of developments since the Gulf War', *RUSI Journal*, Feb. 1992, pp. 35–41

Hirdman, S., 'Sweden's policy on arms exports', *Military Technology*, Nov. 1990, pp. 54–55

Hirst, P. and Thompson, G., 'Globalization and the future of the nation state', *Economy and Society,* vol. 24, no. 3 (Aug. 1995), pp. 408–42

Hofhansel, C., 'German perspectives on export control policy', eds G. Bertsch, R. Cupitt and S. Elliott-Gower, *International Cooperation on Nonproliferation Export Controls: Prospects for the 1990s and Beyond* (University of Michigan Press: Ann Arbor, Mich., 1994)

Ito, T., 'The control of conventional arms proliferation', eds T. Taylor and R. Imai, *The Defence Trade: Demand, Supply and Control* (Royal Institute of International Affairs and Institute for International Policy Studies: London, 1994), chapter 7

Janning, J., 'A German Europe—a European Germany? On the debate over Germany's foreign policy', *International Affairs*, vol. 72, no. 1 (1996), pp. 33–41

Johnson, J., 'Financing the arms trade', *Annals of the American Academy of Political and Social Science*, 535 (Sep. 1994), pp. 110–21

Jones, I, and Wyn Rees, G., 'Britain and post-cold war arms transfers', *Contemporary Security Policy*, vol. 15, no. 1 (Apr. 1994), pp. 109–26

Jones, S., 'EU and US codes of conduct on arms transfers: status and review', *Nonproliferation, Demilitarization, and Arms Control*, fall 1998, pp. 23–31

Kapstein, E., 'Shockproof: the end of the financial crisis', *Foreign Affairs*, vol. 75, no. 1 (Jan./Feb. 1996), pp. 2–8

Karp, A., 'The arms trade revolution: the major impact of small arms', *Washington Quarterly,* vol. 17, no. 4 (autumn 1994), pp. 65–77

—, 'The rise of black and grey markets', *Annals of the American Academy of Political and Social Science*, 535 (Sep. 1994), pp. 175–89

Kelle, A., 'German export controls on nuclear and dual-use goods, 1988–92', eds D. Carlton *et al.*, *Controlling the International Transfer of Weaponry and Related Technology* (Dartmouth: Aldershot, 1995), pp. 203–24

— and Müller, H., 'Germany', eds H. Müller and J. Prystrom, *Central European Countries and Non-Proliferation Regimes* (Polish Foundation of International Affairs and Peace Research Institute Frankfurt: Warsaw, 1996), pp. 119–54

Keller, W., 'Global defense business: a policy context for the 1990s', ed. E. Kapstein, *Global Arms Production: Policy Dilemmas for the 1990s* (University Press of America: Lanham, Md., 1992), chapter 2

Kellman, B., Gualtieri, D. and Tanzman, E., 'Disarmament and disclosure: how arms control verification can proceed without threatening confidential business information', *Harvard International Law Journal*, vol. 36, no. 1 (winter 1995), pp. 71–126

Khripunov, I., 'Have guns, will travel', *Bulletin of the Atomic Scientists*, May/June 1997, pp. 47–51

Klare, M., 'Deadly convergence: the perils of the arms trade', *World Policy Journal*, vol. 6, no. 1 (1989), pp. 141–68

—, 'Gaining control: building a comprehensive arms restraint system', *Arms Control Today*, June 1991, pp. 9–13

—, 'The next great arms race', *Foreign Affairs*, vol. 72, no. 3 (summer 1993), pp. 136–52

—, 'Secret operatives, clandestine trades: the thriving black market for weapons', *Bulletin of the Atomic Scientists*, vol. 44, no. 3 (Apr. 1988), pp. 16–25

Laurance, E. J. and Wulf, H. (eds), *Coping with Surplus Weapons*, Brief no. 3 (Bonn International Centre for Conversion: Bonn, 1995)

Lennon, P., 'Dual-use export controls and the European Community', Paper for the Centre for European Policy Studies/Saferworld conference, Brussels, 18 June 1993 (unpublished)

—, 'Export controls and the European Community', Paper for the Centre for European Policy Studies Meeting on Controlling the Export of Sensitive Dual-Use Technologies, Brussels, 21 Oct. 1991 (unpublished)

—, 'Export controls and the European Community', Paper for a Seminar on Defence Export Controls, Defence Manufacturers Association, London, 3 Nov. 1993 (unpublished)

Levine, P. and Smith, R., 'The arms trade and arms control', *Economic Journal*, vol. 105 (Mar. 1995), pp. 471–84

Lewis, W. and Joyner, C., 'Proliferation of unconventional weapons: the case for coercive arms control', *Comparative Strategy*, vol. 10 (1991), pp. 299–309

Lovering, J., 'After the cold war: the defence industry and the new Europe', eds P. Brown and R. Crompton, *Economic Restructuring and Social Exclusion* (University College London Press: London, 1994), pp. 175–95

—, 'The arms industry at the end of the twentieth century: invading the global economy', University of Hull, School of Geography and Earth Resources, 1994 (unpublished draft paper)

—, 'The British defence industry in the 1990s: a labour market perspective', *Industrial Relations Journal,* vol. 22, no. 2 (1991), pp. 103–16

—, 'Opportunity or crisis? The remaking of the British arms industry', ed. R. Turner, *The British Economy in Transition: From the Old to the New?* (Routledge: London, 1995), pp. 88–122

Lumpe, L., 'Clinton's conventional arms export policy: so little change', *Arms Control Today*, May 1995, pp. 9–14

Lysen, G., 'Some views on neutrality and membership of the European Communities: the case of Sweden', *Common Market Law Review,* vol. 29 (1992), pp. 229–55

Macdonald, G., 'UK arms exports: government policy, procedures and practice', *RUSI Journal*, Oct. 1995, pp. 47–56

McKibbin, W. J. and Thurman, S., 'The impact on the world economy of reductions in military expenditures and military arms exports', *Brookings Discussion Papers in International Economics,* no. 99 (1993)

Maniruzzaman, T., 'Arms transfers, military coups, and military rule in developing states', *Journal of Conflict Resolution*, vol. 36, no. 4 (Dec. 1992), pp. 733–35

Martin, S. and Hartley, K., 'Defense equipment, exports and offsets: the UK experience', *Defense Analysis,* vol. 11, no. 1 (1995), pp. 21–30

Masefield, C., 'Defence exports: the challenge ahead', *RUSI Journal*, Aug. 1995, pp. 15–18

Mayer, H., 'Early at the beach and claiming territory? The evolution of German ideas on a new European order', *International Affairs*, vol. 73, no. 4 (1997), pp. 721–37

Meiers, F.-J., 'Germany: the reluctant power', *Survival,* vol. 37, no. 3 (autumn 1995), pp. 82–103

Miller, D., 'Defense sales and the Scott Inquiry', *Defense Analysis,* vol. 10, no. 2 (1994), pp. 216–18

—, 'The Scott Report and the future of British defense sales', *Defense Analysis,* vol. 12, no. 3 (1996), pp. 359–70

Moisi, D. and Mertes, M., 'Europe's map, compass, and horizon', *Foreign Affairs*, vol. 74, no. 1 (Jan./Feb. 1995), pp. 122–34

Moodie, M., 'Beyond proliferation: the challenge of technology diffusion', *Washington Quarterly*, vol. 18, no. 2 (1995) , pp. 71–90

—, 'Constraining conventional arms transfers', *Annals of the American Academy of Political and Social Science*, 535 (Sep. 1994), pp. 131–45

—, 'Conventional arms control: an analytical survey of recent literature', *Washington Quarterly,* vol. 12, no. 1 (winter 1989), pp. 189–201

Moravcsik, A., 'The European armaments industry at the crossroads', *Survival,* vol. 32, no. 1 (Jan./Feb. 1990), pp. 65–85

—, 'Preferences and power in the European Community: a liberal intergovernmentalist approach', *Journal of Common Market Studies,* vol. 31 (1993), pp. 19–56

Naumann, K. (Gen.), 'From co-operation to interoperability', *NATO Review,* July 1996, pp. 17–20

Naylor, R. T., 'Loose cannons: covert commerce and underground finance in the modern arms black market', *Crime, Law and Social Change,* vol. 22 (1995), pp. 1–57

Neuman, S., 'Arms transfers, military assistance and defense industries: socioeconomic burden or opportunity?', *Annals of the American Academy of Political and Social Science*, 535 (Sep. 1994), pp. 91–109

—, 'Controlling the arms trade: idealistic dream or realpolitik', *Washington Quarterly,* vol. 16, no. 3 (summer 1993), pp. 53–75

—, 'Coproduction, barter and countertrade: offsets in the international arms market', *Orbis,* spring 1985, pp. 183–213

Nield, R., 'After arms control', *Bulletin of Peace Proposals*, vol. 32, no. 1 (1992), pp. 23–28

Nolan, J., 'The US–Soviet conventional arms transfer negotiations', eds A. George, P. Farley and A. Dallin, *US–Soviet Security Cooperation* (Oxford University Press: Oxford, 1988), pp. 510–24

Pearson, F., '"Necessary evil": perspectives on West German arms transfer policies', *Armed Forces and Society,* vol. 12, no. 4 (summer 1986), pp. 525–52

—, 'The question of control in British defence sales policy', *International Affairs,* vol. 59, no. 2 (spring 1983), pp. 211–38

—, 'Of Leopards and Cheetahs: West Germany's role as a mid-sized arms supplier', *Orbis*, spring 1985

—, 'Problems and prospects of arms transfer limitations among second-tier suppliers: the cases of France, the United Kingdom and the Federal Republic of Germany', ed. T. Ohlson, SIPRI, *Arms Transfer Limitations and Third World Security* (Oxford University Press: Oxford, 1988)

Phythian, M. and Little, W., 'Administering Britain's arms trade', *Public Administration,* vol. 71 (autumn 1993), pp. 259–77

Pierre, A., 'Conventional arms proliferation today: changed dimensions, new responses', in *Science and International Security Anthology: Trends and Implications for Arms Control, Proliferation and International Security in the Changing Global Environment* (American Association for the Advancement of Science: Washington, DC, 1993)

Rana, S., 'Small arms and intra state conflicts', United Nations Centre for Disarmament Affairs, Washington, DC, 1995 (mimeograph)

Reinicke, W., 'Cooperative security and the political economy of nonproliferation', ed. J. Nolan, *Global Engagement: Cooperation and Security in the 21st Century* (Brookings Institution: Washington, DC, 1994)

Rimanelli, M., 'The rationale, evolution, and future of arms control', *Comparative Strategy,* vol. 11, no. 3 (1992), pp. 307–29

Roberts, B., 'Arms control and the end of the cold war', *Washington Quarterly,* autumn 1992, pp. 39–56

—, 'Rethinking export controls on dual-use materials and technologies: from trade restraints to trade enablers', *The Arena*, vol. 2 (June 1995)

Ross, A., 'The international arms market: a structural analysis', *International Interactions*, vol. 18, no. 1 (1992), pp. 63–83

Rusman, P., 'A conventional arms transfer regime in the European Community', eds H. G. Brauch *et al.*, *Controlling the Development and Spread of Military Technology: Lessons from the Past and Challenges for the 1990s* (VU University Press: Amsterdam, 1992), chapter 20

Saferworld, 'Arms and dual-use exports from the EC: a common policy for regulation and control', London, Dec. 1992

—, 'Controlling the export of arms and dual-use technology', Submission to the Labour Party's Working Group on Defence Policy, London Sep. 1994

—, 'Policy and practice: UK arms exports 1 May 1997 to 10 May 1998', London, June 1998

— and Institute for Security Studies (ISS), 'Southern Africa Regional Action Programme on Light Arms and Illicit Trafficking', London, May 1998

Sample, S., 'Military buildups, war, and realpolitik', *Journal of Conflict Resolution,* vol. 42, no. 2 (Apr. 1998), pp. 156–75

Santer, J., 'The European Union's security and defence policy', *NATO Review,* Nov. 1995, pp. 3–9

Simpson, J., 'The nuclear non-proliferation regime as a model for conventional armament restraint', ed. T. Ohlson, SIPRI, *Arms Transfer Limitations and Third World Security* (Oxford University Press: Oxford, 1988), pp. 227–40

Singh, J., 'Conventional arms transfers: the search for representative data', *Strategic Analysis,* Mar. 1995, pp. 1481–94

Sislin, J., 'Arms as influence: the determinants of successful influence', *Journal of Conflict Resolution,* vol. 38, no. 4 (Dec. 1994), pp. 665–89

Sköns, E. and Wulf, H., 'The internationalisation of the arms industry', *Annals of the American Academy of Political and Social Science,* 535 (Sep. 1994), pp. 43–57

Smith, R., 'Is Europe pricing itself out of the market?', *RUSI Journal,* Feb. 1994

—, Humm, A. and Fontanel, J., 'The economics of exporting arms', *Journal of Peace Research,* vol. 3 (1985), pp. 239–47

Spear, J., 'Arms transfer regime formation', Paper presented at the annual meeting of the International Studies Association, Washington, DC, 28 Mar.–1 Apr. 1994 (unpublished)

Sperling, J., 'American, NATO, and West German foreign economic policies, 1949–89', eds E. Kirchner and J. Sperling, *The Federal Republic of Germany and NATO: 40 Years After* (Macmillan: London, 1992), chapter 8

—, Louscher, D. and Salomone, M., 'A reconceptualization of the arms transfer problem', *Defense Analysis,* vol. 11, no. 3 (1995), pp. 293–311

Strange, S., 'Political economy and international relations', eds K. Booth and S. Smith, *International Relations Theory Today* (Polity Press: London, 1995)

Taylor, T., 'European cooperation and conventional arms control', Discussion paper, IISS Conference on Conventional Arms Proliferation, 5–7 May 1993 (unpublished)

Thomas, A., 'Attacked from all sides: the UK 20 per cent in the arms market?', *RUSI Journal,* Feb. 1994

Ulin, R. and Young, T.-D., 'Conventional arms control and disarmament: lessons from the interwar period', *Comparative Strategy,* vol. 10 (1991), pp. 205–15

Vetschera, H., 'Comment on Paul R. Viotti's and George J. Stein's comparative articles on the European neutrals', *Defense Analysis,* vol. 6, no. 4 (1990), pp. 413–17

Viotti, P. R., 'Comparative neutrality in Europe', *Defense Analysis,* vol. 6, no. 1 (1990), pp. 3–15

Wallensteen, P. and Sollenberg, M., 'The end of international war? Armed conflict 1989–95', *Journal of Peace Research,* vol. 33, no. 3 (1996), pp. 353–70

Weitbrecht, A., 'The control of arms exports in the Federal Republic of Germany', *Disarmament,* vol. 15, no. 1 (1992), pp. 57–65

Wenzel, J., 'The European Community's approach to export controls', eds K. Bailey and R. Rudney, *Proliferation and Export Controls* (University Press of America: Lanham, Md., 1993)

Weston, D. and Gummett, P., 'The economic impact of military R&D: hypotheses, evidence and verification', *Defense Analysis,* vol. 3, no. 1 (1987), pp. 63–76

Willett, S., 'The dilemmas and contradictions of an ethical arms trade policy', *CDS Bulletin of Arms Control,* vol. 30 (July 1998), pp. 11–19

Williams, P. and Black, S., 'Transnational threats: drug trafficking and weapons proliferation', *Contemporary Security Policy,* vol. 15, no. 1 (Apr. 1994), pp. 127–51

Williamson, R., *Conventional Weapons, Conventional Wars: The Need for an Expanded Arms Control Agenda*, Occasional Paper (Council for Arms Control: London, May 1994)

Wulf, H., 'The Federal Republic of Germany', ed. I. Anthony, SIPRI, *Arms Export Regulation* (Oxford University Press: Oxford, 1991), pp. 72–85

—, 'German arms export policy', Paper prepared for the workshop on the European Arms Trade, Centre for Defence Studies, King's College, London 18–19 Jan. 1994

4. Newspapers, periodicals and journals

Arms Control Today

Aviation Week & Space Technology

Bulletin of the Atomic Scientists

Defense Analysis

European Analyst

Financial Times

Foreign Affairs

Foreign Policy

The Guardian

The Independent

International Affairs

International Defense Review

International Organization

International Security

Jane's Defence Contracts

Jane's Defence Weekly

Journal of Peace Research

The Observer

Orbis: A Journal of World Affairs

RUSI Journal

Security Dialogue

Scientific American

Strategic Analysis

Strategic Digest

Survival: The IISS Quarterly

UN Disarmament Review

Washington Quarterly

World Policy Journal

Index